Sociology

Related titles in the series

Accounting
Auditing
Book-keeping
Business and the European Community
Business Environment, The
Business French
Business German
Business Italian
Business Spanish
Business Studies
Commerce
Cost and Management Accounting
Economics
Elements of Banking
Financial Management
Law
Management Theory and Practice
Marketing
Organizations and Management
Statistics for Business

Sociology

Second edition

Jane L. Thompson and Judith Priestley

MADE SIMPLE
B O O K S

Made Simple Books
An imprint of Butterworth-Heinemann
Linacre House, Jordan Hill, Oxford OX2 8DP
A division of Reed Educational and Professional Publishing Ltd

 A member of the Reed Elsevier plc group

OXFORD   BOSTON   JOHANNESBURG
MELBOURNE   NEW DELHI   SINGAPORE

First published 1982
Reprinted 1992, 1993
Second edition 1996
Reprinted 1996

British Library Cataloguing in Publication Data
Thompson, Jane L.
    Sociology -2Rev.ed
    I. Title II. Priestley, Judith
    301

ISBN 0 7506 1687 3

Composition by Genesis Typesetting, Laser Quay, Rochester, Kent
Printed in Great Britain by Martins the Printers Ltd,
Berwick-upon-Tweed

Contents

Introduction: what is sociology?

Quite simply _definition:_ sociology is the study of the intricate relationship between people and society – how people make and change society; and how society influences and shapes the ways in which people behave and think about themselves. Of course, there are more complicated definitions than this, and as you read on you will understand that the relationship between people and society is by no means a straightforward affair.

History

When thinking about how people 'make society' we also have to remember that we inherit some ideas from the past – from those who have gone before us. A lot of our behaviour – for example, what we consider to be appropriate behaviour for men and women – has deep roots in the behaviour of previous generations.

Diversity

We also have to take into account the massive variety of people in any one society, and the considerable diversity of this variety when placed in the context of the world. The behaviour and beliefs of different people vary enormously within any one society. For example, it is fairly obvious that attitudes to the police are likely to be very different if people are young, black, unemployed or living in the inner city than if they are rich, white, middle-aged and living in rural Dorset.

There are also considerable differences between societies. Levels of expectation and the possibilities for development and change are very different among people living in poor and famine stricken countries of the southern hemisphere, for example, compared with others in technologically advanced and more affluent societies in the north and west.

Culture and sub-culture

When we're talking about people's behaviour and ideas – including their history and language, beliefs and attitudes, and ways of doing and making things – we're talking about what sociologists call **culture**. And, of course, cultures vary enormously between different kinds of societies. The culture of rural tea and cotton workers in India is very different from the culture of American fruit farmers in California, for example.

Cultures also vary within societies, so that, for example, while both are representatives of the wider American culture, the **sub-culture** of American fruit farmers in California is very different from the sub-culture of African–American domestic workers in downtown Los Angeles or New York City.

Differences

Differences based on ethnicity, gender, wealth, class, age and religion affect the ways in which people perceive society, give it shape and are shaped by it. These are all conditions which are very clearly associated with power.

Power

Some groups in society have more power than others, either because they've been born with it or because they've worked or struggled to obtain it. Some are very aware of the need to maintain that power. Others try to become more powerful themselves. Many exist with little prospect of ever achieving power, except in specific personal and individual relationships.

Discrepancies in power are evident between societies (Somalia and Sweden, for example) and within societies (business people and the homeless, for example).

Choice

The idea that individuals exist in some kind of equal relationship to each other, and can do anything they 'choose' to do depending on their own inclinations and initiative, is not a view which would be widely held by sociologists. Even the notion of 'free choice' is greatly affected by the possession or absence of power. The freedom to make choices is clearly related to the amount of power and influence a person enjoys. Lack of money or the means to earn it; lack of influence over others; opportunities restricted by poor education, poor housing, poor health, poor diet – all place enormous limitations on the exercise of so-called 'free choice'. The ways in which these factors which influence choice are themselves influenced by ethnicity, social class and gender are also highly significant.

Individuals and groups

While individuals and their lives are obviously important, sociologists are more interested in how people can be classified into groups. They are interested in the range of beliefs, values and behaviour patterns which 'groups of individuals' appear to share, and in the differing patterns that can be detected between different groups. These may be relatively small groups of individuals who have something pretty significant in common – for example, the same kind of employment, such as prostitution or building cars; or larger groups – related by the shared experience of long-term unemployment or domestic violence.

None of these conditions – prostitution, building cars, unemployment or domestic violence – are either coincidental or arrived at 'by chance'. They are all a consequence of the complicated interplay between people and society. Generalizations can be made about them – for example, in Britain domestic violence is more likely to happen to women than to men; it is rarely an isolated act of brutality; women frequently fail to report domestic abuse to the police, and when they do, the assistance and protection of the state cannot be guaranteed.

Each of the conditions has something to do with the interrelationship of people, power and society: how people – within societies, over time, with different cultures and sub-cultures, in relation to others, with differing amounts of power – are both influenced and 'made' by their society, as well as being continually involved in the process of remaking it and giving it meaning.

Social change

As you read on, it's important for you to remember that the interrelationship between people and society is not a static process. If you look backwards over time, it will be clear to you that your society has changed. If you look forwards you can only guess at what things might be like in a hundred years from now.

Even the present is a complexity of shifts, realignments and rearrangements which are sometimes predictable and sometimes surprising. Things change and are changing, even as you read these words. Your relationship to the study of sociology is already slightly different from what it was when you opened this book. You are already deciding whether to read on and learn more, or close the book and put it back on the shelf.

Sociologists are very preoccupied with social change. Not simply as **historians** might be – in terms of events and changing ways of life. Or as **anthropologists** might be – in terms of how different societies in faraway places sometimes strengthen, sometimes lose their culture over time. Or as **economists** might be – in terms of changes in the ways in which goods are made and distributed and wealth is created and shared. But more in terms of how social change is brought about at all. What causes it? Who influences it? Who benefits? And just as important – what effects does this have on how people live? To what extent is social change brought about by human behaviour and activity? To what extent is human behaviour and activity brought about by social change?

Later in the book we'll look at the significance of social change in relation to some important institutions in society, such as the family, education and work. We'll also look at some of the factors that affect social change, such as economics, ideologies and power; the influence of technology; politics and popular culture; the impact of social class, ethnicity and gender; the distribution of wealth and poverty.

Studying sociology

In each chapter you will be asked to consider the different explanations put forward by sociologists to account for social behaviour and social change; to examine some of the social changes taking place; and to increase your awareness and understanding about how these changes affect people's lives.

You should then be able to:

- describe various examples of social behaviour and social change (for example, how different groups experience racism, the relationship between social class and education, or the rise of capitalism and the changing structure of the economy);
- distinguish between different sociological explanations of how this behaviour and these changes have come about;
- assess the effects of social changes on the way of life of different groups within society.

Words which are part of the special **language of sociology** – words which some people call jargon – will be highlighted and explained as we go along. We'll also be highlighting **key concepts** which we particularly want you to notice, as a way of stressing their importance.

Theories and methods

To help you understand about **theories and methods** in sociology – the important interrelationship between the ideas of sociologists, the research methods they use and the issues they study – we have chosen to introduce these little by little in each chapter, in relation to the topic being studied. In Chapters 9 and 10 an overview is provided to explain about the most common theories and methods in more detail. In sociology textbooks this information is usually given first, so that you can then apply it to what you go on to study. But for absolute beginners, screeds of information about complicated sociological theories may seem rather abstract and difficult at first. You will probably learn more by taking it in a bit at a time, in the context of specific issues and particular pieces of research, until you can see for yourself the differences between different approaches and the ways in which they fit together.

There is nothing to stop you reading either Chapter 9 or 10 next if you prefer. But our advice, if you're a beginner, is to wait a while until you feel more familiar with the kinds of issues about which sociologists are concerned, the special language they use, and some of the different ways in which they record and interpret their information.

Part One

Why aren't all people equal? Why do some people earn seven-figure salaries while others exist on state benefits? Has a woman of Afro-Caribbean origin as much chance of securing a 'top' job as a white, male Old Etonian? Who decides what is a 'top' job?

The study of social stratification and social inequality is one of the most important areas in sociology. The position people occupy within a society and their access to material resources affect all aspects of their lives, from their education, work and health to their behaviour, beliefs and values.

Social stratification refers to the way in which social groups are ranked one above the other in terms of their wealth, prestige or power, rather like the geological formation of rock layers or strata. However, the geological analogy is not entirely appropriate for the following reasons:

- Social groups are not as rigid as this implies, and some people are able, on occasions, to move between the layers.
- In society the top layer is considerably smaller than those lower down, as only a minority of people occupy the pinnacle of the stratification system.
- The relationship between the 'layers' is one of **inequality.** Those in the top layer are more **privileged** – in their life chances – they are more likely to be wealthier, healthier and better educated. They are likely to be seen as more important, to get more respect and have more **prestige** or **status** than other groups. They will also have more **power** over their own lives and over the lives of other people.

Some people are reluctant to accept that this ranking of social groups exists, often referring to the essential humanity of all people regardless of background or position, or to a religious belief that 'all are equal in the eyes of God'. Others may have a strong sense of being 'just as good as anyone else'. These assertions may well be true, but they are beliefs – moral, philosophical or religious propositions – which cannot be proven one way or the other.

Sociologists, on the other hand, have shown that social position affects life chances from birth to death. For example, we know that Americans of colour have, on average, twice the rate of infant mortality of other groups in the USA. In Britain the chances of dying prematurely at every age increase as one moves down the social scale. There is no doubt, then, that social inequality exists, and that it has far-reaching consequences for individuals and for society as a whole.

The main elements in social stratification in modern industrial societies are:

- class and status
- gender
- ethnicity
- age.

In the past justifications were used to explain why poor people, women or non-Europeans were treated unequally in Britain. These explanations frequently claimed that such groups possessed innate or biological characteristics which warranted unequal treatment. For example, the poor were blamed for being lazy or inadequate; women for being weak and emotional; non-European ethnic groups for being less intelligent.

Today sociologists deny these claims, arguing that they have been constructed as excuses for inequality, to preserve privilege, prestige and power for other groups.

The social construction of identity

The study of social class, gender, ethnicity and age is also important in relation to understanding the nature of social identity – about the factors which help to influence people's identity and which also provide the context in which they are able to make sense of their identity. Relatively few things about a person are 'given' at birth in a form which is 'biologically determined' and which cannot be altered. People are born men or women, with differing skin colours, in circumstances of greater or lesser affluence. But the **significance** and **consequences** attached to these circumstances are more important than the circumstances themselves. Rather than being **biologically determined**, sociologists now argue that most of what we associate as male and female behaviour, or the differences which separate people from different ethnic backgounds, are **'socially constructed'**, and as such they are subject to variation and change. Even the maldistribution of resources which makes the discrepancies in wealth and opportunities around the world enormous are a socially created phenomenon, not an act of 'God' or nature.

Women's Liberation Movement

One of the main demands of the **Women's Liberation Movement** in the 1970s and 1980s was for the right of women to 'define their own sexuality and identity' rather than have these definitions 'imposed from outside' by forces which did not necessarily have women's best interests at heart. The demand implied that there is always some kind of struggle going on about what constitutes identity, and that definitions of identity are **contested** or argued about in ways which reflect different interests as well as different ideas. **Bell Hooks**, the black feminist and sociologist, in writing about inequalities and power relations in society, has argued that:

BellHooks

> as subjects, people have the right to define their own reality, establish their own identities, and name their own history.

The extent to which individuals have scope to do what she says is massively influenced by issues of class, gender, age and ethnicity, which both 'give' substance and shape to individual identity and also reflect the meaning which individuals are able to give to their own lives. In considering these factors in subsequent chapters in relation to social stratification, we shall also consider their impact on the social construction of identity.

1   Social class in Britain

Classes are one of the main forms of stratification in modern industrial societies like Britain. In feudal times people were grouped into formal, legally defined **estates** – the nobility, the clergy, commoners, with a mass of people below them living as serfs or landless peasants. Position was largely determined by birth, and movement between the estates was rare. By contrast, social classes have no legal status. In theory at least, we are all equal before the law. Class position is not absolutely determined by birth, and people can move into different social classes by a variety of means. Although there are differences of opinion about what are the precise class groups, there is general agreement about the three main categories:

● upper class
● middle class
● working class.

In recent years some sociologists have recognized an additional group below the usual categories, which some label as an **underclass** of particularly deprived groups and individuals.

One of the first things a sociologist wants to know about a person is 'what social class they belong to.' Terms such as upper class, middle class and working class are ones we all use. But what do we mean by them? Do sociologists mean the same thing? And why does it matter anyway? Before trying to answer some of these questions, stop for a moment and ask yourself what you mean by social class. Here are a few questions to help you.

Test your class consciousness

1 What social class do you think you belong to? Make a note of your main reasons for putting yourself in one social class rather than another. (If you do not think you belong to any social class, jot down the main reasons for your opinion.)
2 Think of one or two people you know very well and imagine you had to decide upon their social class. These are some of the things you might take into account. Rearrange the list in order of importance, putting the most important consideration at the top and the least important consideration at the bottom.

● What kind of education they have had
● What kind of house they live in
● What kind of job their mother did
● The amount of respect and admiration they get from others
● How much money they have
● Their dress and general appearance
● Their general attitude to life
● Their general behaviour and relationships with others

- What kind of job they do
- What kind of neighbourhood they live in
- How much they earn
- What kind of job their father did.

3   Do you think that class differences are very important in Britain today? Do people look up to some, or look down on others, because of their social class? Jot down as many illustrations as you can to support your point of view.

As soon as anyone mentions social class, there is likely to be a full-scale argument about whether or not social class exists or matters these days. Your own answers to the questions above are probably just the sort of thing to get any group of adults agreeing or disagreeing with your point of view. Try it out when you are next in the pub with some friends! Social class is certainly a subject which can stir up a lot of emotions, especially if people associate it with 'too much money','too much power', 'rowdy behaviour', 'snobbish' or 'irresponsible' attitudes. The stereotypes we all have about what is 'typical' of upper-class, middle-class and working-class people are many, and, like all stereotypes, they often contradict each other.

In this kind of atmosphere the sociologist's job is a difficult one: how to make generalizations about social class which are meaningful, as objective as possible and yet sensitive to different people's emotional reactions to the issues involved. Sociologists start from the conviction that not only does social class definitely exist in our society, but also its influence, in all kinds of organizational and personal ways, is very important. While a lot of the different characteristics have changed over the years, and the divisions between social classes are maybe not as clear-cut as they used to be, membership of one social class rather than another still has a tremendous influence on people's life styles, behaviour, opportunities and attitudes.

Before considering some of these, let's return to your thoughts on the matter.

Subjective and objective definitions of social class

Whatever social class you put yourself into, the first thing to notice is that people's views of themselves do not always correspond with the description a sociologist would make. The difference is often referred to as the distinction between **subjective** definitions of class and **objective** definitions of class.

Some people, for example, consider themselves to be 'middle-class' if they think of their occupation as a respectable white-collar job. Others may feel that everyone who works is working class, as Margaret Thatcher asserted in 1988, or they may still feel a part of the working-class family environment in which they grew up, even though education and occupation have changed their social circumstances considerably.

Whatever people's personal or subjective feelings might be, sociologists have rather different criteria for deciding their social class. They use a number of categories such as occupation, income, wealth, education, lifestyle and behavioural characteristics to put people into different social class groupings. In general, the most importance is given to the kind of job people do and how much money they have. The type of house they live in, where their children go to school, what they do in their spare time, how they dress and what they expect from life usually follow from the first two – though, of course, the relationship between them can be more complicated than this.

Criteria of class

Occupation

For official purposes the Office of Population Censuses and Surveys classifies the population according to the Registrar-General's classification scheme. Originally this was a system of ranking people into one of five groups according to the 'standing in the community' of their particular occupation. Since 1981 classification of occupations is now on the basis of the amount of skill needed to perform the job.

Class

1   Professional
2   Intermediate occupations; lower professional
3N Skilled non-manual occupations
3M Skilled manual occupations
4   Semi-skilled occupations
5   Unskilled occupations

The division between working and middle class is seen to be between 3N and 3M.

Look back at your answers to the questions and see how closely they correspond to the Registrar-General's scheme.

John Goldthorpe

Sociologists often use the Registrar-General's scale in their own research, but others have developed alternative scales. For example, **John Goldthorpe** devised a different system when he was carrying out research into **social mobility** (the extent to which people's class positions change). He devised a system based on an assessment of the **market situation** and the **work situation** of people's jobs. By market situation he meant how much money a person could expect to earn in a job and what his or her career prospects were. By work situation he meant how much control that person could expect to have over his or her own work, whether he or she could organize the work at his or her own pace or were tied to externally set work schedules or even to a machine controlled by a supervisor.

His scheme was as follows:

Class

Service:
Higher-grade professionals, administrators, managers and owners of large companies
Lower-grade professionals, administrators, managers and owners of smaller companies

Intermediate:
Routine non-manual, clerical, sales
Small owners, including farmers, self-employed artisans, e.g. plumbers
Lower grade technicians, supervisors of manual workers

Working:
Skilled manual employees
Manual wage workers in semi- and unskilled occupations

Now try fitting your own answers into this scheme.

Some sociologists are critical of this scheme because it fails to recognize that the owners of large companies are usually much wealthier and more powerful than other occupations in their group.

There are two major criticisms that can be made of classification systems like these.

1 First, any system which puts people into classes according to their occupation leaves out anyone without a paid job, including the sick or disabled who are unable to work; the unemployed; the retired; young people; unpaid carers and those doing full-time housework or childcare at home; as well as those who are wealthy enough not to have to work.

2 Secondly, feminists have criticized these schemes for failing to reflect the kinds of jobs women generally do in the labour market and, more importantly, for classifying women according to the occupation of their husbands. Sociologists such as **Michelle Stanworth** and **Sarah Arber** have pointed out that many women are now the only, the main or significant breadwinners for their families. They also argue that because women experience discrimination at work and inequality at home they should be classified in their own right. Some sociologists such as **Christine Delphy** have gone so far as to suggest that women are a different class entirely from men, regardless of their occupational status.

Stanworth and Arber

Christine Delphy

Income and wealth

Accurate information about income and wealth is quite difficult to obtain. In practice, we know who the rich people are, but it is very difficult to find out just how wealthy they are. This is because a distinction is made between income and wealth.

Income is defined as the money earned from paid employment and the dividends received from investments. It has to be declared to the Inland Revenue and income tax has to be paid. But there are all kinds of perfectly legal ways in which people can get tax relief on things like mortgages, life assurance, school fees and business expenses.

Wealth refers to people's other financial assets, such as land, property, stocks and shares. The assessment of liability for tax on these is much more difficult to determine and, consequently, easy to avoid. For example, there are legal ways of transferring wealth before death to avoid paying death duties. Since rich people do not have to divulge the extent of their wealth to anyone, it is almost impossible to find out just how much they own. What is known, however, is that the majority of income and wealth is concentrated in the hands of a relatively small section of the population.

Income

Sources of income include wages and salaries, fees, pensions, gifts, maintenance payments, state benefits, income from property and dividends from shares, interest on investments and sometimes benefits given in kind, such as the value of education or health services. The amount of income earned influences lifestyle and life chances. Those on higher incomes tend to have a better education, live longer and enjoy better health and living conditions.

Government policies can alter the distribution of income by changing taxes and welfare benefits and can be used to redistribute income from the rich to the poor or to favour better-off groups. The Royal Commission on the Distribution of Income and Wealth 1949–79 found that some redistribution of income had occurred, but mainly from the very top towards middle-income groups rather than to poorer groups. Since 1979 this trend towards redistribution seems to have been reversed.

Between 1979 and 1993 the basic rate of taxation has been cut from 33 per cent to 25 per cent, with a special rate of 20 per cent for those on lower incomes. At first sight this would appear to favour less well-off groups, but in fact because the tax thresholds (i.e. the point at which tax starts to be paid) have been lowered, more low incomes are now eligible for taxation than previously, and the reduction in the basic rate has been more advantageous to middle-income groups.

The top rate of taxation has been reduced from 80 per cent prior to 1979 to 40 per cent, immediately increasing the incomes of those on higher earnings and reducing the state's income from taxation.

indirect tax

Since 1979 VAT has gone up from a dual rate of 8 per cent and 12 per cent to a single rate of 17.5 per cent. It has been applied to fuel, which was previously zero-rated for tax purposes. Value added tax is known as an **indirect tax** because it is not deducted from earnings at source but added to the cost of goods and services. Such indirect taxes fall more heavily on poorer groups, who spend a greater proportion of their income on living costs and cannot afford to save. Consequently, they pay tax on a greater proportion of their income than better-off groups.

Local taxes such as the community charge and the council tax, which replaced it in April 1993, both require people on benefits to pay up to 20 per cent. These relatively new taxes, both introduced by the Conservative Government of Margaret Thatcher, have also increased the tax bill for poorer groups.

Government policy between 1979 and 1994, aimed at reducing inflation, partly through the control of public expenditure, has meant that the poorest groups in society, who are most dependent on welfare benefits and services, have seen their incomes fall at a time when others have enjoyed considerable prosperity. By 1991, after a sharp recession, 1 in 7 people were dependent on state benefits for all or part of their income.

Recent figures from the Central Statistical Office suggest that these changes in Government policies have redistributed income **to** the rich. According to the *Guardian*, 23 January 1992:

> Tax changes under the Conservatives have helped the well-off at the expense of the poor, the annual Social Trends statistical survey confirms today in an analysis showing that indirect taxation is taking a growing slice of low incomes.

The survey acknowledges that the share of total income going to the richest fifth of households has grown since 1979 'at each stage of the tax-benefit system'. Meanwhile, 'the share of the poorest fifth has shrunk'.

It would seem, therefore, that in the last two decades of the twentieth century there has been an increase in income inequalities and, some would argue, a strengthening of class divisions.

Wealth

Sources of wealth can be **marketable wealth** – assets which can be sold and their value realized, such as land, stocks, shares, houses, cars, works of art, jewellery, antiques, savings or shares, or **non-marketable wealth** – assets which cannot be disposed of, such as entailed land and property, non-transferable pensions or superannuation schemes.

Because the Government does not collect information on wealth because there is no wealth tax on the living, there are difficulties in obtaining accurate information on the distribution of wealth in our society. The following methods are used, however:

estate duty

1 Information from **estate duty** figures. Estate duty is a tax payable on assets over a certain value on death. However, these figures tend to give an inaccurate estimate of wealth for the following reasons:

inheritance tax

- It is possible to transfer some assets to relatives before death to avoid paying estate duty. Since 1986 **inheritance tax** has not been payable on gifts under a certain size, providing they were made seven years or more before death.
- Estate duty figures tend inevitably to yield information about the wealth of older groups in society, but wealth is not evenly distributed by age so we cannot generalize on the basis of these figures to other age groups in society.

2 Tax must be paid if a capital gain is made on the sale of shares or some forms of property. This information should be available to the Inland Revenue. In 1988 information from a treasury survey found that 21 per cent of adults over the age of 25 owned shares. The effect of Government privatizations in the 1980s and early 1990s has been to increase the number of people owning shares, but the majority of stakes are so small that they are unlikely to exercise any influence on the companies concerned. In fact, Phillips and Drew, the stockbroking firm, estimated that between 1979 and 1989 the percentage of shares in private hands fell from 33 per cent to 18 per cent as financial institutions, insurance companies, etc. increased their holdings.

Changing distribution of wealth

There have been considerable reductions in wealth inequality over the last hundred years, **although most wealth is still concentrated in the hands of a minority**. For example, in 1989 the wealthiest 1 per cent owned 18 per cent of all wealth, the wealthiest 10 per cent owned 53 per cent of all wealth while the remaining 90 per cent shared less than half of all personal wealth in Britain. The most significant redistribution of wealth has been **within** wealthy groups rather than **between** them and the rest of the population. This has occurred as assets have been transferred to younger members of the family to avoid death duties and because of the inheritance of houses, which increased in value as a result of rises in house prices in the 1980s.

Overall, the distribution of both income and wealth in Britain still reflects a considerable degree of inequality. Over the last twenty years the rich have got richer and the poor poorer.

Cultural definitions of social class

So far most of our discussion has been about the distribution of economic resources in society. In your answer to question 2 on page 3, did you place job, money and earnings at the top of your list or choose some other criteria?

Some people would argue that you can tell a person's social class by how he or she talks and dresses, where he or she lives and how he or she behaves. People from different social classes tend to do different things in their leisure time, read different newspapers, watch different programmes on television, feel differently about education, politics and the jobs they do. Or so the argument goes. In other words, the general behaviour, attitudes and lifestyles of people are different in different social classes. When sociologists emphasize these kinds of criteria, they are using a **cultural definition** of social class.

However, cultural definitions can produce problems if they are not applied carefully. The main danger is one of 'putting the cart before the horse'. It is certainly the case that people in the same social class have many things in common – the same monopoly or lack of access to scarce resources, for example; the same good or bad standards of housing; the same access to, or restrictions on, educational opportunity; the same shared experiences of comfort, travel, hardship or enjoyment. But all of these cultural character-istics are the **consequences** of social class rather than the **causes** of it. People's lifestyles are a reflection of their economic condition in society, not the reason for their position.

A second problem with cultural definitions of class is that of stereotyping and 'labelling'. In making generalizations about the behaviour and attitudes of people in different social classes, there is a tendency to assume that **all** working-class people or **all** middle-class people are much the same. And so often these generalizations are accompanied by implicit judgements about the behaviour being described. The fact that the children of working-class parents or of Afro-Caribbean parents are less likely to be successful at school than the children of white, middle-class parents, for example, has focused a good deal of attention on their family background and upbringing. **Doug Holly** captures the flavour of much of this labelling in this extract from *The Invisible Ruling Class*:

Doug Holly

> The working class show only limited interest in education and aren't much good at it. The parents fail to encourage the children at school or provide the right setting at home for educational successes. They don't read many books and they watch the wrong sort of television. Their language, too, we are told, is all wrong. The working class, except for a small group trying to get their children a better start in life, are, in fact, born educational failures.

The kind of labelling which Holly is paraphrasing here has the effect of stigmatizing all working-class backgrounds. By sleight of hand 'cultural definitions' of working class are translated into judgements about 'cultural deficiencies' which can become **self-fulfilling prophesies.**

By comparison, middle-class parents are said to:

J. W. B. Douglas

> ... take more interest in their children's progress at school than working class parents do, and they become relatively more interested as their children grow older. They visit the school more frequently to find out how their children are getting on with their work. They are also outstanding in the use they make of the available medical services. Their children benefit not only from the support and encouragement they can get in their school work but from the excellent personal and medical care they get at home.

In this extract from the influential study *The Home and the School*, by **J. W. B. Douglas** and his colleagues, you can begin to see how the label of 'good' applied to middle class parents came to be established. The effect of sociological research like this has been to stereotype the repercussions of social class divisions in society and to contribute to social prejudices about the supposed cultural superiority of some in comparison to others.

Class theories

Before we look further at the changing class structure of Britain, we need to look briefly at the key theories about social class inequality that have been developed in sociology over the last 150 years. There are three major theories:

1 Explanations based on the theories of Karl Marx.
2 Explanations based on the theories of Max Weber.
3 Functionalist explanations of stratification.

Karl Marx

Marx is the best known and most influential writer on the subject of social class. Although he died before he had fully explored the concept of class, others have worked on his many writings, interpreting and reinterpreting them to provide what is today regarded as a **Marxist** view of class. (Note the distinction, therefore, between the term **Marxian**, which stems directly from Marx's own writing, and **Marxist**, which is an interpretation of Marx's work.)

means of production

For Marx the most important element in society was the economy. He argued that the means by which people made their living – the **means of production** – determined all other social factors. He took a historical perspective, analysing societies from ancient times to Victorian Britain, and arguing that, at every stage of history, one group emerged which was able to control others through its control of the means of producing wealth.

According to Marx, in 'primitive' times people survived as best they could, hunting small animals and gathering berries and nuts. Inequality had its origins in the next stage of development, where sufficient skill had been developed to make tools to begin simple agriculture. This provided a more secure form of subsistence and also created the possibility that some people could expropriate the means of producing food on which the group survived by claiming the land or the tools as their own private property.

This then created a two-fold division into those who owned the means of production and those who were doing the actual labour of producing the crops. So in feudal times, for example, society was principally divided into the landowners – the aristocracy and gentry – and the serfs who toiled on their behalf. This model of a land-owning élite and mass of exploited peasantry still exists today in some parts of the world.

In industrial societies it is industrialists or **capitalists** who own the factories, offices and shops, and workers who must exchange their labour power for wages.

Marx's theory of class

The main points in **Marx's theory of class** are as follows:

In capitalist societies the factory owners or **bourgeoisie** do not pay the workers, or **proletariat**, the full value of their labour because they want to make a profit, selling the product for more than the cost of producing it. This creates what Marx calls **surplus value**, which the bourgeoisie can use as they see fit, either reinvesting it to make more profit or using it to finance a privileged lifestyle. Marx was writing at the height of the Industrial Revolution in Britain, when there were striking differences between the lives of wealthy industrialists and factory workers. Owners were beginning to use their profits to buy mansions on the edge of towns, run by an army of servants, to send their sons to public schools and to find marriageable members of the aristocracy as husbands for their daughters. At the same time their workers were living in overcrowded, insanitary conditions.

Because workers are not paid the full value of their labour they experience **exploitation** and **alienation** from their true natures. They are unable to express themselves through work or to experience any satisfaction from the work they do, working only for extrinsic rewards in the form of their pay packet. This limits their capacity to lead meaningful and creative lives, as they have no sense of control over their own destinies.

As capitalism develops, firms expand. Small businesses, such as shop-keepers or craftspeople, are forced out of business because they can no longer compete with mass production and large businesses. As a result, these intermediate groups sink down into the proletariat, leaving the two main groups, the bourgeoisie and the proletariat, in opposition to each other at either end of the class structure. This process is known as the **polarization** of classes.

The bourgeoisie continue to exploit the proletariat, who become increasingly impoverished. In the endless search for more profit, skilled work is split into a series of smaller, unskilled tasks, or taken over by new machines which reduce labour costs. This process, in turn, reduces the differences between groups of workers on the basis of their superior skill or higher wages, and, as a consequence, the conditions of the proletariat become increasingly similar or **homogeneous**. They increasingly share a common lifestyle and common **class interests** as they are herded together in factories.

In these circumstances the proletariat would then become increasingly aware of their true position as a **class**, not just as individuals. **Class consciousness** would result, as they came to see themselves in a relationship of **class conflict** with the bourgeoisie.

The proletariat would then begin to organize as a **class for itself** and engage in **class actions** to challenge the power of the bourgeoisie by forming a revolutionary workers class which would rise up and overthrow the bourgeoisie and usher in a **socialist** and ultimately **communist** society.

Although Marx predicted that capitalism would eventually give way to communism, in fact those societies which became communist in the twentieth century were mainly semi-feudal societies, such as Russia and Latin America. We can only speculate on what Marx would have made of the upheavals in Eastern Europe, in which so-called communist governments were replaced with free market economies in the late 1980s.

For Marx, then, class is not a result of birth, education, status or occupation, but of one's relationship to the means of production – either an owner or a non-owner. He believed that inequalities of income, wealth and lifestyle were a consequence of class position rather than the cause of it.

Substructure and superstructure

Marx believed that class conflict affected every aspect of social life, not just work experiences. He made a distinction between the economic base or **substructure** of society and what he called the **superstructure**, which refers to other aspects of society. The form the economy takes influences the state – government, parliament, the judiciary, the civil service – and the ideas put forward by what Althusser (see page 99) later called the 'ideological state apparatus' – the education system, the church and mass media. Two important aspects of Marxist theory develop from this distinction.

ruling class

1 Marx argued that those who control the economy, through the ownership of the means of production, also exercise political power through the state. In other words, the bourgeoisie is also the **ruling class** which controls the business of government to serve its own interests, for example by passing laws which protect its power and privilege.

dominant ideology

2 The prevailing ideas and beliefs present in a society at any point in time are likely to be those of the ruling class because they are in a position to have their ideas adopted and put forward via the education system, the church, the mass media and the legal system. Marx uses the term **ideology** to describe this system of beliefs which underlies social action. More recently, the term **dominant ideology** has been used to refer to a set of ideas which justifies the dominance of one group over another. For example, we might say that private property is highly valued in a society which is based on a capitalist economic system, and that it is regarded as 'natural' to want to own and accumulate things. However, there are societies where this is not the case, where things are owned collectively and where generosity is what is highly valued, rather than acquisitiveness. By encouraging people to buy, consume and collect possessions, the interests of business are served and profits increase.

In the 1980s the belief that 'private ownership is best' was vigorously pursued with regard to home ownership, and local councils were ordered to make public housing available for purchase by their tenants. The result was that over 1.5 million council houses were sold. The effects of recession, unemployment and rising interest rates has meant that there have been widespread repossessions by building societies and that people who previously had secure tenancies have lost their homes.

false class consciousness

It could be argued that in this case private ownership was not in the best interests of those people, but because of the significance given to the idea of private ownership in our society this truth was obscured. Marxists refer to such a situation as **false class consciousness**, in which the proletariat hold views which are contrary to their **best** interests, because their **real** interests are obscured by the pervasive nature of dominant ideology. According to Marx, the proletariat must recognize their real interests before revolutionary action can take place.

Criticisms

Many sociologists have pointed out that the polarization which Marx predicted has not (yet) taken place, but rather that the reverse has happened. Although some marginal groups may have disappeared, there has been a growth in professional, managerial and white-collar occupations, with the development of large-scale bureaucracies and welfare agencies, who do not fit neatly into the bourgeoisie/proletariat division. In other words, they disagree with the view that polarization into just two large classes has occurred.

The class consciousness which Marx argued was necessary for real classes to emerge does not seem to have happened. Some argue that both the bourgeoisie and the proletariat have been more prepared to make concessions or compromises than Marx foresaw. The effects of the welfare state in Britain and general rises in the standard of living have reduced the worst excesses of capitalism and consequently taken the edge off class consciousness.

Others, including some feminists, have criticized Marxism for basing class purely on the relationship to the means of production, arguing that there are other sources of inequality besides the economic, such as the inequality between men and women in family life.

Whatever the criticisms, and despite the apparent demise of states based on Marxist ideas, Marxism remains one of the most influential perspectives on social class and has been incorporated into some explanations of other sources of stratification, such as gender and ethnicity. Modern Marxists have paid more attention to the cultural aspects of class rather than the purely economic ones, and as such have moved closer to the theory of Weber, discussed below.

Max Weber

Max Weber was also an early contributor to the discussion on social stratification. Like Marx, he defined people's social class in relation to their economic power, but unlike Marx, he made a distinction between different aspects of social stratification. Weber's major criticism of Marx was that he over-generalized from what is 'sometimes the situation' to what is 'always the situation'. Neither did he believe that class conflict and class consciousness were the inevitable product of the class situation, as Marx suggested, but that a variety of different actions could result, depending on the circumstances. He wrote, in *Class, Status and Party*, 'the direction in which the individual worker is likely to pursue his interests may vary widely' and 'the rise of societal or even communal action from a common class situation is by no means a universal phenomenon'.

Weber took a more pragmatic and **empirical** line than Marx in this respect, and concentrated rather on recording and comparing the different types of action which came from different groups in the class system.

He also drew attention to other dimensions of stratification which Marx tended to assume were all part and parcel of the same thing. Weber believed that not just economic position but also social standing was a significant feature of the way in which people were regarded by society. He referred to this as **status**.

Usually a person's status is a reflection of his or her job and economic position, but the link is not always a direct one. Some groups receive more respect and prestige than others, and, while the criteria change over time, they are usually based on social judgements about occupation, lifestyle, birth, culture and education. The ways in which such 'qualities' are defined and come to be agreed upon make an interesting debate. There seems to be a remarkable consensus in society at any one time about what is thought to be worthy of respect. The questions for sociologists to ask are, of course, 'Who makes these judgements in the first place?' And 'How do they become so widely accepted?' The ways in which ruling groups in society tend to promote and reinforce their own culture as the superior kind, and conspire, through their control of key economic and social institutions, to restrict entry to it, while at the same time setting it as the goal for other groups to aspire to, is a discussion provoked by Marx and Weber's debate and taken up again in the twentieth century by sociologists like Bourdieu and Althusser and the arguments which contribute to the sociology of knowledge and control.

While Marx tended to regard class and status as synonymous, Weber believed that status considerations often cut through and overlapped class divisions – for example, the distinction made between the 'respectable', 'hard-working' and 'aspiring' working class and the 'rough', 'feckless' and 'unreliable' lower orders, or the high status attached to individual craft workers and the sense of vocation attributed to occupations such as nursing and social work, neither of which is reflected in the economic rewards and social power of their holders.

The other dimension in Weber's view of social stratification besides class and status was **party**. For Weber, parties were groups of people who organized themselves to attract and exert power. They might be political parties, but could also be trade unions, pressure groups of various kinds, professional associations or, indeed, any kind of group acting together in some form of collective action. Weber conceded, however, that such groups could well overlap class and status distinctions.

Functionalist explanations of stratification

Talcott Parsons

Functionalist theories of stratification are concerned to demonstrate that stratification systems contribute to the maintenance of order and stability in societies. **Talcott Parsons**, the American functionalist, argued that:

- different parts of societies and different groups are interdependent, and must cooperate if society is to run smoothly;
- there is general agreement about how people should be ranked in society. In Western societies this is generally on the basis of individual achievement, ambition and hard work, so that people with talent or responsible positions are paid more and are highly regarded by others;
- a stratification system in which some people are more highly rewarded and regarded than others is therefore seen as both inevitable and just;
- the power of higher social groups is seen as legitimate because it is used to pursue goals which benefit the whole society.

Increasingly, sociologists have become critical of functionalist theorists like Parsons (see page 39), arguing that:

- stratification can create divisions between groups – the haves and the have-nots – which might disrupt the smooth running of society;
- people in positions of power do not always work in the interests of society as a whole, but for personal gain, sometimes at the expense of others.

For example, on 11 October 1992 *The Sunday Times* reported that:

> Too many captains of industry are massively over-paid for their performance in terms of the return they deliver to shareholders.

Among the many examples quoted in the article was a company chairman, whose salary of £187,849 was over 16 per cent of his company's profit for that year and represented a massive 839 per cent rise on his salary of £20,000 for the previous year. At the same time, the value of shares in that company fell by 27 per cent. The article also gives details of top salaries of £1,813,000, at a time when increasing numbers of ordinary workers were being urged to exercise wage restraint and keep demands for wage increases in line with inflation.

On 3 September 1994 the *Guardian* reported on 'one of British industry's most daringly generous pay packages'. Martin Sorrell, boss of the advertising group WPP, received a package of 'annual salary, performance bonus, shares, private health care and personal insurance' which could add up to more than £8 million a year. Meanwhile, 'the company had just resumed dividend payments to shareholders, with a 1p share payout after a three-year gap'.

High rewards given to some positions are not necessarily approved of or supported by the rest of the population, but are maintained because some groups have more power than others to advance their positions.

Davis & Moore

The most comprehensive development of the functionalist theory of stratification was made by **Kingsley Davis and Wilbert Moore** in an article in *The American Sociology Review* in 1945. We can summarize their arguments as follows:

- All societies need some system of organizing positions, roles and duties. Therefore stratification is **inevitable, universal, functional** and **desirable**.
- Societies need to motivate skilled, able people to fill important and responsible positions in society.
- People differ in terms of their innate ability and talents; not everyone is able to do every job. Ability and skill may be in short supply.
- Positions in society differ in terms of their importance for the survival of society. Some jobs are more important than others and have other jobs dependent upon them.
- Unequal rewards motivate the most able people to undertake these important jobs. High earnings, status and respect are seen as necessary 'carrots' to persuade the 'best' people to undertake lengthy training and arduous responsibilities.

Criticisms

- Sociologists have argued over whether stratification is universal and inevitable. For example, even in societies which have made a deliberate effort to eliminate material and status differences between people it seems that some elements of stratification have emerged.

Eva Rosenfield

In a study of the Israeli kibbutzim, **Eva Rosenfield** found that, despite attempts to create a new and equal society within the kibbutzim, status distinctions began to emerge as they moved from a purely agricultural economic base. This supports the argument that inequalities emerge in complex industrial societies where different technical and managerial skills are required.

However, it is not inevitable that different skills and talents need to be rewarded unequally.

The functionalist theory assumes that people are only motivated by external rewards. Responsible jobs may attract people because they may be more interesting, allow the holders more freedom or authority to make decisions and allow them greater control over their own lives. There are many examples of people choosing lower paid jobs because of the interest they hold or because they attract people with a sense of 'vocation'.

According to Davis and Moore, talented people from any background are able to acquire the qualifications through the education system which are their passport to highly rewarded positions. However, others have pointed out that people with talent and ability do not always achieve the qualifications and occupations of which they are capable. Research into educational achievement (see Chapter 6) indicates that educational 'success' is often itself a **result** of stratification, as class position, financial hardship and the middle-class ethos of educational institutions can all prevent able members of lower social groups from achieving their full potential.

It is not always the case that those who have qualifications always succeed in securing the most highly rewarded jobs. There is much evidence of what is known as 'self-recruitment' to top jobs. Those who occupy the top élite positions in society – in business, government, the civil service, the church, the military – tend to come from the same social backgrounds, sometimes from the same families. Well-qualified people with different social origins may find it very difficult to break into this 'Establishment'. This could apply to class, gender or ethnicity, all of which can operate as barriers to the free recruitment of talent or 'meritocracy' assumed by Davis and Moore.

The idea that some jobs are functionally more important than others is difficult to demonstrate. Are people who make key decisions in boardrooms more important than those workers who produce the fuel – oil, coal, electricity, gas – that powers the industrial, commercial and domestic processes on which our day-to-day lives are so dependent? It is also unclear what Davis and Moore mean by 'the survival of society' – is it to maintain the current system operating in the same way? Or is it to encourage change and development to meet changing circumstances?

The idea that people deserve rewards for undergoing training has been criticized. Some argue that going to college or university is a privilege in itself, providing rewards, not deprivations, compared with the lives of young workers or those young people without work. Davis and Moore also assume that lengthy training is necessary to perform well-paid jobs. This view has been questioned with regard to both manual and white-collar jobs. During the Second World War women learned to be welders in the shipyards after four months' training. Male apprenticeships had previously lasted for six years. Some professions also maintain that lengthy training is required, as this helps to preserve the mystique of the occupation when, in fact, the job could be learned in a shorter period of time.

The functionalist approach ignores the fact that positions carry differing amounts of power and that those with power are able to manipulate the system for their own benefit, erecting barriers to keep others out. The more powerful are able to control the system of rewards in such a way that, far from operating in the public interest and helping to integrate society, they serve their own interests at the expense of others and produce a divided society. In recent years some sociologists have argued that an **'underclass'** of particularly deprived groups is emerging, dependent on fixed state benefits and effectively cut off from the social experiences of the rest of society. Women, ethnic minorities, the young and the elderly figure disproportionately here, suggesting that these groups have unequal access to resources in our society.

The changing class structure in Britain today

Traditionally, the British class structure has been regarded as more rigid than, for example, that of the United States. This has been attributed to the existence of a traditional aristocracy and monarchy, with privileges based on birth, inherited wealth, preserved and transmitted to successive generations, and to hereditary positions such as the House of Lords, all of which have limited upward mobility from other social classes.

At the same time, there has been some redistribution of wealth compared with the nineteenth century, and an increase in the significance of educational achievement and merit as a means of moving up through the system.

Other changes include the impact of technology and large-scale organizations in both the public and private sectors of employment, an increase in the numbers of women and ethnic minorities in employment and the growth of consumerism, all of which have affected both manual and non-manual occupations or lifestyles.

How these changes to the class structure are interpreted depends upon which theoretical perspective is employed.

- **Liberal** sociologists writing about the post-war years have suggested that classes are moving closer together as the distinctive aspects which distinguish manual work and working class lifestyles are disappearing and becoming indistinguishable from those of the middle class.
- Sociologists following Weber have argued that classes have **fragmented** into different positions based on skill, wages, conditions, status, each with their own interests, and that it is no longer meaningful to talk of distinct classes.
- Marxists have examined the class structure for signs of polarization, strong class allegiance and political movements, arguing that Britain is still an unequal society characterized by distinct social classes which stand in opposition to each other.

We shall examine each class in turn for evidence of these views.

The working class

Traditionally, those employed in manual work have been regarded as working class, living in traditional communities, typified by pit villages in the north of England, Wales and Scotland or dockland areas in the East End of London. While distinctions were always made between skilled, semi-skilled or unskilled workers, in general the working class was seen as a distinctive group sharing a common identity, values and way of life, seeing its best interests served by collective action in the trade union and Labour movement.

On the other hand, there have always been those who denied that there were significant class differences, maintaining, as Margaret Thatcher did, that there was no real class system at all. These popular views reflect sociological arguments, too. Sociologists are divided over whether it really makes much sense to study the working class as if this group shares a common identity and experience. Some argue that changes have so altered society that the term 'working class' is itself redundant. For example:

- Changes in the occupational structure brought about by the decline in agriculture, mining and manufacturing industries have resulted in a decline in the number of manual jobs and hence in the actual size of the working class which has shrunk as a result.

- Traditional working-class communities have virtually disappeared, partly as a result of slum clearance and rehousing programmes in the 1950s and 1960s, and more recently as a result of industrial decline. Class solidarity in such communities was reinforced by common working experiences and communal life.
- At the same time, there has been a growth in service industries, providing jobs which have traditionally been regarded as middle-, or at least lower-middle-class occupations – in retailing and sales, catering, care and clerical work, now filled by many who originated in the working class.
- Issues of sex and race discrimination have introduced divisions which throw into question the homogeneity of the working class as a group with a common culture and identity. A young Asian woman working in the computer software industry in Surrey, for example, might be thought to have little in common with a redundant miner in South Yorkshire.

Daniel Bell

Liberal sociologists such as **Daniel Bell,** reviewing the affluent post-war years, argue that the impact of technology has changed the nature of manual work, which now requires greater technical expertise and more responsibility. In other words, the distinctive nature of working-class jobs – heavy, manual, sometimes dirty and dangerous labour – has changed and become similar to white-collar work. Work is less physically demanding, cleaner and allows greater freedom, so that the industrial worker is no longer a blue-coated, overall-clad worker tied to a machine but a white-coated technical operative, supervising smooth-running automated processes.

The effect of such changes, Bell argues, has been the development of a more individualistic outlook and a decline in working-class consciousness. Workers no longer need the group solidarity fostered by extreme working conditions, and become more 'privatized', less concerned with collective strategies and more with consumerism, status, family life and leisure activities.

This kind of argument was found in the debate in the 1960s and 1970s about the supposed growth in affluence among certain sectors of industrial workers, e.g. those in car and chemical production, known as the **embourgeoisement debate.**

Embourgeoisement debate

In the course of the 1950s statistics became available which suggested that a significant increase in the incomes of manual workers had taken place and that many of them were now earning wages which were directly comparable with those of white-collar workers and supervisory staff. Information about consumption patterns also indicated a big increase in consumer spending among manual workers who, in addition to material goods such as televisions, vacuum cleaners and washing machines, also began to buy motor cars and houses, which were formerly the exclusive preserve of middle-class buyers.

Using this information, it was argued that the working-class characteristics of inferior economic resources and consumer power were no longer applicable. The age of the 'have-nots' was written off as a passing phase of industrialization. The stage of development now being attained was one in which the bulk of the population enjoyed middle-class living standards.

Arguments about increased economic parity led to claims that cultural differences would also be removed. As manual workers achieved middle-class incomes, they would also take on middle-class lifestyles. In terms of speech, dress, eating habits, styles of decor, entertainment, leisure activities, child-rearing practices and parental aspirations, they would become indistinguishable from their middle-class neighbours.

Sociologists describing this phenomenon talked in terms of the 'embourgeoisement' of the working class, by which they meant manual workers taking on bourgeois or middle-class lifestyles and joining the ranks of the middle class. The increase in home ownership was seen as particularly significant, in that manual workers would now be able to live physically much closer to their middle-class neighbours. In taking on middle-class lifestyles, it was also assumed that they would take on middle-class attitudes – attitudes which would radically alter their traditional allegiance to the Labour Party and the trade unions, for example. Rather than regarding work relationships with employers and social relationships with the middle class as an 'us and them' situation, they would rapidly forgo their class loyalties and increasingly identify with their middle-class counterparts.

It was these arguments which John Goldthorpe and David Lockwood, together with Frank Beckhofer and Jennifer Platt, set out to investigate in 1962: the extent to which affluent workers in the car industry had become 'middle class' in their behaviour and attitudes as a consequence of earning more money and increasing their spending power. Their research produced three major studies of affluent workers in relation to industrial attitudes and behaviour, to political attitudes and behaviour and to class structure. Their findings are well documented and in essence combine to refute the notion of embourgeoisement. They show how social class differences were changing in their surface characteristics, but they could find no evidence of any radical reshaping of the class structure or alteration in the relationship between different status groups within it.

Developments during the 1970s to some extent confirmed their findings. The enhanced power of the trade unions and the close allegiance between the labour movement and the Labour Government at that time were based on the increasingly vociferous demands of the working class to enjoy economic and material prosperity in line with middle-class standards of living. The point to note here is that the embourgeoisement idea, as it was argued in the 1950s and 1960s, was largely discredited by Goldthorpe and Lockwood's studies. Seen in their historical context, the arguments used to support the theory seem out-of-date. Even the findings of Goldthorpe and Lockwood have been overcome by events. Times change, and the impact of long-term recession and the loss of the industrial base of the British economy affect the class structure in different ways. It is to these events that we now turn.

The beginnings of Thatcherism

1979 saw the election of a Conservative Government brought to power by a significant percentage of working-class votes – some would say evidence of the shift in attitudes among some sections of the working class. It was a government committed to changing the social and economic face of Britain. It pursued a set of policies which have come to be known as 'New Right' policies, aimed at reducing the role of the state in economic and social matters, allowing free market forces of supply and demand rather than central government 'interference' to direct the economy and the provision of social services. It also proposed to reduce the role of the welfare state, encourage the 'self-reliance' of individual families and usher in what Margaret Thatcher called a 'property owning democracy'.

These policies included:

- privatization of nationalized industries such as gas, electricity, water, etc. by sale of shares to members of the public;
- encouragement of home ownership by the sale of council houses; private health care; and private education;
- schemes to encourage unemployed workers to set up small businesses;
- major changes in the benefits system and the organization and funding of the welfare state.

At first sight, these policies appear to encourage the type of embourgeoisement discussed above. It was undoubtedly the case that certain sections of the working class as well as other groups prospered for a time under this government. However, others were less fortunate. Government economic policies, the rise in world oil prices and the resultant recession pushed unemployment to levels not seen since the Depression of the 1930s, at a time when the value of welfare benefits was being eroded. The increase in those experiencing poverty and homelessness led some to argue that Britain had returned to the 'two nations'written about by Disraeli in the nineteenth century. Sociologists began to speak of an 'underclass' of deprived people emerging in late twentieth-century Britain.

What was the impact of these changes on the structure of the working class? Had the working class become increasingly impoverished, as Marx predicted, or had divisions within it become so marked that it no longer made any sense to speak of the working class as a distinct group, as some Weberian sociologists argued? These arguments can be summarized as the **united working class** or the **divided working class** debate, compared with the **disappearing working class** put forward by the proponents of the earlier embourgeoisement debate.

The evidence

Ivor Crewe

Stephen Lukes

Writing in the 1980s after analysing the results of the 1983 election in which the Conservative Party was re-elected with a majority, **Ivor Crewe**, a political scientist, argued that:

> Manual workers can therefore be divided into the 'traditional' and the 'new' working class. In 1983 these two groups voted very differently. ... Among the traditional working class of trade unionists and council house tenants, and in the traditional strongholds of Scotland and the North, Labour remains the first, if not always the majority choice. But among the new working class of manual workers who live in the South, who own their own home and who do not belong to a trade union, the Conservatives have established a clear lead over Labour. Indeed Labour trails in third place, behind the Alliance (now Social and Liberal Democrats), in the first two categories. It is as if the two groups of manual workers belong to **quite different social classes.** (our emphasis)

Crewe believed that voting behaviour was a good measure of class identification and that changes in living patterns indicated that the working class was no longer united. This theme was developed by **Stephen Lukes** in his essay 'The Future of British Socialism'. He argued that work itself had become less significant as a source of identity for many people in the post-war period. It had been overtaken as a central concern by issues to do with consumption. In other words, we no longer define ourselves by what we do but by what we own, where we live or where we spend our holidays. Lukes, like Crewe, maintained that Britain was a society divided in new ways which were different from the old class lines, for example:

- those with a stake in private property (e.g. a house, shares) and those without;
- those who were self-sufficient on earnings and those increasing numbers dependent on welfare benefits;
- those living in prosperous areas, mainly in the south, and those living in declining regions;
- those in secure employment and those who were unemployed or in casual, cash-in-hand employment.

These divisions, he maintained, reflected short-term, instrumental, capitalistic interests, and led to the decline in traditional working-class solidarity where progress was seen in collective rather than in individualistic terms – in other words, the reverse of class consciousness predicted by Marx. According to this view, a skilled worker owning his or her own home and a few shares in British Telecom would be unlikely to identify as part of the same class a single mother dependent on welfare benefits, living in temporary bed and breakfast accommodation.

So far, the evidence seems to support the view that the working class has fragmented. However, Marxists could argue that both Crewe and Lukes were writing in the early 1980s, when the south was relatively untouched by the recession which had earlier devastated industrial areas of the north and Wales. Since then, even the prosperous areas of the south – Surrey, Sussex and Hampshire – have experienced rapidly rising rates of unemployment in the late 1980s and early 1990s. It became apparent that no-one, not even those in middle-class occupations, had 'a job for life'.

At the same time, many of those encouraged to 'go it alone' and set up in small businesses found their limited resources insufficient to protect them from recession. In the early 1990s such businesses went bust at the rate of one every four minutes. Similarly, some members of Crewe's 'new' working class were unable to withstand the impact of rising interest rates or redundancy and found their newly purchased homes being repossessed by building societies.

We must be careful, then, not to overestimate the permanency of the divisions discussed by Crewe and Lukes.

The underclass

The increase in the numbers dependent on state benefits as a result of these changes has led some to argue that a new underclass is emerging which itself reflects, and helps to foster, divisions within the working class, between those employed and those who are marginalized and dependent. The term 'underclass' is an imprecise one, which entered popular journalism in the 1980s. It echoes earlier distinctions between the respectable, hard working and deserving members of the lower orders and those defined as lazy, work-shy, trapped in poverty by their own irresponsible attitudes. It is variously used to include groups as diverse as single mothers, old-age pensioners, the homeless, ethnic minorities, the unemployed, drug-users and New-Age travellers.

Sociologists are also disunited on the significance and even the existence of an underclass. We can summarize these into three distinct views:

1 The New Right view
2 The Weberian view
3 The Marxist view.

The New Right

Charles Murray

This view has been expressed by Conservative politicians and by sociologists such as the American, **Charles Murray**. Writing in 1989, he identified an underclass both in Britain and the United States, arguing that the poor can be divided into two groups, one which merely lacks money and another which is trapped in poverty by its attitudes and behaviour. He characterizes the latter as being drunken, unable to hold down work and having high crime levels. He also attacks the single-parent family or, more accurately, lone mothers who are dependent on the state and some young people who, he argues, choose not to work but exist on a mixture of casual jobs, illegal activities and some benefits.

Basically, this view blames people for their own misfortune, and has been criticized as a view which has been rejected in the past but from time to time is reconstituted as an explanation for disadvantage.

Others are critical of this use of the term because the various groups said to constitute the underclass have little in common other than insufficient money on which to live. For a group to form a class there must be some common culture, or at least a common explanation for their predicament. Clearly, the reasons why a pensioner may have a poor standard of living would differ from those for lone mothers or New-Age travellers.

The Weberian view

Rex & Tomlinson

Unlike the New Right, this position does not blame individuals for the underclass, but examines the structure of society for clues to its emergence. This view has been used to explain the disadvantaged position of ethnic minorities and women. For example, **John Rex** and **Sally Tomlinson**, in an important study in Birmingham, argued that ethnic minorities were disproportionately trapped in an underclass as a result of their weak market situation. They considered that racial discrimination made ethnic minority workers less likely to be given opportunities to train for skilled work, confining them to low-paid, unpopular and less secure jobs, trapping them in the underclass and denying them access to the more desirable jobs within the working class proper.

The strength of this argument is that it pays attention to the structural factors which may explain the deprivation of a particular group. One criticism is that clearly not all members of ethnic minorities are in this position.

The Marxist view

lumpen proletariat

Marxists are unhappy with the term 'underclass' because it implies that the working class is a divided rather than a united group. Marx himself did identify a particularly disadvantaged group which he named the **lumpen proletariat**, but this was still considered to share the same interests as the rest of the proletariat. Marxists have been criticized for underplaying the particular injustices experienced as a result of sex and race discrimination in their desire to maintain that all disadvantaged groups share common interests because of their relationship to the means of production.

In more recent years, Marxists like **Miles, Phizacklea** and **Amrit Wilson** have acknowledged the significance of discrimination arguing, for example, that black women form a particularly disadvantaged 'class fraction' or 'sub-section' of the working class.

Summary

From this brief summary of recent writings on the working class we can see that sociologists are attempting to make sense of social changes and to assess their effect on the class structure of Britain.

On the one hand, there seems to be much evidence of real divisions within the working class and little evidence of concerted class action to challenge inequality and privilege.

On the other, there are signs of increasing impoverishment, with more than 1 in 7 people dependent, at least in part, on means-tested benefits. Women are particularly disadvantaged – 61 per cent of all welfare claimants are women. There has also been an increase in homelessness, a decline in the number in work and a material and cultural deterioration of life for some sections of the community. Some commentators pointed to the urban riots of the early 1980s, the miners' strike of 1984 and the poll tax demonstrations of the early 1990s as evidence of increasing unrest. But whether these could be taken as examples of a class-based challenge to the power of the bourgeoisie is another matter.

The middle class

Traditionally a distinction is made between those who work with their hands in physical labour and those who do non-manual work. In the days when levels of literacy were low, those employed in work requiring these skills were regarded as superior when compared with other workers. Clerical workers, sales personnel, professionals and administrators did not own the means of production, and therefore were not part of the bourgeoisie, but their working experiences, life chances and position were all different from those of manual workers. Generally speaking, such groups have greater job security, shorter working hours, better chances of promotion, longer holidays and better pay. Sociological research has revealed that such workers and their families have better health, a longer life expectancy, own more goods, do better at school and are less likely to be convicted of a criminal offence.

petit bourgeoisie

Although Marx recognized the existence of an intermediate group – the **petit bourgeoisie** – between the two main classes, he believed that, as capitalism developed, this group would drop down into the proletariat and the bourgeoisie and the proletariat would become increasingly polarized. Instead, we have seen the massive expansion of 'middling' occupations as a result of the development in large-scale bureaucracies employing increasing numbers of administrative staff and providing the impetus for the development of new and expanding professional and managerial groups. Rather than seeing the middle class as a small group of professionals and clerical workers squashed between two larger groups, we now have a situation where more people are employed in non-manual occupations than any other kind of work. These changes have raised important questions about the definition and composition of the middle class and its position relative to the working class. The embourgeoisement debate discussed earlier raised questions about the relationship between affluent workers and white-collar employees, suggesting that the pay advantage of some so-called middle-class positions, relative to skilled manual workers, had declined in the post-war years.

The key debates concerning the middle class are as follows:

1 The middle class now contains such diverse groups as top professionals, such as barristers, and low-level clerical workers, and it is no longer possible to see all non-manual workers as a distinct and united group. Their working situations, their financial positions and their social standing are so different that the middle class has become fragmented into a variety of different status positions. This is a view adopted mainly by sociologists following a **Weberian** perspective.

*Weberian versus
Marxist view*

2 The simple distinction between manual and non-manual work as the dividing line between the working and middle class is no longer appropriate. The expansion of routine white-collar work and service industries has created a situation where many non-manual workers are now employed in large open-plan offices, tied to machines such as computers, with little personal autonomy in the organization of their work. White-collar occupations have become increasingly filled by female workers who receive low pay, low status and few opportunities for promotion. These changes have prompted some sociologists to advance what is known as the **proletarianization thesis,** arguing that the position of such workers is no different from that of manual workers. This is a view adopted mainly by sociologists following a **Marxist** perspective.

There is no consensus among sociologists about the position occupied by the middle class or, indeed, about whether such a class exists at all. According to the Registrar-General's classification, the middle class can be subdivided into three parts:

1 The upper middle class, consisting of top professionals, senior managers with major companies, successful business people, top administrators, bishops, government ministers.
2 The 'middle' middle class, consisting of lower professions, managers, engineers and scientific workers.
3 The lower middle class, consisting of white-collar workers, clerical and sales personnel.

Make a list of the different groups of workers that **you** think are part of the middle class.
For each group in your list make a note of the following points:

1 How much control over their work do you think they have? (its pace, when to start or stop work, the order in which jobs are tackled, whether they are heavily supervised or not?)
2 What are their working conditions like? (are they in a room with others? do they have their own office?)
3 What payment do they receive and how is it paid?
4 Are there any 'perks' attached to their jobs?

You have probably found many differences among the groups you listed. How would

a) Functionalists
b) Marxists
c) Weberians

explain these differences?

Whatever our particular view of the middle class, we can see that the term is often used to include groups with a wide divergence of experiences, remuneration and power. An important question is whether or not these diverse groups share a common class identification, or whether some of them have more in common with other classes. For example, some Marxists have argued that the middle class is polarizing, so that at the lower end clerical and retail workers rightfully belong in the working class, whereas some top-level managers, professionals and administrators should be seen as part of, or at least as the functionaries of, the bourgeoisie.

Anthony Giddens

Other sociologists have been concerned to clarify the definition of the middle class. For example, **Anthony Giddens** argues that the middle class is united by the possession of educational qualifications which equip them with **mental** labour power to sell. This distinguishes them from the working class, who sell their **manual** labour power, and from the upper class, who **own** the means of production.

On the other hand, as we saw earlier, John Goldthorpe does not see the ownership of the means of production as a means of distinguishing between an upper and a middle class. He sees no separate upper class. For him, the main distinction is between professionals, managers, etc. on the one hand and lower white-collar workers on the other. He has been criticized for underestimating the wealth, power and influence of those at the pinnacle of the British class system by placing them in a larger group of employed professionals and managers.

fragmented middle class

An interesting study was made by Roberts *et al.* in *The Fragmented Middle Class* in 1977 using a subjective view of the middle class. They examined the class images of 243 male white-collar workers and discovered four distinct views of the middle class:

1 *The middle mass image*: 27 per cent saw the middle class as the bulk of the working population, with a small, poorer, lower class on one side and a small, rich and powerful upper class on the other. This group was inclined to see the middle class as a united group with no clear-cut divisions within it. This view tended to be held by middle-income groups.
2 *The compressed image*: 19 per cent saw the middle class as a small group sandwiched between two large and powerful groups on either side. Owners of small businesses were most likely to hold this view.
3 *The ladder image*: 15 per cent saw society as a ladder with several rungs, with movement between the rungs being possible. This view was most frequently held by well-educated professionals who did not identify with a particular class and who often rejected the notion of distinct social classes altogether.
4 *The proletarian image*: 14 per cent saw themselves as part of the working class, which they saw as the largest of all the classes. They identified common interests with manual workers rather than with management. Not surprisingly, it was routine white-collar workers who were most likely to hold this view.

These results led the researchers to argue that the middle class is now so fragmented that it is no longer possible to talk of the 'middle class' as a distinct social class.

This view has come in for some criticism – for ignoring the views of women, for relying solely on subjective class images and for ignoring objective differences between the working class and middle class.

Since that study was completed, some would argue that the middle class has experienced a revival under successive Conservative governments, pledged to preserve their interests.

Further research on the middle class has tended to concentrate on the groups at the extremes – the top professions and lower white-collar workers.

The professions (see also pages 193–4)

The long-established traditional professions such as medicine and law have been held in high esteem and have had significant power and influence. The lengthy training period conferred upon practitioners a licence to practise that profession and thereby prevent others from encroaching on their territory. This control over the numbers entitled to practise has maintained the scarcity, and thereby the power, of these traditional professions and their position within the class system. Their specialist training has been seen to give them an independent judgement and a specialist skill, denied to others, which will be used in the service of clients.

Originally such groups were independent, fee-paid practitioners, seen to operate for the general good of society rather than in the service of the ruling class. Functionalists such as **Bernard Barber** have viewed the professions in this light as being more concerned with public service than personal gain, strictly controlled by a set of ethical guidelines such as the Hippocratic Oath for doctors which safeguards the rights of patients. The high status and rewards given to these groups are seen as just returns for lengthy training, knowledge, expertise, independence and public service.

Bernard Barber

In recent years, however, this uncritical view of the professions has been questioned. For a start, there are few professions which can claim the degree of independence of earlier times; most doctors work within the NHS, at the moment at least, and many lawyers, architects and accountants are employed directly by large companies. In addition, new professions have grown up as a result of the growth in administration and social services as well as scientific and technical developments. Advertising, television, teaching and social work all claim professional status for their practitioners, but are a long way from enjoying the privileged position of the older established professions.

Generally, it is the older professions which have been able to organize themselves and to control who joins the profession; the training and supervision of members; the regulation of the profession and the handling of complaints against individual members; and who are the ones who still enjoy the most privileged positions. Doctors, for example, have been able to control their market situation very effectively since the British Medical Association was formed in 1832. Social workers, on the other hand, are subject to much greater control by government and government agencies, and do not enjoy the same status, pay or power as the more traditional professions.

Ivan Illich

Nowadays, professions are not immune to public criticism. Doctors can be sued for malpractice, architects criticized by the Prince of Wales. **Ivan Illich**, the radical sociologist, has gone so far as to claim that professions, far from acting in the interests of society as functionalists suggest, actually work against the interests of society. In his attack on the medical profession in *Medical Nemesis* (1975), he argues that, by claiming that they alone can 'cure' illness, doctors damage society by obscuring the fact that the real causes of ill-health lie in poor housing, sanitation, bad nutrition and poor working conditions. He argues that improvements in health in the West predated modern medical developments such as vaccinations and antibiotics and were brought about by improvements in the standard of living. In a far-reaching attack on modern industrial societies, he argues that alienating work, stress on acquisitiveness, competition, greed, lack of genuine opportunities for creativity or control over our own lives are the real roots of ill-health today. Doctors, by treating individuals, obscure these real causes and thereby contribute to poor health rather than the reverse.

Weberians are also critical of the claim that professions act in the interest of the general good. They argue that in fact they operate in their own interests to work towards a situation whereby they can exercise the greatest degree of control over the profession. By controlling entry to, for example, the law, its practitioners can claim more money. In recent years, the high fees charged by solicitors for conveyancing during house sales have been criticized, since this work is generally delegated to legal clerks and requires a minimum of legal skills. Books appeared informing the general public on how to do their own conveyancing and thereby save a lot of money. These moves were resisted by solicitors, who continued to claim that only they had the expertise to perform this task and hence were justified in charging high fees.

Weberians such as **Parry and Parry** in *The Rise of the Medical Profession* (1976) show how the medical profession has been able to organize to its own advantage, compared with the teaching profession where the state has been able to exercise greater control over training and employment.

Marxists are critical of both functionalist and Weberian claims about the professions. Some claim that professionals serve neither their own nor society's interests so much as the interests of the ruling class. Groups such as lawyers and accountants are frequently employed by capitalists to advise on contracts or taxation to further their position. Teachers are employed to control the working classes and prepare them for employment in capitalist organizations. Doctors dispense pills to get the workers back on their feet as soon as possible. Social workers and media people patch up or divert the working classes, thereby helping to prevent political dissent which could challenge the bourgeoisie. A new professional managerial class has emerged according to Marxists such as **B.** and **J. Ehrenreich** in *The Professional Managerial Class* (1979) which, while not owning the means of production, sees its interests as best being served by pursuing those of the ruling class. This view is a far cry from the notion of professionals as independent practitioners, claiming rather that this group is merging into the upper class.

professional managerial class

Other Marxist sociologists such as **Harry Braverman** have argued that some professional groups have become proletarianized. Those marginal professions which have never enjoyed the privileged position of the long-established ones have found that their position has deteriorated in recent years. For example, teachers, engineers, technicians may have experienced a drop in status as their work has been fragmented into separate tasks. Even in the established professions, the position of some members has been affected by employment in large-scale organizations. For example, the position of junior hospital doctors, who have recently fought to restrict their working week to 84 hours, bears little resemblance to the privileged position of doctors in private practice before the setting up of the NHS. Some point to the growth of trade unionism among such groups as evidence of a shift downwards in their social position.

Harry Braverman

White-collar workers

The massive increase in the numbers of these workers has led some sociologists to argue that they should no longer be regarded as part of the middle class, but that their working conditions, pay and prospects have more in common with the working class – that they have become proletarianized.

Braverman argues that specialization and mechanization have resulted in a deskilling of clerical and personal service work (see page 189). For example, clerical work has been reorganized so that tasks have been broken down into small specialist jobs which follow set routines. The introduction of word processors has removed much of the typist's skill. Letter layout and spelling are taken care of automatically, and consequently someone with less skill and fewer qualifications can be employed to do the job. This process of deskilling has occurred gradually over the century, and at the same time clerical workers have become employed in greater numbers in large offices which resemble factories, they have less direct contact with top management and generally less control over their working environment than in the small office situation. Over this same period, clerical work has become a predominantly female job. Whether this reflects the fact that this work now carries less pay and respect, or those changes are partly a result of this feminization, is open to question.

Other sociologists, particularly Weberian ones such as David Lockwood and John Goldthorpe, have argued that, while the position of clerical workers has declined during the course of the century, they still maintain some advantages over the working class. Lockwood argues that clerks are in a position of 'status ambiguity' somewhere between the middle and working classes. Goldthorpe argues that this is a relatively fluid group falling between the middle class proper and the working class, which does not have a strong sense of class allegiance and may be in the process of moving from one class to another.

social stratification and occupation

This last point is also studied by Stewart *et al.* in *Social Stratification and Occupations* (1980). They argue that 'clerk' is a position which male white-collar workers may occupy temporarily en route to a higher-status post. So the young man behind the bank counter may be on the first rung of the management ladder and so should be regarded as middle class. However, this ignores the position of the vast numbers of clerical workers who are women. Are they as likely to get promotion as their male counterparts? If women form the majority of white-collar workers, most of whom will remain at that level of work, the fact that a handful of men may be upwardly mobile does not affect the class position of clerical workers as a whole. Studies of the subjective view of clerical workers, such as that by Crompton and Jones in 1984, suggest that many white-collar workers feel that they have little control over the work process, follow established routines and have little skill.

The upper class

So far, we have made little reference to the upper class. Classification systems generally make no reference to this group. Doug Holly makes this point in *The Invisible Ruling Class*:

> The notion put about by many sociologists is that we live in a two-class society. How strange we hear so much of the middle class and the working class whilst we hear almost nothing about any upper class.

The British upper class has its origins in feudalism, in the survival of aristocratic titles dating back to the Norman Conquest when some soldiers were given titles and land in return for military service. The idea of an aristocracy may seem to be a bit old-fashioned in today's Britain, although people with titles do still exist and are extremely wealthy compared with many other people, living in large country houses on vast rural estates as their fathers and forefathers did before them.

The merchant class of the Middle Ages expanded and developed into the international traders and financiers of the eighteenth century who made money out of colonization which was then used to finance the Industrial Revolution in Britain. This group of financiers became closely linked with the traditional land-owning aristocracy, helping them to diversify into mining and railways. They sent their sons to public schools and became part of the upper class through inter-marriage with aristocratic families.

The third element to make up the upper class were the industrialists of the nineteenth century who became assimilated into the upper class as they bought country estates and acquired honours and titles.

John Scott and 'The Establishment'

John Scott, a Weberian sociologist, argues that there is a particularly privileged and powerful group within the upper class – **the Establishment** – which is based on the following institutions:

- the Conservative Party
- the Church of England
- public schools
- ancient universities
- the legal profession
- the Guards regiments
- the London gentlemen's clubs.

The Establishment consists of core families linked by marriage, public schools, the conduct of social contacts through country house life and key events in the social calendar such as the Henley Regatta, Ascot and Glyndebourne. This group differs from other classes in society in that it is a cohesive group, with little movement between it and other classes.

self-recruitment

Sociologists call this **self-recruitment**, meaning that present members of the upper class have usually been born into that class.

Despite enormous changes in society during the last century, the upper class still manages to reproduce itself. For example:

It has been able to transfer economic capital across generations so that each new generation does not have to make its own way but can maintain the standard of living enjoyed by the older generation. (See the earlier section on the distribution of income and wealth for a full discussion of how this works.)

cultural capital

It is able to maintain a common culture through the public school system. This is sometimes referred to as the reproduction of **cultural capital** rather than of economic capital. A public school education provides more than academic instruction – it is an induction into an élite way of life, so much so that anyone without that privilege might find it difficult to gain entry into that group regardless of qualifications or money.

It is important not to over-exaggerate the significance of this cultural capital. Clearly, talented individuals from more humble origins do sometimes make it into the upper class. Members of the Royal Family have friends from the world of showbusiness; even criminals from other classes can be found with business or social connections with the upper class. However, much research reveals the career advantages of a public school education.

Giddens found that 73 per cent of the directors of large companies, 83 per cent of the directors of financial institutions, and 80 per cent of all judges, Anglican bishops and top army officers had attended public school.

Jeremy Paxman

Some argue that the Thatcher Revolution in the 1980s brought newer business wealth into the upper class, which meant that the public school declined as the only way to success in top careers. The journalist **Jeremy Paxman** carried out interviews with more than 150 powerful members of the Establishment, from the aristocracy, the City, big business, the government, the church, the armed forces, the judiciary, the civil service and the arts to assess the effects of these changes on elite self-recruitment to the upper class. While he detected some shift to the 'meritocrats', with more members of Margaret Thatcher's 1979 cabinet coming from grammar schools than previously, he concluded: 'Approximately fifty years since the introduction of free, high quality secondary education for all, the public schools seem as secure as ever.'

hogomany

There is a high level of inter-marriage within the class – what is called **hogomany**. A young man or woman used to an upper-class lifestyle is most likely to choose to marry someone from a similar background. This means that the upper class is not just a social category, but a distinct group aware of its own culture and its social boundaries.

The monarchy legitimates the system of titles and honours which come to symbolize social superiority. This maintains a non-democratic element in Parliament in the form of the House of Lords, and confers additional political power on the upper class.

Class and power

This raises one of the important questions we need to ask about the upper class – do they also monopolize political power? In other words, we know that the upper class is extremely wealthy; as we saw earlier – in 1989 the top 1 per cent of the population owned 18 per cent of all marketable wealth – but does it also have a disproportionate amount of political power and influence? Is the upper class also a ruling class in the way that Marx claimed?

Giddens, although not a Marxist, has demonstrated the predominance of the upper class among the directors of major companies and financial institutions. According to Marx, those who own the means of production also control political decision making so that it reflects their own interests rather than the interests of the population as a whole.

To prove that the upper class is also the ruling class is very difficult, and at the end of the day depends on the perspective taken. However, there are close links between those who dominate the business world of Britain and its political life.

Social mobility

The degree of movement between social classes is important when examining the changing structure of the class system in Britain. Sociologists are interested in social mobility because:

- the amount of social mobility might affect the formation of social classes and the level of class solidarity among its members. If classes are very fluid structures, with people constantly moving in or out of them, it is unlikely that distinctive class consciousness or ways of life will develop;
- the amount of social mobility provides us with information about life-chances and the degree to which one's class origins determine these chances. In societies with very little movement between classes, an individual's opportunities are more circumscribed by birth than in a more fluid system;
- the amount of mobility tells us something about the degree of openness in a society, important in a democratic society claiming to encourage equality of opportunity.

The functionalist theory of stratification maintains that modern Western societies operate as meritocracies in which those with talent and dedication will rise to the top regardless of their social origins. This philosophy has been espoused by Conservative politicians, notably John Major, himself a product of the state education system.

Studying social mobility, however, presents problems for sociologists.

Firstly, the researcher has to decide which criteria will be used to determine a change in class membership. Essentially this presents the same problems discussed earlier on how we determine a person's class position in the first place. Most researchers have tackled this in the same way, by using occupation as the indicator of class. However, different researchers have used different occupational scales, which means that their results are not directly comparable. For example, an early classic study of social mobility by **David Glass** in 1954 used socio-economic status as the means of classifying a person's position. Goldthorpe, in his 1980 study, used his classification discussed on page 5 and other researchers have used the Registrar-General's classification system.

David Glass

Although these studies differ in detail, they all suggest a reduction in the number of unskilled manual workers, an increase in non-manual groups, but little evidence of significant changes in life-chances for the majority.

Secondly, these studies have been criticized for either ignoring women altogether or assuming that the patterns of social mobility are the same for women as for men. Consider the following case:

> Marion left school with four GCSEs and worked for five years as a VDU operator, during which time she met and married Mark, a computer programmer in the same office. She took the next five years out of work when their two children were small. During this time she had no money to call her own unless she saved a bit out of the housekeeping. Mark, on the other hand, continued to have his nights out with the boys and always took the family car to work.
>
> When Marion went back to work she found that her skills were outdated, and she was employed at a lower level than when she left. Mark, meanwhile, had got promotion.
>
> Two years later Mark left Marion to live with a new VDU operator from the office, and despite Mark's good salary Marion was forced to supplement her income with Family Credit.

Reviewing Marion's career, list the ways in which her class position was different from Mark's. Were she and Mark socially mobile and, if so, was it upward or downward mobility?

The assumption that a woman's class position is the same as her husband's has been challenged by feminists who point out that:

- not all women are married or remain married; therefore, they should be studied independently of male occupational measures;
- sex discrimination against women means that they are more likely to be found in lower-level occupations and therefore are less likely to experience upward social mobility;
- married women may not share the same class as their husbands because they may have less access to family resources than men, particularly if they are not in paid work;
- marriage itself may confuse social mobility measurements. Generally people tend to marry a partner from a similar social position, but there is some evidence that men are more likely to marry someone slightly below them in both class and educational terms. On the other hand, many male

manual workers are married to women who are clerks, VDU operators, etc. who, according to some classification schemes, would be regarded as belonging to a higher social class than their husbands.

A third problem facing the social researcher is to decide at what point in a person's life should the measure of social mobility be carried out. Consider the following case:

> Stanley comes from a working-class background and does a manual job for many years, while doing GCSEs and A Levels at night class. He then decides to go to university. Afterwards he does some professional training and becomes a personnel manager with a good salary and company car. A few years later his firm is taken over and he is made redundant.

Clearly, the extent to which Stanley could be said to be socially mobile would depend on the point at which he was included in the research.

Two main measures of mobility are used:

1 **Intra-generational** mobility, which measures how far a person moves in his or her own lifetime.
2 **inter-generational** mobility, which compares an individual's position with that of his or her parents, usually fathers (the most usual method).

A fourth point which must be borne in mind when studying social mobility is that there have been major changes in the occupational structure of Western societies which may exaggerate the real extent of social mobility achieved by individuals. International studies suggest that there has been considerable inter-generational mobility in Western countries between manual and lower-level occupations. In other words, considerable numbers of people from working-class backgrounds have moved into the lower middle class.

At first sight, this seems to suggest that societies have become more egalitarian and open, but in actual fact this movement reflects the process of industrialization itself. As industrialization proceeded, there was a massive increase in the number of workers needed to fill administrative and social welfare positions created by the growth of organizational bureaucracies. Many more white-collar jobs were created than there were recruits from the middle classes to fill them. The expansion of state education enabled these workers to be recruited from the working class.

structural and elite mobility

This process is called **structural mobility**, and contrasts with what is called **elite mobility**, in which individuals move of their own accord across class lines. Most mobility in Britain has been as a result of this structural change. Elite mobility tends to be lower than in both the USA and the former USSR and across a shorter range of positions. The 'rags to riches' kind of social mobility is rare in Britain, despite the meritocratic rhetoric of politicians and some well-publicized examples of 'success stories'.

Summary

- Most social mobility from manual to non-manual occupations has occurred as a result of changes in the occupational structure.
- The relative chances of long-range upward mobility between social classes other than by structural mobility has not increased significantly in the last sixty years.
- The usual route for social mobility is via the education system and, as such, usually begins early in a person's career as he or she acquires qualifications.

- As most movement has been into the middle class, this group tends to have less class solidarity – as new people join it, there is less opportunity for a distinct class culture and class identity to flourish.
- The upper class and the working class both experience less movement than the middle class and, as such, may have a stronger sense of class culture.
- There is little evidence of any significant reduction in inequalities – there are still very real barriers to social movement which reflect class inequalities as well as inequalities based on gender and ethnicity.

Social class – Some thoughts for the future

For over 150 years the notion of social class has been a crucial, some would say the most crucial, concept for analysing social relationships. The tremendous influence of the works of Marx and Weber, and the subsequent refining, redefining and criticism of their theories, have been critical to the development of sociology as a discipline.

The supremacy of such overarching theories which maintain that human social behaviour is largely the result of external social structures such as the class system has been challenged in the last two decades of the twentieth century by the movement known as post-structuralism, discussed above and in detail in Chapter 9.

Here we want to consider how the worldwide changes of these years have shifted our understanding of the British class system and its influence on the lives and life chances of the population.

Many British firms are now part of multinational corporations, and British industrialists and financiers part of an international capitalist class making decisions about which regions of the world to invest in or pull out of. Some commentators suggest that these corporations have such considerable economic power that they can influence the economic and political decisions of national governments. By deciding to pull production out of a particular region or country they could contribute to unemployment, recession and social unrest. Like a plot for a Superman movie, they could have the potential to destabilize a national economy, bringing down governments.

Altering the local economy by laying off labour helps to shift the class structure. We have already seen that the shift from manufacturing to tertiary industry in Britain has altered the size of the working and middle classes and the relationship between them, as well as contributing to the creation of an underclass.

The relationship between management and workers shifts as a result. Workers are unable to stand up to management in disputes with transnational companies that they have no hope of winning. In Britain, legislation to weaken trade unions, high unemployment and a growing underclass have all reduced the militancy of trade unions as organizations to defend the rights of the working class. Multinational corporations have been able to demand no-strike agreements before investing and providing much needed jobs in depressed areas.

Some argue that class consciousness and class militancy cannot flourish in this situation, so that class interests are superseded by other interests – some of global significance, such as the threat of nuclear war, world poverty or environmental pollution. Other 'sectional' interests come to the fore – nationalist movements as in the former USSR, or ethnic wars as in the former Yugoslavia, transcend class struggles.

A sense of class based on occupation becomes less meaningful in a world where work itself assumes less significance. **Mike O'Donnell** makes the point that:

Mike O'Donnell

> people are now more interested in spending than earning. This apparent shift in popular focus from work and production to leisure and life-style is a further aspect of the decline in the salience of class consciousness.

It may be premature to sound the death knell for social class, however. There are still many people around for whom class is a significant source of identity. There is ample evidence to show that there are considerable inequalities of wealth and income which are the root cause of severe disadvantages, incompatible with social democracy. A low-class position brings with it poorer health, a lower life expectancy, unequal treatment throughout life – in school, in housing, before the law – together with an impoverished quality of life.

Sex, gender and sexuality

For most of the preceding 200 or so years, in which sociologists have been concerned to explain the nature of society and, in some cases, argue for social progress and social change, they have done so in ways which:

- seem to assume that society is made up entirely of men (and mostly white men);
- seem to assume that generalizations made about men can be equally applied to women;
- fail to take account of the variety of disadvantages, inequalities and oppression experienced by women in the world compared with men, and which derive from different experiences, different access to resources and different degrees of power.

The re-emergence of the women's movement in the West in the 1960s gave rise to considerable agitation for social and political change on behalf of women. Feminist ideas began to influence the academic debates in a variety of subjects which had previously been dominated by the concerns of men.

Sociology was a fairly male-oriented and male-practised subject before the impact of feminism and before the questions raised by feminism about the lives and relationships and social conditions of women began to be taken seriously. Few studies were undertaken about the social behaviour and experiences of women. Descriptions of essentially male-oriented experiences, such as industrial labour and delinquency, and the use of paid occupations (which did not include housework) to determine social class, were assumed, by default, to apply equally to women, although women were rarely mentioned.

Now the picture has changed. Not only has the subject content of sociology become considerably more concerned with the recognition of gender issues in society, but many more women are studying, writing, teaching and researching sociology in their own right. Feminist perspectives have become an essential element of sociological theory (see pages 43–4).

Working definitions

One of the main contributions made by feminism to sociology and to the deeper understanding of social processes and social behaviour in society has been to confirm the central significance of **sex, gender** and, to some extent, **sexuality** in explaining human activity. There is a distinction, however, in the ways in which these terms are used.

Sex means quite simply the biological (physical and genetic) differences which distinguish men from women. In practice, like 'race' differences, these are quite small. Physically people have much more in common with each other, in terms of how their bodies work, than physical characteristics which make them different.

But sex differences are clearly important. The fact that women menstruate and can give birth is of obvious significance, as is the fact that men can do neither of these things. But what is probably most important is the cultural significance attached to these characteristics, the meaning given to them in different societies and the way they are used to make statements about men's and women's roles and identities. It could be argued, for example, that it is precisely because men cannot give birth that, in Western cultures at least, they have taken considerable trouble to control the terms and conditions within which childbirth takes place, through their dominance of medicine, gynaecology and reproductive technologies, for instance. They have ensured that children's legitimacy and inheritance is associated with relationships to the father. They have established the recognition of 'father rights' in even the most fleeting associations. They have enormously influenced social constructions of motherhood in different cultures in ways which in the West, for example, ensure that it is experienced and practised in some relationship to men, and under both direct and indirect male supervision and control as fathers, as officials of the welfare state, as 'experts' of various kinds and as advertising men. It is clear that to be the sex which can give birth and play the major role in the reproduction of life brings potential power and authority, which could become 'the organizing principle' for distributing power throughout society. Since men can't do it, it has become imperative in *patriarchal societies* **patriarchal societies** (see below) to control, manage and organize the ones who do.

Some physical differences which are assumed to be biologically determined, like height and physique, for example, are less significant. They are neither immutable nor automatically related to sex differences. For example, north-western European women are likely, on average, to be taller than South-East Asian men. Body size and weight is considerably affected by diet and exercise, both of which are influenced by cultural and gender-related assumptions about who should be given the biggest portions of food and what constitutes appropriate exercise and sporting activities for growing boys and girls. Whether you live in the first world or the third world is also an important consideration. In addition, physique and bodily strength respond to training, and can be changed or increased in either men or women. In practice, however, it is not so much the physical differences as the social significance attached to the differences between men and women which is important.

Gender means the accumulation of roles, related behaviour and attitudes which are conventionally associated with males and females in any given society. The kinds of identities which we develop as part of our social identity as either men or women are 'learned', 'constructed', 'built up' in the process of living our lives in particular societies, with specific cultures, at specific points in time. Gender roles and identities are not 'natural' or 'determined by our biology', they are 'socially constructed' and learned in the process of social interaction.

Neither can gender be regarded as a 'fixed' condition. Gender roles change over time; they vary in different cultures. We do not inherit them wholesale, like brown eyes, which we then have to live with and cannot change. Gender is best understood as being immensely flexible within a series of social constraints. Social constraints such as social class, culture, religion, education, etc. all serve to influence gender roles and identities. Money is made for the economy, order is preserved for the state, individual men and women benefit in various ways if they can be persuaded to behave and respond in certain ways rather than others. But, like all constraints, social 'rules' and 'norms' are implemented to advance some people's interests at the expense of others. In these circumstances it is likely that what is commonly regarded as 'appropriate behaviour' for either men or women has to be questioned and possibly resisted.

And, of course, 'resistance', though difficult, is possible. Individuals are not simply the creations of society, they are also its creators. They make decisions about their lives, they can think and act and relate to others in various and complicated ways, at a variety of levels. Each new recruit into society not only inherits considerable amounts of information from what has gone before, but immediately begins to remake and renegotiate what he or she has been 'given' in a continuing and changing process of negotiation and interaction with significant others. This is not to imply that every individual has the opportunity to become whatever and however he or she wants to become. We know that the social constraints of poverty and power and institutionalized inequalities, for example, are hard to overcome, but social beings are not simply socially determined by their circumstances, they are also involved in individually and collectively determining those circumstances.

Sexuality includes all those aspects of identity, behaviour, attitudes and expression associated with sexual activity, both for reasons of pleasure and procreation. The characteristics of male and female sexuality, however, appear to be very different, and the extent to which these differences are the result of biology or social construction invite considerable controversy, as we shall see later. As an issue, sexuality becomes very important in sociology in the study of, for example, male violence and aggression towards women and children; definitions of, and attitudes towards, prostitution; debates about pornography; discrimination practised against lesbians and gay men.

Key perspectives

Nature and culture

Early sociologists, writing against the backdrop of the Enlightenment, the so-called Age of Reason and the Industrial Revolution, assumed that there were considerable natural and biological differences between men and women (and between whites and blacks). Men, who dominated intellectual, scientific, economic and governmental activity at the time helped to construct and disseminate and pass on to those men who came after them theories about men as 'rational' and 'logical' beings, who 'employed reason' and 'exercised judgement', who could 'create culture' and 'control nature'. It was claimed that men were fitted by their nature to be leaders and actors and doers, innately aggressive and dominant and, by definition, superior.

Women, on the other hand, were considered to be limited by their nature. Because of their ability to bear children, it was increasingly assumed, in Western cultures at least, that they should be the ones responsible for mothering and childcare. Women were depicted as fragile, weak, temperamental, passive, dependent. The middle-class 'ideal' associated with women was that they should be rather like Shakespeare's notion of woman as 'patience on a monument, smiling at grief'. They should be 'the angel in the house', who was 'pure' and 'above reproach', 'decorative' and 'devoted'. Menstruation and childbirth were thought to contribute to women's increasing weakness. Undue exercise or intellectual activity would sap their strength. 'Protective' and restricting ideas about the 'natural incapacities' of women kept them like comfortable prisoners in the middle-class households of their fathers and husbands, where a retinue of servants was employed to undertake the reality of household chores and childcare, but the 'lady of the house' was expected to manage them. Severe restrictions were imposed on women gaining an education or serious paid employment. They were not able to own or inherit property in their own right until 1882. Divorce was legally and socially impossible, and domestic violence was commonplace.

The list of women's 'deficiencies', of course, took no account of the constant pregnancies and hard physical labour undertaken by the majority of working-class women at the time, or the ways in which men's power over Victorian women was more likely to be responsible for their social confinement than any deficiency of their biology.

As the Industrial Revolution began to change patterns of working and family life, sexual divisions which existed in pre-industrial times were consolidated in ways which helped to separate out the spheres of influence and activity in which men and women operated. Increasingly, men became associated with the **public sphere** of paid work, social responsibility and public activity, while women became increasingly contained by expectations about their domestic and dependent role in the **private sphere** of household and family. When middle-class feminists campaigned for education, entry to the professions, the vote and an end to male sexual exploitation, they were derided as harridans and spinsters and freaks of nature. When working-class women worked 'in service' and sweatshops and as prostitutes, their work was invisible, their morals were condemned and they were still expected to assume major responsibility for keeping their own homes and families together.

As Britain developed its Empire overseas, notions of white male supremacy were extended to diminish respect and concern for 'subject populations'. They were considered 'heathens' who needed to be 'civilized' by British culture and traditions as well as Christianity. Like women in general, native populations were thought to be 'closer to nature' than their British conquerors. Racist assumptions about the intellectual and cultural inferiority of other races were compounded at this time. In America, where black slave-holding communities were still common in the mid-nineteenth century, black men were caricatured as lazy and work-shy, while women were seen as exotic and sexually promiscuous.

Genetics and evolution

Tiger & Fox

A hundred years later, writing in the 1970s, anthropologists like **Lionel Tiger** and **Robin Fox** still insisted upon the significance of biological and natural material in the production of human behaviour. They argued that human beings are not the product of their culture nor of what they have learned during their socialization, and they accused sociologists of ignoring the genetically-based predisposition of human beings to behave in certain ways. These predispositions were not the same as instincts, since they could be influenced and modified by culture, but they acted as basic influences on human behaviour. Tiger and Fox referred to these 'genetically-based influences' as human **biogrammars**.

Although the biogrammars of men and women contained some similarities, they were essentially different in what might seem like fairly predictable ways. These were comprised of characteristics which were acquired during 'hunting and gathering' periods of prehistory, when men were hunters and gatherers and women were carers. It was this legacy which, according to Tiger and Fox, caused men to be aggressive and the custodians of power in society, and women to be closely bonded to their children and naturally responsible for their welfare and well-being.

Those who believed, like Tiger and Fox, that gender roles were rooted in biogrammars, claimed that any attempts to abolish gender roles would 'go against nature'.

Sociobiology

A second intellectual fashion which has attempted to relate gender differences to biology and evolution is sociobiology, first developed by E. O.

Darwin's theory of natural selection

Wilson and subsequently applied to sex and gender by David Barash. Based on **Darwin's** original nineteenth century **theory of natural selection,** sociobiologists believe that human development is a consequence of 'the survival of the fittest'. In the process of social change and development, those who adapt most successfully to their environment are most likely to survive and flourish.

Sociobiologists go further than Darwin, and argue that it is not just physical characteristics which are subject to natural selection but also behavioural characteristics. Constant comparisons are drawn between human behaviour and the behaviour of animals, as if the fact that humans are also thinking, speaking, conscious and reasoning beings is of no significance. Differences in male and female behaviour are attributed to the different sexes using different strategies to maximize their chances of survival and reproduction.

Barash & Wilson

Barash and Wilson assert that different reproductive strategies in men and women create different social roles. Men are more likely to be promiscuous because they produce millions of sperm, while women are more chaste because they only produce one egg at a time. Wilson says: 'It pays males to be aggressive, hasty, fickle, and undiscriminating. In theory it is more profitable for women to be coy, to hold back until they can identify males with the best possible genes'. Barash talks of men 'playing fast and loose'. Wilson claims that rape by men can be explained in this way.

Sociobiologists attempt to support their sweeping and somewhat amazing claims with studies carried out on animals, which lead to stereotyped views of human behaviour, dubious correlations between the animal kingdom and humanity, little account being taken of cultural differences in human behaviour and considerable sexism. Barash denies that the prescriptive views held by sociobiologists are sexist and admits that men and women are not obliged to behave in the ways in which their biology dictates. However, if they deny their biological imperatives it makes them 'less efficient' at maintaining the species.

Prejudices based upon these views are wheeled out intermittently to assert that 'women who do men's jobs' damage their reproductive capabilities and 'men who show emotion' lose their masculinity.

Functionalism

The functionalist view of society relies on the assumption that 'the way things normally are is the way they ought to be'. Aberrations or dysfunctions prevent the kinds of cohesion and continuity which enable societies to continue and reproduce themselves most effectively. Functionalist explanations of gender roles and gender differences in societies allow for greater flexibility than biological and evolutionary explanations and for the recognition of cultural influences. **George Murdock**, for example, explains the sexual division of labour as a matter of practicality and convenience in which each sex is best suited to the tasks allotted to it. Writing in the 1940s, **Talcott Parsons** explains the roles of men and women in modern industrial nuclear families as 'complementary'. Like Freud before him, he regarded sex role differences as essentially 'natural'. Parsons characterizes the woman's role in the family as 'expressive' – that is, she should provide warmth, security and emotional support for husband and children. The man's role, on the other hand, is seen by him as 'instrumental' and concerned mainly with 'breadwinning'. Since this is a role which leads to undue stress and anxiety for men, the woman's emotionally supportive function is clearly complementary. Like 'love and marriage', a 'horse and carriage', 'yin and yang', the two fit together perfectly. Although functionalists like Parsons move a

Talcott Parsons

John Bowlby

long way from biology in the development of their theories, it is certainly the starting point from which most of their assumptions about the sexual division of labour originate.

John Bowlby in *Child Care and the Growth of Love*, examines the role of women from a sociopsychological perspective which was extremely influential in the 1950s and 1960s. Like Parsons, he declares that a woman's place is in the home looking after children. But he goes further than this, asserting that children who have been deprived of a close and continuing bond with their mothers in the formative years of life will develop personality disorders and social problems in later life.

The cultural perspective

Margaret Mead and socialization

Liberal feminist Ann Oakley

The influence of anthropologists like **Margaret Mead** have played a significant part in alerting sociologists to the impact of culture on gender roles and identities. Mead's work in the South Pacific set out to show that there is no universally prescribed expression of masculinity and femininity. Male and female roles are learned during the process of **socialization**, and vary from culture to culture and at different periods of time.

Ann Oakley, writing as a **liberal feminist** in the 1970s and 1980s, and making extensive use of anthropological studies, including those of Murdock and Mead, did much to advance the cultural perspective on gender roles and on gendered behaviour and attitudes. Her distinction between sex and gender is fundamental to this approach. She says that sex differences are biological in origin whereas gender differences are culturally produced. This leaves gender difference considerably dependent upon influences within the wider society, potentially malleable and clearly subject to variation and flexibility between different cultures and over time. Oakley claims: 'Not only is the division of labour by sex **not** universal, but there is no reason why it should be. Human cultures are diverse and endlessly variable. They owe their creation to human inventiveness rather than invincible biological forces.'

Oakley is especially critical of Parsons' and Bowlby's work. She dismisses Bowlby's assertion that children need intimate and continuous contact with their mothers in order not to become juvenile delinquents with illustrations from other societies in which such contact is not the norm. She accuses Bowlby of inventing ideologies designed to keep women out of the labour force in Western industrial societies at a point in time when women's labour was not particularly required, and quotes alternative studies which show that working women who are not tied to constant child care and domestic routines are likely to be less irritable and more engaged with their children than 'full-time' mothers when they do spend time together. Rather than becoming social disasters, children who learn to relate to other responsible adults and experience 'sheltered independence' in nurseries and good daycare facilities are likely to be better prepared for school and for future independent behaviour.

Oakley also accuses Parsons, and his views about the 'expressive' nature of the role of women as an ideological justification for the domestic oppression of women. In challenging much of the conventional wisdom to date about the biological and functional nature of roles, and in showing the ways in which previously assumed 'natural' conditions like 'motherhood' and 'domesticity' were, in fact, cultural constructions, she helped pave the way for the massively influential intervention by feminists into the whole debate about the extent to which the social distribution of power and resources in societies is related to sex and gender inequalities.

Gender socialization

If human behaviour and the attitudes and practices associated with male and female roles are not innate or biologically produced, but are the consequence of culture, then, it is argued, they have to be learned. The process by which new recruits into any given society learn their gender roles is called socialization.

The family

The first significant and influential series of relationships in a child's life is experienced within its immediate family and wider kinship group. Traditional patterns of gender socialization in family groups distinguish sharply between males and females in matters of dress, toys and play activities, reading materials, forms of physical contact, language used, expectations and role models, etc. While some of the worst excesses of this differentiation have become modified in some cultures as a result of the attention drawn to its effects by the women's liberation movement, the pervasiveness and subtlety of strongly held and deeply embedded attitudes and assumptions about males and females in any given culture make the process of stereotyping and social conditioning difficult to overcome. While it is relatively easy in the West to refrain from dressing male children in blue and female children in pink, for example, significant adults are not nearly so alert to the extent to which they coax girls into nurturing and emotional and servicing roles, while allowing boys greater freedom of manoeuvre, play activities which, in the guise of adventure, condone aggression, and the licence to absent themselves from household chores. In addition, any attempts by concerned or enlightened parents to counteract the worst effects of early gender socialization are further impeded by the continuing and pervasive influence of other socializing agents in the wider society.

School
Dale Spender and
sexism in schools

The impact of gender socialization in education, and of treating pupils differently on the basis of gender, was also identified and considerably attacked by feminist sociologists in the 1970s and 1980s. **Dale Spender**, for example, was extremely influential in revealing the extent to which the school curriculum frequently reproduces male-centred knowledge, how subject 'options' tend to be gendered in ways that entice boys and girls in different directions, and how boys receive preferential treatment, in terms of attention and teachers' time, compared with girls (see page 156). The consequences of all this, as in early family socialization, is to prepare boys and girls for different roles in society, with different attitudes and expectations, which in turn reproduce differing degrees of power and influence. While the influence of feminist sociologists and educationalists at the time played a big part in modifying some of the worst excesses of school sexism, the re-election of a Conservative Government and the changing emphasis in education away from 'equal opportunities' and towards 'new vocationalism' have meant that much of the concern about sexism in schools has 'gone underground' and thus frequently remains unchallenged.

Work

Although in the 1990s young women are now leaving school with as good, if not better, qualifications, than boys, compared with twenty years ago, they are still likely to end up in 'typically female jobs' such as office work, retailing, nursing, social work and childcare.

In the current economic climate it is now expected that women will be available for paid work outside the home. Women in Britain currently comprise almost 50 per cent of the paid labour force, not counting the voluntary sector and the unpaid domestic labour force. This is more than at any other time in our history. It does not represent a victory for feminism, however. Despite equal pay and sex discrimination legislation in the mid-1970s, women still earn on average only 70 per cent of the average male wage, and are still concentrated in a segregated labour market in which women's jobs are regarded as routine, largely unskilled, easily replaceable and worthy of little financial reward. Furthermore, when women work in the same or similar occupations to men, e.g. in teaching, banks or administration, they are likely to be concentrated in the lower grade, least influential and worst paid positions.

Stereotyped notions of what constitute men's jobs and women's jobs; popular prejudices about the greater significance of men's jobs than women's jobs, even when increasing numbers of men are unemployed and increasing numbers of women are the sole breadwinners in families; and so long as different degrees of status and financial rewards are attached to jobs done by men and women – then the processes of socialization at work all help to retain unequal practices and possibilities so far as men and women are concerned.

Mass media

However powerful the influence of family, school and work might be on reproducing men and women who conform to accepted gender roles and who in turn assist in the business of inducting and influencing others in the same ways of being, all this is made so much easier and more effective by the pervasive influence of the media. In the 1970s feminists used to worry about the sex stereotyping in children's reading schemes and comics and involve themselves in campaigns about sexist adverts on billboards and the conformity to domestic slavery encouraged in most women's magazines. Today these examples might seem relatively harmless. But they were all evidence of gender socialization at work, which helped to confirm attitudes and behaviour patterns consistent with 'appropriate' behaviour patterns for boys and girls, men and women. Twenty years later, the mass media has become more sophisticated, more pervasive, more influential and, in terms of inducing conformity, potentially more dangerous.

Controversy reigns about the extent to which television, videos and computer games, for example, actually influence or determine human behaviour. Human beings have minds of their own after all, which can presumably be used to exercise judgement and discretion. The issue is most usually debated in relation to the incidence of sex and violence and general misogyny in the popular media, and in relation to the sensationalism and trivialization of reporting associated with the tabloid press. The media is a business and, as such, is concerned with making money. The tension between 'responsible public broadcasting and reporting' and 'the profit motive' is consequently enormous. In the United States, where anything up to an average of fifty different television and cable channels compete for viewers, producing wall-to-wall adverts, interspersed with sound bites masquerading as programmes, the emphasis on profit is probably most obvious. Even the integrity of diverse and distant cultures is not exempt from the potential domination of Western ideas and practices communicated by satellite and software through the international media.

Although it remains unproven whether or not there is a direct link between the male violence and aggression displayed on television, in films and increasingly in computer games, CD-Roms and virtual reality, and male violence and sexual aggression towards women and children in real life, there can be no doubt, at the level of gender socialization, that omnipresent images of men doing daring, violent, dangerous and destructive things, whether as cartoon characters directed at children, popular heroes in soap operas and blockbusters, animations on CD-Roms or midnight movie thugs, does little to encourage young men and boys to 'reconstruct' their gender identities in ways which emphasize gentleness or caring personalities. The role models presented to young women and girls through the widespread portrayal of women as bimbos and victims, whose sexuality is defined and limited by the constant presentation of various kinds of verbal and physical abuse as being virtually synonymous with everyday heterosexuality, leaves little scope for self-definition or the realistic expectation of social equality.

Even if programmes like *Neighbours* and *Home and Away* are merely the backdrop or 'the wallpaper' against which countless Western youngsters sit on settees, eat their tea or do their homework, the subliminal, stereotyped messages about approved forms of masculinity and femininity cannot fail to have their impact.

Gender and inequality

Gender differentiation might be of less concern if it simply reflected diversity and the possibility of creative responses to personal and collective identity, if it was simply to do with people being different but equal. The problem identified by sociologists, however, especially feminists, is that gender represents a form of **social division** which is related to varying amounts of power, resources and opportunity in societies.

Men and women, on the whole, have access to differing amounts of power, resources and opportunity simply because they are men or women. Men monopolize the most money and the best jobs, compared with women of the same social class and ethnic group. Men themselves, or their (male) representatives, exercise the greatest influence in high places such as the judiciary, academia, big business, the media, religions, governments, the military, etc. At a personal and domestic level, men can expect to be 'looked after' by the women who give birth to them and bring them up and become sexual partners with them, in the name of something called 'love' or 'duty'. They can expect more or less the same kind of services from women, whether they demonstrate or deserve love or not. In return, men are expected to assume economic responsibilities for women in most Western cultures and, even when they don't, women's wages and financial relationship to the state are based on the assumption that they do.

Young recruits into existing societies are conscripted into gender roles which anticipate different ways of life and different opportunities for boys and girls. They are not equal. There are very few, if any, contemporary societies in which social power, authority and influence is monopolized, or even shared equally, by women. In societies in which men work hard, women work harder. In societies in which men are poor, women are poorer. It is for these kinds of reasons that sociologists, and especially feminists, are concerned about the origins of gender inequalities and about the ways in which these are sustained and highly resistant to significant change in contemporary societies.

Feminist perspectives

Feminist perspectives on the relationship between gender and social inequality all agree that the two phenomena are closely related.

Most feminists assume that gender is socially constructed rather than biologically determined, although different kinds of feminists explain the connection in different ways and some, for example **Linda Birke**, claim that, while women's biology does not determine their lives, the fact that women menstruate and give birth does have an actual and material impact upon their lives in ways which cannot simply be 'wished away'. Others, for example **Juliet Mitchell,** argue that gender and identity are not simply the product of socialization and social construction, but are also a consequence of complex psychological patterns and emotional responses which exist in the subconscious. The extent to which these 'originate' in the subconscious and then operate their influence on our personalities; or can be explained as 'particularly profound' consequences of our social learning experience, which have become so 'well-embedded' in our ways of thinking about ourselves and the ways in which we give meaning to the world that they become 'almost second nature', 'taken for granted', 'seemingly instinctive', remains a lively debate within feminist theory.

The important principle to understand about feminism is that, while feminism implies considerable agreement about, and opposition to, the oppression of women, the ways in which this oppression is explained is the subject of considerable disagreement. This has led to the development of a number of feminist perspectives which are not mutually exclusive but which certainly emphasize different causal factors, and which in turn lead to different recommendations for action. If you believe that gender inequality is a matter of ignorance and 'old-fashioned ideas', for example, picked up during a particularly 'unenlightened' childhood, then the remedy might seem to lie in initiatives which concentrate on education and changing attitudes. If you take the view that gender inequality is related to the concern of capitalism to exploit women workers and to benefit from the free provision of domestic and emotional labour which helps to reproduce the male labour force and gets them to the factory gate on time, then the remedy might seem to lie in initiatives which modify, change or do away with capitalism.

Liberal feminism

The explanations and related recommendations of liberal feminists are typified by the ideas of Ann Oakley. Since gender roles are not innate or inevitable, they can be changed. Since they are learned as a consequence of socialization, socialization practices can be modified and changed. Child-rearing practices, education, attempts to 'feminize' the media, etc. can help to change traditional ideas. Pressure on governments to introduce legislation to make sex discrimination illegal, to insist upon equal opportunities policies in schools and workplaces and to create a general legislative framework in which the oppression and abuse of women is prevented are all seen as ways of 'changing society from within'.

Improving the general status of women in society, and making sure that the barriers which prevent women from entering the professions and traditional male jobs are recognized (e.g. lack of proper training and decent childcare support) would all help to increase the participation of women in the public sphere and enable them to take on the kinds of influential public roles (e.g. in government, industry and trade unions) where decisions are made and influence is exerted.

These are all arguments which assume that, while gender inequality is widespread it is not automatic. It can be challenged, and 'where there's a will', it can be overcome. Much of the energy expended by liberal feminists in the 1970s and 1980s was concerned with 'getting into government', 'getting into management', with 'establishing equal opportunities policies' and 'joining Parent–Teacher Associations', with 'speaking out' against sexism and 'raising anti-sexist children'. It certainly helped to establish a climate of opinion in which some of the most obvious and immediate examples of sexism became subject to criticism and became part of a more general public awareness about the issues.

It is debatable whether much was changed, however. Some modifications to the language and a few examples of positive action in education and training programmes are unlikely to wipe out generations of institutionalized inequality, in which the general power of men in society to monopolize positions of influence and the greatest access to resources is stubbornly resistant to anything other than superficial change.

Marxist and socialist feminism

Marxist and socialist feminist perspectives draw on Marxist theory to account for women's oppression and inequality within society. The economic structure of society is seen as crucial in determining the material conditions and circumstances within which people live. The rise of capitalism and the increasingly transnational nature of its influence and power over people's lives is held to be at the heart of women's oppression. Arguments originally produced by Marx and his followers to explain the unequal relationships of production; the creation of social classes with conflicting interests to defend; the maldistribution of resources, especially wealth and profit; and the use of ideologies as methods of thought control were adapted and developed by feminists to show the ways in which women's domestic labour in the family has been 'appropriated' by capitalism at nil cost to ensure the domestic servicing of the current labour force and the social reproduction of the future labour force.

Not only are men and women engaged in a 'sexual division of labour' which benefits capitalism's need for workers and the free use of related support services, but women also act as a supply of cheap and intermittently available labour, who can be drawn into the workforce and laid off again at whim, like a 'reserve army', when it suits the needs of capital to have more or fewer workers.

In this respect, it is argued, women have interests in common with the working class. Both are on the receiving end of capitalist exploitation, and their social and political circumstances can only be relieved and improved by collaborative resistance to the attempts by capital to exhort yet more work and profit out of their waged and unwaged labour.

Part of the implication of this argument is that women are somehow different from the working class. Some, of course, were also part of the working class. This apparent confusion lies in the tendency of Marxists and socialists (and many sociologists) of the time to define social class in relation to 'the relationships of production' and to men's occupations. Women who are not 'technically' or 'actually' working class, e.g. middle-class women and members of ethnic minority groups, should, however, see their interests lying in common with the working class, who will act as the kind of vanguard against capitalism which, when it is overthrown, will lead to a much more just and egalitarian society for all.

In the 1970s and 1980s Marxist and socialist feminists, most of whom could be regarded as middle class, were active in left-wing political groups, trade unions and the Labour Party, in an attempt to improve the terms and conditions of women in paid work and to highlight the problems associated with domestic labour, housework and childcare, in an attempt to make them part of the political agenda of at least the Labour Party. In a shifting political climate which witnessed the spread of Thatcherism, the demise of trade unions and the softening and shifting of the left to more moderate ground, the claims of anyone to be Marxist, and even socialist, decreased. Often the battle to 'withstand Thatcherism' took precedence over specifically feminist issues to do with women's position in society, although a considerable effect of Thatcherite policies was to weaken the position, increase the poverty and confirm the dependency of women even further.

Today Marxist and socialist feminists (increasingly called socialist feminists) are still likely to explain the main cause of women's continuing inequality in economic terms, which are considerably exacerbated by capitalist relations, but their analysis has broadened to take account of what radical feminists have to say about **patriarchy** and what black feminists have to say about **racism.**

Radical feminism

Kate Millet and patriarchy

An early contributor to the re-emergence of Western feminism in the 1960s was **Kate Millet,** whose book *Sexual Politics* was one of the first of its generation to focus on **patriarchy,** or male domination of women, as the root of women's oppression. She defined patriarchy as 'power-structured relationships' in which one group of people – women – were ruled and controlled by another – men.

Radical feminist analysis is based on the same conviction, i.e. that it is men's domination of women, in all aspects of society, that explains the roots of women's oppression and inequality. According to radical feminists, inequality between men and women existed before capitalism, and has continued to operate in cultures and economies which are not based on capitalism. If capitalism exploits women, it is because capitalism is a man-made institution.

Patriarchal relations operate rather like a **caste system** according to Millet, in which one sex – simply by being born men – enjoys greater power, and power over, the other sex – women. Christine Delphy, the French sociologist, uses the Marxist notion to describe gender as 'a class in itself'. By virtue of their common material conditions and their relationship to the means of production and reproduction and to men, women share a similar 'class' relationship. Just as Marxists see different class groups as being inevitably 'in conflict' with each other, because they have different and conflicting interests to defend, so, too, are the social, economic and political interests of women 'as a class' in conflict with those of men 'as a class'.

Delphy and Millet have both been criticized for assuming 'common' and 'universal' characteristics in women's oppression which take no account of ethnic and cultural differences, for example, and for over-generalizing about the universality of male power, which also takes no account of first world/third world differences and 'race' differences. Delphy has subsequently refined her theory to take account of greater complexity and diversity, but she still combines Marxist methodology and terminology with a radical feminist analysis to great effect. (See, for example, *Familiar Exploitation* – a book about the economic relationships of marriage and family life, written with Diana Leonard.)

Although not all men share the same amount of social power and influence e.g. upper-class and working-class men, white and black men, etc. they all have shared patriarchal interests in common. They all benefit to some degree from the dominant position of men in society, and derive privileges from their maleness in societies in which maleness is most valued. Although they may have other interests to defend, which may be in conflict with each other (e.g. conflicting financial interests as either workers or capitalists; opposing religious and ethnic interests as Serbs or

Muslims, etc.) they still share common understandings about the position of women (in relation to rape, for example) and may collude to advance male interests at the expense of women's interests, even when the women are from their own class or ethnic group (e.g. the long-standing perpetuation of the pay gap between men's and women's wages is preserved by the mutual agreement of male-dominated trade unions, male-dominated employers' organizations and the male-dominated government (whether Conservative or Labour)).

While it could be argued that some women (especially middle-class and white women) have greater access to wealth and resources and social power than some men (especially working-class and black men), it is also the case that most middle-class women's resources are dependent upon their relationship to middle-class men. They are also conditional upon 'good' and 'dutiful' behaviour in patriarchal marriages and patriarchal employment. Divorced women from the erstwhile middle class are notoriously poorer unless they remarry someone of similar status. Middle-class women in well-paid jobs are usually dependent for promotion and tenure on predominantly male management and employers. Middle-class women and white women are generally no safer than any other group when it comes to domestic violence or physical attack. Working-class and black men do not simply seek revenge for their exploitation and brutal treatment by confronting white, upper-class supremacy, they often use violence against the women of their own groups and continue to expect the kinds of domestic and sexual servicing that keeps women in inferior economic and social positions to themselves.

According to radical feminists, oppressive and unequal relationships between men and women originate not in the wider society but in the intimacy of personal relationships, in sexual partnerships and families and domestic households of various kinds. Personal relationships are also 'political' relationships, in that they are based on different and unequal amounts of power which is determined by sex, and which is both recognized and reinforced in the wider society, in every aspect of culture, government and organization. Religion, law, tradition, education, the media – all reflect the patriarchal leadership, ideas and power which stem originally from the power of individual men over individual women and which has become institutionalized in the wider society. Sometimes the exercise of power is benign and respectful towards women. Sometimes it is 'enlightened' and concerned to demonstrate good intentions with regard to equality and anti-sexist attitudes. But it is nonetheless 'in charge'. Those who benefit from patriarchal societies are unlikely to agree to giving up their benefits and privileges without a fight, particularly within the family and within the intimacy of personal and private relations.

Crucial to radical feminist explanations of the preservation of men's power over women are assumptions about the significance of sexuality and the use of violence. Patriarchal definitions of women's sexuality are used to control women and keep them as the 'property' of men. Women are expected to be 'available' to men, to 'belong' to individual men, to respond to men's sexual needs, to dress and behave in ways which appeal to men's definitions of sexual attractiveness. This may vary in different cultures, but the same principle of women's sexuality being defined in relation to what pleases men at any one time is almost universal.

Similarly, male violence and sexual aggression may take different forms in different cultures, but it is widespread and commonplace. According to radical feminists, male violence reflects the naked exercise of male power over women, and the inducement of fear, which attempts to keep women 'in their place' when all else – such as economic dependency and ideological 'brainwashing' – fails. Even when women are not noticeably trying to rebel or to extricate themselves from patriarchal and heterosexual relations, the threat or possibility of male violence and sexual abuse are a continuing characteristic of such relationships.

Radical feminists are among the few contemporary feminists who have taken seriously the feminist idea that 'the personal is political', and have concentrated their studies on the power relationships which are experienced 'in private'. Delphy and Leonard point out that socialist and heterosexual feminists have yet to produce any serious studies of sex in marriage and cohabiting relationships, and are much more likely to express solidarity with working-class women, whose productive labour is being exploited at work and whose domestic labour is being exploited at home, than consider the ways in which the socialist and sometimes 'anti-sexist' male partners and colleagues of middle-class female academics and feminists also collude in the 'appropriation' of women's intellectual, domestic and emotional labour, in ways which perpetuate women's dependency and exploitation.

Criticisms made of radical feminism by socialists and black feminists, which suggest that an analysis based on the universality of patriarchy as the fundamental cause of women's oppression and inequality under-estimates the exploitation of poor groups generally; of colonial situations in which the greatest damage to people's lives has been done by imperialism rather than patriarchy; and of the impact of racism, which is usually blamed as the 'main enemy' by the majority of those who experience it, have caused radical feminists to recognize the ways in which other forms of oppression do intersect with male domination in ways which are not always straightforward. Most contemporary radical feminist theory, including that produced by black women who also define themselves as radical feminists, takes pains to acknowledge the diversity of different women's experiences and to accept that multiple oppressions do occasion complicated and sometimes contradictory loyalties. Some may even see individual men as 'victims' rather than perpetrators of patriarchal attitudes and practices. Others may acknowledge the steps taken by some men to absent themselves from the behaviour patterns and rewards which generally accrue to men in a patriarchal society. But this does not prevent them from attributing primary significance to the social construction, development and consolidation of male power as being the main cause of women's oppression and inequality.

Black feminism

Black feminists make two major criticisms of white Western feminism in general and discussions on gender matters in particular.

The first is that, because of racism, most Western-derived theories, including feminism, tend to be **ethnocentric**, that is, they see things from the point of view of their own historical and cultural experience, without considering that other cultural experiences and histories might lead people to other conclusions; or over-generalize from their own culturally specific and subjective experience in ways which assume that experience is universal and that what counts for white women in the West is also true for all women in other cultures, give or take a touch of language difference or the odd 'curious' tradition; or overlook and ignore completely the experience of women who do not constitute the 'dominant group'. **Audre Lorde** has said:

Audre Lorde

The oppression of women knows no ethnic nor racial boundaries, true, but this does not mean it is identical within these differences. Nor do the reservoirs of our ancient power know these boundaries. To deal with one without alluding to the other is to distort our commonality as well as our difference. For then beyond sisterhood is till racism.

Similar criticisms were made about early feminist theory by working-class women, who said that it reflected middle-class rather than working class experience and priorities; and by lesbians, who said that it assumed that all women were 'straight' and involved in intimate relationships with men. Both were distortions of the complexity and diversity of women's experience which, like racism, made understanding 'our shared commonality' more difficult.

The second main criticism is about 'ignorance' and making statements about black experience which are simply not true, or only partly true, or only true in some circumstances. In other words, the problems of any group 'thinking it knows about' someone else's experience, and even becoming an 'authority' on it, in circumstances in which it would be more appropriate to listen and try to learn rather than assume understanding.

So long as racism is institutionalized in societies like ours, and white groups remain dominant and in the majority, the problems of racism are likely to persist. But it would be true to say that feminists, and feminist sociology, have taken the criticisms of black feminists seriously, and do increasingly try to take account of cultural diversity and pay serious attention to the different experiences of ethnic minorities, as well as attempt to confront and overcome racism in their own attitudes and working practices.

Social divisions

In terms of social divisions in society, black feminists have been among the first to point out the ways in which different forms of inequality, brought about by different oppressions, actually intersect.

Kum-Kum Bhavani says:

When comparing racism to sexism, which is more fundamental? The question is unanswerable, for it is like asking of the product of a multiplication which of the numbers is more fundamental to the answer. Racism and sexism inform each other – all women are racialised and all human beings are gendered. In other words – each structures the other, with both being inscribed within class relations.

Third world women

The early use of anthropological studies to demonstrate cultural diversity were not necessarily based on anti-racist assumptions.

Amos and Parmar, in *Challenging Imperial Feminism*, say:

Whilst one tradition has been for black women to have remained invisible within feminist scholarship ... another tradition has been the idealisation and culturalism of anthropological works. Often we have appeared in cross-cultural studies which, under the guise of feminism and progressive anthropology, renders us as 'subjects' for 'interesting' and 'exotic' comparison.

Sexuality

The social construction of sexuality is influenced by 'who makes the definitions' and to what extent women are free 'to define their own sexuality' outside of patriarchal and racist social relationships. Whereas it has taken radical and lesbian feminists to point out that dominant forms of male and female sexuality are not 'given by nature', black feminists have also explored the racist connotations of the definitions. Phoenix, in *Theories of Gender and Black Families*, says:

> black men of Afro Caribbean origin do not fit the stereotype of the powerful male in western societies. Instead they are stereotyped as feckless, violent, criminal and over sexed, even to the extent that they are likely to be seen as rapists. While 'normal' males have some degree of aggression and strong sexual drives, to be too aggressive and have too much sexual drive. . . is not to be super male but rather to be bestial.
> Black women similarly are stereotyped as having some 'feminine' character-istics to excess, but also some 'male' characteristics. Thus black women are perceived as being easily available sexual objects who are prone to prostitution. The mythology of black women as having different sexuality from white women has served to permit the rape and sexual exploitation of black women . . . without the public outcry being equivalent to when white women are raped. Black women are also stereotyped as matriarchs who are tough and who can be expected to work hard.

Hazel Carby says:

> One important struggle, rooted in these different ideological mechanisms (i.e. racism and sexism) which determine racially differentiated representations of gender, has been the black woman's battle to gain control over her own sexuality in the face of racist experimentation with the contraceptive Depo-Provera and enforced sterilisation.

Dual systems perspectives

Increasingly, the points of demarcation between patriarchy and capitalism as having distinct and separate responsibility for creating gender inequalities, with 'greater significance' being attributed to one rather than the other, are breaking down. Most contemporary socialist, radical and black feminist writing takes account of the interrelationship of systems of oppression which feed and inform each other. Clearly it makes no sense to study capitalism, for example, without recognizing that it exists in a kind of 'twin town' relationship with patriarchy and racism.

Heidi Hartmann, in *The Unhappy Marriage of Marxism and Feminism*, exerted an early influence on the feminist sociology of work (see pages 198–9) by pointing out that patriarchal relations at home and capitalist relations at work went hand in glove so far as the exploitation of women's labour was concerned.

Sylvia Walby, in *Theorising Patriarchy*, has shown how patriarchal relations existing in the private sphere are reproduced and consolidated in the public sphere. She also shows how patriarchy continually reconstitutes, reinvents and represents itself in different forms to 'keep on top of the competition'.

In *The Road to Wigan Pier Revisited*, Bea Campbell, while making a socialist feminist analysis, uses a radical feminist perspective on patriarchy to describe the political and social betrayal of working-class women by the men of their class who, as part of the 'men's movement', collude with male employers and government in defence of so-called men's jobs and wage rates and domestic privileges.

Delphy and Leonard, in *Familiar Exploitation*, use the economic focus and methodology of Marxism to support a radical feminist analysis of the ways in which men appropriate and exploit women's labour in the home, to create personal and private power relations which promote and support patriarchal interests in both private and public relationships. Although they do not hold capitalism primarily responsible for women's oppression, but rather men behaving as capitalists and men informing the practices of capitalism, they make considerable use of the concepts employed to study capitalism in their arguments.

Post-modernism   The contemporary intellectual preoccupation with post-modernism became fashionable in British sociology in the 1980s. It was associated, among other things, with a growing interest in cultural studies in university sociology departments and a sideways shift from women's studies to gender studies. The developing emphasis on 'gender' rather than 'women' enabled the study of **masculinities** to be included. The shift had political connotations, and reflected the less radical climate of the 1980s in which feminism was becoming increasingly the subject of a right-wing, some would say patriarchal, backlash (see e.g. *Backlash*, Susan Faludi).

Post-modern perspectives in sociology have continued in that sociological tradition which is more interested in interaction and subjective experience rather than wide-ranging and structural explanations of social organization and behaviour; in the tradition which recognizes 'multiple realities' rather than 'single truths'; in the tradition which recognizes the capacity of thoughtful human beings to 'give meaning' to their world, in their own way, and who are actively engaged in making and remaking their own identities, despite the wider social context. Because such views rely on 'taking personal experience seriously', 'recognizing diversity' and 'challenging traditional forms of authority and knowledge', they have received a sympathetic response from some feminists. But they have also been subject to fierce criticism.

So far as gender is concerned, post-modernists are interested in the flexible nature of gender and gender identity. They have been keen to dismantle and 'deconstruct' all taken-for-granted 'categories', 'types' and 'forms' which attempt to make any generalizations about common experiences of gender. This is sometimes referred to as a process of 'fragmentation', in which there is no such thing as structures or truth or fixtures or permanence. Gender, like everything else, is always in a state of 'becoming', so that as soon as you try to classify and label it, it has moved on and changed. Not only does the person who inhabits the gender have the capacity to remake it and recreate it all the time, but all those who witness the presentation are likely to have differing and changing responses to it.

Some post-modernists go so far as to claim that there is no such thing as the categories 'man' and 'woman'. Some men do, and all men could, create and develop more of the so-called 'feminine' characteristics of identity or any other characteristics they chose, and vice versa. Studies of masculinity and femininity in forms of popular culture such as music, film, soap operas and romantic fiction, for example, reveal a variety and diversity of possibilities. Identity is not simply something which is 'given' it can be 'created' and 'played about with', almost as a conscious act of subversion.

While this analysis is quite fun, and is certainly useful in counteracting some of the 'over-determinist' tendencies of certain structural explanations of human behaviour, it may seem a rather odd, and not very relevant, question to ask a single-parent mother of three, living on inadequate state benefits on a run-down council estate somewhere in the north of England; 'What do you mean by "woman?"'

Any sense that there are determining forces in society, like systems of inequality based on social class; or that there are structural barriers based on sex discrimination and race discrimination which exercise controls over people's freedom to be 'whatever they choose'; or that ideologies which serve the interests of powerful groups are continually used in ways which influence and direct the so-called 'free' consciousness of people, even against their own interests, are discounted by post-modernists as 'inadequate' and 'unsatisfactory' explanations of cultural diversity and resistance and multiple realities.

Key debates

Major debates about the characteristics and consequences of gender inequality will be taken up in subsequent chapters. We have chosen to concentrate on those to do with the **family**, **education** and **work**.

Sexuality

Sociological debates about sexuality are concerned with the extent to which human sexuality can be said to be biologically determined or socially constructed. In general, those theoretical perspectives which assume that human behaviour is:

● programmed by biological biogrammars; or
● determined by biologically-based strategies to ensure the most efficient reproduction of the species; or
● moulded by culture to reflect the complementary and functional interrelationship of men and women in society

assume that patterns of human sexuality are rooted in nature and possibly interpreted by culture to reflect different religious and moral considerations.

Arguments about 'male sexual aggression' and 'female passivity' are linked to the assumed effects of genetic and hormonal differences and to observations about the different social roles which it is assumed men and women are required to play in society – in simple terms, man as hunter-gatherer and breadwinner; woman as birth-giver, nurturer and carer.

It is also true that in almost every attempt to discuss human sexuality – in historic or contemporary terms, in academic or lay person's language, in mono cultural or multicultural context – the heavy hand of ideology is rarely absent. What people 'think about' sexuality is always closely tied in with definitions of what sexuality 'is said to be'.

Descriptions of sexuality can be:

● thinly disguised rationalizations of subjective desires and preferred requirements
● justifications for particular forms of sexual practices compared with others
● moral and religious imperatives
● practical solutions to population requirements.

Radical feminism and sexuality

According to radical feminists, the focus on sexuality is one of the main ways in which patriarchal power relations are organized and sustained.

Human sexuality is seen by radical feminists as being potentially immensely flexible. But it becomes channelled and reproduced in fairly rigid and predictable ways.

There is no reason why sexual identity, behaviour and attitudes need **automatically** to be associated with procreation and reproduction. Reproduction of the species **could be** a simple technical issue concerned with fertilizing eggs and birthing babies. It doesn't need to be associated with 'love' or 'marriage' or sexual fidelity – indeed, in some cultures it is not. The fact that, in Western societies at least, sex and reproduction are sometimes seen as synonymous, attempts are made to control the expression of sexual activity, which is 'merely' for pleasure, within religious beliefs, moral codes and relationships, which imply responsibility.

Sexual activity is also a significant feature of relationships which preserve male power over women. The institution of **heterosexuality,** according to radical feminists, is a social institution, socially constructed and man-made. It is presented to new social recruits in ways which make it seem 'almost compulsory', and is widely regarded as the 'natural' and 'normal' way to express desire and organize sexual activity.

Firmly established over time and in different cultures, heterosexuality has become the accepted way in which sexual desire and sexual activity are channelled towards forms of sexual expression involving the opposite sex. In Western culture, the ideology of 'romantic love' has been invented and promoted to encourage and legitimize the sexual relationships that develop. Religions, popular culture and the mass media all help to build and sustain the ideology. It becomes a very effective way of organizing people into couples for the purposes of procreation, and then into households for the purposes of raising children; in turn providing and sustaining a labour force, and in the process controlling people by virtue of their many responsibilities towards each other.

Of course, as anyone who knows anything about sex will tell you, while this may be the 'ideal', it is often not the reality. Sexual activity is not always associated with love or responsibility. It is not always a 'pleasure'. It is not always entered into through freedom of choice (e.g. in cases of rape or child sexual abuse).

Because of patriarchy there is rarely 'complete equality' between the participating adults. Indeed, heterosexuality is to a large extent based upon the eroticization of power differences between 'strong' and 'commanding' men, who 'initiate' the action and 'demand' compliance (see the countless examples in popular culture) and 'weak', 'grateful' and 'compliant' women. Power inequalities are intensified when differences are also multiplied by class, 'race' and age. We should not be surprised, therefore, when research suggests that by far the largest number of child sexual abusers (over 90 per cent), are heterosexual men. Or that rape and sexual abuse are not regarded as serious crimes, especially when the 'victim' is poor, black or considered in some way to be responsible for what has happened to her.

Sexuality and ideology   A further characteristic of the ideology surrounding male and female sexuality is that men are seen to operate rather like a faulty tap which, when it has been 'turned on', cannot be turned off. This rather crude analogy finds expression in the comments of numerous judges who dispense light and suspended sentences to rapists on the grounds that 'they couldn't help themselves', 'they were led on', 'the woman was "asking for it"', 'the child was "no angel"', etc.

Women, on the other hand, are frequently assumed to be largely responsible for what happens to them. They wear 'provocative clothes'; they 'wander the streets late at night'; they frequently give men 'mixed messages', saying 'no' when they really mean 'yes'; they 'use sexuality' to 'get what they want'; they 'like men to be the boss'. Blaming the victim in this way acts as a means of excusing men for the worst excesses of their sexual behaviour.

Considerable effort is made to promote sexual intercourse as the main form of sexual activity, despite numerous forms of sexual expression which may be more pleasurable for women and which certainly would be safer and healthier. Considerable effort is made to encourage women to look to men for sexual approval and to dress and behave in ways likely to appeal to men's taste in women. Wives and ex-wives and girlfriends are ranged 'in competition' with each other for 'the man of their dreams'. All of which does a lot to advance and sustain the social and political power of patriarchy.

Lesbian and gay sexuality

In totalitarian and closed societies, like most of Eastern Europe until the recent collapse of communism, alternatives to compulsory heterosexuality were not allowed and were violently suppressed. In circumstances in which alternatives were not known about, they didn't happen very much, or at least only in secret. And yet there were lesbians and gay men in the former Eastern bloc – East Germany and the Czech Republic, for example – who, since the revolution, have begun to 'come out' and live their lives more openly.

In countries like Britain and the United States, lesbian and gay culture is more visible, but there are still criminal and legal discriminations applied to gay people which are not applied to heterosexuals. In Britain, since **section 28** of the Local Government Act was passed in **1988**, it has become illegal 'to promote lesbian and gay lifestyles' in schools, when no legal prohibitions are placed upon promoting other kinds of lifestyles. Sex between men over 18 and men under 18 is a criminal offence, as is attempting to arrange sexual encounters, i.e. so-called 'soliciting' and 'importuning'. Recent campaigning activity during 1994 by gay rights organizations managed to get the age of consent for gay men reduced from 21 to 18. But it remains at 16 for heterosexual men and women. Kissing and holding hands in public is not likely to get heterosexual people arrested or ridiculed or beaten up. 'Chatting up' members of the opposite sex with a view to arranging sexual encounters is a fairly standard and commonplace practice in everyday heterosexual social relations. Lesbians who are mothers face enormous discrimination in the courts over custody of children (see page 119).

Gay and lesbian workers have no statutory rights against unfair dismissal if they lose their jobs because they are gay. Lesbians and gay men working in social services, teaching, the police force and the armed services often do so 'in secret' for fear of reprisals or of losing their jobs. Between 1990 and 1994, 260 army personnel were sacked on grounds of their sexuality, including captains, majors, a squadron leader and two chaplains.

Public prejudice against lesbians and gay men is considerable. Sometimes called homophobia, it is not so much about an 'irrational fear' of homosexuality as a profound hatred. The **civil rights** pressure group **Liberty** confirms that 25 per cent of lesbians living in London have experienced violent assault due to other people's prejudice about their sexuality. Incidences of 'gay bashing' and 'queer bashing' are common in our larger cities.

Section 28

Civil Rights and 'Liberty'

Cause and effect

Explanations concerned with 'the 'causes' of lesbianism and homosexuality vary. The commonly held view, endorsed by a long history of dubious theories and assertions, is that homosexuality is some kind of aberration or abnormality which is genetically determined. The search for the 'gay gene' in modern science is legendary. What is interesting is the vast amount of trouble taken to find some physical explanation for a pattern of behaviour which could just as easily be a matter of diversity, illustrating the flexibility of human sexuality, or a matter of choice.

'gay gene' theory

Gay men's politics has always tended to favour the **'gay gene' theory**, believing that if their behaviour can be found to be biological in origin then they can't be held responsible for what they do. In a tolerant and liberal society their sexual difference would be accepted and forms of social discrimination against them would be abolished. It's a double-edged argument, however, because in a repressive society the identification of a 'gay gene' could also lead to calls for 'selective breeding', which would eliminate its carriers at birth!

personal choice

Lesbian feminists put forward a different theory, believing sexuality to be a matter of **personal choice**, informed by a political commitment to women and a preference for the company and intimacy of women. Because human sexuality is socially constructed, it is quite possible, though not always easy, to resist the pressures which promote heterosexuality, especially when there is a strong political and social commitment to women. Furthermore, because human sexuality is flexible there is no reason why sexual activity and sexual expression can't be focused on members of the same sex rather than the opposite sex. This second part of the argument helps to explain why lesbians who are not feminist choose women for other than 'political' reasons.

Attempts to quantify the numbers of lesbian and gay men in society vary. Kinsey, writing in the 1960s, quoted 1 in 10 as a rough estimate. But figures are unhelpful. If homosexuality and lesbianism are a consequence of genetics, then they will happen in all societies and all cultures in direct relation to the incidence of the so-called 'gay gene'. If lesbianism and homosexuality are social constructions then they will happen any society and in any culture in which some degree of choice or resistance, however secretive, is allowed. The knowledge that alternative patterns of sexual activity, and the creation of alternative kinds of sexual identity, are possible will extend the possibility of more people choosing such options in the future.

3   Ethnicity

Race and ethnicity have emerged as a central concern of sociology in the second half of the twentiethth century. Earlier sociologists like Durkheim, Marx and Weber had predicted that divisions along the lines of race and nationality would give way to those based on class or status. However, research on the position of black people in Britain, the USA and Southern Africa in the 1960s indicated that widespread inequalities existed between ethnic groups.

In Britain, full employment in the immediate post-war years led to the recruitment of workers from the colonies, soon to be 'New Commonwealth' countries of the West Indies, India and Pakistan.

In the USA, studies of the black population in the years leading up to the civil rights movement raised awareness of ethnicity as a dimension in the social stratification system. Widespread segregation operated in public places and in education. Black people generally suffered considerable overt discrimination and were largely confined to lower-level work, doing the jobs that were too dirty, dangerous or unpleasant for white workers, in a period of full employment. They were also concentrated in poorer housing, in rural areas or in overcrowded conditions in the slum areas of northern cities.

Sociology as a discipline responded with a debate about whether black people were a particularly deprived part of the working class or whether the concept of class itself was inadequate to explain the position of ethnic minorities.

In Britain, sociology has now also begun to reflect the concerns of its own multi-ethnic population. Generalizations can no longer be made about 'society' or 'the population' unless they hold true for all ethnic groups. Issues to do with ethnicity in the study of society should not be ignored, or side-tracked into separate sections of books about sociology. For this reason you will find references to ethnicity throughout this book. In this chapter, however, we are examining the impact of ethnicity on the stratification system so that we can assess the extent to which social position is determined by a mixture of social class, gender, ethnicity and age.

Terminology

There is no universally accepted meaning of the term 'race'. Increasingly, the term itself is seen as a relic of a period in which it was thought possible to divide the world's population into different, clearly identifiable and biologically distinct racial groups. Influenced by theories of evolution and advances in biology, some nineteenth century thinkers attempted to classify the world's population into a hierarchy of racial types, making a link between certain physical characteristics and differences in ability, intelligence and temperament. In much the same way as biological sex differences between men and women were thought to give rise to different natures and capacities, racial stereotypes were constructed in which black people were defined as 'closer to nature', 'more physical', 'sexually aggressive' and 'less intelligent'. According to Hazel Carby, the objective of stereotypes is 'not to reflect or represent a reality but to function as a disguise, or mystification, of objective social relations'. Controlling images based on stereotypes are designed to make things like racism, sexism and poverty appear to be natural, normal and inevitable. The power of these stereotypes continues today – the music business and sport are two of the few areas of human endeavour in which black people are encouraged to excel.

Modern genetics, however, has moved away from this notion of fixed racial groups which are biologically based. Work based on archaeological material suggests that human beings come from the same genetic stock and that population groups are not static but are constantly changing, adapting and mixing. Furthermore, it is pointed out that as much as 85 per cent of all genetic differences between human beings – height, hair colour, blood type, shape, etc. – can be found within the same 'racial' group. There are, in fact, few biological differences between races, and this concept, like that of gender, has been 'socially constructed'. A particular difference, skin colour, has been 'selected' and given 'social significance'. A set of other characteristics – of personality and aptitude – are associated with it, and the idea of separate races constructed.

Dangerous doctrines of genocide, slavery, apartheid and, more recently, 'ethnic cleansing' are based on the belief that there are 'pure' racial types which can be separated. The constructed differences between them are then used to justify treating less powerful groups as inferior or sub-human.

Scientists now reject this understanding of 'race'. In 1967 the world's scientists, meeting in UNESCO, declared:

> Current biological knowledge does not permit us to impute cultural achievements to differences in genetic potential. Differences in the achievements of different peoples should be attributed solely to their cultural history. The peoples of the world today appear to possess equal biological potentialities for attaining any level of civilisation.

Although this quotation begs the question of what is meant by 'achievement' and 'civilization', it unequivocally makes the point that culture is more significant than biology. Sociologists therefore prefer to use the term **ethnicity** which refers not to nationality or race but to the **learned culture** or **way of life** of a group which includes customs, beliefs, tradition and language. Although it is not a perfect concept, because it assumes there is a shared culture in each group, it does avoid the biological connotations of 'race'. The term **minority group** is also sometimes used when it is an accurate description.

It is important to remember that not all ethnic minority groups in Britain share the same culture or experiences. While the experience of discrimination may be shared, its impact, and the responses to it, may vary.

Historical background

When the Romans invaded Britain almost 2000 years ago the population of these isles was already a mixture of Britons, Celts and Picts. There were black people in those invading armies, some of them commanders. We know, too, that Britain's population was further diversified by Angles, Saxons, Danes, Jutes, Vikings and Normans, and by Jews, who arrived from the Middle East soon after the Norman Conquest.

Throughout the last four centuries there has been documentary evidence about a continuing black population in Britain which reached a peak of about 15 000 in the early seventeenth century before declining until the early twentieth century. This population consisted of Asian seamen employed on

British ships, escaped slaves from America and the West Indies, the children of African chiefs sent to Britain for education and the offspring of white plantation owners. We now have available studies which show that black people were found in all stations of life, from paupers and servants to academics and companions of the aristocracy and royalty. This does not mean, however, that there was a 'Golden Age' when prejudice and discrimination were unknown.

Liverpool was a centre for the slave trade, and prospered accordingly. Most menial employment in Britain, as opposed to the colonies, was carried out by whites, but there were black slaves in Britain who were mainly personal servants. Although the existence of the early black population of Britain has been well documented, most people are still unaware that Britain was anything other than 'white' prior to black immigration in the period after the Second World War.

The sixteenth- and seventeenth-centuries voyages of so-called 'discovery' – to the Caribbean, India, Australia and America – saw a time when traders brought back food, raw materials and mineral wealth, and missionaries set out, intent upon converting 'heathens' to Christianity. This period was followed by colonization, in which the newly 'discovered' lands were annexed to become part of the empires of European countries such as France, Holland, Germany, Spain, Portugal, Belgium and, the largest of all, Britain.

During this bloody period of European history thousands of indigenous people were exterminated or transported into slavery. Their families were torn apart, their lands stolen, their religious and spiritual sites were desecrated and their customs, traditions and languages were overridden or outlawed. The careful harnessing of natural resources, such as forests, rivers, lakes and land, which had taken place for centuries, was overturned in the drive for cash crops and mineral wealth, resulting in what we now recognize as grave environmental damage.

Abundant natural resources, such as gold, diamonds, rubber, oil, zinc and uranium, and crops, such as coffee, cocoa, sugar and cotton, as well as antiquities, were removed from the colonies over the centuries. The resultant wealth was used to finance the Industrial Revolution. Goods manufactured from raw materials were sold back to the new and vast markets provided by colonization, producing an even greater contribution to Britain's standing as the foremost industrial power of the time.

Britain, therefore, has had a long and inglorious association with the countries which later provided soldiers in wartime and low-paid workers in the post-war industrial expansion after the Second World War. In the words of one immigrant: 'We're here because you were there'.

After the Second World War there was a labour shortage, as Britain began to rebuild the economy and introduce the new provisions of the welfare state. Using its colonial populations as what Marxists would call a 'reserve army of labour', recruiting officers for organizations such as London Transport and the National Health Service, as well as private companies, went to the Caribbean and Indian sub-continent to enlist workers.

Most who came in those years were either single, or came leaving families behind, because they expected to earn enough to save up and return with capital to invest in their home countries. However, the types of jobs available and the rates of pay provided, meant that few were able to do so, and they increasingly came to see their futures as being in Britain.

In 1962, responding to anxiety about unplanned migration to Britain, the Conservative Government passed an **Immigration Act** restricting entry to only those people with employment vouchers which matched the need for

Immigration Act

workers. This Act prompted more immigration before 'the door was closed', so that this year was the **only one** in which immigration has ever exceeded emigration. Over the next two decades other Immigration Acts were passed which now effectively made it very difficult for black (but not white) immigrants to come to Britain unless they are the dependants of breadwinners already here.

Robert Moore has argued that these laws are essentially racist, or at least play into the hands of racists, by defining black people as a 'problem' whose numbers must be limited.

The practice of assimilation and integration

Since the 1950s sociologists have developed a variety of perspectives to explain the position of ethnic minorities and their effect on the stratification system and society as a whole, in particular, the extent to which a 'minority culture' can or should be absorbed into the wider culture of British society. The variety of possibilities has been expressed as a continuum from 'complete absorption', through 'integration', 'multi-culturalism', to 'separatism', in which ethnic groups live totally separated from each other.

Assimilation

Assimilation describes a situation in which a minority group is completely absorbed into a majority culture so that it becomes indistinguishable, rather like the French Huguenot refugees in Britain. In this situation the minority group adopts the values and patterns of behaviour of the majority or 'host' society. The process can involve changes on behalf of both groups as each adapts to the other's beliefs and behaviour, but usually the greatest change is expected on the part of immigrants to 'fit in' with the host society. This model usually involves a consensus, or **functionalist perspective**, of society. The majority is seen to share a 'common culture' based on agreement about the basic values on which society is based. Differences of class, age, sex and other potentially divisive factors are minimized, and the society is depicted as harmonious, cohesive and homogeneous.

This cultural consensus is initially disturbed by the arrival of groups with a noticeably different culture – religious practice, dress, language, family structure, etc. It is said to 'threaten' the equilibrium of society, but interaction between incomers and the host society results in a process of adaptation, whereby the new arrivals settle in and gradually adjust their behaviour and attitudes to be more like those of the host society. This process continues into the second generation, who are more easily accommodated because they have been socialized into the norms and values of the majority culture. So goes the theory.

Sheila Patterson

Sheila Patterson, in *Dark Strangers* (1965) presented an example of this approach. Studying West Indian immigrants in London, she described the 'cultural gap' between them and the local community, despite similarities of language and religion. The culture of West Indians is presented as more outgoing, laid-back and, in some ways, less 'respectable' than that of their white neighbours, creating potential conflict. However, she argued that, if West Indians would be willing to 'learn important aspects of British culture', like waiting in queues or getting married, the host society would be prepared to 'accept' them. She acknowledged that Britain was insular and 'mildly xenophobic', but claimed that, as a society, it also 'respected personal liberties and individualism'. She argued that anti-discrimination legislation should be passed to prevent inequality in jobs and housing. This study represents a view of 'race relations' that was very common among liberals in the 1950s and 1960s.

The doctrine of assimilation was more apparent in the USA than in Britain, where successive waves of immigration – from Eastern Europe, Ireland, Latin America, the Caribbean and the Far East – were urged to become 'Americanized' in some gigantic 'melting pot'. The second generation was to be socialized into the American way of life through the education system and contact with other Americans. By the second generation, the process would be complete. In practice, such a process could only happen if the 'host society' was willing to provide complete access to all spheres of life for minority groups.

integration

In Britain in the 1960s it was **'integration'** that was stressed – the process which Roy Jenkins, then Labour Home Secretary, defined as not 'a flattening process of assimilation' but one of 'cultural diversity in an atmosphere of mutual tolerance'. According to this process, the immigrant group would retain certain aspects of their cultural heritage, but would also learn to participate fully in the British way of life, by speaking the language and joining mainstream organizations such as political parties, trade unions and other groups. In this way the presence of ethnic minorities was seen to 'add something' in a positive way to society.

multi-culturalism

Slightly further along the continuum came the term **multi-culturalism**, in which it was acknowledged that cultural diversity existed in Britain which must be reflected in the school curriculum, in teaching materials, in celebrations and in religious practices. A genuinely **pluralist** society would be one which recognizes no one 'dominant' culture as being superior, but a multiplicity of different cultures which should be given equal regard.

This notion of pluralism has created considerable controversy in recent years, however. Some politicians on the right have argued that Britain should continue to be regarded as **primarily** an Anglo-Saxon, Christian country, and the values which support this 'prefered' culture should be those which are given significance. Inevitably, perhaps, it has been in the area of education that this controversy has been most fiercely contested.

1988 Education Act

Arguments over whether white children should learn about Hindu or Muslim festivals led to them being removed from a school in Bradford. Some parents and head teachers in predominantly white areas said that it was 'unnecessary' to teach about other cultures in their schools because 'there weren't any ethnic minority children in them'. Some Muslim parents protested about rules against girls wearing trousers. Under the **1988 Education Act** it was decreed that there should be a return to daily acts of Christian worship, from which other religious groups could be withdrawn if their parents wished. This led to an outcry from many schools about the potentially divisive effects of such a move, as well as its impracticality. By 1994 the majority of schools were not complying with the Act, according to the independent inspectorate. At the same time, the curriculum in History, English and Religious Education has been changed to present a more restricted and ethnocentric perspective.

Meanwhile, some ethnic minority groups have been expressing concern about the effect of these changes upon their children. There has been much evidence to suggest the extent to which ethnic minority group children have been disadvantaged in the education system (see Chapter 6), and certain groups have begun to provide Saturday or after-school classes for their children as a self-help response. Some Muslim parents, especially ones following a more fundamentalist approach to religion, have demanded the right to separate Muslim state-assisted schools, along the lines of Roman Catholic ones.

ethnic separatism

This kind of development moves us further along our continuum towards **ethnic separatism**. This term describes a situation in which ethnic groups co-exist within the same society, but follow separate lives and participate in separate institutions such as schools. The founding of an Islamic Parliament, and the Salman Rushdie affair, have highlighted to what extent a distinct cultural group is bound by the same conventions and laws as other members of the population. Sometimes demands for separateness come from the dominant group, as in South Africa, and at other times they are a response on the part of an oppressed minority to their under-privileged position, for example, calls by black Muslims in the USA in the 1960s and 1970s for a separate state, and the development of Rastafarianism in Britain.

Ethnicity and the class struggle

Marxist sociologists place less importance on the concept of ethnic culture. They argue that an emphasis on cultural difference is potentially divisive, plays into the hands of the ruling class and diverts attention away from the real divisions in society, between those with wealth and power and those without. Marxists have assumed that most ethnic minorities are part of the working class. Class interests, therefore, should unite different ethnic groups, whether black or white, Muslim or Serb.

Marxists argue that concentrating on ethnic and cultural differences leads to **false consciousness** and to deep and dangerous divisions between groups who, in class terms, ought to have interests in common. Nationalism in Eastern Europe in the aftermath of the break-up of the USSR and Eastern bloc, or tribal divisions in Rwanda fostered during colonization, are reminders of the devastating consequences of ethnic and cultural divisions.

In capitalist societies like Britain, the white working class have been encouraged to identify with the ruling class, in seeing Britain's colonial past as a period of great and glorious triumph, and to hold prejudiced and racist attitudes towards ethnic minorities.

In practice, there seems to be some truth in this argument.

- In 1990 the London Research Centre found that there had been an increase in racially motivated attacks in inner-city areas, and that 48 000 ethnic minority households had experienced racial harassment of some kind, mainly from people living in the same area.
- Home Office figures show that racial attacks increased from 4383 in 1988 to 7780 in 1991.
- The Anti-Racist Alliance claim, from their records, that only 1 in 10 attacks are reported, which, if this is correct, suggests that the real number of attacks would be more in the region of 70 000.
- The Newham Monitoring Project, which helps people who have been harassed, suggests that only 1 per cent of all attacks it has dealt with have been the result of extreme right-wing groups; the rest have been carried out by neighbours and acquaintances.
- A report by the Commission for Racial Equality in 1992 pointed out that racial harassment is not confined to inner-city areas. Eric Jay documented accounts of racial attacks and widespread prejudice in the rural south west of England – Cornwall, Devon and Somerset.

British National Party

The growth of fascist organizations, such as the **British National Party**, Pro-Fascist Action and Combat 18 may be the result of an alienated and disaffected minority, affected by recession and unemployment, being increasingly drawn to such groups. In 1993 it was reported in the press that the BNP was recruiting in the East Midlands among the ranks of unemployed miners. It had already set its sights on unemployed youth and football fans. Neo-Nazi groups have been banned in Germany, and there is pressure on the British Government to do likewise.

Some sociologists maintain that there are also cultural consequences of treating a particular ethnic group unequally. A group which is economically disadvantaged for racial reasons is likely to develop cultural supports and patterns of behaviour in response. Studies of Rastafarians, Islamic militants or young, male, unemployed Afro-Caribbeans are all examples of cultural responses to the reality of racism. Some sociologists have argued that racism has led to the development of a **black underclass** which also has cultural consequences as well as a profound effect on the stratification system.

black underclass

Racism

Although there is no universally accepted meaning of the term 'race', the concept of racism is an important one in understanding the relationship between dominant and minority ethnic groups in Britain and elsewhere. By 'racism' we mean the 'dogmatic belief that one race is superior to another'. This rests on the questionable assumption that there are identifiable racial characteristics which affect behaviour, such as intelligence. Racism is an ideology – a set of commonsense assumptions which are used to explain and justify the unequal treatment of some groups. It has been used to justify the processes of colonization and slavery, the Holocaust, 'ethnic cleansing' in the former Yugoslavia and the slaughter of millions in Rwanda.

To support the ideology, racists draw on the Bible and other religious tracts, 'science' and 'history' to demonstrate their case, in much the same way that the so-called inferiority of women was also ideologically constructed. In *Learning about Racism*, produced by the **Runnymeade Trust** in 1993, it is pointed out that:

Runnymeade Trust

> To support racism some people pointed to the Bible and the passage about Noah's Ham, who was cursed by God and whose descendants were condemned to be slaves and servants for all eternity. Black people, it was said, were Ham's descendants and were ... destined to be slaves ...
> Later philosophers and scientists tried to prove that black people were inferior to white people. Such people claimed, for instance, that black people had smaller brains or were more suited for manual work or needed the 'guidance' of white people.

The language reflected these perceptions, in which black came to be associated with evil, sinister or unpleasant practices such as blackmail, black magic, black leg, while whiteness is associated with goodness and purity.

Such doctrines stress that one group is the 'chosen' or 'righteous' people. This is then used to justify political systems such as **apartheid** in which races were to be kept separate as much as possible. At its height the institution and organization of apartheid led to the widespread movement and incarceration of many of the African population in spurious 'homelands', and to the denial of basic citizenship to non-white peoples. The teachings of the Dutch Reformed Church were used to justify this process because its members believed themselves to be the chosen people.

apartheid

Racism can be expressed individually, in racially prejudiced attitudes and in racial discriminatory behaviour. A **prejudice** is a 'prejudgement' made about individuals or groups, in this case on the basis of their colour or ethnic group. **Racial prejudice** is often based on a **stereotype** of a black person, which continues to be held even when evidence is advanced to refute it. Such firmly held stereotypes can contradict each other – the view that all blacks are lazy scroungers living on the dole co-exists with the contradictory stereotype that they also cause unemployment by taking jobs that belong to whites. The fact that racial prejudice is largely irrational still makes it difficult, though not impossible, to change.

Racial discrimination occurs when a person or institution puts **prejudice into action** and treats an individual or group unfavourably on racial grounds. Discrimination can be **direct** – for example, when a black person is refused a house or a job purely on racial grounds – or **indirect** – when a condition is applied to all people but affects one particular group unfairly – for example, a school uniform rule which insists that school caps must be worn would unfairly affect Sikh boys wearing turbans.

Bernard Coard

Institutional racism refers to the situation in which an institution or society is so riddled with racist assumptions that racism has become part of the culture and structure of that institution or society. For example, **Bernard Coard** argued in 1971 that the British education system actually made West Indian children 'educationally sub-normal' by presenting negative stereotypes of black people in books, in language and in the content of the curriculum.

Studs Terkel

When racism is institutionalized it becomes both a cultural and a structural feature of society. Social position and life chances are affected by a racist ideology which results in differential opportunities and life experiences. In *Race* (1992) **Studs Terkel** writing about America, quotes a 1990 survey in which:

> 53% of non blacks believe that African-Americans are less intelligent than whites; 51% believe they are less patriotic; 56% believe they are more violence-prone; 62% believe they are more likely to 'prefer to live off welfare' and less likely to 'prefer to be self-supporting'.

The **ideology of racism** fuels individual racist attitudes, to produce commonly held stereotypes. These attitudes are part and parcel of the cultural institutionalization of racism. Terkel goes on to quote a 1991 study in which it is shown that:

> Black males have the lowest life expectancy of any group in the United States. Their unemployment rate is more than twice that of white males; even black men with college degrees are three times more likely to be unemployed than their white counterparts. About one in four black men between the ages of twenty and twenty-nine is behind bars. Blacks receive longer prison sentences than whites who have committed the same crimes.
> Suicide is the third leading cause of death for young black males. Since 1960, suicide rates for young black males have nearly tripled, and doubled for black females. While suicide among whites increases with age, it is a peculiarly youthful phenomenon among blacks.
> Many black males die prematurely from twelve major preventable diseases. Nearly one-third of all black families in America live below the poverty line. Half of all black children are born into poverty and will spend their youth growing up in poor families (from a 1991 report of the 21st-Century Commission on African-American Males).

These statistics are not the result of an unhappy coincidence, but the evidence of the structural implications of institutionalized racism, whereby the life chances of whole groups are adversely affected and the population, class and power structure of society is also considerably affected.

So far as Britain is concerned, there are opposing views about whether racism is institutionalized. On the one hand, there is the popular view that

Charles Husband

Britain is a liberal society with a strong sense of fair play. On the other hand, there is the view that Britain is not as liberal or tolerant as the conventional view suggests. **Charles Husband**, writing in 1975, argued that:

> Our record of tolerance is clearly not compatible with our image of ourselves as a liberal and tolerant nation ... we must divest ourselves of the comforting myth of our national tolerance and painfully recognise that Britain is an endemically racist society.

This more radical stance is one in which **a conflict model** is employed to demonstrate the extent to which racism is an inevitable outcome of Britain's imperial past and its capitalist imperatives.

Racism – the evidence

Over the past thirty years sociologists have been investigating the extent of prejudice, discrimination and disadvantage experienced by ethnic minority populations. When black immigrants came to Britain after the Second World War, it is often said that they were surprised by the level of hostility which faced them. As citizens of the British Empire and British passport holders, many believed they were coming to the 'mother country'. In the 1950s and early 1960s black people could be refused service in shops, entry to public places such as swimming pools and were regularly denied jobs or houses. Sociologists responded with studies which provided firm evidence of discrimination, which was then used by pressure groups and politicians to press the government for **anti-discrimination legislation**.

1965 Race Relations Act

In **1965** the first **Race Relations Act** was passed, prohibiting discrimination in public places. However welcome, it did not cover the crucial areas which affected the well-being of the black population – employment, education and housing. Political and Economic Planning (PEP), later to be merged with the Policy Studies Institute (PSI), conducted early research into discriminatory practices in these areas.

W. W. Daniels

In 1968 research conducted by **W. W. Daniels** was published, which used a variety of methods including interviews, questionnaires and situation tests. In the latter, three actors were employed – a white person, a white immigrant such as a Hungarian, and a black immigrant – and were then sent after jobs, houses and mortgages. The tests were applied to 500 different people who were in a position to discriminate, to see whether they actually did so. Each actor in turn applied for the same job or flat using equivalent details of income, qualifications, etc. The black immigrant was discriminated against in two-thirds of all cases, leading Daniels to conclude that discrimination varied 'from the substantial to the massive' in many important areas of life. While this discrimination could not be 'explained away' in terms of language deficiencies, or length of stay in Britain, it was shown to be directly related to a prejudiced and racist response to skin colour.

1968 Race Relations Act

In **1968** a second **Race Relations Act** was passed, which outlawed discrimination in employment, housing and education and in the provision of goods and services. The Race Relations Board was set up to administer complaints.

Another PEP report conducted in the mid-1970s showed that, while discrimination had diminished, there was still cause for concern. People were discovering ways to circumvent the 1968 Race Relations Act, by using **indirect** discrimination. Evidence indicated that in the area of housing, especially council housing, black applicants were predominantly found in older and inferior accommodation.

In 1976 another Race Relations Act was passed, which made racial discrimination also unlawful in the disposal and management of premises, and tackled indirect as well as direct discrimination. When a Liverpool store owner told a careers officer not to send any applicants with the kind of post codes which indicated they lived in areas where predominantly black people lived, he was taken to an industrial tribunal, which found evidence of indirect discrimination.

The Act set up the **Commission for Racial Equality** (CRE) to enforce the law and promote equality of opportunity and good relations between people of different racial groups. The CRE was also given a general responsibility for advising the Government on the workings of the Act and providing information and advice to the general public.

Many commentators feel that race relations legislation needs to be strengthened. For example, the Government is actually excluded from the implications of the Race Relations Act and is itself free to pass racist legislation.

The Scarman Report in 1981, in the wake of riots in Liverpool and Brixton, argued that there were numerous unresolved problems regarding racism, one of which was to do with the way that ethnic minority communities were policed. Stuart Hall and others have referred to police acting like 'armies of occupation' in black communities, and of using the 'Stop and Search' clauses of the Prevention of Terrorism Act to harass young black men on the streets.

Bea Campbell on the 'sus' law

Bea Campbell, writing in *Goliath* about the behaviour of the police in ethnic minority communities, describes one person's reaction:

> A white woman living and working in South London before the 'sus' law was abolished in the eighties recalled with shame seeing these young white policemen who had been given permission to run their hands all over these young black men's bodies in the street. I remember thinking it was like the slave owners. No one could stop them: it was sanctioned in a liberal society, apparently in the name of crime prevention, for white men in the street to intimately touch black men's bodies. Of course, a white person touching a black person's body has a historical significance for all of us.

Only 4.3 per cent of stops under the 'sus' law actually resulted in arrests. Criminologist Richard Kinsey argued that its efficiency was questionable and its use positively harmful in causing great resentment against the police.

Despite anti-discrimination laws, only about 1 per cent of police officers are black. It has been estimated that the Metropolitan Police Force needs ten times more ethnic minority officers to match the proportion of ethnic minority people in its population. According to a report in the *Guardian* in November 1989, 90 per cent of all ethnic minority police officers were in service at the lowest rank.

In a report by Fiona Millar in the *Guardian* in May 1992, evidence from the CRE was published which suggested that, despite the legislation, discrimination in key areas of life was still high. In many professions, such as the civil service, law, teaching and social work, as well as management jobs, black people were under-represented. There were, in 1994, only six out of 651 black Members of Parliament.

The CRE claimed that:

> Unless the law is significantly sharpened, and as a matter of urgency, the rate of progress towards equality in Britain will be dispiritingly low.

The CRE criticisms of race relations legislation have been directed in part to its administration. Discrimination is difficult and expensive to prove, especially when care is being taken to avoid detection. The Commission argues that it needs new powers to investigate institutionalized discrimination in employment, housing and education. **Ethnic monitoring** is not, as yet, a legal requirement under the Act, but its introduction could help the CRE to investigate the employment record of firms. The CRE has also suggested that legal aid should be extended to cover cases in industrial tribunals investigating racial discrimination, but cuts in public spending already applied to the legal aid budget makes this unlikely to happen, at least in the short term.

If the European Commission was to introduce directives to outlaw racial discrimination Britain's legislation could be strengthened.

Alongside the race relations legislation, which is designed to tackle discrimination, albeit not very effectively, there has also been passed a series of Immigration Acts which have been accused of being racist. Because the Crown is exempted from the Race Relations Act, legislation passed by the Government and administered by the civil service continues to be racist.

Sociologists like Robert Moore have argued that successive governments have responded to racist demands and become obsessed with 'the numbers game' in the attempt to control black immigration and residency in Britain. The racist language and attitudes of politicians have encouraged them to pass discriminatory legislation which restricts the entry of mainly black, but not white, immigrants, and which continues to define black people as a problem.

Theories of a 'pure, white race', 'swamped' by 'alien races' have been around for centuries. In recent decades one of the most famous uses made of the terminology was by Enoch Powell, MP in 1968 when he referred to 'rivers of blood' and the 'swamping' of British culture. In 1979 Margaret Thatcher used similar language. In 1990 Norman Tebbit, MP implied that many immigrants and black British did not have primary allegiance to Britain or to something known as 'the British way of life'.

It could be argued that, rather than mounting a swift and effective attack on racism, there has been an ambivalent approach by both governments and opinion leaders, in which racism has been awarded a degree of respectability. Anti-discriminatory legislation has not been strong enough or positive enough to create a genuine climate of equal opportunities and anti-racist strategies.

The effect has been to ensure that, while discrimination is outlawed, disadvantage and inequality in life chances and power remain. More recent research by the PSI has concentrated on investigating these patterns. We shall examine the results in two areas: housing and employment.

Employment – the evidence

PEP/PSI studies from 1973 to 1993 using a variety of research methods, including situation tests, have documented the unequal position of ethnic minorities in the labour force. The Government Labour Force Survey 1993 revealed higher rates of unemployment for black workers than white workers:

Afro-Caribbean   28 per cent
Asian   35 per cent
Bangladeshis   48 per cent.

Between summer 1992 and 1993, 3.7 per cent of ethnic minority workers lost their jobs, compared with 0.5 per cent of white workers.

Young black workers and women are most badly hit by unemployment:

- In the 16–24 age group, 35 per cent of ethnic minorities are jobless, compared with 17 per cent of young white people.
- Average unemployment among ethnic minority women is three times the rate for white women. In June 1994 an Equal Opportunities Commission (EOC) report showed that ethnic minority women were the most disadvantaged group in the labour market, showing the impact of both racism and sexism on job opportunities.

Trevor Jones

A more detailed examination of the 1993 PSI study shows that patterns of inequality are not evenly spread across different ethnic minority groups. In his research, **Trevor Jones** showed that, despite continuing discrimination against ethnic minorities, some ethnic groups have made progress throughout the 1980s. Jones comments:

> The disparity can no longer be adequately summarised by a simple contrast between relatively well-off 'whites' and poorly-off 'blacks'.

In his analysis of the Labour Force Surveys he showed that more young people of Indian, African-Asian and Chinese origin stayed on in full-time education and were achieving some of the highest examination results across all ethnic groups, including whites. This was slowly being reflected in the higher numbers occupying professional jobs such as medicine, accountancy and computing. Jones comments:

> This is a major change from earlier studies which generally found even well-qualified people from ethnic minority groups were more often confined to lower job levels than similarly qualified whites. ... There is evidence of a strong dynamic among ethnic minority communities driving them to develop beyond the social and economic niche they filled for the first 20 years.

His analysis relates to the type of jobs occupied by ethnic minorities and to changes in the structure of the labour market over the past twenty years, in which there has been a decline in manufacturing jobs, in which many ethnic minority group members worked, and an increase in professional and service sector jobs. Skill shortages in some of these 'newer' areas meant that well-qualified ethnic minority workers were able to fill them.

Jones also relates the progress of some groups to the development of business links within the Indian and Chinese communities.

Young people from Afro-Caribbean, Pakistani and Bangladeshi backgrounds have had the least educational success (see Chapter 6), are more likely to be in low-paid, semi-skilled and unskilled work and to experience higher rates of unemployment. Afro-Caribbean girls do better in school than boys. Bangladeshi youngsters and their parents face the most intense discrimination of all groups.

Jones's study found less discrepancy between women workers from different ethnic groups than between men, demonstrating the persisting effects of sexism on all women. However, research carried out by other sociologists such as Annie Phizacklea and Irene Breugal has shown that there are different experiences within different groups, and that some ethnic minority women work longer hours, are more likely to do shift work and to be doing work for which they are over-qualified. Some groups of Asian women, for example, are involved in home-working, a

*Annie Phizacklea &
Irene Breugal*

traditionally low-paid and exploitative type of employment. The EOC survey (1994) also revealed that black women workers were the lowest paid of all workers in the labour market.

Thus, while the evidence suggests that all ethnic minority groups face discrimination, their actual positions are also affected by the structure of the labour market, skill and qualification levels, age and gender, as well as the amount of time they have been resident in Britain.

Some sociologists and other commentators argue that, as time passes, ethnicity will cease to be the crucial factor determining employment prospects, and that class factors will take over, as some members of ethnic minority groups move into the middle class, while others appear confined to the lower levels of the working class.

Housing – the evidence

At the time of black immigration in the post-war period, and for the subsequent decades, the housing conditions of black people were very poor. In 1961 one-half of Commonwealth immigrant households were in shared dwellings, while two-fifths of Afro-Caribbeans and one-tenth of Asians were living in overcrowded conditions. Discriminatory practices by private landlords, building societies and council housing departments forced most immigrants into expensive but poor-quality multi-occupied houses in decaying inner-city areas.

The 1966 PEP Report revealed evidence of direct discrimination, where landlords openly displayed in their windows signs saying 'no coloureds'. In two-thirds of situation tests, black applicants were discriminated against.

Elizabeth Burney

In 1972 Elizabeth Burney, studying the effects of the 1968 Race Relations Act, found substantial evidence of discrimination by landlords, building societies and estate agents. 'Red-lining' practices were used, in which a line was drawn around certain inner-city areas. Black applicants for mortgages on houses not in these areas were turned down. Practices like these led to the development of areas with higher than average concentrations of black people, who were then accused of creating ghettoes. Home Office research in 1983 also revealed that they were being charged higher than average prices and rents on properties in these areas.

In 1982 the study *Black and White Britain* found that:

> the separation of the jobs and residential locations of the British people from those of Asian and West Indian origin is so firmly established that it generates among both whites and blacks assumptions, expectations and behaviour that perpetuate it.

In practice, different ethnic minority groups have solved their housing problems in different ways. Those of Afro-Caribbean and Bangladeshi origin have been more likely to apply for council properties, while those of Indian and Pakistani origin have tended to buy their own houses, often outright. These different kinds of 'solutions' reflect the range of options available for different groups, as well as cultural differences.

In some Asian communities family groups have clubbed together to buy a house outright, avoiding their potential rejection by building societies. These houses have often been larger Victorian homes in inner city areas, in which more than one family lives together, sharing expenses and saving to buy another property for the second family to move into. This kind of practice demonstrates the ways in which family support has been used to overcome racist practices in the housing market.

Afro-Caribbeans are less likely to be able to call on this family network, and have turned instead to local authority accommodation. But properties have not been allocated on the basis of equal opportunities. The evidence shows that Afro-Caribbeans and Bangladeshis have been over-concentrated in older, unmodernized properties. Five times as many Afro-Caribbeans and Bangladeshis live in high-rise flats than white tenants. Generally, 20 per cent of white households are housed in detached properties, compared with 5 per cent of ethnic minorities. Thirty-three per cent of Bangladeshis, representing one of the most recently arrived and poorest minority communities, live in overcrowded conditions, compared with 1 per cent of whites.

The 1988 Labour Force Survey showed that 78 per cent of Asians, compared with 66 per cent of whites and 40 per cent of Afro-Caribbeans, were in owner-occupied properties, whereas 43 per cent of Afro-Caribbeans, compared with 23 per cent of whites and 12 per cent of Asians, were in council property.

In both employment and housing, therefore, both crucial and connected areas of life, there are clear patterns which demonstrate the generally less favourable position of ethnic minority group members in comparison to whites. In other areas – education (see Chapter 6), social welfare (see Chapter 8) and the law similar patterns are apparent.

Social stratification: Sociological theories and explanations

Sociologists have been particularly interested in the effect which these patterns of disadvantage and inequality have on the social stratification system. There are four main perspectives which attempt to theorize the relationship between ethnicity and social class – liberal, Weberian, Marxist and feminist.

The liberal perspective

The liberal perspective argues that the stratification system is like 'a ladder of opportunity' up which people are able to climb, depending on their abilities and perseverance. In the 1960s liberals argued that the over-representation of ethnic minorities in low-level employment and poor housing was a function of their recent arrival, poor command of English and lack of appropriate qualifications and skills.

Although the prejudice of some whites was acknowledged as a factor, it was thought that, as time passed, anti-discrimination legislation, education and a willingness to adapt on the part of immigrants would remove the ethnic dimension in the stratification system. It was thought that racism as a barrier to social advancement would be overcome and that recent immigrants and their children – 'the second generation' – would be represented in proper proportions at all points of the stratification hierarchy, depending on their abilities and hard work.

The New Right and the 'classless society'

This 'opportunist' view of the class system has also been promoted by the **New Right** in recent years, for example John Major's vision of a **classless society**, which is better regarded as a meritocracy.

Recent research indicating the improved educational and employment 'success' of some Indian, Pakistani, Chinese and African-Asians could be used to support this view. However, the overwhelming conclusion of research evidence seems to suggest that, while some progress has been made, and some individuals have been able to 'move up the system', ethnic minorities are not proportionately represented in many areas of life. They are over-represented and marginalized in low-paid work, poorer housing and the ranks of the unemployed.

In 1990 a Government-sponsored report conducted at Sheffield University found that, while proportionately more young Asians completed further education and training courses than whites, they had only half as much chance of getting a job as white students with the same qualifications.

In the 1992 general election a black lawyer and Tory Party candidate, **John Taylor**, stood for election in the safe Conservative seat of Cheltenham. The seat was lost to the Liberal Democrats, as voters and members of a party which claims to see Britain as a meritocracy changed their allegiance and voted for a white candidate from another party – a result which indicates that racism is more enduring than the liberal analysis claims.

It is an analysis which has always been more popular in the USA than in Britain, where successive waves of immigration throughout the past century enabled those who had arrived earlier to move up the scale, as positions at the bottom became occupied by more recent arrivals. This theory does not explain, however, why native Americans, who have been residents for the longest time of all, or black Americans who arrived as a consequence of slavery, have been largely bypassed in the so-called 'moving-up' process.

However useful this perspective might be, immigration policies in Britain have effectively closed the door on any further black immigration, so it may be that black ethnic minorities remain trapped at the bottom of the stratification system.

The Weberian perspective

The Weberian perspective owes its sociological inspiration to the ideas of Max Weber (see pages 235–6) who argued that social position is not just the result of economic position but also of social status and the degree of power which different groups possess. John Rex has developed these ideas through research into housing and employment experiences to explain the position of ethnic minorities in Britain.

Working with Robert Moore in the 1960s, he studied the housing patterns of ethnic minorities in the Sparkbrook area of Birmingham, an area with a higher than average proportion of ethnic minorities.They argued that there were three distinct housing zones. The poorest, which was nearest to the city centre, was where most members of ethnic minorities lived. Other groups had gradually been able to move out to more desirable housing in the suburbs.

Moore and Rex went on to argue that the position of any group was determined by competition between different groups over scarce resources, in this case housing. As a result, there were 'housing classes', or groups, which occupied different bargaining positions in the competition for houses.

They also argued that the 'market position' of immigrants in this competitive situation was low – they had lower wages and lower social status because of racist attitudes and practices towards them. They were often the victims of racial discrimination, which could be direct or indirect, as in the case in which some local authorities used 'length of residence' criteria rather than 'need' in the allocation of homes. Their only solution was to live in the inner-city zone in overcrowded and dilapidated accommodation. As a result, they were accused of 'taking over' these areas, whereas in reality they were trapped in them by discrimination. Rex and Moore comment:

Being a member of a housing class is of first importance in determining a man's associations, interests, life-style and his position in the urban social structure.

Despite the sexist language, they demonstrate how the situation of black immigrants is structurally distinct from that of the white working class and that, by means of discrimination in housing, their position in the stratification system is determined.

Rex and Moore have been criticized by Marxists about their claim that housing is somehow independent of the wider class structure, and by others who have argued that Sparkbrook was not typical, and that in other areas ethnic minorities were able to move into other housing areas.

dual labour market theory

Working with Sally Tomlinson in the 1970s, Rex went on to examine why the employment position of ethnic minorities affected their social position. They applied **dual labour market theory** (see page 192), a theory originally developed to explain the position of black workers in the USA, to the employment experiences of black immigrants, this time in the Handsworth area of Birmingham. They found that about half of the non-white population of Handsworth was employed in semi-skilled and unskilled work, and less than 10 per cent in white-collar jobs, compared with one-third of whites.

Ethnic minorities were more heavily represented in the least desirable work – dirty and dangerous jobs, or those with unsociable hours – and were under-represented in professional, scientific and administrative work. Black workers had to work longer hours and do nightshift work to earn wages approaching the levels of white workers in the same companies.

Rex and Tomlinson argued that these findings suggested the operation of a dual labour market, in which ethnic minorities were trapped in the less privileged secondary sector. Although they admitted that the two labour markets were not entirely distinct, their evidence suggested that there were two types of job situation, and that whites and blacks occupied different ones.

Again, the argument was based on the assumption that this unequal situation arose because of the 'weaker market situation' of black workers, who are seen to possess less desirable qualities, judged to be inferior and to have a lower social status. They were thus trapped in their position by discriminatory practice.

Rex went on to argue that, as a result, there existed an **ethnically differentiated underclass**. By this he meant that ethnic minorities formed a disadvantaged group which did not share the same position, status or privileges of the white working class. He argued that there existed what he called a '**structural break**' between the black and the white working class, consisting of housing class, poor education and secondary labour market position, all of which effectively marginalized them as a group into a separate and distinct underclass. He then went on to predict that, as a result of this marginalization, they would develop separate institutions – places of worship, shops, theatres and cinemas, schools and separate political groups – to represent their interests.

In practice, most politically active ethnic minority people have tended to vote Labour, seeing this as the party most likely to represent their interests, although there is some recent evidence of more affluent people shifting their allegiance to the Conservative Party. However, many disaffected younger people do not vote at all, and others prefer involvement in campaigning and self-help groups within their own communities. The demand in the 1980s for a black section in the Labour Party and in some trade unions, and the setting up of the Islamic Parliament, suggest that, for some at least, the need for some degree of independence from 'mainstream' political representation is thought to be desirable.

The Marxist perspective disputes the existence of a marginalized underclass. On the whole, Marxists have tended to consider ethnic divisions as being less significant than the wider divisions between social classes. They have argued that the position of most ethnic minority group members in the stratification system is the result of their class position as exploited workers who do not own or control the fruits of their own labour.

According to Marxist argument, capitalist societies, in the drive for increased profits and larger markets, colonized other countries and used their populations as either slaves or, more recently, as a reserve army of labour to draw upon in times of economic expansion and prosperity. Local workers were able to move into more congenial jobs and their place was taken by migrants who were forced to take low-paid, unpleasant work by unemployment and hardship at home, originally created by the colonial process.

Castles & Kosack

Castles and Kosack developed this argument in 1973, claiming that their analysis applied equally to the experiences of British passport-holding immigrants to Britain as well as to the experiences of migrant or 'guest' workers from countries such as Turkey or North Africa, allowed only temporary residence in the affluent countries of northern Europe. Both groups of workers unwittingly helped to divide the working class along racial lines and therefore further served the interests of capitalism.

Unlike the liberal view, Marxist analysis acknowledges that the 'host' society is not a homogeneous and harmonious one. Immigrants do not 'create' divisions in an otherwise cohesive and stable structure, because the society is already hierarchically stratified and divided by class interests. But they do alter the class structure by helping to divide the working class. This process can only happen because the white working class has been socialized to accept the dominant ideology of racial superiority, and so regards the newcomers as a threat, rather than as allies in the struggle against the ruling class.

Westergaard & Resler

Other Marxists such as **Westergaard and Resler**, have criticized this theory. They claim that concentrating on the particular problems of ethnic minorities and racism obscures the real divisions between the bourgeoisie and the proletariat. They prefer to focus on the notion of a **united** working class, in which the commonality of experience and position between the white and black working class should be explored and emphasized. It is a view which has been criticized for seeming to imply that the experiences of ethnic minorities are the same as those of the white working class and for overlooking the effects of racism on the position of black people.

Robert Miles

Robert Miles has agreed that class stratification is the fundamental division in capitalist societies, but recognizes that different sections of the working class have additional experiences of oppression. He argues that there are **racialized class fractions** – each with their own interests. While he acknowledges that racism is important in understanding the position of ethnic minorities, their condition constitutes a particularly disadvantaged position within the working class, rather than being construed as an underclass. Sociologists like Rex have exaggerated the effects of discrimination at the expense of class factors.

Miles points out that, although most ethnic minority members are concentrated at the bottom of the stratification system, not all are, and those within the middle class can also be seen as a 'racialized fraction', with their own interests and experiences, as a result of their ethnic group.

In recent years, feminist writers have added to this array of explanations by attempting to unravel the relationship not just between ethnicity and class but also between ethnicity and gender.

Amrit Wilson

In 1978 **Amrit Wilson**, in *Finding a Voice*, a study of Asian women in Britain, argued that working-class Asian women comprised one of the most deprived sections of the working class:

> Asian women are the worst off of all British workers. They are at the bottom of the heap. They come unprepared, easy victims to unscrupulous employers. ... Neither their husbands and families, nor white trade unionists nor middle class Asians are keen to help them.

As a result, Asian women workers have developed a reputation for organizing themselves very effectively in long-term and bitter disputes with their employers. In describing their role in the long-running dispute with Grunwick, the film processing firm, she helped to contradict the passive stereotype often put forward about Asian women.

Wilson was also one of the first writers in recent years to direct attention to the experience of women home-workers whom, she argued, should be considered as a 'sub-proletariat' because of the extremity of their economic exploitation and deprivation:

> In Britain there has been for many years a sub-proletariat, a sub-class of the working class who are far worse off than the main body, consisting of sweat shop workers and home workers, people who are treated by employers as though they have no rights at all.

Sallie Westwood

In *All Day Every Day*, **Sallie Westwood** examined the relationship between ethnicity, gender and social class in the lives of Asian women hosiery workers, whose economic position in the labour market, and cultural response to life on the shopfloor and to their possibilities generally, were inextricably linked to their experiences of class and gender oppression in the context of widespread racism.

Bryan, Dadzie & Scafe

In *Heart of the Race*, **Bryan, Dadzie and Scafe** place a similar emphasis on the inter-connectedness of oppression deriving from racism, sexism and class inequalities in the lives of first- and second-generation black women in Britain.

After at least twenty years of debate within feminist political groups and feminist theory, few contemporary feminist sociologists would now underestimate the significance of ethnicity in structuring women's experiences and women's oppression, and would see the urgency of refining feminist theories to take account of both diversity and commonality in women's lives and of the ways in which ethnicity, gender, social class, sexuality and age all help to shape the pattern of women's experience and the making of women's identity.

4   Age

In January 1993 Age Concern launched its poster campaign concerned with challenging negative stereotypes about ageing. 'How long before people start calling **you** names?' the posters asked, and in an accompanying leaflet:

> At some point in your life you will find that people start to characterise you by one single dismissive criterion. Your age. Your abilities won't matter. Years of experience will count for nothing. Your achievements won't matter. Your personality won't matter.

It may seem as though the case is 'overstated' by a pressure group committed to campaigning on behalf of the elderly, but age is becoming an increasingly important factor in the distribution of resources and opportunities in societies like Britain, partly because people are living longer and partly because attitudes to ageing are changing.

In times of recession and the restructuring of the labour market (see page 170) it is harder than ever for over-40s to get a job. 'Early retirement' is widely on offer at 50, although state pensions don't take effect until age 65. Although it goes against the spirit of equal opportunities legislation, almost half of all job adverts specify an upper age limit for applicants, usually 35. According to Anita Higginson of the Brook Street Employment Bureau:

> Perceptions about the 'right age' for jobs are dyed-in-the-wool 25–30 for the perfect secretary, under 35 for 'front office' staff, over 50 for cleaners. The vast majority of employers are looking to fill their vacancies with under-25s, which is crazy. People are being invited to retire early at 50 and that's when they think of ageism beginning. But frighteningly, it starts at 25 to 35.

So that 'being old' seems to be getting younger!

A survey carried out by the Brook Street Bureau also revealed that women with the same qualifications and skills as men were more likely to be discriminated against on grounds of age.

Eric Midwinter

Dr Eric Midwinter, in a 1991 report on attitudes to ageing, said that part of the problem was to do with 'old' being the opposite of 'new' as well as 'young', so that the term itself had become 'overlaid with grey colourings'. Negative attitudes about old age are common, and seem to be based on the association between old age, sickness and dependency. A review by Lehr in 1983 found that:

> the aged are perceived as ill, retarded, tired, slow and inefficient in their thinking: they are seen as asexual, or even if showing sexual interests, as ridiculous.

David Field (*Elderly People in British Society*) comments:

> Because an old person has difficulty with walking and eyesight, she or he is also presumed to have difficulty in understanding others, to be unable to make everyday decisions, and to have lost interest in world affairs and their own sexuality. As with other stereotypes, the contradictory evidence of able and competent old people who manage their lives successfully is explained away, for example, by claiming they are 'exceptions'.

Third Age Lifestyles 1993

According to a 'lifestyle survey' published by the market research group Mintel in 1993, nearly a half of men and a third of women said that they were happier when they were younger. Although 'well-off' 50-somethings were likely to be richer once they had reached their top earnings, their mortgage was paid off and their children had left home, this apparent affluence hid the fear and poverty of those who reach middle age facing long-term unemployment and dependence on state pensions. In 1994 the state pension was worth only 16.5 per cent of average male earnings in real terms.

The Mintel survey (**Third Age Lifestyles 1993**) also revealed a significant divide between the so-called 'baby boomers' born just after the Second World War, who would be aged around 50 in the mid 1990s, and their parents' generation. Previously, over-45s shared traditional values and attitudes, and were said by sociologists to become 'more conservative' as they got older. But at least some of today's recruits to middle age were once the rebellious teenagers of the 1960s who helped to shape some of the great changes taking place in social and sexual values and spending power. Their views frequently have 'more in common' with 35-year-olds according to Mintel, although they do not enjoy the same social and economic opportunities, especially in relation to jobs.

It is not simply the middle-aged and the elderly who are arousing interest, however. There has been considerable talk in the press during the early 1990s about what has happened to childhood. In 1994 a rapist was given a particularly light sentence because his 8-year-old victim was said by the judge to be 'no angel'. In 1993 a 13-year-old boy raped his teacher in a school classroom in Wimborne. James Bulger was beaten and kicked to death by two boys who were barely teenagers. The tabloid press was full of headlines about 'the young monsters in our midst'.

Calls were made for 10-year-olds to be punished as if they were adults and government ministers began to consider special prisons in which to incarcerate 'out-of-control' children, not only to punish them but also to blame single mothers for failing to provide them with the male role models they needed to keep them 'on the straight and narrow'. Legislation was quickly introduced to control the sale and hire of so-called 'video nasties'. In the process the big horror stories of a slightly earlier period – about child sexual abuse, the scandals in children's homes, the high rates of youth unemployment and the lack of opportunities for inner-city kids, especially if they are black – all got conveniently swept under the carpet.

Karl Mannheim

In such circumstances it is easy to rely on stereotypes, and sociologists have been as guilty of this as anyone else, but in an effort to avoid stereotyping it is perhaps useful to remember **Karl Mannheim's** refinement of the concept 'generation' in 1952. He distinguished between a generation as **'location'**, i.e. the simple age group of 15–25-year-olds or 45–55-year-olds, and generation as **'actuality'**, which emphasizes the importance of the collective social and political experience of age groups, leading to forms of 'shared consciousness' and 'world views' which are unique to that group – views which, in a changing society, may lead to differences and conflicts between people in different age groups.

Mannheim also pointed out that **sub-groups** within a generation also experience the world in different ways, because of differences in social class, gender, ethnic background and even region of residence. So while youth unemployment, for example, rose to record levels in the early 1980s, not all young people felt alienated and rejected. Levels of youth unemployment varied, depending on whether young people lived in the north or the south of Britain, whether they were males or females, whether they were middle class or working class, whether they were black or white.

Mannheim used the idea of a generational unit to take account of diversity **within** age groups, which makes it easier to consider potential conflict **within** generations as well as **between** generations. It also helps to avoid stereotyping particular generations and age groups as all having the same 'world view'.

In this chapter we are going to review some of the shifts and changes in sociological accounts of why age and generation studies are important to our understanding of the relationship between social behaviour and society.

Childhood

Philippe Aries

Childhood, as so much recent sociological literature makes clear, differs enormously according to time and place. At some times and in some places it does not exist at all.

The sociologist most influential in charting the 'emergence' of childhood was the French demographic historian **Philippe Aries**. According to Aries, 'In medieval society ... the idea of childhood did not exist ... as soon as the child could live without the constant solicitude of his (sic) mother, his nanny or his cradle rocker, he belonged to adult society.

Ann Oakley agreed that childhood was not, as earlier and some contemporary psychological theories suggest, based on 'fixed development phases' which progress 'in stages', but was 'socially constructed'. What is expected of children varies according to time, culture and location. According to Oakley, 'childhood', like the role of 'housewife' emerged in Britain at least during the nineteenth century, when children became a threat to adult wages and legislation took them out of the factories and mines. Fears about revolution sent them to school as part of the process of 'gentling the masses' and teaching them 'appropriate values' and 'just enough knowledge' to become compliant workers in their turn.

Prout and James continue the debate arguing that:

- biological immaturity is not the same as childhood;
- there is no universal notion of childhood in other cultures – it depends on tradition, ethnicity, gender and economics, and is marked by different customs, e.g. tribal rites of passage and the Jewish Bar Mitzvah ceremony for boys;
- sociology in the past has largely ignored children and the concept of childhood. Talcott Parsons, for example, exemplified functionalist assumptions that children were passive recipients of socialization imposed on them by adults and other agents in the wider society;
- children should be seen rather as 'active participants' in the creation of their own experiences and should be studied independently of adults;
- anti-positivist research methods should be used when studying children.

This growing awareness of children as 'people in their own right' has been paralleled in social work approaches to some extent. The recent Children's

Act, for example, places a greater emphasis than ever before on children's rights rather than parents' rights.

Cultural diversity

Mead & Malinowski

The work of **Margaret Mead** and **Bronislaw Malinowski** has been used to demonstrate different ideas about childhood and different childhood experiences in different cultures. Among the Manus people of the Admiralty Islands, studied by Margaret Mead in the 1920s, for example, marriages were arranged in childhood or adolescence and the couple were not allowed to speak to or see each other until their wedding day. The Arapesh of New Guinea treated babies as 'soft, precious, vulnerable little objects, to be protected, fed and cherished'. The Mundugamor women of New Guinea actively disliked child-bearing and child-rearing. In traditional Samoa, children were handed over, almost as soon as they were weaned, to the care of relatives and other young girls until they could fend for themselves. Malinowski describes childhood among the Trobriand Islanders as a period of relative freedom in which children took responsibility for themselves, regarded parents more as companions than carers, and during which time there was a relatively easy and early initiation into adulthood.

In third world economies based on subsistence levels of agricultural production and survival, life expectancies are short and the work needing to be done is labour-intensive. In these conditions, children are an economic asset and child labour is still common. In some societies – parts of India, for example – girls are viewed as an economic liability in poor families because they require dowries to be paid to the families of prospective husbands on marriage and their labour power is lost to their families of origin. In such extreme circumstances of poverty, and with traditions which prefer boys and give power to men, girl foetuses are more likely to be aborted and girl babies left to die at birth.

The interference and financial interests of Western economies creates problems for children in third world societies. In societies in which the mal-distribution of resources in the world leads to poverty, which in turn encourages child labour, and where rich Western men come as tourists and business travellers, the incidence of child prostitution is increasing – in Thailand and the Philippines, for example. It would be wrong to assume that child sexual abuse of this kind is confined to third world economies, however. The statistics concerning the numbers of children who are abused in societies like Britain are hard to come by, for reasons of fear, family privacy and male power, but they are estimated to be considerable.

Family life

Most studies of the family have concerned themselves with the functions of the family and the relationships between adults. However, there has been some attention paid by feminist writers such as Ann Oakley and Carol Smart to the ways in which the responsibility for looking after children was shifted onto women once they became an economic liability rather than an economic asset, in ways which coincided with attempts to get women out of the paid labour force and confined to the home.

Others, such as Liz Kelly, have carried out extensive research into child sexual abuse, claiming that it continues to be widespread in predominantly heterosexual families, but, for reasons of institutionalized male power, both in the family and in society generally, goes largely unreported and unpunished.

More recent concern expressed about the 'undue influence' of lone mothers, and the absence of father figures as 'agents of discipline and control', has been expressed by New Right sociologists such as **Charles Murray** and has led to government action and political pressure by right-wing campaigning groups like **Families Need Fathers** to 're-establish' fathers' rights in decisions taken about abortion, in divorce and custody cases and in disputes about child maintenance payments. Feminists explain these developments as part of a wider backlash against women in the 1980s and 1990s.

Stephen Wagg, writing from the perspective of the New Right sees the family as the cornerstone of society in which any 'deviation from the norm' poses a threat, including the influence on children of drugs, the media, left-wing teachers, youth cults and premature advice about contraception, etc. The danger is that 'disobedient children' challenge parental authority, leading to civil disorder and **anomie**.

But although the focus of these discussions is about 'what happens to children', the emphasis remains largely on the rights of adults **over** children rather than on the rights of children themselves. Hood-Williams refers to this as a form of **age patriarchy**, which acts as a system of control by adults. He argues instead for the **empowerment** of children, with more attention being turned towards their experience of physical care, abuse and punishment.

Education

Interactionists writing in the late 1960s and 1970s such as Hargreaves and Keddie began to depict children as actors with their own perceptions, and helped to fuel progressive and egalitarian ideas about child centred education and comprehensive schools. Feminists such as Dale Spender pointed to the ways in which boys and girls were treated differently in the school system in ways which ensured that boys received preferential treatment. Paul Willis made a detailed study of how working-class boys arrived in working-class jobs. The education and schooling studies of the time which related education to social class, and subsequently to gender and ethnicity, were generally 'progressive' in orientation and concerned about the ways in which certain children were prevented from fulfilling their true potential by the operation of class bias, sexism and racism.

The arrival of successive Conservative Governments in 1979, and the philosophy of the New Right, took an altogether different view of the education system and about what needed to be done to raise the educational standards of children's achievements and to create more choice for parents in their children's schooling. The New Right favoured 'traditional teaching methods', and used their influence in government to change the content of the school curriculum, increase the testing of children, promote competition between children and between schools by the publication of league tables, encourage schools to opt out of local authority control and make arrangements for the local management of schools. Recent government pronouncements about 'truancy watch schemes' have been criticized by civil liberties organizations like Liberty as being an actual infringement of children's rights so long as truancy is not a criminal offence.

While all of these 'reforms' have claimed to improve standards and increase parental choice, they have also contributed to a view of children as the passive receivers of education rather than activists in their own learning.

The media

Children's broadcasting used to be scheduled at specific times, and the major broadcasting companies had special budgets and remits with regard to

Neighbours and Home and Away

children's broadcasting. Now there is less of a distinction between what constitutes 'children's programmes' and 'adult programmes'. The growth of teatime soaps, for example, like *Neighbours* and *Home and Away*, consciously include a lot of youthful characters and story lines to attract young viewers, while also including supposedly 'adult' material. The more the presentation of programmes becomes aimed at a wider age range, the harder it is to retain distinct differences between what children and adults are able to watch. Children and young people provide a ready market for films and videos, in which story lines and material are increasingly presented in ways which make little distinction between adult and child viewers. The so-called 'watershed', or informal agreement made by television companies to keep programmes containing explicit sex and violence off the air until after 9 p.m., is not always adhered to, but is built upon some implied responsibility of parents to also monitor their children's viewing.

Children are the main viewers of television and, as such, they also provide a potentially lucrative market for advertisers. The scheduling of toy adverts in the run-up to Christmas, and adverts of convenience foods and snacks at times when children are most likely to be viewing, helps to induct children into the values of a consumer-oriented and fast-food society, as well as increasing the pressure on parents to respond to children's demands for particular toys and products. It may help to increase the alienation and hopelessness of children living in poor families, who cannot afford to spend lots of money on consumer durables and fashionable foods, and may be related to levels of teenage theft.

The debate about whether violence on television, video nasties, computer games which increasingly feature sex and violence as part of their animation and the imminence of virtual reality CD-Roms are responsible for 'increasing the lawlessness and violence' of young people is fraught with prejudice. Certainly it is young people and their 'feckless' parents who are blamed when crimes are committed. But vast amounts of money are made out of the manufacture and distribution of videos and related technologies, which appear to be distributed with only cursory attempts made to apply or enforce 'parental guidance' ratings. The most distasteful of computer games and videos are frequently simply 'more explicit' versions of already pretty sordid tales of sexist abuse, racist stereotypes and mindless entertainment, which is unlikely to encourage the critical intelligence or political enlightenment of those who regularly use them. Otherwise affluent societies, in which increasing numbers of poor people, with few prospects and little status, have few reasons to share in collective values of responsibility towards property, may also account for high levels of crime and violence in urban and deprived areas. Certainly there is a relationship between poverty, street crime, gender and ethnicity, which is more complicated than a simple 'copy cat' response to watching violent TV and videos might suggest.

Youth

As with childhood, one of the concerns of sociologists studying youth has been to establish that it is a 'social construction'. In modern societies youth has become an increasingly clearly defined period in a person's life. But the transition from childhood, through youth, to adulthood does not necessarily take place **at the same time** or last for **the same period of time** in all societies, and even within the **same** societies variations occur over time.

In Britain, theories about the social construction of youth became popular with sociologists in the 1950s and 1960s, partly because of the good employment opportunities for young people at the time, the prevalence of the so-called 'affluent society' (just before poverty was 'rediscovered' in the

1960s) and the birth of the 'teenagers' who were targeted by the advertising and manufacturing industries as consumers of fashion, magazines, popular music, leisure activities and cosmetics, etc. Functionalists such as Mark Abrams recorded these developments as a process of transition from childhood to adulthood without any distinction being made between different social class or ethnic groups and with no reference to gender in **the content** of youth culture. He noticed that working-class youth was more likely to be involved in spending and middle-class youth was more likely to stay longer in education. He also noted that boys had more to spend than girls. In *The Teenage Consumer*, Abrams showed that young people's real earnings increased by 50 per cent in the period 1938–58. Teenage spending, as a percentage of all spending, also increased after the Second World War.

Youth culture

The growth of mass commercialism in the 1950s was seen as encouraging the growth of youth culture. As different youth cults became the subject matter of sociological studies, it became evident that there was a clear class, gender and ethnic difference in the content and style of different youth cults, and that these factors – class, gender and ethnicity – continue to affect young people, structuring their experience of youth differently.

Clarke & Jefferson

John Clarke and **Tony Jefferson**, from the Centre for Contemporary Cultural Studies at Birmingham University, writing in 1973 described the creation of youth culture as the attempt by the young 'to exert some control over one's life situation'. What characterized youth cults of different kinds, according to them, was the search for excitement, autonomy and identity – the freedom to create 'cultural meanings' rather than simply accept what was presented by those representatives of adult officialdom and authority.

Youth in Western contemporary societies can best be seen as the time in which young people, in different ways, depending on their social class background, gender and ethnicity, attempt to negotiate their own definitions with their elders, within the context of a society in which dominant and mainstream culture is the arbiter, and in which the creation of wealth and the distribution of economic resources resides increasingly in the hands of multinational corporations.

Theories of youth

Functionalist theories, such as those of Eisenstadt and Parsons, explain youth as a period of transition from family roles which are based on 'particularism, ascription and collectivity' to adult roles based on 'individualism, achievement and universalism'. Social agencies exist to help this transition take place, such as education, but informal youth organizations and peer groups also play their part in the process of 'socializing' children into adolescents. Functionalists also maintain that youth is a period which is characterized by lower status and power because it is a training period – a time of rehearsal – for adulthood. Discrepancies of power and status and discrepancies between physical maturity and social maturity are regarded as potential 'dysfunctions' which can lead to friction, but which are usually resolved as part of the 'growing-up process'.

Marxist theories place a different interpretation on the growth and development of youth and youth cults. Hall and Jefferson see youth cults as a response to the domination of ruling-class ideology. They represent potential conflict, rather than 'the chance to let off immature steam before consensus is maintained', as functionalists suggest. Marxist writing has concentrated on working-class male youth cults, such as rockers, skinheads and soccer hooligans, and described them as a form of 'resistance' through various 'ritual forms' of behaviour, to middle-class and ruling-class ideologies, in which resistance helps to create identity. The potential of working-class youth cults, in resisting mainstream values and dominant culture, to be 'truly oppositional' poses a serious threat to ruling-class interests, however. Often their behaviour is 'incorporated' and 'made safe' by a commercialized version of the real thing. Commercially promoted pop culture – clothes, music and leisure activities – not only makes profit out of teenage spending but can serve to distract youngsters away from a potentially more dangerous (to the ruling class) and authentic oppositional culture, along avenues which make the consumption of mass-produced pop culture 'seem like' the challenge they want to make to society. **Professor Laurie Taylor**, writing in *The Times* in 1984, went so far as to suggest that 'the music' had also 'grown safe along with the culture'. The fact that ultimately the commercial interests which mass-produce pop culture for young people emanate from the same economic concerns as those which seek to preserve a hierarchical society in which profit can flourish illustrates the pervasiveness, variety and effectiveness with which ruling groups exercise their control and reinforce their power.

Laurie Taylor

Clarke and Jefferson found it hard to identify any youth cultures which are 'truly oppositional' in the sense of having a 'political dimension'. Opposition tends to be confined to the area of leisure. They are not geared up to the total transformation of their social conditions as political groups might be. Paul Willis reveals how working-class lads can be mightily resistant to the dominant culture of schooling (see pages 144–6), but has to conclude that the counter-culture of schooling is flawed by both sexism and racism and has yet to be transformed into any kind of generalized political resistance to the organization and practices of an unequal society.

Stan Cohen

Interactionists such as **Stan Cohen**, writing in the early 1970s, looks at societies' response to youth and youth cultures. He made a detailed content analysis of the media's response to mods and rockers in the 1960s and identified a kind of 'moral panic' at work which exaggerated, in ways which bordered on hysteria, the danger to society of their deviant and threatening and challenging behaviour – the same kind of tabloid hysteria which has more recently referred to 'Acid Crackdown' and the 'Lush Life Lure that Snared Ecstasy Girl', and to 'out-of-control children 'as 'monsters in our midst'. According to Cohen, 'panics' served to partially divert attention from 'real' and 'underlying' explanations of behaviour, such as poverty, or even completely from other social factors such as recession, and by indicating the threat posed by individuals to society, thereby helping to avoid too close an inspection of more general concerns such as government policies or the unequal distribution of resources in society generally.

Feminist theories have pointed to the sexism of classic studies carried out on male working-class youth such as Learning to Labour. Sheila Rowbotham and Ann Oakley have drawn attention to the ways in which women have been 'hidden from history' and are 'invisible in sociology'. With the exception of promiscuity and prostitution, they have been largely ignored in studies of deviance, criminology and youth cultures. During the period in the 1960s and 1970s when working-class youth cults were being placed under the sociological microscope, and the press was full of panics about vandalism, gang fights, soccer hooliganism and clashes with the police, because these were the kinds of behaviour from which girls were excluded, it was assumed that girls did not take part in youth cults.

While in the 1950s and 1960s working-class boys were moving into the workplace, the pub and the football ground, girls' attention was still focused

McRobbie & Garber

more on the home, on boyfriends and getting married. Girls certainly did 'dress up' to go out and get boyfriends, but they would have been less likely to hang about street corners than they are today, and would have been allowed less licence than their brothers in relation to staying out late and sexual relationships. **Angela McRobbie** and **Jenny Garber** suggested that a good deal of girls' culture happened 'within the culture of the bedroom' – experiments with make-up, listening to records, reading magazines, sizing up boyfriends, gossiping, dancing – even if the room was uneasily shared with an elder sister. Subsequent studies have looked in more detail at the effects of teenage magazines and television on girls' sub-cultures.

Paul Gilroy & Stuart Hall

Black sociologists, for example, Paul Gilroy and Stuart Hall, have paid close attention to the ways in which black youth are presented as a serious threat to social order and stability. Others have examined the content of black music cults, e.g. rap and reggae, for expressions of resistance to white domination and for content that could be said to be sexist and homophobic.

Postmodernists suggest that previous theories of youth cults, especially in the 1950s, 1960s and 1970s, assumed that 'beneath the surface' was something 'real' and 'authentic' and 'oppositional'. 'In-depth' analysis is claimed to be no longer appropriate because cultures are, in fact, characterized by 'shallowness, flatness and hyper-reality'. While teds, beats, rockers, mods, skins, hippies, rudies and rastas were generally applauded by 1970s sociologists for their 'signs' of resistance and rebellion to contemporary society, they have become increasingly 'manufactured' by the media. Post-modernists argue that, because current versions of pop culture can be seen to be obviously 'manufactured' – who is to say that all the others were not similarly constructed, in ways which seem to invalidate about thirty years of previously orthodox theory.

Economic options

The years of recession and economic restructuring in the 1980s and 1990s mean that jobs are no longer so easy to come by for young people, and the amount of money they have to spend is less, in real terms, than in earlier periods.

Young people are more likely to stay on longer at school or college because of poor employment prospects. State benefits for 16- and 17-year-olds have been withdrawn and those paid to 18–24-year-olds have been reduced. Youth Training Schemes carry an element of compulsion. Housing benefits and housing options have been reduced. Grants to students in higher education have been severely cut back. Instead of moving steadily towards economic and social independence, increasing levels of unemployment, low student grants and reductions in state benefits all mean that young people, even those in their early 20s, are likely to be dependent for longer on their families of origin. However, increased levels of family poverty generally during the 1980s and 1990s, exacerbated by the strains put upon families by domestic violence and family breakdown, youth unemployment and declining opportunities for those in particularly vulnerable and discriminated-against groups, have led to increases in homelessness and financial hardship among the young, especially in large and run-down urban areas. **Beatrice Campbell** (*Wigan Pier Revisited*) argues that, for many young women, having a baby is one of the few ways in which they can still make the 'transition to adulthood' in a society which has increasingly closed down their other options. For young men, the options are different and sometimes more deadly. In *Goliath* Campbell writes about young men with few prospects of work turning to car theft and joyriding as an alternative.

Beatrice Campbell

She describes the 'daring nature' of the crime as providing a reputation for showmanship:

> In Blackbird Leys (in Oxford) where men's employment in making cars had given way to young men's enjoyment in stealing them, the car was the fetish par excellence. . . .

For young people denied real employment and the chance to acquire marketable skills, having a baby or stealing a car can become public ways of achieving status. One father, speaking after the death of his son in a car chase by the police, and in an attempt to dignify his son's short life, claimed that he was 'no ordinary joyrider' but 'a professional car thief'. He said:

> I tried to talk him out of it but if kids don't see sense what can you do? He had no job and he told me he did it to make money. I know whatever he was involved in, he was not a joyrider.

Social change

There is now a much greater time-span between biological and emotional maturity. Improved diets and healthcare, for example, have led to earlier puberty in Western societies. Psychologists argue that this has increased the likelihood of emotional stresses and strains. Young people are more vulnerable than adults to adult pressures, and may be less able to cope. Research estimates suggest that no fewer than a quarter of adolescents in the United States have significant emotional difficulties to do with eating disorders, depression and sexuality which are likely to cause them problems as adults. These are no doubt compounded by pressures to conform to gender stereotypes, especially in relation to young women.

The elderly

In 1850 less than 5 per cent of the population of Britain was aged over 65. Today the figure is more like 18 per cent with a projected increase to over 23 per cent in the next forty years. It is a mistake to lump all those over 65 together, however, given the wide age range involved and the ways in which social class, gender and ethnicity are likely to create different experiences and opportunities when it comes to ageing.

Sociology in Britain has traditionally studied the elderly as a **problem** and in terms of 'the burden' presented by 'their dependency', 'the cost to the nation', the detrimental effects of 'an ageing society'. It is said to be the time when 'functions' and 'abilities' are lost in ways which appear to affect all groups in the same way. However, in other societies age is assumed to lend wisdom and frequently gives status and position.

As with childhood and youth, ideas about old age should also be treated as social constructions. Retirement from paid employment at 65 is an invention of the twentieth century. The transition to old age is affected by increasing longevity and decreasing optional ages of retirement. With 'early retirement' now being possible in some jobs, including teaching, at 50, and growing numbers of people living well into their 80s, at what point does 'being old' begin? The issues for a 60-year-old are different from those for an 80-year-old, but still involve the replacement of one kind of status for another. As the pressure group Age Concern has asked, 'How long before people start calling **you** names?'

Most elderly people (77 per cent) live with their spouse or on their own in their own home. Elderly women are more likely than men to be single, widowed or divorced. About 5 per cent of elderly people live in institutions such as old people's homes or nursing homes, although single people, and therefore women, are more likely to do so than those who are married.

Sarah Arber

Sarah Arber (*Class and the Elderly*) claims that the experience of old age in Britain is related to social class. Two different theories help to explain how:

- *Proletarianization theory* – in which the elderly are seen as a homogeneous group of low-paid, deprived people who form part of the underclass
- *Labour market continuity theory* – in which the inequalities derived from previous jobs, income levels and exit from the labour market affect the status and economic position of people in their old age. Middle-class workers will be less likely to be solely dependent on the state pension, for example. Early retirement may be a positive experience which is anticipated and planned, whereas redundancy usually represents a negative experience involving insufficient resources.

The General Household Survey of 1986 found that amenities and consumer durables were less likely to be 'well provided for' in 'elderly households, especially single person households'. A study by Plank in 1977 into waiting lists for old people's homes demonstrated that, in the view of social workers, at least one-third of the elderly really needed rehousing rather than residential care – a circumstance which still appears to be true today.

VAT on fuel

The dismantling of many of the services of the welfare state, in order to make public spending cuts in the 1980s and 1990s, has meant the reduction in 'meals on wheels' provision, day care for elderly people and local-authority-run homes and sheltered housing. The imposition of **VAT on fuel**, and the decline in real value of state pensions (worth 16.5 per cent of the average male wage in 1994 and well below the income support level), all add to reductions in living standards for those who have few savings and no additional sources of income.

Elderly people are one of the main groups to be living in poverty in Britain. Some elderly people (but not women) are in receipt of occupational pensions, but the main source of income for elderly people is social security – either as a state pension or income support. In comparison with other European countries, pensions in Britain are not generous.

There are also gender issues involved. Because of women's greater longevity, they comprise two-thirds of all those over 65 in Britain, a proportion which becomes greater with increasing age. Women tend to live longer than men and to be poorer than men. They are not poorer because they live longer. The social expectation of women's financial dependency on men lays the foundation for their material disadvantage throughout life. Welfare state benefits and insurance contributions introduced after the Second World War were organized and based on this assumption, and elderly women still live with the consequences of these assumptions having been made.

Women's poorer position in the job market means that they are less likely to have occupational pensions, savings schemes, redundancy payments or private healthcare insurance. They are also less likely to be car drivers and car owners and are more likely, as are all women, to fear attack in public places: a factor which 'keeps women off the streets' and renders them more likely to be socially isolated than men.

The effects of their relative poverty compared with men increases as they get older, and at a time when their health may be deteriorating. Elderly women are much more likely to experience bereavement than men, which is in itself one of the major causes of death among old people. Elderly women are much more likely to be living on their own than men, which can increase stress levels at an increasingly vulnerable time, and they are more likely to be looking after someone else than being looked after themselves.

Government legislation designed to shift the responsibility for elderly and other 'potentially dependent' groups back onto their families or into privatized 'community care' schemes has increased the responsibilities of women within families. Women in middle years are now much more likely to be looking after elderly relatives, without additional financial assistance or state support, at a time in their lives when they might have expected that their caring and domestic roles should be becoming easier.

Among ethnic minorities in the population elderly people face particular problems, especially if they have to rely on institutional care. Minority religious practices, language and diet are all sensitive areas, which homes for the elderly don't usually take into account. It is unclear whether stereotypes of the 'all-caring' Asian family are true or false. Certainly patterns of migration have contributed to the breaking up of extended family units. The 1981 census revealed that extended families were typical of households headed by people from the New Commonwealth or Pakistan, but that elderly people from ethnic minorities comprised only 4 per cent of these households. Older people are often less likely to speak English, which may cause extra difficulties in their use of health and other statutory services. Elderly women still have to produce considerable documentation to demonstrate their entitlement to benefits in Britain, more so when their husbands have died, in a system which is administered with a good deal of racism. Their lowly position in the labour market leads to related economic deprivations which intensify with age.

As 'elderly people' also 'get younger', however, views about the elderly will undoubtedly change. The prospect of large numbers of 'relatively young' older people provides a potentially lucrative consumer market, both for goods and services such as education and leisure activities. Attempts to 'marshall' elderly people into pensioners' pressure groups and unions in recent years, concerning issues to do with pensions and VAT on fuel, indicate the potential for 'older voters' to become a significant political force if they get themselves organized.

Part Two

Households, families and marriage

What is a family?

The family seems, at first sight, to be one of the simplest of sociological concepts to understand. It is a term used in everyday language; almost everyone has some personal experience of family life. We are used to hearing the term used by politicians from all parties, claiming to be supporters of the 'family' and 'family values'.

In practice, however, the term is not as simple as it may seem when it comes to definitions; when we want to define the various living arrangements we would describe as 'families'.

One of the main debates which has preoccupied sociology in recent years concerns the best definition of a 'family' and whether families can be distinguished in any way from other kinds of living arrangements. A distinction is sometimes made between a 'family' and a 'household'. For instance, a group of students may share a common dwelling and living expenses; they may cook together or separately; they may go to the pub together; they may give each other support during their exams or other emotional crises; but we would not generally consider them to be a family. This is because we think of a family as consisting of people who are related to each other, either by blood or by a primary, intimate, sexual relationship which is often based on marriage and which has a greater degree of permanency about it than other types of living arrangements.

But what about a married couple without children – are they a family? Or a widower bringing up children on his own?

George Murdock

In 1949, **George Murdock**, a functionalist sociologist, after examining accounts from 250 different societies, defined the family as:

> a social group characterised by common residence, economic co-operation and reproduction. It includes adults of both sexes, at least two of whom maintain a socially approved sexual relationship, and one or more children, own or adopted, of the sexually co-habiting adults.

Using his definition, neither of the two examples mentioned above would be considered a family. You might like to think about what other types of living arrangements would be excluded by Murdock's definition. These could include lone-parent families; cohabiting couples with or without children; lesbian and gay couples with or without children; an elderly couple whose children have grown up and left home; or people living in a commune.

Anthony Giddens

More recently, **Anthony Giddens** has defined the family as:

> a social unit made up of people who support each other in one or several ways e.g. socially, economically or psychologically (love, care, affection) or whose members identify with each other as a supportive unit.

This broader definition moves away from the biological base of Murdock's and would include those arrangements left out of his definition. It also allows for more self-selection. In other words, any group which considers itself to be a family could be included.

This highlights an important debate within sociology and within society at large about what kind of living arrangements are to be defined as 'real' families and therefore to be encouraged as 'natural' and desirable.

Social security and other legislation generally deals with families as units rather than directly with individuals, and while common-law relationships are now generally recognized, some other kinds of relationships are not, and are positively discouraged. For example, in the 1980s in Britain, the Conservative Government launched an attack on what it called 'pretend families', targeting lesbian and gay families as undesirable and not proper families. The **Lesbian Custody Support Group** within the organization Rights of Women documented the difficulty of lesbian mothers retaining custody of their children who were born in a previous heterosexual relationship. Changes in policy about the right to artificial insemination and in-vitro fertilization have made it extremely difficult for lesbians or, indeed, any unmarried woman, to receive treatment.

Lesbian Custody Support Group

All of this suggests that defining some, and not other, kinds of households as families is not as straightforward as we might imagine. It suggests that the family is not a 'natural' unit but a 'socially constructed' one, which reflects particular political views about what is considered desirable or 'normal'.

Popular understandings of what is meant by the term 'family' are also influenced by the stereotype of the 'typical family' portrayed in advertising, consisting of husband, wife and two children, which is presented to us as a kind of 'norm', so that, although a variety of other arrangements exist, this norm becomes viewed as somehow 'more real'.

In reality, studies of family life in different societies, at different times and within the same society reveal a variety of behaviours, attitudes and organizational characteristics. Cultural and ethnic diversity within society also helps to challenge prevailing notions of what constitutes a family. Families may cross more than two generations; in some societies it is common to find large households crossing three generations, living with their relatives in an independent and almost self-sufficient community.

polygamy and monogamy

In some societies and groups, marriage is the usual basis for family life, but in others there is greater tolerance of other arrangements. In Nigeria, among the Tiv people, a man may have more than one wife. In other societies, a woman may have several husbands. These kind of **polygamous** relationships contrast markedly with contemporary British society in which **monogamy** – the marriage of one man to one woman at a time – is the only legally permitted matrimonial relationship, although the pattern of divorce and remarriage, which is becoming increasingly common, is referred to as **serial monogamy**.

In some societies or cultural groups, a fair amount of free choice in the selection of marriage partners is allowed. In others, however, there is considerable pressure to marry within a particular religious faith, ethnic group or social class. Arranged marriages are the preferred type in some groups.

The permanence or impermanence of marriage also varies. Traditional Christian teaching depicts a relationship which endures until death. The divorce law of many countries has been changed this century to make divorce easier, although in Britain in the 1990s there is discussion about reversing some of this legislation.

Relationships between parents and children also vary. In some societies child-bearing is seen to be a woman's responsibility; in others fathers play an important role. In yet others, children are looked after in a more communal way by relatives and kinsfolk. The status of children within a society and within the family also varies. In the past in Britain children were seen as the possessions of their fathers, and it was not until 1839 that fathers' property rights over their children were limited and children gradually became seen rather more as dependants, in need of care and protection. In earlier times, childhood was a brief period until children could look after themselves sufficiently to contribute to the work carried out by the rest of the family. Today extended education and limited job opportunities mean that young people sometimes remain dependent on their families until their twenties.

Children in Western society are more likely to be seen as financial liabilities – requiring vast expenditure on disposable nappies, special foods, toys, books, branded trainers and sports equipment – in contrast to the economic asset they represent in societies where child labour remains prevalent.

In some societies children, like wives, are a measure of a man's virility and status. In others, like traditional New Guinea, the Mundugumor women actively disliked child-bearing and rearing. In traditional Samoa, children were handed over into the care of relatives as soon as they were weaned. In many societies it is not uncommon for children to be reared by adults other than the children's parents. For example, in the British upper class it is still quite common for the day-to-day care of young children to be entrusted to an employee and for children to be sent away to boarding school at around eight years of age.

All of these illustrations – and there are many others – merely serve to show that family organization and behaviour are immensely flexible. Economic circumstances, law, religion, education, custom and tradition all influence our personal relationships and living arrangements. Therefore, far from being a natural and instinctive set of relationships, the family is more accurately seen as a social and economic arrangement, considerably affected by the prevailing economic and social characteristics of the society in which it operates.

Is the family universal?

Until quite recently it has been common to find the family referred to in many textbooks as 'a universal institution'. While acknowledging that the precise form of the family might differ, or that the customs surrounding marriage and child-rearing may vary, the basic family structure, consisting of man, woman and children, was said to exist in every known society. Murdock's anthropological study led him to believe that all known societies showed a remarkable degree of similarity despite the differences we have mentioned.

Murdock argued that in every society it is necessary to regulate relationships between people so that the needs of society can be met. For example, the regulation of sexual relations, the procreation and rearing of children, the production and distribution of economic resources and the socialization of members, particularly the children. This argument assumes that the ties within family units are the most significant and fundamental ties that exist between human beings, because they are based on blood, or a socially and/or religiously significant relationship, such as marriage. It also assumes that they are different in type and strength from those with people outside the family – the idea expressed in the saying that 'blood is thicker than water'. In other words, he argued that the important unit for providing *nuclear families* the necessary functions which promote social stability is the **nuclear unit**, consisting of man, woman and children, regardless of variations in customs and practices. This view, that the family as defined by Murdock is universal, has now been challenged by both anthropologists and sociologists.

Murdock's argument rested on an examination of anthropological studies of more than 250 societies. He has been criticized for an ethnocentric bias, in which the practices of widely differing societies from the past, or from distant parts of the globe, were interpreted through the filter of mid-twentieth century Western experience. His view was also an essentially conservative perspective because it suggested that there was some 'biological imperative' about the family which placed it beyond criticism.

It is this aspect of Murdock's work which has been most fiercely criticized by both Marxists and feminists, who have sought to show that the family is a 'social construction' serving a particular set of interests, rather than an inevitable and naturally occurring phenomenon. They would also be critical of contemporary definitions of the family which omit more common living arrangements, e.g. mother-headed, lone-parent families.

Some anthropologists and sociologists have cited evidence of a vast array of living arrangements which did not coincide with Murdock's definition. For example, the Nayar tribe of Northern India made no link between intercourse and conception; women lived independently of men, and paternity was not a consideration. The Trobriand Islanders, studied by Malinowski, did not consider fathers as blood relatives of children, while the Lakker tribe of Burma considered mothers as merely a vessel for children prior to birth and as having no blood relationship with them after birth. In other societies, children were adopted immediately after weaning, and Margaret Mead claimed that some adoptive mothers even breast-fed their adopted children. In Tahiti, it was common for young girls to have children with whom the relationship stopped after birth. The Nuer tribe studied by Evans-Pritchard practised 'ghost marriages' where, if a man died without children, a close male relative would marry his widow and any children born would be seen as the children of the dead man. If an older woman had no children she would marry a younger woman and be seen as a parent to her children.

Whether we are to consider these practices as examples of families or not depends upon whether we accept the definition of the basic family core of man, woman and children put forward by Murdock.

An alternative view is argued by Yanina Sheeran:

Yanina Sheeran

> There is an enduring belief among sociologists that biological parents and children are the universal core unit of 'family' life, despite recent research which suggests that child-rearing 'households' take many forms. In addition, the definition of the nuclear family as the core unit automatically makes a single mother family an aberrant type of household rather than the well-recognised and enduring form it has always been, even when disapproved. ... There does, however, appear to be a universal core to 'family household' life in its myriad forms, and that it is best described as a 'female-carer core unit'. The centrality of the woman in family household life holds true today in Britain, and also when we examine historical and cross-cultural evidence.

She goes on to show that, whatever the particular family structure, there is usually a woman (not always the biological mother) and children core unit, and that this unit, rather than the nuclear family of man, woman and children, should be seen as the universal family form.

Whether we regard the family as a universal institution depends on how we define the term 'family'. It is clear that all societies face questions about how to organize relationships so that both personal and societal needs are catered for. Marxists argue that, in modern industrial society, the ideology of the nuclear family claims to meet our needs for love, privacy and security, but in fact serves the interests of capitalism in a variety of ways (see below).

As a result, there have been a variety of attempts to replace the family with a less individual and more communal system.

Attempts to eliminate the family

USSR after 1917

In both the USSR and China the family has been regarded as a **bourgeois institution**, representing all that was retrogressive about pre-revolutionary life. In the **USSR**, after the Bolshevik Revolution in **1917**, one of the first actions taken was to try to curtail the power of pre-revolutionary forces, such as religion, which governed family life. Family life itself was said to encourage individualism and, as such, served the interests of capitalism.

In 1918 civil marriage was substituted for religious marriage and divorce was made easier to obtain. A wife was no longer bound to live with her husband or to take his name, and legal discrimination against illegitimate children was abolished. Marxists believed that capitalism created a form of family in which men were encouraged to dominate women, just as the bosses dominated the workers, and these traditional views were seen to hinder the progress of true socialism. They also wanted to release more women for paid employment to play their part in the reconstruction of the post revolutionary economy.

But it took more than a change in the law to alter relationships within the family, and a variety of developments in the 1920s, partly stimulated by political ideals and partly by political expediency, produced a very confusing period in which family relationships and responsibilities appeared to be in chaos. According to most Western observers, the results of 'new sexual freedoms' were disastrous. The Soviet press of the 1930s reported that promiscuity flourished and that juvenile delinquency was on the increase because of irresponsible parents and broken homes. A familiar cry in Britain in the 1990s!

It became clear that, while the bourgeois and religious domination of family life under Tsarist rule had supported the economic and social exploitation of the vast majority of the population, the answer was not to undermine the family but rather to encourage it to reflect more socialist and egalitarian ideas. It was still the most efficient unit for organizing reproduction and child-rearing. This resulted in the passing of stricter marriage and divorce legislation and laws making parents more responsible for the actions of their children. The government was concerned about the drop in the birth rate as a result of the earlier changes, and now wished to reverse that trend by legislation seen to support the family, while at the same time providing state childcare facilities to enable both parents to work outside the home. Whether we should interpret this as a sign of the 'inevitability' of the family is unclear, as the whole society was in such turmoil at the time.

China after 1949

In **China** one of the first things the new Communist government did in **1949** was to introduce new marriage laws to weaken the power of husbands over wives. In pre-revolutionary China women were among the most oppressed in the world. The rules of Confucius, who lived 500 years before Christ, still demanded that women were subservient to men. Weddings were arranged for them, child marriages were common and young girls could be sold into prostitution. The main duty of the wife was to produce children, and from an early age their feet were bound to restrict their movement and to be a sign of their slave-like existence. Husbands could end a marriage at any time. There was an old Chinese saying: 'Noodles are not rice and women are not human beings'.

The new laws ended the sale of women and the forcibly arranged marriages. Young people were encouraged to marry late, partly as a form of population control but also so that they could devote themselves to their work rather than to the family. During the cultural revolution in the 1960s the family came under great attack as a reviled institution, and children were encouraged to denounce their parents for anti-revolutionary activity. Although today marriage ceremonies are simple civil affairs, family planning, abortion and sterilization are freely available to support the one-child policy, and nurseries, public dining rooms and washing facilities are provided – the family itself is seen as an important institution.

Kibbutzim

Another attempt to create an alternative to family life was created by the **kibbutz** system in Israel after the Second World War. In a desire to stress the needs of the society rather than the individual, and in the push to create a new society, family ties were to be weakened by a variety of measures. Both men and women were needed to work, so children were to be cared for collectively within children's houses on the kibbutz, rather than within individual families. Parents would spend some leisure time each day with their offspring, but for the rest of the time they were brought up communally. This was thought to foster loyalty to the kibbutz rather than to individuals. Meals for all members were provided communally, and private space was kept to a minimum. However, it was found that many young people had to look outside the kibbutz for a partner because they regarded their peers, with whom they had been brought up, more like siblings. Although most kibbutzim do not operate along these strict lines today, and children now sleep with their families, research has indicated that children were as well-adjusted as those brought up more traditionally, and that child-rearing could be carried out effectively by institutions other than the traditional family.

Communes

Other alternatives to the family have been **communes**. There have been experiments in communal living for centuries, especially among religious communities. They are usually based on the ideals of sharing a collective style of living, which poses an alternative to the individualistic, consumer-oriented mainstream society. More common in the USA than in Britain, they are usually relatively short-lived. Andrew McCulloch studied British communes in 1975 and found that out of 67 only six lasted for more than five years. Although the values espoused by commune inhabitants do represent a challenge to traditional family life – 'free love' and 'joint child-rearing', for example – their small numbers mean that, on the whole, they do not suggest a viable alternative to family life for most people. It remains to be seen whether groups such as travellers and itinerant 'New Age hippies' present a 1990s alternative to family life, or whether they are themselves a response to unemployment and homelessness.

Key debates

There are five key debates within the sociology of the family which we shall consider.

1 The first examines the **functions** the family performs for a society, and is linked to the discussion about whether the family is universal **because** it performs vital functions for society. In this section we shall look at the contribution made by different theories to the debate about the functional importance of the family.
2 The second examines the **structure** of the family. It explores the argument already touched on in the introduction, about whether the **nuclear family** is the predominant family form and about the relationship between it and the **extended family** and **kinship network**. This debate was popular in the 1960s and 1970s in Britain as sociologists began examining the impact of

post-war slum clearance schemes and welfare state policies on family life.

3 The third debate examines the **roles and relationships** within the family, particularly relationships between men and women. This debate was stimulated by the re-emergence of feminism with the **Women's Liberation Movement**, and has given rise to a whole new sociological analysis of family life.

4 The fourth debate, already touched on in the introduction, concerns the **diversity of family forms and types,** looking at the variety of family types, including lone-parent families, reconstituted families, ethnic diversity and same-sex relationships. This debate became popular in the 1980s and presents an alternative view of families and households to the earlier functionalism of family sociology.

5 The fifth debate is linked to the previous one, but examines divorce legislation and social policy concerning **marriage and divorce**.

Family functions

We are used to thinking about the pros and cons of family life from a personal perspective, but most of us are less used to standing back and considering what part the family plays for the wider society. We are so familiar with living the way we do that it is hard to imagine living any other way. Functionalists have taken this particular view and argued that the family performs vital functions for society which no other social institution could perform so effectively. It is this 'functional importance' which led functionalists like Murdock to argue that the family must exist in all societies.

According to this analysis, families serve a number of important functions for their members and for society, and thereby assist in both the preservation and recreation of social life. Functionalism sees society as a social system with interrelated parts, each making a positive contribution to the stability and order of the whole. According to this view, the family must relate to, and be integrated with, other important elements in the system, such as the economy or the education system. The type of family form at any one time, therefore, must dovetail with the needs of these other social institutions.

All societies have basic functions which must be performed if they are to operate efficiently and harmoniously. The population must be reproduced, nurtured and taught the norms and values of the society. The functions performed by the family for society are said to include:

● the organization and regulation of sexual behaviour;
● the reproduction of children within a socially approved setting;
● the care of children until they are capable of caring for themselves;
● the socialization or informal training of children to exhibit the kind of behaviour, values and attitudes which are expected of them by society;
● the organization of a 'division of labour' between man and wife in terms of breadwinning, household maintenance, child-rearing and so on, so that the family group can operate as an efficient and interdependent unit;
● the definition of roles such as wife, mother, father, husband, grandparent, son, daughter, etc. – all of which enable family members to develop appropriate expectations of each other and to learn in turn what is expected of them;
● the provision of love, care, emotional security and shelter for all members of the family, which, unlike other groups to which people might belong,

ensures an intimate, enduring and responsible base in an otherwise impersonal and often alienating society;
- the provision of leisure and recreation for family members and a unit within which to share celebrations and significant occasions such as births, marriages and deaths.

According to Murdock, these can be summarized as four main functions which ensure the survival of society. These are:

- the regulation of potentially disruptive sexuality within a socially approved system of control such as marriage;
- the reproduction of offspring with readily identifiable and responsible parents;
- the production and distribution of resources such as food, clothing, livelihood to sustain the population;
- the education of members so that the culture of society is transmitted from one generation to the next.

He argued that the family makes a significant contribution to each of these vital functions and that this explains why, according to Murdock, the family is found in all societies.

The family is also said to function positively for individual members of society as well as the social system. Thus he argued that each of the functions works best for individuals when structured within families. For example, the sexual function provides for personal satisfaction while clarifying rules about sexual relationships within a particular society. It also helps to create bonds between husband and wife which makes the family a more effective and close-knit institution. This leads **Haralambos** and **Holman** to comment:

Haralambos & Holman

> Murdock's picture of the family is rather like the multi-faceted, indispensable boy-scout knife. The family is seen as a multi-functional institution which is indispensable to society. Its 'many-sided utility' accounts for its universality and its inevitability.

As such, it is an over-enthusiastic view of the family in which widely varying societies are perceived as requiring the self-same functions regardless of period or place. Murdock fails to consider whether these functions could be effectively performed by other institutions or by a more communally organized system of provision. In common with many functionalists, he does not consider the possibility of conflict emerging within families, for instance between parents and children or between spouses. He has also been accused of 'biological determinism'. For instance, he argues that, in carrying out the economic function, it makes sense for men and women to specialize in different activities, and he thus assumes a gender division of labour to be both inevitable and desirable. This aspect of his work has been fiercely criticized by feminists for assuming that a biologically determined gender division of labour similar to that in the West exists in all societies.

This type of analysis was taken further by Talcott Parsons, who related the perspective to modern, industrialized societies such as the USA. Parsons' account is an attempt to explain how the family has adapted to the change from an agricultural to an industrial society.

Modern societies need more specialized institutions. Thus in pre-industrial times family members worked together on the land and at their crafts in a joint endeavour. The family taught the children all they needed to know to survive, and determined their status and position within that society. As societies became more complex, specialized places of work, such as factories, developed; schools took on the task of teaching the more sophisticated knowledge and skills needed in society and the workplace; and young people increasingly left home to establish their separate identity and position on the basis of their own talents and skills. In other words, the family lost some of its functions to other institutions, and therefore continued to specialize much more in those things which could be done only by the family.

Ronald Fletcher

In Britain this type of analysis was popular in the early 1960s, when some commentators were arguing that the provisions of the expanding welfare state would strip the family of its original functions. Some British sociologists like **Ronald Fletcher** claimed that the new provisions of the welfare state, rather than undermining the family, would work in partnership with the family, supporting it in ways which would enable it 'to work even better'. It was a very optimistic view of both the post-war welfare state and the family.

While functionalist-inspired sociologists like Fletcher and Young and Willmott agreed that the family was no longer a **productive** economic unit in the way it had been in pre-industrial society, they argued that it still functioned as an economic unit in terms of **consumption.** Family members now worked outside the home, to earn the money to spend on an ever-increasing range of consumer goods for home and family use.

Parsons argued that, in modern societies, the functions that 'only the family' can perform had been honed down to two vital tasks:

● the primary socialization of the young;
● the stabilization of adult personalities.

Primary socialization remained important because it is through this process that the culture of society – its norms, values, customs and language – are passed on. Parsons argued that in the family this was more than a simple form of socialization because, by being introduced to these aspects of culture during the formative years, the child absorbed them more profoundly and so they became 'part of his or her personality. This helped to ensure that, within any society, the key beliefs which were commonly shared and valued were perpetuated, and the socialization process served to create a consensus about basic understandings which united the society and minimized conflict. In American society these values were typically those of individual achievement, competition and patriotism. In other societies they might be bravery, generosity, respect for elders, concern for the common good, etc.

This process, according to Parsons, was reinforced in adult life by marriage and the creation of a new family. Within marriage, partners provided the close emotional support and security needed to cope with the inevitable strains of modern competitive societies. The family provided 'a haven of safety, love and relaxation' in which spouses had complementary but equal roles and in which individuals could satisfy their personal needs.

There are obvious criticisms of this type of analysis, which in turn help to account for its lack of popularity among sociologists today:

● It begs a lot of questions about the 'unacknowledged assumptions and values' underpinning the analysis.
● It ignores the fact that other institutions could, in theory, perform the same functions equally well, e.g. the kibbutz.

- It assumes that there is general public consensus about the basic values to be taught. In fact, in any society there is usually disagreement about these, sometimes reflecting the different religious, ethnic, social class, political or age groups to which we belong. For example, feminist critics of the Conservative Government's campaign about 'family values' in the 1990s would argue that the 'traditional family', in which the man is seen to be the 'head of the household', can create unhappy, unequal and unsafe families.

R. D. Laing

- It paints a picture of 'normal' family life as happy, secure, enduring and unproblematic. In practice, many people's experiences suggest that family life is not that easy. It can be a source of pain, guilt and conflict – families can be split apart by broken marriages, plagued by jealousy, unfulfilled expectations, resentment and violence. **R. D. Laing**, writing in the 1960/70s, argued that family life could even trigger mental illness, such as schizophrenia.
- Others have claimed that it encourages an inward-looking and selfish society, concerned only with the immediate family rather than the good of society as a whole.
- It fails to take account of the economic characteristics of a society, the implications of economic factors in terms of family structure and behaviour and the interplay between economic needs, family organization and social change.

Marxist perspectives on the family

Friedrich Engels

Marxists would agree with functionalists about the way the process of socialization works, but they would see this as a **negative** rather than a **positive** function of families in capitalist societies. According to Marxists, the mode of economic production is what structures the pattern of family life. **Friedrich Engels**, a friend and collaborator of Marx, provided a Marxist-inspired account of the 'origins of the family'. In it he argued that families emerged at the same time as private property, as a mechanism for handing on accumulated property to the next generation.

Marx's analysis of the relationships of production in capitalist society has been used and adapted to show how the family serves important functions not for society as a whole, but for those who own the means of production – the capitalist class or the bourgeoisie. For example:

A division of labour between men and women in the family and the workplace means that the main workers (the men) can be looked after, fed, clothed, cared for by women working for love. In other words, women provide these functions which benefit the boss, by producing a happier, fitter workforce, at no additional cost. They also bring up the next generation of workers in the same way.

In times of labour shortage women provide a 'reserve army' of labour which can be drawn into the work force only when the owners need them and dispatched back to the home when they are no longer required.

Herbert Marcuse

By encouraging people to live in small units, more of the products of production are sold – every home needs a washing machine, video, microwave, fax – and this produces more profits for business. Rather than perceiving this as 'a happy fit' between the economy and the family, as functionalists usually do, neo-Marxists like **Herbert Marcuse** (*One Dimensional Man*) claim that under capitalism we are encouraged to seek personal satisfaction in home and family life and the accumulation of consumer goods. False needs are created through ideological conditioning from an early age and from a variety of sources – family, religion, education, mass media – i.e. the process which functionalists refer to as socialization.

Encouraging people to think about their own family before all others means the workers are less likely to join with others to overthrow the bourgeoisie. This represents a form of 'false class consciousness'. **Louis Althusser**, writing in 1971, argued that the family is part of what he called the 'ideological state apparatus' (ISA) (see page 240) which controls the masses to prevent any challenge being made to those in power.

Louis Althusser

A Marxist analysis of family functions, therefore, sees the family as a bourgeois institution, supporting the interests of the ruling class and encouraging individualism rather than collectivism, in which we come to see the family as the one area of our lives in which we will be personally fulfilled.

We are caught in a double bind – in order to be 'happy' we need to satisfy our 'false needs'. We see faces smiling out of advertisements which tell us that Oxo/Ariel/Toyota will improve our family lives. In order to buy these goods we have to work in what Marcuse calls 'exhausting, stupefying and inhuman slavery'. In every area of our lives, then, we are alienated, and in the process we lose the capacity for creativity and fulfilling personal relationships.

Critics of the Marxist analysis would point to the lack of success Marxist-inspired governments have had in coming up with a viable alternative to the family, for the organization of reproduction and satisfaction of personal and emotional needs in complex industrial societies. Although it is relatively easy to provide childcare, mass education and social security if the political will exists, it is less easy to provide a meaningful alternative to intimate and enduring personal relationships.

Feminist perspectives on the family

Feminists are critical of Marxists for failing to pay sufficient attention to what actually happens within families. Like functionalists, Marxists analyse the relationships between the family and other institutions on a macro scale, but pay scant attention to what actually goes on within families. They also ignore the way in which individual men as well as capitalists benefit from the exploitation of women.

Betty Friedan and 'the problem which has no name'

Women's dissatisfaction with the reality of their experiences within families was one of the triggers for the Women's Liberation Movement in the 1960s. When **Betty Friedan** wrote in *The Feminine Mystique* about '**the problem which has no name**', thousands of women throughout the Western world knew precisely what she meant. Women had been told that they would be happy if they 'got their man', lived in a nice house and had two children. They were not told how to satisfy their own needs, or find their own potential outside the family. Women, especially white, middle-class women, were supposed to be 'fulfilled' by family life. But many were left with a craving for something more.

The main contribution of feminist analysis to our understanding of the family, missing from functionalist and Marxist perspectives, has been the examination of the 'interior life' of families and the nature of the relationship between family members. For the first time, these relationships were identified as 'political', a term previously applied only to the public sphere of institutions such as political parties and governments. Kate Millett, in her book *Sexual Politics*, referred to the relationship between men and women in the family as 'power-structured relationships' of domination and subordination. We shall look in detail at this analysis later.

For radical feminists like Kate Millett, the family in modern society represents the cornerstone of patriarchy, the system in which men dominate women. The functions which the family performs are those which support this patriarchal system.

Socialization

It is within the family that children receive their **primary socialization**. According to Ann Oakley this socialization affects a child's 'self-concept', so that children acquire all the attributes considered 'appropriate to their sex' within their particular society. Masculine and feminine traits are learned, not inborn, and help to provide boys with a 'dominant temperament' which in later life allows them to exercise control over women. Through this process of socialization the **interior colonization** of women takes place, in which they come to see themselves as inferior and so accept their allotted roles within the family and their unequal position in society. Patriarchal power is thereby legitimized.

Patriarchal power

The family also plays an important part in Western cultures in the continuation of patriarchy, by allowing men **personal** domination over women as well as in the wider society. Children have a 'known' father, so that 'legitimate heirs' are guaranteed and power and privilege can be passed on through the male line. Women and children take their social and class status in society from the male head, so the family reinforces an unequal stratification system. Through the family, women come to see their main role in life as caring for others, and become economic dependants of men, which further reinforces their inferior status.

For black women, the effects of patriarchy are also mediated through racism.

Changes in the structure of the family

The family and industrialization

In describing family patterns in societies like Britain, sociologists usually make a distinction between nuclear families and extended families. The nuclear family is usually depicted as a modern phenomenon which has come about because of industrialization, and the factory system, geographic mobility by people in search of work, birth control and the emancipation of women from the home have all encouraged smaller families which are not dependent on social relationships and support from other relatives. The nuclear family, therefore, refers to a unit made up of husband and wife and their dependent children.

The extended family, on the other hand, is a term frequently used to describe the kind of family arrangements where several generations of the same family and relatives live together, or in close proximity to each other, sharing in each other's social, emotional and economic lives, on a fairly regular, day-to-day basis.

For a long time it was the accepted orthodoxy in sociology that the extended family was the predominant form in pre-industrial times, but that this had given way to the nuclear family, which was seen to fit the needs of modern industrial societies. For example, Talcott Parsons argued that the nuclear family was more functional for industrial society, encouraging geographical and social mobility and weakening the ties of kinship obligations which hindered geographic and social mobility. Within the nuclear family, the emphasis is on individualism and the relationship between spouses, rather than with the wider kin. As state agencies assume the responsibility for functions such as education and health care, the family is given greater scope to specialize in the essential functions of socialization and stabilization of adult personalities.

William Goode

Another functionalist, **William Goode,** argued that, in modern societies, the extended family had less to offer individual members because success increasingly depended upon individual, rather than collective, endeavour. The extended family may continue to function effectively among the upper class, where families are able to offer more in the way of wealth, influence or contacts, but elsewhere nuclear units are freer when they are no longer responsible for restricting obligations to the extended family.

Criticisms

During the past thirty years or so this analysis has been criticized for being too simplistic. More recent research has suggested that family structure has always been more complex than these ideas suggest.

Lawrence Stone

In 1977 **Lawrence Stone,** examining European historical material from medieval times to the present day, argued that:

- In medieval times there were small household units which were deeply embedded in the wider community, and these community ties were more important than the ties between spouses. Survival depended on communal cooperation, obligations and responsibilities.
- In the early sixteenth century nuclear families became more separate from the community with the growth of individualism. Relations between spouses and children became stronger and men's power over women increased.
- By the early eighteenth century a nuclear family, with close relationships, domestic privacy and marriage based on romantic love, began to emerge.

Stone explains these changes in family life as resulting from changes in the economic structure. In earlier times the family and community were an integrated production unit. As large-scale commercial farming developed in the seventeenth century, followed by industrial production in the eighteenth century, the separation of home and workplace developed, and family units became smaller and relationships within them closer. The ideology of women as 'natural' carers and men as 'breadwinners' grew, and the family became a private sphere of existence, separated from the more public sphere of work, politics and public life.

Peter Laslett

Peter Laslett, writing in 1977 (*The World We Have Lost*) using data from parish records, helped to demolish various myths about the pre-industrial family:

- there was little evidence of early marriage – the average age in Elizabethan times was 24 for women and 28 for men;
- life expectancy was low;
- fertility levels were low;
- the average household size was 4.75;
- it was a young society – the average age was 25.4;

- more than 70 per cent of households contained children;
- there were few elderly people.

It doesn't take much to calculate from these facts that the number of people living in extended families, consisting of more than two generations, was not that great. People simply did not live long enough to see their grandchildren, and only 1 in 20 households had more than two generations living together.

These figures led Laslett to suggest that in fact the **nuclear form** was the most predominant family form in north-west Europe long before industrialization, but that households were often 'extended' by the presence of non-kin such as lodgers, apprentices, skivvies or servants.

Michael Anderson took issue with Laslett, claiming that there has always been a greater variety of family types existing than either Laslett's, or earlier work by functionalist sociologists, suggested. Using data from the 1851 census in the town of Preston in Lancashire, he found an increase in the number of households where parents lived with their married children. He argued that, as life expectancy increased, this system was more likely to emerge among the working class, where sharing of household costs and work provided benefits for all. Rather than industrialization breaking down the extended family, he argued that the reverse might have been the case, at least in Preston.

Willmott & Young

In 1957 **Peter Willmott** and **Michael Young** (*Family and Kinship in East London*) suggested that, in traditional working class communities, the extended family persisted well into the middle of the twentieth century, providing support and the exchange of services between the generations. Although, like other functionalists, they believed that the extended family was the predominant family form **before** industrialization, and the nuclear family the predominant form **after** industrialization, their work was important at the time because it suggested that a variety of family patterns could co-exist at the same time. They went on to study the impact of slum clearance and rehousing policies on extended families in the East End of London.

Their work also demonstrated the separateness of men's and women's lives, even within marriage, where men spent most of their waking lives in the company of other men at work or in the pub, while women were closer to their mothers and sisters.

Throughout the next two decades there were a series of studies which supported the view that, while nuclear families were common, their ties with extended kinship networks were still significant. For example, research by Colin Bell in Swansea found that regular contact was maintained between married children and their parents within the middle class, where parents continued to give grown-up children financial support. Graham Allen's work, in a commuter village in East Anglia, suggested that there were few class differences in the degree of contact with the extended family.

Studies of the family structure of ethnic minorities in Britain also revealed that extended family ties are very durable, sometimes in spite of separation across thousands of miles.

It is probable that there have always been a variety of family structures existing at any point in history. Certainly the ties of kinship appear to remain strong in many families. A recent study in Britain found that 32 per cent of respondents said they lived less than an hour away from other family members. Only 9 per cent lived more than five hours away. Eleven per cent of respondents saw their mother daily and 58 per cent phoned, or kept in touch by letter, every week. **Haleh Afshar's** study of Muslim women in

Haleh Afshar

West Yorkshire, published in 1994, was carried out among women living in three-generational families, where grandmothers continued to exercise a fair degree of control over their grandchildren. Extended family ties have also been well documented among Afro-Caribbean, South Asian and Cypriot families living in Britain.

community care

Recent changes in health and welfare policies in Britain have implicitly placed responsibility for family members upon the extended family. The Conservative Government's policy of **community care** increasingly relies upon the unpaid labour of grown-up children, usually daughters, to care for aged parents. The 1990 General Household Survey Carer's Report showed that 10 per cent of adults were caring for their parents or parents-in-law. Similarly, cuts in benefits and services to young unemployed adults or single mothers suggests that the onus of responsibility lies not with the state but with the extended family.

The simple assertion by functionalists, therefore, that the extended family was the predominant form before industrialization, and that it was superseded by the nuclear family because it was better fitted for modern industrial society, is not borne out by the facts.

Changes in roles and relationships within the family

Men and women

Functionalists such as Murdock and Talcott Parsons argued that the modern family was characterized by **joint conjugal roles** compared with the **segregated** roles of earlier times. The growth of romantic love as a basis for marriage and the supposed development of the nuclear family had led to greater closeness between partners who are regarded as equal partners in a modern marriage. However, functionalist arguments assume that it 'makes sense' for each partner to specialize in those particular functions which relate to the biological differences between men and women. They argue that because women give birth to children it is 'natural' for them to be the ones who look after them and also to apply the same 'caring skills' to look after husband and home. Parsons saw women's role in the family as 'expressive', i.e. concerned with nurturing, whereas men's role was 'instrumental', i.e. concerned with providing for wife and children. Although he did recognize that not all women would be happy to be confined to this role, he argued that this type of specialization made sense. The roles were complementary and in no way unequal because each was mutually dependent on the other.

Functionalist theories are sometimes called 'march-of-progress' theories because they imply that, as societies develop, they get 'ever better'. In this example, families would become more egalitarian, taking joint responsibility for family decisions and spending their leisure time in shared activity.

Willmott and Young, in their studies of the East End of London, also argued that, as families moved away from their relatives, the roles and relationships between men and women would become more equal.

Elizabeth Bott and conjugal roles

Elizabeth Bott, in her research *Family and Social Network* in 1957, argued that there were two types of **conjugal roles** – **segregated** and **joint**.

Segregated conjugal roles existed where husband and wife led relatively separate lives, as in those families described by Willmott and Young. Segregated roles, both inside and outside the home, were strictly demarcated, so that men were breadwinners but not shoppers, or would repair the pram but not push it.

Joint roles, on the other hand, existed when husbands and wives spent more time together, sharing some tasks, interests and decisions. In her small-scale study of twenty families in London, she found that joint conjugal roles were more common among middle-class families, who had moved away from their families of origin and so had to rely more upon each other for support. This tied in conveniently with march-of-progress theories, which saw greater equality between spouses emerging as the nuclear family became the norm.

In *The Symmetrical Family* in 1974 Willmott and Young developed their earlier work to provide a theory to explain changing relationships within the family. They carried out research using a sample of 1928 people living in the Greater London area, and argued that the segregated roles of the extended family had all but disappeared. A new type of family was emerging, which was home-centred, self-contained and in which the husband and wife made equal contributions, rather than 'the family' being seen as the wife's sphere.

However, they did not see men's and women's roles as interchangeable – they believed, like Parsons, that it was possible to have equality between husbands and wives at the same time as a gender-based division of labour. They saw the family as a 'haven' in which men could recover from boring and alienating work in factories and find personal satisfaction in their non-work lives.

They went on to suggest that this type of family pattern could change. They predicted changes in technology which would take over dirty, physically demanding work so that more work would assume a servicing or supervisory nature, carrying greater responsibility and opportunities for greater satisfaction. In this case, they argued, more men might become 'work-oriented', like those already working in executive positions. They studied a smaller sample of managing directors, finding that their high level of commitment to their work led to a greater degree of specialization between husbands and wives and to **asymmetrical roles**.

asymmetrical roles

This theory was out of touch with the spirit of the times, however. The technological revolution did not noticeably improve the quality of work, but made people redundant and led to a growth of low-paid service jobs, in which it was mostly women who were employed. It also coincided with the re-emergence of feminism.

Feminist criticisms of conjugal role theory

Feminist theory is critical of functionalist perpectives on the family because it has failed to examine what actually happens inside families. Theories about equality between men and women were promoted without any attempt to test the theories empirically. They also failed to take account of the impact of inequality between men and women in other social institutions – in education, at work, in public life or in the distribution of wealth, power and status.

It has only been as a result of feminism that family life and relationships have been subjected to detailed scrutiny and a coherent theoretical perspective. The impact of feminism has shifted 'the sociology of the family' firmly away from earlier functionalist explanations. The assertion that 'the personal is political' means, in essence, that even the most private and personal relationships inside the family cannot be divorced from wider systems of gender inequality, and that these relationships, therefore, carry different degrees of power.

In recent years, the power dimension of family roles and relationships has been examined in terms of:

● the division of labour – who actually does what in the family?
● the distribution of money and other resources between family members;
● the decision-making process;
● violence.

Who does what in terms of housework?

The question of who does the housework has been a focus of discontent for women for a long time, but it was only with the emergence of a feminist analysis in sociology that housework was seen as a proper area of concern for sociologists. Even now it is studied as a part of family sociology rather than the sociology of work.

Since the early 1970s there has been a wealth of research on the topic as well as discussion in the popular media. At times it is said that the 'New Man' has emerged, who shares the household chores equally, or that there are a growing number of 'househusbands' who have done 'role swaps' with their partners. However, the bulk of evidence continues to show that, despite more than thirty years of feminism, women (and sometimes children) do the bulk of the cooking, caring, shopping and washing that goes on in families. Furthermore, it seems that, while more women have taken on 'male' roles of breadwinner, painter/decorator, etc. they still do more housework than men.

In 1994 the consumer research organization Mintel published the findings of a survey of 1500 men and women. It had wanted to study couples who shared equally household tasks such as shopping, cooking and laundry, but was forced to abandon its preferred line of research after finding that only 1 man in 100 did his fair share of the housework. Only 20 per cent of working women said their male partners shared housework and 85 per cent claimed that they almost always did all the laundry, ironing and cooked the main meal.

Does it really matter who does the housework so long as someone does? Feminists would argue that it does. They point out that women frequently spend hours on this work, often in addition to their paid work. It is akin to a **second shift,** so that rather than being 'a haven of peace and relaxation', home, for most women, is a site of continous labour. The hours taken up with housework, and with the more emotionally demanding tasks associated with childcare, serve to disadvantage women in their paid work. Women are seen as only 'partial' workers or as 'unreliable' workers because of these responsibilities. They are more likely to take part-time work or work near home or forgo the kinds of promotion which involve long journeys or relocating the family because of their domestic work. In other words, doing housework contributes to economic inequality between men and women.

In addition, housework and paid work do not have equal status in society, despite the lip service paid to 'the vital work' carried out by wives and mothers. Phrases such as 'Just a housewife' are still recognition of its lowly status in our society. Furthermore, clearing up after other people, who may regard home as a place to relax, reinforces the menial and servicing position which many women occupy in their paid jobs. So housework becomes in many ways symbolic of the inequality in money, status and power which women frequently experience. Of course, this analysis does not carry the same weight for all women – it applies mostly to heterosexual women, who are married or living with a man. But lesbians and single women, especially if they have children, may still be 'judged' (i.e. in court, in custody disputes) by their ability to perform these tasks.

In 1974 Ann Oakley, in *The Sociology of Housework*, took issue with functionalist analysis of the family. She re-examined the anthropological texts used by Murdock, claiming that his conviction that the nuclear family, based on a division of labour between men and women, was inevitable had led to a misinterpretation of the 'evidence' he studied. In her own work she provided an 'alternative reading', in which she claimed that a wide variety of living arrangements existed, in which it was by no means 'always the case' that women 'specialized' in domestic work.

Oakley argued that the role of housewife was 'socially constructed' and emerged during industrialization, driven and accompanied by a powerful ideology of domesticity and femininity. Prior to industrialization women did a wide variety of jobs not associated with the kinds of things commonly linked with women today – they were bookbinders, ship-builders, brewers and farmers. But as early as the sixteenth century women were being squeezed out of profitable areas of work, and this process continued during industrialization. It became the norm among the middle class for women to be seen as fragile, dependent creatures unsuited for the cut and thrust of working life, in need of care and protection from their husbands.

Although this ideology took longer to take hold among the working class, particularly as these were the women who formed the servant class for the middle- and upper-class households, by the turn of the twentieth century it was also becoming more common for working-class women to remain at home on marriage.

In other words, Oakley's analysis challenged the assumption that the division of labour between men and women in the family was biologically based, and showed that there are many cultures in which women performed other roles. Within Britain itself, the housewife role was a relatively new one.

Oakley was particularly critical of Willmott and Young's work on symmetrical families, because she claimed that they did not properly examine the division of labour. They chose to base their claim about 'greater equality' between spouses on one question – about the extent to which husbands helped with housework. The question was:

Do you/does your husband help at least once a week with any household jobs?

As she points out, any man who set the table once a week or ironed his shirt would be included in the 72 per cent who were claimed by Willmott and Young to share the housework.

In her own primary research she interviewed forty married couples with young children and found that in only 15 per cent of cases did husbands have a high level of participation in housework. In only 25 per cent of cases did they share childcare. She also found that many women regarded housework and childcare as 'their responsibility' and thought it 'unmanly' if a man undertook these activities. She comments:

as long as the blame is laid on a woman's head for an empty larder or a dirty house it is not meaningful to talk about marriage as a 'joint' or 'equal' partnership. The same holds true of parenthood. So long as mothers and not fathers are judged by their children's appearance and behaviour ... symmetry remains a myth.

*Heidi Hartmann and
the double shift*

In 1981 **Heidi Hartmann** summarized much of the research on housework carried out in the USA. She found that housewives averaged between fifty and sixty hours of housework per week, rising to seventy hours in households with small children. When women worked outside the home, their hours on housework dropped, but their overall working hours increased because they were then doing a **double shift**, one at paid work and one in the home.

The re-entry of women into the paid labour market appears not to be matched by men's increasing participation in the home. Men on average do eleven hours per week, including gardening and car maintenance. In households with young children men do more childcare, increasing this to fifteen hours, but reducing the time spent doing other domestic work.

Research has been carried out which looks at families where husbands and wives have jobs of equal status to see whether, in a situation of greater financial equality, men do more housework. But it does not seem to be the case. Elsdon, in a study of male and female doctors, found that shopping, cooking and looking after sick children were still seen as a woman's responsibility.

dual-career families

Husband and wife team Rapoport and Rapoport looked at **dual-career families**, and found that men tolerated their wives working so long as they still took prime responsibility for housework and childcare. In these situations 'help' is more likely to be paid for, but the responsibility for engaging and dealing with nannies and cleaners usually rests with the woman.

Mary Boulton

Mary Boulton pointed out that asking respondents who does certain tasks, does not always reveal who takes ultimate responsibility. In her sample, less than 20 per cent of men played a major role in childcare.

Alan Warde

In 1988 **Alan Warde** carried out research in north-west England, questioning 250 families. He asked 'who usually' did 'certain tasks' and then 'who last did' a particular task. His first question revealed that, while women did more routine household and childcare tasks, there was a belief that tasks were shared. However, the second question revealed a much more rigid division of tasks. The question of 'who last cleaned the toilet' decisively revealed that 'women do more of that sort of thing'. It was the most firmly gendered task of all. When asked 'how fair' they thought this division of labour was, only one woman thought she did less than her fair share of housework, compared with 42 per cent of men. This suggests that men, as well as women, pay some lip service to the ideal of equality, but that their behaviour has not changed accordingly.

Angela Hughes, the research manager of the 1994 project 'Woman 2000' carried out by Mintel, commented:

> men seem to set out with good intentions to share the domestic chores, but the catalyst appears to be the arrival of children. At this stage the man appears to abdicate responsibility for his share, regardless of whether his partner is working.

Marxist feminists have emphasized, in the discussion about housework, the extent to which housework is a form of production which, like industrial production, benefits the ruling class. They have used Marxist analysis to show how both capitalism and patriarchy are supported and sustained by the unpaid domestic labour of women.

While there are some significant differences between domestic labour and wage labour – domestic labour is unpaid, it implies no clear demarcation between work and non-work activities and is not included in the calculation of Gross Domestic Product (GDP) as making an economic contribution to a society's economy – it does nevertheless have a real value to capitalism. The work of maintaining the workforce would have to be paid for by employing outside agencies if wives and mothers did not provide these services for free. Insurance companies have rejected policy schemes to insure housewives which would pay for their services if they were unable to perform them through illness or injury, because the high cost of providing for the collective labour of a cook, childminder, cleaner, driver and housekeeper would price such policies out of the market.

James and Dalla Costa

Some Marxist feminists, like **Selma James** and **Maria Dalla Costa** in *The Power of Women and the Subversion of the Community*, have argued that housework is productive labour because it produces labour power in the form of workers. Women are therefore doubly exploited by capitalism, as they are the 'slaves of wage slaves'. They make out a case for 'wages for housework', and for domestic labour to be seen as a proper part of the economic system.

Christine Delphy and Diana Leonard in *Familiar Exploitation* employ a radical feminist analysis but a Marxist methodology. They analyse the family as part of the economic system in which women's exploitation serves to support the patriarchal order. They see the work done by women in the family – housework, emotional and sexual labour – as supporting men's economic and political supremacy over women. They say:

> Our focus is, therefore, the practical, emotional, sexual, procreative and symbolic work done by women for men within family relationships. This includes housework, work on men's occupations, emotional servicing of family members, childcare, the care of sick and frail family members, sexual servicing of husbands and the bearing of children.

Delphy and Leonard argue that just as capitalism, according to Marxism, steals the labour of the proletariat, within the family men appropriate the labour of women. They claim that this applies not just in relationships between husbands and wives but that all women – daughters, cohabitees, single women and lesbians – are affected by the economic relations within the family, and that the inequalities within paid work and public life which affect all women have their origin within the economic exploitation of women by men within the family. They go further than the dual-system approach adopted by Heidi Hartmann or Sylvia Walby discussed in Chapter 7 because they believe that it is patriarchy which benefits primarily from the economic exploitation of women.

The distribution of money and other resources

According to George Bernard Shaw:

> The truth is that family life will never be decent, much less ennobling, until this central horror of the dependence of women on men is done away with.

Early work on the family, and much of our social policy, has assumed that women are, and should be, financially dependent on men. The functionalist perspective assumes that, although men are 'breadwinners', their earnings are shared out equally, taking full account of the work that women do within the family.

It is interesting that there is much less research on this aspect of family life than there is on housework, and that the **division of resources** remains a relatively unexplored and private area of family life.

There is historical evidence to suggest that women in poor families were less well nourished than men or children and therefore prone to nutrition related diseases, such as tuberculosis. Even today it is predominantly women who carry the burden of poverty in the struggle to make ends meet. Mothers of young children are likely to be among the most economically dependent groups in society. Less than 10 per cent of all women with pre-school children are in paid employment, although this figure is higher among Afro-Caribbean women, who are less likely to experience financial dependency on a man.

Many women are either dependent upon a partner or upon the state. In some ways, women who are dependent upon state benefits are 'better off'. The money, although insubstantial, is always there, and if they are living alone, or with children, they are free to manage it in the way they see fit, whereas when women live with a man, the control lies elsewhere. In theory, two-parent families are 'better off' than one-parent families, but this may disguise the fact that resources are not usually equally distributed between partners. Research indicates a variety of ways in which resources are divided within families and, most importantly, who retains control of these resources. The management of money and the 'stretching of wages' to cover all the household bills most frequently falls to women.

1994 Woman 2000

The **1994** Mintel study '**Woman 2000**' found that eight out of ten women say they share big financial decisions equally, but only four out of ten have their own bank accounts.

Hilary Graham

The most common system of resource division, according to Hilary Graham, is one in which the control and the management of resources is split. An allowance is given to the woman for 'housekeeping' and the man retains the rest of the wage. In her study mothers described a system in which expenses to 'outside bodies', such as housing departments, electricity and water boards, were met first, with remaining income being used to meet the expenses of food, clothes, transport, etc. In such a system women sometimes do not know what their husbands earn and have no personal money to spend on themselves. It also means that the major responsibility for managing family debt falls on women – leading to increased levels of stress.

Research by the Child Poverty Action Group shows that men who are high earners are just as likely not to tell their wives exactly what they earn as other men. One woman interviewed by Hilary Graham said:

> I haven't the faintest idea what he earns. I really haven't. He's a managing director and if he pays the bills I don't ask, I've no need to. He gives it to me monthly … but I need my child benefit weekly. I wouldn't be able to budget otherwise.

Another said:

> His hobby is fishing and do-it-yourself things and he'll just go out and buy the tools and I think, 'Oh, that money, what I could have bought for that money.' So I will budget and go around the markets and that, and find the best buys, and he'll just go to the best shops because it is convenient, so yes, we do disagree about money.

myth of 'joint money'

Lee Comer, in *Wedlocked Women* argued that the notion of '**joint money**' is often a **myth** – women don't feel they can spend money on things other than the children or the house, whereas men are used to 'putting something in their pocket' to spend at the pub or on their hobby.

Vogler and Pahl

Vogler and Pahl in 1993 examined the different methods of budgeting in families, and related these to the level of partners' satisfaction within the marriage. The highest level of dissatisfaction with marriage, especially on the part of wives, occurred in marriages where men controlled all the finances. As Pahl points out:

> We cannot be certain whether 'husband control' leads to unhappiness or whether marital discord provokes the husband into taking control of finances. However, there was a very significant association between male control of money and marital unhappiness, which applied to both men and women.

It is being increasingly recognized that, within 'a marriage', there are sometimes 'two different marriages', in which women have less access to money, transport, space and time than men. The lack of control which married women sometimes experience reinforces their inequality.

Duncan Thomas

International evidence suggests that paid work and an independent income are important not only for the well-being of women but also for their children. If a woman works, she is likely to have a greater say in how her earnings are spent. The evidence suggests that more income in the hands of women means a larger share of the family budget will be spent on food, health and education. **Duncan Thomas** from the University of California, in his study of families in the USA, Brazil and Ghana, found that more income in the hands of women led to better educated and healthier children, whether the family was rich or poor. Children's weight in Brazil was eight times greater if extra income was controlled by women. In addition, while fathers tend to direct their money towards their sons, more money in mothers' hands has a greater impact on the health and education of their daughters.

Decision making

Perhaps the degree of equality in the family is best judged not so much by the division of labour or resources, but by the capacity of each partner to determine the course of their shared life. Control of money also involves making decisions about how to spend it, or whether to save. In Pahl and Vogler's study one man justified his role in decision making like this:

> Because the biblical principle is that the man is the head of the home and it relieves my wife from these emotional pressures, I would take the strain off those things and pressures which God didn't intend her to carry.

His wife commented:

> I found it hard initially – thinking that the man's going to do it all, sort of thing. From being single to doing things together. Pete thought it was right for the man to do it, and it worked out all right. But when you've been independent, it seemed a bit hard, sort of thing.

Middle Class Couples

Stephen Edgell, in his study *Middle Class Couples*, asked respondents about who made the decisions and which decisions they saw as being important. His study demonstrated an imbalance of power between husbands and wives. Issues which provided a framework for the family, such as decisions about financial management, moving to another area or buying a house, tended to be taken by the man alone. Women, on the other hand, made decisions about day-to-day things, such as interior decoration, domestic spending and children's clothes. Decisions about children's education and holidays were more likely to be shared. Both spouses tended to justify this as the legitimate use of male power. This power was seen to be derived from the man's economic role of provider. He who earns the money has the right to make important decisions.

The 'Woman 2000' study found that, although more than half the women in their sample had full-time jobs, they were paid on average 29 per cent less than men in comparable jobs. The earning gap between men and women was greatest between the ages of 40 and 49, after the period when mortgages were being paid and children were being educated.

Popular culture suggests that this is a widely unquestioned prerogative. Jokes about 'hen-pecked husbands', 'nagging wives', 'feminine wiles' used to 'get round him' indicate that men's dominance in decision making has been seen as part of the natural order of things.

Jessie Bernard, in *The Future of Marriage* (1982), points out that, in the past at least, the state, the church and the courts all conferred this authority upon men in marriage. Women as well as men were socialized to accept it, so that male power was legitimized as rightful and unquestioned authority.

More research is now needed to see whether the increased employment of women has led to women challenging this authority and playing a greater part in decision making.

Violence

The ultimate exercise of power within the family is the use of violence to exercise control over both women and children. Domestic violence is a mode of behaviour which has had tacit acceptance throughout much of Western history, and rape within marriage was only made an offence in Britain in 1993. Historically, English law has supported the notion that women and children are part of men's property and that men have the right to treat them as they like without outside interference. Concern over the plight of battered women first came to the attention of the public in the early 1970s, when women's groups began campaigning against violence and the National Women's Aid Federation was set up as a self-help organization to coordinate provision of refuges for battered women and their children.

Despite some commentators who have attempted to blame domestic violence on the behaviour of a small number of deranged men or on some alleged 'psychological need' on the part of some women, most research has analysed domestic violence as the ultimate form of control that men exercise over women in a patriarchal society. W. J. Goode, in *Explorations in Social Theory* (1973), described the family as 'a power system' based on force, in which the authority of the male resulted from his greater economic power and prestige outside the family. It was argued that in this context husbands often resort to violence as a way of regaining dominance when they feel their authority is threatened.

The Women's Aid Movement

Jalna Hanmer, in *Women's Aid and the Women's Aid Movement In Britain*, points out the extent to which battering occurs as a consequence of the unequal relationships between men and women, both in the family and in society generally, and which is also expressed in terms of income, access to housing and the degree of protection guaranteed by the law. The more that women are dependent – i.e. those with small children – the more powerless they are and the more likely they are to experience violence at the hands of men.

As Jan Pahl (*A Refuge for Battered Women*) makes clear, 'No reliable evidence is available about the amount of violence within marriage in general'. For reasons of fear, shame and guilt, women often do not report domestic violence. In addition, women have low expectations of police and state assistance. Official figures, therefore, represent only a fraction of the real incidence of domestic violence. Like child abuse, we can only estimate its true extent.

Dobash and Dobash, in their study *Violence Against Wives* (1980), relate wife assault to the cultural expectations about male authority in marriage. They found that it tended to happen when wives had not responded to men's immediate needs, e.g. a hot meal on the table, or when women had questioned men's actions or opinions. They found that an argument between spouses commonly ended when the man decided it should, and if the wife persisted, violence could result. They found that women from all classes were affected, and that it was not the result of action by disturbed individuals but by men who were regarded as 'normal' in all other respects.

It is only relatively recently that this kind of attack has been openly condemned by the courts and the police. The law was strengthened in the 1970s to make provision for **injunctions** and **non-molestation** orders to be issued. However, in recent years courts have proved reluctant to issue such orders if it means removing men from their homes. In practice, it is still most often women and children who are forced to leave, although refuges are woefully inadequate and usually dependent on short-term funding from local authorities.

Whose interests?

Jessie Bernard

Following such an analysis of family life we might wonder whose interests such an institution serves. **Jessie Bernard** drew attention to the different experiences of men and women within the family. She argued that within any marriage there were, in effect, two marriages – the wife's and the husband's – and that the two experiences were very different. She pointed out that men, despite jokes about being 'dragged to the altar', like marriage better than women do, and derive greater benefit from it. Certainly we know that more than 75 per cent of all divorces in Britain are initiated by women which, given the economic hardships often faced by divorced or separated women, is surprising.

She also pointed out that married men live longer and have better mental and physical health than single men, whereas for women the reverse is true. She argued that marriage can actually damage women's health, and that many married women suffer from what she calls 'the housewife syndrome'. Comparing the health of housewives with working and single women, she showed that they are more likely to suffer from nervous breakdowns, headaches, fainting, heart palpitations, panic attacks, depression and other symptoms of psychological distress.

Criticisms of feminist perspectives on family relationships

Rhodes Boyson

In the course of this section we have presented a feminist analysis of gender roles and relationships within the family which is radically different from that put forward by functionalists and from the view which is often expressed in everyday discussions. We are usually persuaded to think about the family as a 'good thing', except in a minority of cases where inadequate or violent parents physically or psychologically harm their offspring. We are generally unused to an analysis which talks about the family as a 'social institution' which can be harmful and exploitative. But, not surprisingly, such an analysis also has its critics.

It is criticized by those holding a New Right political and social perspective. Politicians like **Rhodes Boyson** and Graham Gardiner-Webster have claimed that the family is being undermined by feminists. Others, like the American sociologist Charles Murray, would argue that a feminist critique of the family is wrong, and that society needs strong families with male heads in control. Those who share this perspective see the traditional nuclear family being undermined by 'alternative living arrangements' which do not adequately perform the functions needed for the 'smooth running' of society (see below) or, as feminists would interpret it, the 'smooth running of a patriarchal society' which rests on the unequal treatment of women.

The radical feminist analysis of family relationships has also been criticized by some black writers for presenting a picture of family life which ignores class and ethnic differences. It is arguably a form of racism to present an analysis as if it applies to **all** groups when, in fact, it reflects the experience of only one ethnic group. For example, **Hazel Carby**, in *The Empire Strikes Back*, argues that the history of colonialism and imperialism has affected the structure of many Afro-Caribbean families. These families are much more likely to be headed by women (31 per cent, compared with an average of 15 per cent in other groups) and that women are more likely to be financially independent of men and are not confined to motherhood and domesticity:

Hazel Carby

> The use of the concept of dependency is also a problem for black feminists. It has been argued that this concept provides the link between the 'material organisation of the household and the ideology of femininity'. How can we then account for situations in which black women may be heads of households or where because of an economic situation which structures high black unemployment they are not financially dependent on a black man? ... How can it then be argued that black male domination exists in the same form as white male domination?

Afro-Caribbean women are more likely to work full-time and to rely for help with children not on male partners but on female kin and friends. They are less likely to perceive themselves as dependants and, as a result of high levels of black male unemployment, may be major breadwinners in two-parent families. She argues that, as a result, the family life of black women is less likely to feel exploitative.

Hazel Carby shows how, rather than being a site of struggle between the sexes, the family can provide support and resistance to the racism of the wider society, and this could also apply to the family experiences of other ethnic groups:

> We would not want to deny that the family can be a source of oppression for us but we also wish to examine how the black family has functioned as a prime source of resistance to oppression. We need to recognise that during slavery, periods of colonialism and under the present authoritarian state, the black family has been a site of political and cultural resistance to racism.

Radical feminist analysis, which emphasizes the unpaid nature of domestic labour, has also ignored the fact that in some societies domestic labour has also been a significant source of black women's paid work in the homes of white women.

In recent years, feminist thought has struggled to understand the different experiences of different women, especially when the experience of race, class or sexuality makes a difference, and feminist theories are now much more likely to recognize the significance of diversity – although there is still some way to go. The main concern of feminism still remains to understand (and change) the various ways in which women are unequal to men in society.

As a character in Zora Neale Hurston's novel *Their Eyes were Watching God* explains to her granddaughter:

Honey, de white man is de ruler of everything as fur as Ah been able tuh find out. Maybe it's some place way off in de ocean where de black man is in power, but we don't know nothin' but what we see. So de white man throw down de load and tell de nigger man tuh pick it up. He pick it up because he have to, but he don't tote it. He hand it to his womenfolks. De nigger woman is de mule uh de world so fur as Ah can see.

Parents and children

The debate about family roles and relationships has concentrated on the relationships between men and women, but has paid much less attention to those between parents and children. For example, the domestic labour debate has concentrated on the division of labour between men and women. However, some research suggests that children's contributions also need to be recognized, and that daughters are more frequently expected to carry out household tasks than their brothers.

It took the emergence of a feminist analysis to raise questions about the relative powerlessness of women within the family. The even greater powerlessness of children has only recently been addressed by sociologists.

It is often said that one of the ways in which the modern family differs from the family of the past is that it is 'child-centred'. The fall in infant mortality and in the size of families has meant that more time, attention and money can be lavished on children than in the past.

Changes in the size of the family have been accompanied by an ideology of child-centredness in which families are charged with not only the physical care of young members but also with their intellectual and emotional development. In practice, of course, as we have already seen, the sexual division of labour means that it is mostly women who are expected to prioritize the emotional and physical needs of children, whilst men are expected to provide financially and dispense discipline as necessary.

In the post-war period, the theory of maternal deprivation developed by John Bowlby warned of the dire psychological consequences of separating mother and child, even for a short space of time. In retrospect, we can see this as a part of the push to get women back into the home after the Second World War.

In their paper 'From Disregard to Disrepute: the Position of Women in Family Law', Julia Brophy and Carol Smart chronicle the changing legal relationship between children and parents. Until the early nineteenth century, fathers had supreme rights over children, who were seen as their possessions. Even children's earnings belonged to their fathers. The emphasis was on the **rights** fathers had over children rather than on their **responsibilities.** The **1839 Custody of Infants Act** marked the first legal link between mothers and their children, by allowing women legal custody of a child up to the age of seven in certain cases. This marked the recognition of the 'nurturing' role of women and introduced the concept of an 'unfit' parent as a check on the **absolute** rights of fathers.

Brophy and Smart went on to show how women gradually acquired more 'rights' over children, providing they were 'blameless' women, at the same time as children became excluded from paid labour and became dependent upon their parents. In other words, men had **rights** over children when they were economic assets, while women acquired **responsibilities** for children once they became economic liabilities. This period coincided with the development of the ideology of female domesticity and femininity referred to earlier.

1839 Custody of Infants Act

The twentieth-century provisions of the welfare state, such as the development of the National Health Service, free state education and child benefits, all sought to support the family to improve the upbringing of children.

Since the Second World War the rights and responsibilities of parents and children have been the subject of much legislation, culminating in the **1989 Children Act**, in which the rights of children, and their need for protection and care, were carefully balanced with the rights and responsibilities of parents. In this Act, the law recognized that the welfare of children should take precedence over other considerations, and for the first time authorities were charged with taking account of the wishes of children themselves. In family cases involving custody or care proceedings, for example, children can be independently represented by a **guardian ad litem** so that their interests can be assessed independently of the local authority or their parents.

The 1989 Act sought to provide a relationship in which both parents and the local authority acted in partnership in 'the best interests of the child', rather than in obtaining exclusive custody over him or her.

The background to this legislation was the public concern over cases of child abuse and neglect, and about the insensitivity of some local authorities in their response.

Beatrice Campbell, in her study of the Cleveland child abuse controversy in the 1980s, *Unofficial Secrets*, pointed to the 'moral panic' about child abuse in which the 'villains' were to be seen as 'interfering and authoritarian' social workers and doctors who 'rode roughshod' over the civil rights of the 'victims' – the families of the abused children. She argued that this response helped to obscure the real issue – that children get abused within so-called 'child-centred' families.

The Butler-Schloss Inquiry into **Child Abuse in Cleveland 1987** recommended more collaboration between doctors, nurses, social workers, teachers and the police in all matters of child sexual abuse, and this multi-disciplinary approach was included in the provisions of the 1989 Children Act.

Sociologists have also attempted to provide explanations for the physical and psychological abuse as well as the neglect of children. We could point to the effects of long-term recession, to resulting poverty and poor housing, which make it difficult to maintain the high standards of childcare expected of parents today – except that we know that child abuse does not only occur in economically deprived families. From information and statistics provided by the NSPCC, Childline and Rape Crisis, we know that, like domestic violence, it occurs across the entire social spectrum.

Feminists such as Liz Kelly (*Surviving Sexual Violence*, 1988) argue that child abuse is part of 'a continuum of violence' which includes indecent exposure, verbal abuse, rape and murder. That this abuse, generally perpetrated by men, against those who are seen to be less powerful, is an expression of male supremacy in a patriarchal society. According to figures supplied by the **Zero Tolerance Campaign** against domestic violence generally, one in three girls under the age of 12 and one in two young women under the age of 18 will experience some form of sexual abuse in Britain using Kelly's definition.

Valerie Yule, in her paper 'Why are Parents Tough on Children', argues that there may be an established pattern of behaviour towards children that involves brusqueness and lack of respect in this culture which can lead to abuse. She observed interaction between 85 adult/child pairs, and found that in two-fifths of cases the interactions were negative and the adults took little notice of the children. Although it is impossible to draw conclusions from such small-scale research, she seems to be suggesting that generally, despite the rhetoric of 'child-centredness', children have a low status in Western society.

On the other hand, Westwood and Bhachu claim that in the Asian family: 'Children are welcome and highly valued, and relations between parents and children are warm and physically close' – a comment which might equally apply to other cultures.

Family diversity

This important debate took off in the 1980s, but relates back to earlier discussions about what constitutes a family. We have already seen that family structure varied in the past, despite the rather rigid views of functionalists about extended and nuclear families. We are now going to consider the extent to which the so-called nuclear family, consisting of a married, heterosexual couple with dependent children, based on a sexual division of labour in which the man is the principal breadwinner and the woman the principal carer, can really be said to be the contemporary 'norm'.

General Household Survey 1993

According to the **General Household Survey 1993**, the most common domestic arrangement is not the one described above, but a couple without children. Twenty-eight per cent of households consist of a married couple without children, whereas 24 per cent consist of married parents and dependent children. In addition:

- One couple out of every five living together is not married.
- One family in seven is headed by a lone parent.
- One family in twelve includes step-children.
- Ninety per cent of lone-parent families are headed by women.
- Sixty per cent of women work outside the home.
- Thirty-one per cent of Afro-Caribbean families are headed by a lone parent, compared with 15 per cent of white and 5 per cent of Asian families.
- Forty per cent of Hindus and Sikhs aged 16–25 born in Britain would accept an arranged marriage.

Statistics like these suggest that there is much greater organizational diversity in families than is usually claimed, or preferred by governments, and this is further increased by differing ethnic, regional and social class patterns.

Lone parent families

In the mid-1990s this debate escalated, because of government concern about 'the demise of the traditional family' based on marriage, and the increase in lone parenting, divorce and common-law arrangements.

In the USA Charles Murray, a New Right sociologist (see above), expressed concern that 48 per cent of live births to black women occurred outside marriage. This led some sociologists to argue that the 'mother-headed' family was an adaptation on the part of people denied marriage during times of slavery and denied decent jobs more recently. In these circumstances, it was claimed, marriage was not regarded as an important basis for family life. Yanina Sheeran (see above) argues that, rather than seeing this pattern as an 'aberrant type', it should be viewed as the **real basic family core** consisting of female carer and dependent children.

Whatever the definition and explanation, the increase in lone-parent families in Britain to 1.3 million in 1991, of which 1 million relied on income support, has been taken by some to indicate:

- a deterioration of 'family values' within society;
- a contributory factor in lawlessness among the young;
- a massive financial drain on the state.

In Britain a leaked cabinet document in November 1993 revealed plans on the part of the Conservative Government to curb the growing number of lone parents. The paper revealed a plan by Social Security Secretary, Peter Lilley, to:

- curb 'incentives' to become lone parents;
- encourage lone parents to support themselves through work and child maintenance from absent fathers;
- increase the responsibility of a young lone parent's own parents to provide support.

This last point suggests a return to the extended family and would be accompanied by a withdrawal of benefit to young women while allowing maternal grandparents to claim additional benefit for their daughter and grandchild if necessary. Although the parents of the child's father might also be required to contribute, the paper acknowledged that this provision would be highly controversial.

Several pages of the report were devoted to the importance of providing additional childcare facilities, but, as the cost was estimated at between £100 million and £200 million, this was not seen as an 'immediate priority'.

Hilary Armstrong, Labour MP, to whom the document was leaked, commented:

> Lone parents do not need more lectures from ministers: what they need is practical support so they can provide a decent upbringing for their children'.

John Redwood

The leak caused a major furore, in which politicians and other pundits joined in the public debate about single parents. The then Welsh Secretary, **John Redwood**, branded single parents 'one of the biggest social problems of our day'.

The chief reason for the increase in lone-parent families was not, as many politicians seemed to suggest, a rise in teenage pregnancies, but an increase in divorce, from 1000 in 1918 to 192 000 in 1992. Even the Royal Family reflected the national trend, with three out of four children divorced or separated. But while single parenthood cuts across class divisions, the consequences are clearly worse for poorer households.

John Patten

There has been much concern expressed about the consequences of all this for the future. **John Patten**, then Minister for Education, argued that the decline in two-parent families would affect the educational future of Britain.

National Child Development Study

Sociologists have become embroiled in arguments about whether or not children from one-parent families do less well in education. As yet the answer is unclear. Mavis Maclean looked at the educational status of children at age 18, drawn from one of the famous 'cohort' studies – the **National Child Development Study** of children born in the first week of March 1946. She found that of those children from two-parent families, 26 per cent were students, compared with only 10 per cent of children from divorced parents and 20 per cent of children whose parent had died.

Elsa Ferri

Elsa Ferri recently undertook one of the most detailed pieces of research on the subject, using 1958 cohort material and a large sample of 17 000 people. She compared scores in English, Maths and 'emotional adjustment', as judged by teachers. Like Maclean, she found that children from lone-parent families fared less well. But she went on to explain:

> Simply to compare test results doesn't make any sense because there were also economic differences between the families. We found out that when we took these other factors into account the difference between lone and two-parent families was reduced dramatically.

Her results showed that when the **financial background** of lone-parent and two-parent families were the same, the children performed equally well. It would seem that academic performance is more related to poverty, but then, as most single parents are poor, any moves by government to remove financial support, in some kind of punitive attempt to dissuade women from becoming lone parents, would only make matters worse.

Reconstituted families

Another impact of divorce has been the formation of what have come to be known as **reconstituted families** – those formed by divorced adults remarrying new partners, together with their respective children. In 1991 8 per cent of families with dependent children contained one or more step-children.

The majority of reconstituted or step-families, 86 per cent in fact, consist of a couple with at least one child from the wife's previous relationship, together with other dependent children. Six per cent of reconstituted families consist of at least one child from the husband's previous relationship, together with other dependent children. In 6 per cent of cases, both partners bring children from previous relationships.

Other research making use of the 1958 National Child Development material compared the experiences of children who became part of a reconstituted family, and found that children did **not** fare any better than those in lone-parent families. Malcolm Wicks, Director of the Family Policy Studies Centre, says:

> Those who have been eager to proclaim the supposed inferiority of the lone parent family should ponder the evidence on step families, before again declaring that two parents in the family are necessarily better than one'

1991 General Household Survey

The research showed that girls were more likely to become 'unmarried mothers' and boys more likely to get poor school results. However, these results could also be related to financial hardship, as the **1991 General Household Survey** showed. A quarter of step-families were living on less than £200 per week, compared with 15 per cent of other families.

Cohabitation

British Panel Survey

In Britain marriage rates among men have fallen by almost a third and among women by almost a quarter, although more couples now cohabit. The annual **British Panel Survey**, based on interviews with 9000 people in 5000 households, and published by the Economic and Social Research Council (ESRC) in 1994, revealed that over half of all 25-year-olds in Britain had cohabited with a partner, compared with 1 or 2 per cent 25 years earlier.

Kieran & Estaught

The increase in cohabitation and child-bearing outside marriage has been studied by **Kathleen Kieran and Valerie Estaught**. They found that:

- Cohabitants tend to be young – seven out of ten are under 35.
- Two out of three have never been married.
- By 1989 26 per cent of single people were cohabiting compared with 3 per cent in 1979.
- By 1991 the number of births outside marriage was 30 per cent.
- The period of cohabitation tends to be short-lived. A third of couples had been together for less than a year, while 16 per cent had been together for longer than five years.
- Those who decided to get married had higher rates of divorce than other couples generally.

Cohabitation is even more popular in Northern European countries such as Sweden, Denmark, Norway and Finland. In Sweden 50 per cent of children are born outside marriage. However, even in Sweden, 75 per cent of women in their thirties, living with partners, are married, which seems to suggest that cohabitation is more common in the twenties, but does not necessarily indicate a widespread rejection of marriage in the long term.

Lesbian and gay families

We don't know how many **lesbian** and **gay families** there are. Information is difficult to collect because of the widespread discrimination against such families. In most lesbian families the children come with their mothers from previous heterosexual relationships, although some are born as a result of self-insemination. Courts are still reluctant to grant custody or adoption and fostering orders to gay families.

In *Learning the Hard Way* by the Taking Liberties Collective, one lesbian mother writes:

> In divorce most women are granted custody of their children because, consistent with popular ideology, there is a 'natural' bond between a mother and her children, stemming from some 'innate maternal instinct' that makes her automatically the best carer. Except when she's a lesbian. Then it seems the 'natural' bond between a mother and her children becomes 'a problem' and has to be severed, because, consistent with popular ideology, a lesbian mother is judged to be an 'unnatural' one.

A lesbian mother quoted in *Social Issues for Carers* by Webb and Tosell explains what happened to her:

> Losing custody of my child was the most devastating experience of my life so far. The welfare officer who made the report on us for the court told me that my daughter was one of the sanest children he had ever met – which he said must be to do with the way I had brought her up – yet he still recommended that she would be better off in a 'normal' family.

Courts still frequently remove children on the basis of unproven fears about inappropriate gender role socialization and fears about 'moral danger'. We know of no research that supports either of these claims. Evidence about child abuse suggests that it is generally carried out by men in heterosexual nuclear families.

Ethnic diversity and
family structure

As a result largely of immigration there is now considerable ethnic diversity in Britain which has made its own contribution to the variety of family types. We have already seen that the percentage of 'mother-headed' families is higher among Afro-Caribbean households, and Jocelyn Barrow has described how 'traditional support' from relatives has been replaced by 'informal help' from neighbours and from 'community self-help' play-schemes.

Sallie Westwood and Parminder Bhachu (*Enterprising Women: Ethnicity, Economy and Gender Relations*) warn against selective and stereotypical beliefs about 'the Asian family'. They point out that the term covers a variety of diverse cultures, and is often used pejoratively as shorthand to signify an authoritarian, extended and 'abnormal' family type. They point out that generally Muslim, Pakistani and Bangladeshi households are larger than white households (4.6 compared to 2.3) because more households contain children, not because they are extended. The pattern of migration has meant that because it was young people who emigrated to Britain, the Muslim, Pakistani and Bangladeshi population consists of more families with children and fewer single-person households than among the indigenous 'white' population. Extended families are more common among Sikhs and East African Asians, though usually this means living in adjoining houses.

Roger Ballard, studying South Asian families in Britain, describes a **stem-family system**, organized around father and sons and their wives, in which there are strong family ties with a greater degree of parental control over children, despite modifications in the process of adaptation to life in Britain.

Robin Oakley studied Cypriot families, describing strong ties with the extended family, in which children played a less central role during childhood.

Colin Francome, in his survey among young Hindus and Sikhs, shows how Asian family patterns shift and change in the adaptation to life in Britain.

A 34-year-old Hindu woman, quoted in the *Guardian* of 25 June 1994, explains that, although she chose her own marriage partner, she has not rejected the traditional family patterns of her background:

> I was introduced to quite a few boys, because my mum would have loved me to have an arranged marriage. I didn't like any of them, and couldn't bring myself to do what she did. Even though I was brought up with many Asian values, I still wanted to have a career and be an individual. .... Just because I've married the man of my choice doesn't mean I am rejecting Asian culture. It has some very positive sides to it, and I want to maintain them and pass them on to my children.

However, her mother fears that these changes may lead to the destruction of the extended family:

> Young Asians are rejecting the extended family. Girls who have been born here and studied here don't want to live with their in-laws, and that's leading to a lot of loneliness and misery for my generation.

This highlights how family patterns change as social circumstances change.

The debate within sociology is really about whether or not these diverse family forms mean that the traditional nuclear family is no longer the norm.

Robert Chester argues that changes in the family have been over-estimated, and that, when the whole family lifecycle is examined, most people spend some time in a typical nuclear family:

> Most adults still marry and have children. Most children are reared by their natural parents. Most people live in a household headed by a married couple. Most marriages continue until parted by death.

neo-conventional families

He argues that the only really significant change from the nuclear family described by functionalists is that most women now work outside the home. He therefore argues that most people live in what he calls the **neo-conventional family**.

To a certain extent his argument rests on the difference between the percentage of different types of households and the number of people living in those households. For example, while only 24 per cent of all households consisted of a married couple with dependent children in 1992, 39.9 per cent of people lived in this type of household. This discrepancy is partly because of the increase in single-person households. Twenty-seven per cent of all households in England consist of one person, but they represent only 11.1 per cent of the population.

If we compare figures since 1961, we see that the percentage of people living in the 'typical' nuclear family has declined from 52.2 per cent in 1961 to 39.9 per cent in 1992. For the same period, the percentage of people in lone-parent households has increased from 2.5 per cent to 10.1 per cent.

It would seem, from a consideration of family trends in Britain, that there is sufficient diversity of family types to question whether a single family type can claim to be 'the typical family' in the 1990s.

Marriage and divorce

The reasons for divorce

As we have seen, the rise in divorce is the most common reason for the increase in lone-parent families, and is one of the most obvious indicators of family stress. In the past marriages were more likely to be terminated by premature death of a partner. If the marriage did break down, most people had to either continue life together, in what were called 'empty-shell' marriages, or obtain 'legal separations', because the cost of divorce placed it beyond the reach of most families.

Divorce in Britain was actually illegal until 1670, and until the middle of the nineteenth century it was necessary to have a private Act of Parliament passed. Throughout the nineteenth and early twentieth century the grounds for divorce were extended and financial orders for wives and children included. But it was not until 1923 that the grounds for divorce on the basis of simple adultery became equal for men and women. Until that time a man's adultery was insufficient grounds for divorce, revealing the 'double sexual standard' of the times.

Until 1969, the legal principle which informed divorce legislation was the 'fault' principle, in which one partner had to prove that the other was 'at fault' and guilty of one of three matrimonial offences – adultery, desertion or cruelty. Any suggestion of collusion between husband and wife to procure a divorce was enough to prevent the divorce being granted.

The 1969 changes in the legislation came into effect in 1971, and involved the 'no fault' clause, by which partners had to prove that their marriage had 'irretrievably broken down'. A divorce could then be granted after two years if both partners consented, or after five years if one party objected.

Although, when it was introduced, it was heralded as the 'Casanova's Charter' it did help to remove a lot of the shame and misery of divorce. The result, however, has been a rapid rise in divorce. In 1989 the OPCS estimated that 37 per cent of all new marriages are likely to end in divorce. The rate per 1000 marriages has increased from 2.1 in 1961 to 13 in 1990.

The improved social position of women, and their increased but unfulfilled expectations of marriage, have also contributed to this rise. In 1987, 60 per cent of married women were in employment, and this growing economic independence of women has made it somewhat easier for them to leave unsatisfactory marriages. Sociologist **Stevie Jackson** argues:

Stevie Jackson

> Women are generally more dissatisfied with marriage than men, although women seem prepared to put up with quite a lot. ... But most express discontent over the quality of their emotional relationship. Women can be on the verge of divorce, having counselling, and their husbands ask, 'What's the problem?' ... Men find it difficult to establish the closeness that wives want.

In the heated discussions about the increase in lone-parent families, these fundamental problems facing the institution of marriage and the organization of family life have rarely been heard. Instead, the Lord Chancellor produced proposals in 1993 to make divorce more difficult to obtain for couples with children, perhaps to include a compulsory 'cooling-off period' during which the couple must attend a conciliation service. The report requests ministers to explore ways of 'making marriage more attractive', according to a report in the *Independent* on 10 November 1993. These are thought to include tax incentives to married couples to induce more people to marry and, once married, to remain so.

Also anxious to be seen as 'the party of the family', the then Shadow Secretary for Social Services, David Blunkett, maintained that the Labour Party wanted 'more support for traditional two-parent families' through housing allocation policies and family planning, education and advice services. The then Leader of the Labour Party, the late **John Smith** said:

John Smith

> We can best strengthen family values by attacking unemployment, building new homes, and providing better health and education services. Instead of scapegoating single mothers the Government should offer training and childcare. Responsible individuals and families must be supported by a caring and opportunity-creating society.

The consequences of divorce

Undoubtedly, for some families divorce is very beneficial. Children can be protected from rowing parents and sometimes from the fear of abuse. Although 'hard-up', some women prefer being in charge of their own finances and making their own decisions. But at the level of society concern is expressed about:

● the financial costs of divorce
● the effects on children.

The financial arrangements on divorce vary, but courts apportion assets according to the means of each partner and their needs, taking particular account of the needs of children. Increasingly, women do not claim maintenance for themselves, but those who do could find their behaviour being taken into account by the courts. Blameless wives are more likely to be awarded maintenance. Although in theory either spouse could be required to provide maintenance for children, in practice it is more likely to be fathers. This reflects the prevailing ideology about family roles. Children are most likely to live with mothers, whose earning capacity is generally less than that of their ex-husbands.

Child Support Agency

In the past it was very easy for men to avoid paying maintenance. Politicians, concerned about the high cost of benefits paid to divorced women and children, instituted the **Child Support Agency** in April 1993. The Agency uses a formula to calculate how much the absent parent should pay, taking account of income and expenses. It has achieved some notoriety in the mid-1990s for demanding large contributions from prosperous fathers deemed to be making too small a contribution to their children's upkeep, rather than pursuing the 'feckless and irresponsible' absent fathers who pay no maintenance at all. Considerable political pressure from influential groups such as Families Need Fathers, the Network Against the Child Support Act, the Campaign Against Parental Exploitation and Strike Back began to organize. They were given considerable media attention and as a result the Child Support Agency was presented as being 'under attack', in ways which forced the government to make changes.

Ros Hepplewhite

In September 1994 the Chief Executive of the CSA, **Ros Hepplewhite**, resigned with a meagre, in the circumstances, £25,000 pay-off. In many ways she was the scapegoat for legislation which was unacceptable to the interests of better-off men.

Modifications were quickly introduced, and the Agency was charged with the pursuit of more than 1 million absent parents whose ex-spouses were dependent on state benefits. Performance targets for 1994–95 were set at £460 million Social Security savings. The recovery of these payments would make no difference to lone parents, however, as they were to be deducted at source from any state benefits received.

Critics of the policy argue that what lone parents need is help with childcare costs and retraining facilities to enable them to get work, rather than to continue to be regarded as the dependants of ex-spouses.

The evidence about the effects of divorce on children is more difficult to unravel. We have already seen that research about educational attainments of children brought up in lone-parent families is contradictory, but seems to suggest that it is the poverty faced by many divorced families which creates most problems.

Research specifically on the effects of divorce on children has been carried out by Wallerstein and Kelly (1980). They studied the children of sixty divorcing couples, initially at the time of the divorce, then eighteen months later and then again after five years. Almost all of the 131 children experienced intense emotional disturbances at the time of the divorce, but at the end of five years two-thirds were coping well. The other one-third were dissatisfied and upset but, as the researchers point out, we have no way of knowing what their emotional state would have been if their parents had stayed together.

The conventional wisdom that divorce is better than constant rowing has been challenged by one study. Dr John Tripp interviewed 152 children aged 9–14 and their families, half of them from families which finally split up. Those from divorced families were more likely to suffer low self-esteem, difficulties with friends or school and a range of psychosomatic health problems. 'On average, poorer outcomes were reported by children whose parents had divorced than by those whose parents had remained married to each other.'

At a societal level sociologists are interested in whether high levels of divorce indicate a general breakdown in the family as a social institution.

In the 1990s the divorce rate is 13 per 1000 of the married population. In 1990 36 per cent of all marriages in that year were remarriages, but the statistics show that one in four divorces now involve a partner who has already been divorced. There is considerable ethnic variation in divorce statistics, with much lower rates of divorce among Indian, Pakistani and Chinese couples than among 'whites', but higher rates among African, West Indian and Bangladeshi couples.

Britain's divorce rate is the second highest in Europe, but so is its marriage rate. Generally, though, marriage rates have fallen between a quarter and a third and cohabitation, especially among the young and divorced people, has increased.

The average number of children per family has gone down to 1.8, and women, despite all the scaremongering about 'teenage pregnancies', are delaying child-bearing. The average age for a woman to have her first child has gone up from 24 in 1971 to 27.5 in 1991. About a third of all children are born outside marriage.

The number of single-person households has increased. The greater independence of women is shown by the fact that only one unmarried woman in four is living with a man.

Whatever sense we make of these statistics, it is clear that family life is changing. These changes impact on social policy – on the need for housing and for different types of housing; for community care provisions; for child care; for tax, pensions and benefits legislation.

It remains to be seen whether future governments will introduce laws to encourage a return to the traditional nuclear family norm, or whether they will respond to the challenge to accept the diversity of contemporary family life in all its myriad forms.

6   Education

The issues

For most people, education is what happens in schools and colleges and all other easily identifiable institutions which are part and parcel of the education system. So far as sociologists are concerned, most of their attention has been focused on schooling and related issues, as the only part of the education process which is both universal and compulsory. But education is also about the transmission of ideas and values and about the reproduction of certain kinds of social relationships between adult learners in society.

The concerns of those studying the sociology of education have changed over the years, and a variety of different perspectives have been employed to study the processes and practices of what counts as education.

Until the 1950s the education system was seen mainly as an instrument of socialization – taking over from where the family had begun – to induct and train new recruits into society. The role of education was seen to be closely related to the promotion and maintenance of social order and control.

In the late 1950s came surveys and statistical studies concerned with the ways in which educational achievement was related to occupational selection and social mobility.

In the 1950s and 1960s the issue of access to educational opportunities and arguments about equality were paramount – especially in relation to social class. Discussion focused on why working-class children did less well in schools than middle-class children of similar measured abilities. Although sociological studies in this period revealed the persistence of class inequalities in educational opportunities and achievement, it was felt that reforms in the education system could remove most of the worst excesses of inequality. Policy decisions to abolish streaming, introduce comprehensive schools and provide compensatory education were all measures which, it was assumed, would help to create a more equal society and reduce the waste of human potential identified by studies of underachievement.

In the 1970s equality was still an important issue, but by then questions of gender and race were added to the equation, revealing the extent to which girls, and black children generally, were seriously disadvantaged in the schooling system. Increasingly, sociologists relied less on huge statistical surveys to prove the point and turned more to matters of classroom interaction and curriculum organization to uncover the ways in which schools delivered different kinds of experiences to different kinds of pupils. Studies became increasingly radical, for example Michael Young's work on the curriculum and Bowles' and Gintis's study of the relationship between schooling and capitalism which suggested that the main purpose and practice of schooling was to reproduce the social relationships of capitalist production.

In the 1980s and 1990s the education debate was greatly influenced by the return to power of successive Conservative Governments and the emergence of the New Right. This development has been described as new vocationalism, and is associated with the reintroduction of arguments about increased parental choice, competition and standards in education, the introduction of the national curriculum and a renewed emphasis on training and links with industry.

Key perspectives and debates

There are several perspectives operating in the study of education over this period.

1 Until the 1950s discussions were dominated by the ideas of functionalist sociology, especially the legacy of Durkheim. It was Durkheim who saw education as a means of preserving social order. Mannheim took a related view, describing education as a way of ensuring social harmony and resolving social problems.
Functionalists believe that:

- the education system does what it claims to do – i.e. it selects people according to their abilities and qualifies them accordingly;
- there is a rough correspondence between intelligence and achievement;
- education is the device which ensures that the most able people get the most responsible and best paid work.

2 Marxists agree with functionalists that education operates to socialize individuals and groups into the requirements and demands of society. But because, in our society, this means capitalism, and because Marxists are opposed to capitalism, they are immensely critical of the ways in which young people are schooled into conforming to the requirements of a capitalist society. Bowles and Gintis, for example, argue that schools are not meant to maximize potential but to produce uncritical, passive, docile workers who accept their lot in life.
Braverman argues that, rather than teaching children specific vocational skills, the hidden purpose of education is to prepare children for the tedium of work. The education system is less important than the economic system, according to him. As a result of deskilling, most occupations don't need much skill and can be learned 'on the job'. The real purpose of schools in a capitalist economy is to socialize and child-mind while parents are at work.
Marxists regard debates about equality as being dependent upon gross inequalities in the class system – which they see schools operating to reproduce in both economic and cultural ways. They argue that anything other than superficial changes in the education system need a fundamental realignment of power in the wider structures of society, especially economic relations.
Marxists believe that:

- education contributes to the continuation of the class system and class inequality;
- education reproduces a labour force which is socialized to accept its lot in life, which accepts its 'failure' and the 'success' of the middle class as legitimate;
- a small minority of the working class is allowed to 'make it' – in order to reinforce the impression that the system is fair.

3 Liberal (reformist) ideas are based on the notion of individuality, and the assumption that every individual should be encouraged and enabled to fulfil his or her personal potential. Central to these arguments is the opportunity to achieve equality and the optimism that reforms in the system can go a long way to achieving this aim.

Liberal critics of the education system are critical of the emphasis placed upon academic achievement and examination success as a priority, preferring a view of human potential which embraces emotional, creative and social considerations.

4 The social democratic perspective in the sociology of education can be identified with commentators like A. H. Halsey and J. W. B. Douglas, and is enshrined in policy documents like the Plowden Report on primary education. The notion that policy changes such as the abolition of streaming, the 11-plus and the tripartite sytem could be used to engineer greater equality in society was very influential in the 1960s and early 1970s. The introduction of comprehensive education by successive Labour Governments, and the identification of **educational deprivation** as a condition that could be cured by **compensatory education**, owed much to the sociological studies of educational attainment and social class carried out in the 1950s and 1960s.

5 With the return to power of the Conservatives in 1979 came monetarist or free market economics and the philosophic and political ascendancy of the New Right. The New Right approach to education is to emphasize freedom of choice in education and forcing schools to compete with each other to win the allegiance of parents and pupils. Increased competition, it is assumed, will improve standards. The local management of schools, in which the educational and financial control of schools is given over to school governing bodies, together with the inducement to individual schools to 'opt out' of local education authority control, are seen as policies which will increase consumer choice and efficiency.

The other main focus of New Right thinking in relation to education is the stress placed on industry and the needs of the economy. This is reflected in the encouragement given to local employers to get involved in school governing bodies and in the emphasis placed on training and vocational objectives in the school curriculum.

6 While Marxist, Liberal, Social Democratic and New Right perspectives in education have their roots in political ideas and political policy making, the other familiar perspective in the sociology of education is less obviously political. Small-scale studies of individual schools and class-rooms have been undertaken employing an **interactionist** perspective and using **ethnographic** methods in order to examine the nature of classroom relationships.

These studies have helped to highlight the ways in which classroom interaction is affected by external social factors such as social class, race and gender, and how these interactions in turn serve to influence the actors experience outside school. They have contributed to our understanding of the reasons why working class children get working-class jobs, for example, and how girls are silenced by boys in mixed-sex classrooms.

For example:

1 Hargreaves (*Social Relations in a Secondary School, 1968*) relied on participant observation, and looked at the ways in which 'academic and delinquescent school sub-cultures' were related to the systems of streaming and labelling used in schools.

2 Lacey (*Hightown Grammar 1971*) made a study of the effects of streaming in a grammar school.
3 Ball (*Beachside Comprehensive*) showed how banding contributed to pro- and anti-school cultures and how labelling can continue even when banding is abolished.
4 Willis (*Learning to Labour*) placed the process of labelling and the role of the school into a wider socio-economic context. The academic failure of 'the lads' helped to provide new recruits to manual labour and to maintain the capitalist system.
5 Keddie (*Tinker Tailor – The Myth of Cultural Deprivation*) showed how intelligent working-class children get mislabelled as troublesome – which then becomes a 'self-fulfilling prophecy' if the child accepts the label. She argued against any suggestion that working-class culture is inferior, referring to 'the myth of cultural deprivation'. She also argued that the education system should be based on working-class culture rather than middle-class culture (see page 139).
6 Mahony (*Schools for the Boys*) influenced by the work of Dale Spender in, e.g. *Learning to Lose* and *Invisible Women – The Schooling Scandal*, showed how boys monopolize space, time and attention in schools to the detriment of girls and begin to rehearse the oppressive relations of patriarchy in terms of bullying and sexual harassment.

The social functions of education

Functionalist ideas about the character and purpose of education derive originally from the ideas of Durkheim, and are concerned with the ways in which the education system operates to induct new recruits into the prevailing culture, norms and values of their society. According to Durkheim, 'each society, considered at a given stage of development, has a system of education which exercises an influence upon individuals which is usually irresistible'. The notion that the education system serves a variety of functions for society dominated the sociology of education until the 1950s. According to functionalist sociologists like Talcott Parsons, the process of education could be seen as serving four distinct functions:

- economic
- socially selective
- political
- socially controlling.

Education and the economic system

A major responsibility of education is to provide the necessary workers for the prevailing system of production and level of technology which a society requires. The school system acts as a kind of 'sorting agency' or 'clearing house' for employment, largely through the workings of its examination system.

The old divisions into public, grammar, technical and secondary modern schools performed this function much more visibly, with each type of school preparing workers for a different level of future employment.

While public and independent schools continue their traditional function of schooling the future ruling groups in society, the state system has increasingly moved towards comprehensive schools, which theoretically provide a common experience of education for varying and diverse groups of children. However, systems of streaming and banding are the usual devices used within schools to channel children of differing abilities towards different examination outcomes, which in turn helps to 'grade' them into prospective professional, skilled and unskilled workers.

As youth unemployment has become a 'growth industry' in advanced capitalist societies, schools have passed on the responsibility for those for whom there are no jobs to various government training and vocational schemes.

Education and the social system

In Chapter 1 it was argued that all societies have ways of organizing the distribution of the resources which they value by one form of social stratification or another, and that in Britain resources such as wealth, property, power and specialist skills are distributed in differing amounts to members of different social classes.

Social mobility

One of the main differences between a class system and other forms of social stratification, like slavery, feudalism or the caste system, it is said, is that individuals can shift their position to some degree by their own efforts.

Functionalists argue that in order to make the best use of human resources in the pursuit of economic progress:

- there needs to be a certain amount of movement of individuals between different occupational and class categories;
- there needs to be the kind of 'encouraging' social climate which suggests that 'getting on' and 'doing well' in terms of job prospects and lifestyle is perfectly possible for talented and hard-working individuals.

Part of the function of the education system, it is argued, is to both reinforce social class divisions and also to provide limited opportunities for some degree of social mobility. Bright working-class children can do well at school, pass A levels, go to university and qualify as doctors, lawyers or accountants, for example.

Most of the movement happens lower down the social scale – between skilled manual and white-collar occupations and between upper-working-class and lower-middle-class social classifications. But the shift is probably more technical than real. A good deal of the apparent improvement in individuals' class position is to do with changes in the occupational structure of society and the growth in white-collar, administrative and social welfare occupations rather than any real alteration in class power.

As we argued earlier, it is not so much to do with the 'embourgeoisement' of the affluent worker as the 'proletarianization' of the white-collar worker. Considerable restructuring of office and clerical work and the application of new technologies over the years have resulted in the deskilling of white-collar work so that, like manual labour, it becomes increasingly characterized by the fragmentation of tasks and the dependency on machinery, routine and automation. This has led to the convergence of the lower-middle and upper-working class.

In earlier decades achievement in education was seen as the spur to social mobility, especially in an economic climate in which jobs were relatively plentiful. During the last fifteen years, however, that climate has changed. The enterprise culture promoted by the New Right regards business acumen and financial success, rather than education, as the key to social advancement. The expansion of education and training, especially in the post-compulsory sector of further and higher education has, it could be argued, more to do with keeping administrators and teachers in jobs, and the jobless off the streets, than any great commitment to facilitating social mobility.

Class difference

One of the major preoccupations of the sociology of education in its formative years was to demonstrate the extent to which the prevailing education system reflected and acted to reinforce the class system.

- The private sector in education allows those who are already in superior social positions to ensure that, for the most part, their children remain in superior positions.
- The state system perpetuates, through its methods of streaming, curriculum arrangements, examinations and social location in specific neighbourhoods, a way of continuing to educate the children of middle-class, working-class and ethnic minority groups more or less separately.

It was the evidence which supported these kinds of observations provided by J. W. B. Douglas (*The Home and the School*), for example, and Brian Jackson (*Streaming – the Education System in Miniature*), in the 1960s that did much to enhance the arguments for comprehensive reorganization in the 1970s, as a way of equalizing the educational opportunities for working-class and black children.

It was possible to demonstrate in the 1970s that the proportion of working-class children going on to university had not changed in fifty years, and that working-class children were much less likely than middle-class children to find themselves in the then grammar schools, top streams and examination classes, or staying on past the official school-leaving age. Explanations for this phenomenon were sought in the characteristics of different children, their upbringing and environment, and in the selection procedures and underlying assumptions which were employed by teachers and schools. But whoever was 'to blame' – the home or the school, or, indeed neither – the facts were inescapable. Schools were seen to be reflecting and reinforcing the social class divisions of the wider society.

Education and the political system

The ability or inability of education to change society brings us into the realm of politics. Politics, of course, is a very loaded word which is usually approached with caution when people are talking about education in case it is associated with indoctrination. But in the sense that all government activity is political in its aims, and is concerned with formulating policies about the ways in which society should be run, introducing legislation and working through social institutions to implement it, education is just one of the many support systems which serve a political purpose.

The reorganization of schooling along comprehensive lines, for example, was done partly for educational reasons, but also to attempt to bring about greater social equality. The introduction of the local management of schools, the National Curriculum, regular achievement tests and schools opting out of local authority control have all been concerned with applying free market political philosophies of competition, choice and consumerism to make schools more responsive to the needs of industry and to get rid of what are regarded as the worst excesses of egalitarianism.

Attempts to achieve political goals through the education system are by no means always successful, however. Some would argue that they are not meant to be, and are merely there to give the impression that something is being done.

In the USA schools were used to help bring about racial integration in the 1970s, and thousands of millions of dollars were poured into pre-school and nursery provision in an attempt to reduce the social, economic and cultural deprivation said to be exhibited by poor white and black Americans in urban ghettos like Harlem. But in many cases the forced integration of schools was accompanied by riots, murder and policing of school campuses, and ten years after 'Headstart' and other projects designed to provide positive educational discrimination in areas like Harlem, researchers could find no visible signs of any change in the distribution of social advantage or opportunity.

Whether or not attempts to achieve political ends through educational means are successful, the important point to note is that the attempt is made. Government policies, implemented through schools, whatever they may be, illustrate the essentially political nature of education and the important role of teachers as the people responsible for putting them into practice.

The role of teachers

1 According to Marx, teachers fall into that category of petit bourgeoisie which he saw as existing somewhere between the ruling class and the proletariat. According to Marxist analysis, teachers, like social workers, fulfil the role of **functionaries**, in that they help to implement the day-to-day management of the lower classes on behalf of the ruling class. Marxist analysis has been very critical of the imputed custodial and repressive role of teachers in the service of capitalism.

2 Liberal analysis has also been critical of teachers in terms of their propensity for crushing individual spontaneity and creativity in pupils in the name of examination orthodoxy and unnecessary rules and regulations.

3 Social democratic analysis has seen the role of teachers as frequently misguided rather than repressive. The high profile given to sociology in teacher training, and the enthusiasm with which many cooperated with comprehensive reorganization, led to the optimistic belief that, once teachers realized how their behaviour might 'inadvertently' reinforce class disadvantages, they could be persuaded to change their behaviour, and the problems of inequality could be overcome.

4 Currently, teachers are in a state of great dispute with political policies promoted by the government. Conservative education policy has required teachers to adopt very different attitudes to education from those which were popular in the 1960s and 1970s.

- Organizational changes have shifted the balance of power in education away from classroom teachers towards politicians, managers and industrialists.
- Teachers have been required to demonstrate the 'success' of education at precisely the same time as the social circumstances which affect the behaviour and life chances of many of their pupils have been deteriorating.
- Rather than revering teachers as 'custodians' of the young, the New Right tends to depict them either as 'woolly liberals' with out-of-date ideas about equality, or 'dangerous socialists' who, like other 'extremists' in the trade unions and local Labour councils, are using their power and influence over the young to preach revolution.

Education as an agency of social control

The other characteristic of education, according to functionalist sociologists, is to encourage socially acceptable norms and values.

Durkheim emphasized the role of ritual in forming patterns of behaviour and reinforcing values. Sports teams, for example, encourage competitiveness, while assemblies encourage religiosity and even patriotism. He also pointed to the less overt ways in which children are socialized. Hierarchies among staff, for example, remind children that head teachers are more powerful than language assistants. Caretakers are more powerful than cleaners. Men, in general, are more powerful than women. Unconsciously these are 'lessons' which, according to Durkheim, children will later come to apply in their responses to hierarchies in society generally.

Marx described the influence of education as a system of ideology which acted to service and support the prevailing economic system in society. In describing the structural characteristics of society. Marx made a distinction between the 'base' or 'substructure' and the 'superstructure'.

The base in society is depicted by Marx quite simply as the prevailing economic system, its characteristic means and relationships of production.

The superstructure, on the other hand, is made up of those systems and institutions in society which are developed to encourage the political, social and ideological circumstances in which the needs of the economic system, and in particular its owners and controllers, can best be supported and reinforced.

The essence of this view of the relationship between base and super-structure is that:

- An economically powerful group uses its power to define the values, attitudes and beliefs of the various support systems in the superstructure.
- These in turn operate to both reflect and reinforce the interests of the economically powerful, so that any real challenge to their authority is made both difficult and unlikely.

Marxist structuralism

The Marxist structuralists Althusser and Bourdieu derived some of their inspiration from Durkheim and some from Marx.

Althusser argued that the education system is largely determined by the needs of the capitalist economic system. Schools are middle-class institutions, run by middle-class people (teachers), in which middle-class pupils are usually enabled to succeed. So far as the workers are concerned, they must be socialized to accept their required place in the class system.

Bourdieu introduced the terms **cultural capital** and **cultural deficit** to explain why middle-class children usually do better in schools than working-class children of the same measured ability.

In middle-class institutions like schools, the values, attitudes and behaviour of middle-class pupils are more closely in tune with teachers' expectations and the demands of the examination system than those of working-class pupils.

'cultural deficit'

As a consequence, middle-class children can be said to benefit from 'cultural capital' whereas working-class children may exhibit '**cultural deficit**'.

He does not mean to imply, however, that working-class culture is necessarily inferior to middle-class culture – merely that it is non-academic. In terms of schooling this means that working-class children are at a disadvantage.

Bourdieu also discussed the significance of the examination system in schools as a form of 'ritual' or 'ceremonial', in which the cultural capital of the middle classes is ratified as 'success' and is made to seem legitimate. It is a system which also ratifies the cultural deficit of the working class and defines it as 'failure'.

Examinations are not fair competitions, according to Bourdieu, although they are perceived as fair by both the middle and working class, and are thought to be neutral. As a result, the middle class are generally assumed to have earned their just rewards and the working class to have got their just deserts.

'symbolic violence'

Bourdieu calls this illusion a form of **symbolic violence**, in which middle-class power is maintained not by physical force but by superiority in communication, especially language. The ability to manipulate language and to use it in different forms of literature and logic and artistic expression is just as much a weapon in the class struggle as economic power.

Untrained and inexperienced in these concerns, working-class people become overawed and intimidated by them, in ways which create self-perceptions of failure and inadequacy. This kind of 'symbolic violence' done to the culture and self-esteem of working-class people helps to explain why they are often persuaded to put up with boring and repetitive roles.

Some would be reluctant to describe the relationship between cultural and economic power and prevailing values in quite these terms, since it seems to suggest the manipulation and control of the majority by the cleverness and power of the few, in pursuit of selfish interests.

cultural determinism

Bourdieu is accused of **cultural determinism** and of believing that class culture is inevitably passed on from one generation to the next, without allowing for the fact that working-class people might choose to alter their social and cultural awareness by becoming scholars and writers and artists themselves. But he sees the freedom of expression enjoyed by individual artists and intellectuals as largely irrelevant in the struggle to change inequalities in the class system.

Functionalism

Conventional functionalists do not share this conflictual view of society. They emphasize instead:

- the organic nature of society;
- the interdependency of each part of the whole with the other parts of the whole;
- the search for integration and cohesion between systems;
- the need to organize socialization and control as a way of preserving society and ensuring its maximum efficiency.

Social interactionism

Those sociologists influenced by Weber and a social action approach prefer to concentrate on socialization and the development of social meanings and behaviour in an interpersonal rather than a structural context.

They are reluctant to acknowledge the influence of 'huge' and 'impersonal' forces like institutional ideologies on human behaviour, but do accept that individuals are very susceptible to being moulded and influenced by subconscious messages and symbols in the process of social interaction.

The hidden curriculum

Although it is generally agreed that schools assist in the business of socialization and social control, it is not assumed that children learn moral values and attitudes in the same kind of overt way in which they learn history or geography, for example. Rather, schools serve to recognize, reinforce and stand for mainstream values through the kind of atmosphere, rewards, punishments and attitudes which underpin the relationships of schooling.

- Competition in sport and academic achievement symbolized by prizes, badges and merit points, for example, and the sanctions placed upon those who 'let the school down' are simple illustrations of the 'hidden curriculum' in operation.
- The separation of boys and girls for different activities, and the varying behavioural expectations that are attached to each of them, are both covert preparations for their future lives as adults in a society which 'defines gender roles differently.
- The presentation of knowledge in subjects which are taught as if they are separate and distinct from each other, and which are taught in different contexts to different pupils, help to make distinctions in status between those who are mainly exposed to 'academic' subjects such as languages and science and those who are encouraged to concentrate on 'practical' and 'vocational' skills. In later life, these distinctions are reflected in pupils' employment opportunities and occupational status.
- The 'hidden curriculum' also has the effect of communicating to pupils which of them are regarded as 'successes' and which 'failures' in society's terms, and what kinds of behaviour will be expected of them in the future.

The high levels of truancy and disruption in some schools may lead to the conclusion that schools are not always very successful in inculcating 'appropriate' behaviour. But, of course, control, in the sense of allocating future workers to different levels of employment, with the opportunity to exercise different degrees of initiative and responsibility, does not require them all to be 'successful' in the school's terms. If they were, they might expect better employment prospects than society is prepared to provide.

Even unemployment, as socially unpopular as it appears to be, acts as a useful 'regulator' of the labour market, enabling wages to be kept lower than they might otherwise be, and keeping a reserve pool of labour always on hand to service the ups and downs of the economy's need for expansion and recession.

This kind of interpretation of the relationship between schooling and control does not explain disruptive behaviour as a threat or an indication of the school's failure to exercise the degree of ideological control demanded of it by vested interests. Rather, disruption, like apathy, is seen as a manifestation of alienation. Both are preparations for the alienation which workers, deprived of any kind of control over their labour or their lifestyles, experience in the work situation.

According to this view, it is the price society seems prepared to pay, as a means of preserving the prevailing economic system based on the unequal distribution of wealth and social justice. The education system operates as a way of 'regulating' and 'controlling' the process on behalf of the economically powerful and at the expense of many of those who are kept powerless by its activities. And of course, at a simple and strategic level, the children of the powerful can be removed to the kinds of schools and educational environments in which they need have very little contact with children who might be expected to be disruptive and troublesome.

Social factors affecting educational failure

During the 1960s and 1970s sociologists of education were preoccupied with questions of achievement in the education system and explanations of 'failure' in schools. As you consider these arguments, you should be able to recognize rather different approaches and assumptions being used – both in

Table 6.1 Differing explanations of educational failure

Assumptions	Types of explanation	Location of 'the problem'	Key concept used	Remedy
1 'Children fail because they're inferior.'	*Pathological: Psychometric* Failure arising from low IQ – innate psychological and mental inadequacy, transmitted from one generation to the next and capable of being measured by IQ tests.	In the mental deficiency of the individual.	Low ability.	Remedial education.
2 'Children fail because they're deprived.'	*Pathological: cultural deficit* Failure arising from the 'deficient' cultural experiences and social pathology of 'deviant' groups.	In the social deficiencies of individuals, families and 'deviant' groups.	Deprivation.	Compensatory education and social work intervention.
3 'Children don't fail – bad schools fail them.'	*Technical/maldistribution* Failure arising from the malfunctioning of some schools and the unequal distribution of resources and opportunities.	In the relationship between institutional and administrative 'mistakes'.	Disadvantage.	Institutional change and positive discrimination policies.
4. 'Society uses the education system to "create" and perpetuate failure. So long as failure exists, education is succeeding!'	*Structural* Failure arising from the need to protect an economic system based on private profit.	In the relationship between the working class and the political, economic and social structure.	Exploitation.	Redistribution of economic power and control in society.

the definition of terms like 'failure', 'achievement', 'success', 'ability', etc. and in the social factors which are considered to be significant.

It is perhaps too simple to reduce the different arguments to those shown in Table 6.1 but it may help you to begin to see the differences between them and the shifts in argument from one type of explanation to another.

Pathological: psychometric

This type of explanation of educational failure went more or less unchallenged for at least the first half of this century. It relied on the view that most – some would have said all – of a child's ability was based on genetic intelligence which was both innate and inherited.

Modifications to this view over the years conceded the influence of the young child's family environment, and recognized that social factors could stimulate or restrict the development of ability.

Notions of 'intelligence' and 'ability' were rarely defined in this type of explanation. They were often used interchangeably, and it was assumed that everyone knew about, and agreed upon, what they meant. If challenged, they would probably have been defined as those qualities of 'mental dexterity', 'verbal fluency' and 'logic' which make the 'learning of knowledge' relatively easy.

Cyril Burt

Cyril Burt, writing in 1933, explained:

> By intelligence the psychologist understands in-born, all-round intellectual ability. It is inherited, or at least innate; not due to teaching or training. It is intellectual, not emotional or moral, and remains uninfluenced by industry or zeal. It is general, not specific, i.e. it is not limited to any particular kind of work, but enters into all we do or say or think. Of all our mental qualities it is the most far reaching. Fortunately it can be measured with accuracy and ease.

So sure of their ground were early psychologists like Cyril Burt that a battery of Intelligence Quotient (IQ) tests were devised and used to measure this intelligence. On the basis of the results, decisions were made about the type of school and level of stream which would be 'best suited' to the intelligence of the children being tested.

Children who performed badly in the tests and who failed were considered to be lacking in the 'mental dexterity', 'verbal fluency' and 'logic' necessary to learn very effectively. They were termed children of 'low ability', who, in extreme cases, would need specially planned, remedial education to help them make the best of their 'mental handicaps'.

There were many criticisms levelled at this type of explanation of educational failure which seemed to concentrate almost exclusively on the personal mental deficiency of individuals.

> One of the main criticisms was the unproblematic way in which concepts like 'ability', 'intelligence' and 'failure' were used. It seemed as though 'intelligence' was something that was fixed and could be measured only by IQ tests, and that ability was somehow defined as a result of an individual's response to such tests.

> Research also showed how biased and one-sided apparently neutral tests could be. It was argued that they favoured the cultural experiences of white, Anglo-Saxon, middle-class children, and consequently it was not surprising that black, West Indian, working-class children, for example, did not always do very well in them.

> Similarly, research showed that, in completing IQ tests, a certain amount of 'practice makes perfect'. Children were likely to do better in the tests if they were given lots of experience of them beforehand.

> Criticisms were also made about the explanation of educational success and failure based on apparently sound scientific principles which did not take into account the significance of social and emotional factors which were likely to be operating.

> Researchers in the 1970s and 1980s, revisiting some of Burt's earlier records, found that many of the findings from tests were misrepresented to fit in with his preconceived theories of intelligence, in ways which were both élitist and racist. Substantiating articles in learned journals,

purporting to corroborate his conclusions, were found to be fraudulent and written by Burt himself under an assumed name.

While his work is now considerably discredited, largely for these reasons, Burt's contribution to the psychometric measurement of intelligence affected, in a detrimental way, the educational opportunities of millions of schoolchildren in Britain for almost forty years.

Pathological: cultural deficit

This type of explanation of educational failure was rooted in the reports and sociological writings of the 1950s and 1960s which emphasized the links between social class and educational achievement. (See, for example, the following reports: *Early Leaving* (Cyril Burt, 1954), Crowther (1959–60), Newsom (1963), Robbins (1963–64), Plowden (1967); and the following sociological texts: *Social Class and Educational Opportunity* by Jean Floud, A. H. Halsey and C. A. Martin (1956), *The Home and the School* (1964) and *All Our Future* (1968) by J. W. B. Douglas *et al.*, and *The National Child Development Studies* (1st Report 1966, 2nd Report 1972) by the National Children's Bureau.)

The outcome of all this research was to stress the significance of the home in the educational process and to suggest that the home was, in fact, more important than the school in determining educational success and failure. The argument went something like this.

There are several characteristics which contribute to a 'good' home, including financial security, reasonable comfort, space and a pleasant physical environment. They also include family stability and parents with a good understanding of educational play and the importance of language development. As the child starts school, a 'good' home continues to provide supportive educational experiences and a lot of encouragement and interest in what the child is doing at school.

A 'bad' home, on the other hand, is one in which there is no financial security, overcrowding and lack of space. There are often too many children and sometimes a broken marriage to contend with. 'Bad' parents do not have the 'proper kind of attitudes' about education, or 'the right aspirations' for their children. Their language, and the language they teach their children, is 'restricted' in its vocabulary and sentence structure, and provides a poor preparation for the child's subsequent learning experiences in school. Children from 'bad' homes have parents who show little interest in their schooling and are usually very reluctant to visit teachers and to discuss their children's progress.

This is obviously an over-simplification of how 'good' and 'bad' homes were depicted, but the more you read the literature of the time the more you'll be able to identify these kinds of judgements being made. In the National Child Development Study *From Birth to Seven*, for example, these comments were made:

From Birth to Seven

A great deal – if not the major part – of learning takes place outside the school and much of it is accomplished even before the child enters school. The vocabulary and concepts used by those around him (sic) are vital in providing a framework within which his own intellectual growth can take place. If the framework is bare or impoverished, his own development is likely to be slow, a rich framework of words and ideas will provide the food for more rapid growth. More advanced or abstract thought processes are usually clothed in more elaborate and highly structured language (Bernstein 1961). A home conducive to learning is one where there is a feeling for the spoken and written word as a tool for conveying precise meaning; and where children are stimulated to question the world around them and receive explanations appropriate to their age.

There are two senses in which a child comes from such a home ready to learn. He is intellectually ready in that his language and concepts are already well structured, so that the school is building upon established foundations. But he is also psychologically ready to acquire new skills. For example, he has learned that reading provides pleasure and wants to be part of the literate community as soon as possible. His whole attitude to school is conditioned by his parents' high regard for education.

This kind of home is certainly not the monopoly of professional or other non-manual workers. However, it is more frequently found amongst occupational groups which possesses a high level of education and skill. (author's emphasis)

Because the association of 'good' and 'bad' homes was linked with research about social class and educational achievement, the two become linked into the association of 'good' homes with middle-class lifestyles and 'bad' homes with working-class lifestyles. In other words, it became widely assumed that middle-class children did better in school than working-class children because they came from better homes and their parents made a better job of bringing them up.

This explanation of failure was firmly located in the social, cultural, linguistic and educational deficiencies which were said to be 'typical' of a good many working-class people. Children brought up in such circumstances were said to be 'seriously deprived' compared with their 'more fortunate' brothers and sisters from middle-class backgrounds. Terms like **the culture of deprivation** were used to link the various characteristics of a way of life which seemed to spell disaster.

The sense of deprivation being passed on from one generation of 'feckless' and 'deprived' individuals to another was communicated in the use of the term **the cycle of deprivation**, in which it was thought to be almost inevitable that 'poverty and ignorance' would breed 'poverty and ignorance'.

In terms of remedies, this kind of pathological explanation of failure presented two alternatives.

1 It was thought that, in terms of heredity, parents' occupation and education, family size and the physical circumstances of the home, there was little that could be done to change things, certainly not by means of education.
2 However, in terms of the 'cultural environment' of the home, parents' attitudes, their knowledge of the education system, their use of language and the help they gave to their children, some positive intervention could be made.

It was these kinds of beliefs that encouraged social work initiatives, especially in pre-school activities in the home, and also in the notions of **'compensatory education'** for deprived children to help repair the 'cultural damage' done by their upbringing.

compensatory education

One weakness of this explanation and its remedies lay, of course, in the uncritical way in which the relationship between the home, the school and social class was treated; and in the tendency to simplify, and, indeed, stigmatize, vast numbers of individuals, their families and their home circumstances because they did not conform to the prevailing norms defined and agreed upon by the researchers and the report writers. The other major weakness lay in the recommendations made about 'social intervention' and 'compensatory education'.

Basil Bernstein

In a famous article by Basil Bernstein ('Education Cannot Compensate for Society') in which he tried to put right the way in which his earlier analysis of language had been used to reinforce notions of middle-class cultural superiority and working-class cultural deficiency, he argued that education could not be expected to compensate for society. If the prevailing social structure was unequal in its distribution of resources, and operated a class system which discriminated against working-class people, no amount of educational compensation could alter the experience of social and economic disadvantage. He also challenged the notion of 'cultural deprivation' arguing that, since everyone has a culture, no-one can be said to be deprived of their culture.

Nell Keddie

Nell Keddie developed his argument in her introduction to *Tinker Tailor – The Myth of Cultural Deprivation*. She argued that:

- the cultural background of so-called deprived groups reflected **different** assumptions and practices about child-rearing, not **deficient** ones;
- she showed how in schools it was teachers who defined what was meant by ability, success, failure, achievement, etc. in ways which reflected their own middle-class, cultural values, and then organized schools to reflect these definitions. They were the same definitions that served the interests of powerful groups in society;
- once these became the yardstick, used to measure educational achievement and educational potential, it was hardly surprising that the children of socially powerless groups failed to match up to the criteria being applied;
- with the added authority of sociological research and, for example, the writings of Bourdieu, 'cultural deficit' explanations of educational failure became virtually institutionalized. As a result, children became progressively disadvantaged. Since they were thought to be 'deprived', little was expected of them from the day they entered school. The remedy was not 'compensatory education' or 'social intervention' to change children's cultural behaviour, but rather the fundamental reform of the assumptions, practices and educational values that operated in schools;
- according to Keddie, the responsibility for children's failure lay in the organization of schooling, not in the deficiency of individual children and their upbringing.

Technical/
Maldistribution

Both of the pathological versions of educational failure relied upon a micro analysis of social behaviour and assumed that failure was somehow located in the individual. The technical/maldistribution model takes a slightly broader perspective.

One version of this kind of explanation echoes Nell Keddie's view that schools are 'middle-class institutions' which represent assumptions, values and behaviour that alienate working-class children and which, in a variety of obvious and less obvious ways, systematically ensure that the majority of them fail.

Sources of failure are looked for in the ways in which the schools operate. It may be that:

- the curriculum is badly organized or badly taught;
- rules and regulations may be inappropriate;
- the 'hidden curriculum' of teachers' attitudes may have the effect of denigrating the ability and potential of many of the children.

An examination of specific schools like Lumley (*Social Relations in a Secondary School*, Hargreaves, 1968) and Hightown Grammar (*Hightown Grammar*, Lacey, 1971) illustrated some of the ways in which the organization and expectation of the schools helped to administer success and failure to different pupils.

The implications of this kind of analysis was that, if the values and practices which caused failure could be identified, they could be altered. This was a view which relied a good deal on the assumption that failure had to do with 'technical' weaknesses in the system which could be remedied. The failure was in the failure of parts of the system to operate effectively or fairly. Once it was accepted that 'systems failure' created, or at least contributed to, pupil failure, then institutional changes should be able to improve matters.

This type of explanation and remedy was more appealing to liberal-minded people than explanations that relied on blaming individuals for their cultural deficiency. It seemed less daunting to change the attitudes and practices of a few thousand teachers and schools than to change the cultural behaviour of several million children.

But a lot of teachers and some sociologists still argued that institutions like schools were no more in a position to check the distribution of failure in society than those who experienced it. Schools and teachers were seen as pawns in an altogether more complicated game.

Another version of this explanation looked at the distribution of educational and other resources in society. The argument presented by Byrne, Williamson and Fletcher, for example, in *The Poverty of Education*, showed how different social classes, located in different areas of the city and in different parts of the country, received different resources. In practice, this meant things like the age and quality of the schools, the amount of money spent on equipment and materials, the size of the staff/pupil ratio, the provision of pre-school nursery classes, educational grants to help needy families, good sixth-form facilities, etc.

In *The Poverty of Education* the writers showed how uneven was the distribution of these resources between schools and between local education authorities. Like the more general resources of housing, transport, health facilities, employment and environmental planning, middle-class areas and more prosperous regions tended to be much better served than working-class neighbourhoods and poorer and more remote parts of the country.

The writers did not, however, consider the availability of these resources in relation to black communities in Britain. As will be obvious to the observant reader, most of the research and the arguments we have been considering so far have taken little or no account of gender or ethnicity in their formulations.

Many of the decisions about the allocation of resources are dependent upon local and national government policies, and in times of economic crisis the tendency is to make cuts in those areas in which there will be the least effective opposition and the least organized resistance. In practice, this hits black and working class communities particularly hard.

The effects of unequal resource distribution according to Byrne, Williamson and Fletcher was to exacerbate the social and educational differences between children from different social environments, because the performance of the neighbourhood schools in which they found themselves was thought to be directly related to the kinds of resources they received, as shown in Figure 6.1.

In this argument educational success and failure were directly related to local authority spending, which in turn was affected by local and national government decisions. The assumption was that different decisions and

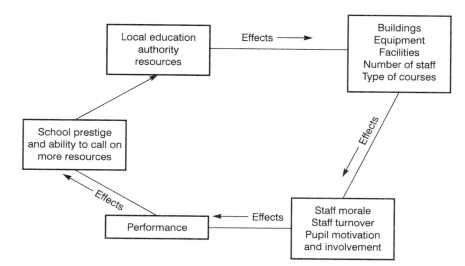

Figure 6.1 Resources and their effects

positive discrimination

more spending could reduce the amount of educational failure recorded in poor areas and badly resourced schools. The remedy was seen to be in terms of **positive discrimination**, so that schools in disadvantaged areas, in which pupils and their families experienced the cumulative effects of the maldistribution of society's resources, should receive proportionately more education funding, better facilities and more favourable staffing ratios to restore the balance between them. In other words, a significant reallocation would occur – not just in education, but in other social and environmental provision, too – to counteract the prevailing inequalities which kept some communities in a state of serious disadvantage.

Structural

All the explanations so far have assumed that educational failure was either a personal or a technical problem which could be remedied, compensated for, altered by institutional change or modified by positive discrimination. In every case failure was regarded as 'regrettable', and reforms were advocated to ameliorate its effects.

Those sociologists who advanced a structural explanation of educational failure, however, took a more pessimistic view of the source and persistence of failure in our society. Key contributors to this kind of explanation in the 1970s were the American historian Clarence Karier and the political economists Bowles and Gintis. All three emphasized the central importance of the economic system in society.

Karier, for example, argued that, through the tool of education, schools in the United States had been used principally to teach the attitudes and skills necessary to 'adjust' pupils to the changing needs of the economic system and to reinforce the values of the 'business ethic' in American society.

Bowles and Gintis developed this view in their book *Schooling in Capitalist America* which, although argued in terms of American society, was considered to be highly relevant to the experience of all advanced industrial nations. According to them:

the education system in society existed to produce the labour force for capitalism, both in terms of the qualities and skills needed and also the attitudes and values likely to endorse capitalist practices;

the function of education was to anticipate and reproduce the conditions and relationships which exist between employers and workers in the relationships of production;

capitalism had advanced considerably since Marx first identified its characteristics in the nineteenth century. In those days, a view of education to 'gentle the masses' on behalf of the ruling class seemed a simple correlation between education and society;

increasingly, the relationship has become more complex as the massive expansion of capitalist influence and state intervention in people's lives has become commonplace;

the experience of work has been transformed over the last hundred years. The majority of workers in manufacturing and production are the employees of vast multinational and transnational concerns, with factories and investments in various countries, operating outside the control of individual governments. Their local managers have in turn become very small cogs in incredibly big wheels;

automation and new technologies have developed to such an extent that machines and computers have gained precedence over workers in the work process and altered and eradicated many of the jobs they once did (see Chapter 7);

economic and social changes are both extensive and rapid. Education is used to maintain order and control;

far from being 'egalitarian' and 'reformist', as so many educators suggest, schools are about 'inequality' and 'repression';

capitalism does not require everyone to fulfil their educational potential or become highly qualified and intellectually critical. In fact, any of these indicators of 'educational success' would, on a large, scale seriously challenge the distribution of employment, profit and power in a capitalist society. People have to be educated just enough to become dutiful workers, citizens and consumers, but not enough to understand, or seriously challenge, the prevailing economic and social system;

the key term is **behaviour modification** – the skills and attitudes which schools reward are docility, passivity and obedience;

there is a correspondence between the social relations of production and the social relations of education, so that children in school begin to learn the values and functions they will later repeat as workers. This is achieved by schools modelling themselves on the economic divisions of society, so that the relations of schooling 'replicate' the relations of production (see, for example, Figure 6.2).

Bowles and Gintis do not attribute the responsibility for creating an unequal society to the school system, however. The root cause of inequality is firmly attributed to the structural divisions of a capitalist society, which needs to maintain its working-class labour force. And just as capitalist society exploits the labour power of the workers, and controls so much of their social and cultural lives, so, too, does schooling exploit the child workers

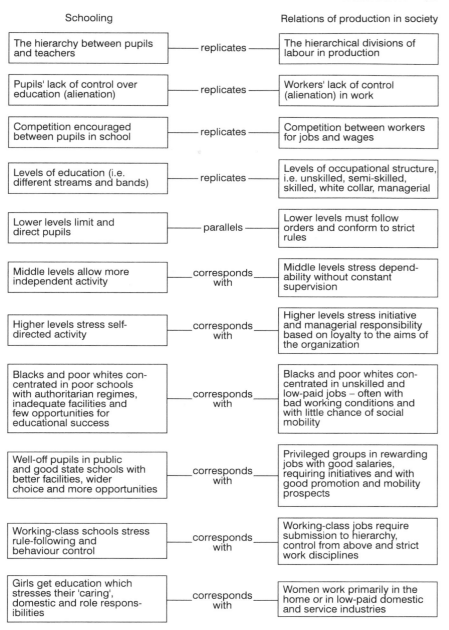

Schooling | Relations of production in society

Schooling		Relations of production in society
The hierarchy between pupils and teachers	— replicates —	The hierarchical divisions of labour in production
Pupils' lack of control over education (alienation)	— replicates —	Workers' lack of control (alienation) in work
Competition encouraged between pupils in school	— replicates —	Competition between workers for jobs and wages
Levels of education (i.e. different streams and bands)	— replicates —	Levels of occupational structure, i.e. unskilled, semi-skilled, skilled, white collar, managerial
Lower levels limit and direct pupils	— parallels —	Lower levels must follow orders and conform to strict rules
Middle levels allow more independent activity	corresponds with	Middle levels stress dependability without constant supervision
Higher levels stress self-directed activity	corresponds with	Higher levels stress initiative and managerial responsibility based on loyalty to the aims of the organization
Blacks and poor whites concentrated in poor schools with authoritarian regimes, inadequate facilities and few opportunities for educational success	corresponds with	Blacks and poor whites concentrated in unskilled and low-paid jobs – often with bad working conditions and with little chance of social mobility
Well-off pupils in public and good state schools with better facilities, wider choice and more opportunities	corresponds with	Privileged groups in rewarding jobs with good salaries, requiring initiatives and with good promotion and mobility prospects
Working-class schools stress rule-following and behaviour control	corresponds with	Working-class jobs require submission to hierarchy, control from above and strict work disciplines
Girls get education which stresses their 'caring', domestic and role responsibilities	corresponds with	Women work primarily in the home or in low-paid domestic and service industries

Figure 6.2 Bowles' and Gintis' Correspondence Theory (copyright Open University Press, E202, Unit 32)

and ensure their alienation from real learning. In different schools and in different streams, the future managers and shopfloor workers are rehearsing their future roles as organizers and organized.

All the while, a façade of equal opportunity and meritocracy exists to confirm that educational success is alive and well, and to explain failure in terms of poor motivation and personal deficiency.

Bowles and Gintis were pessimistic about remedies couched in terms of 'remedial education', 'compensatory education' or even 'positive discrimination', when in practice the sums of money involved were derisory compared with the size of the problems which needed to be tackled. Since most educational problems were not caused by the school system but by the workings of the capitalist economy, reforming institutions in a piecemeal kind of way, without changing the wider political and economic structures in society, was, in their view, doomed to failure. They argued that liberal reformers in all walks of life, not just education, repeatedly failed to understand this, behaving as though social problems could be ameliorated by the sympathetic intervention of the state and trying to reform individuals and institutions by social welfare and legal initiatives, but without questioning the basic structure of poverty and power in economic life, which were at the root of such problems. None of these reforms, according to Bowles and Gintis, placed social problems in the context of the way in which capitalism operates to institutionalize inequality, poverty and educational failure as a means of surviving and flourishing.

Schools and the education system play such an important role for capitalism in this respect that they are unlikely to change in any radical way unless there is the most massive political onslaught on the economic and political base of capitalist society. Failure will never be eradicated from the school system so long as capitalism requires schools to reproduce the majority of its labour force with limited horizons and limited achievements. The most that schools can attempt to do if they actually want to challenge the function they have been given by society is to alter their relationships, so that instead of replicating the social relations of production and helping to perpetuate the capitalist system, they dedicate themselves root and branch to promoting the personal development of all their pupils and social equality between them.

How working-class kids get working-class jobs

'The lads'

In his book *Learning To Labour* Paul Willis drew on the structural perspectives of Marxist writers like Bowles and Gintis and on the research methods of ethnography (the study of cultural behaviour through detailed observation – see pages 259–61) to study why working-class kids persist in allowing themselves to be shunted into working-class jobs. He was writing in the 1970s before youth unemployment had taken on its recent dimensions. If he were writing now, he would probably want to frame the question in terms of why working-class lads allow themselves to be shunted into dubious government training schemes and then unemployment.

Research methods

The usual approach of sociological studies which have set out to examine why working-class youngsters fail in the education system have tended to examine their performance and behaviour from an objective rather than a subjective perspective. Some researchers have made use of questionnaires, structured and unstructured interviews and the extended observation of classroom behaviour to corroborate their conclusions.

Willis's study is different, in that he attempted to build up a picture of 'the lads' counter-school culture in the words, images and responses of 'the lads' themselves, rather than take as given the interpretations made by teachers.

Counter-school culture

The cultural responses which he described, and which 'the lads' actively reproduced in their day-to-day relationships with each other and in opposition to the dominant culture of the school, were those which are usually described in terms of violence and indiscipline in the classroom. They were the kinds of responses which are commonly attributed to 'troublemakers' and which, in their extreme forms, encourage a number of schools to set up special classes, withdrawal units and even quite separate 'sanctuaries' for those whose behaviour becomes 'uncontrollable' in the conventional classroom.

In practice, this meant that 'the lads' did not regard school as a place in which education, learning and deference for teachers had much meaning. School was a necessary evil that had to be 'endured' and 'got through' as pleasurably as possible. The 'pleasure principle' usually revolved around the creation of opportunities to 'have a laugh'.

It was not that school was a place of torture or an institution which inflicted real or symbolic violence upon its victims – at least, not in 'the lads' eyes. They expected nothing from school, nor from teachers. The rules and rationalizations, the moral imperatives and rituals of schooling were there to be resisted. They had no significance and rarely penetrated the cultural experiences or subjective realities of 'the lads'.

The best thing about school was the opportunity to rehearse, with other working-class youngsters, the loyalties and possibilities for defiance and resistance which would later sustain them as wage labourers on the shop floor. Wage labour, like school labour, would be for them essentially meaningless. Exhortations to 'industry' and 'commitment to the company', to 'productivity and loyalty', to 'hard work and self-sacrifice' – indeed, to the whole work ethic which is continuously and variously expounded by those who stand to profit from its acceptance – was largely meaningless to them.

According to Willis, when 'the lads' arrived on the shopfloor they did not need telling to 'take it easy', 'take no notice', or that 'they' (the management) 'always want more', or that 'you've had it if you let them get their way'. Their experiences of schooling had attuned them to the relationships of work.

Hammertown boys

The evidence on which Willis's study was based was a group of twelve non-academic, working-class lads from a working-class council estate in a working-class Midlands town, which he called Hammertown. They attended an all-boys school, and were selected on the basis of their friendship with each other and their behaviour which displayed visible opposition to the mainstream culture of the school.

Willis was in close contact with 'the lads' for their last two years at school and their first six months at work. He also held detailed discussions and interviews with their teachers and parents.

The teachers' view

According to the teachers, 'the lads' attachment to a counter-school culture was 'blatant', as they proceeded to 'lord it about' and display 'wrong attitudes' as a result of 'bad influences'. Their behaviour was generally explained in terms of character deficiencies which encouraged the majority of 'misguided' and 'impressionable' kids to be 'led astray' by a small but disruptive 'minority of troublemakers'.

In the face of such difficulties the teachers often resorted to belittling and sarcastic encounters which exacerbated the distance between them and 'the lads'. Willis refers to the manifestations of this as the 'class insult', which occurred 'in class' but for which the reference point was 'social class'.

In the conventional teaching exchange an important dimension is the respect of one side for the other. But in these circumstances 'the lads' stopped being polite to staff and the staff lost respect for the pupils. Teachers provoked into exasperated and ridiculous outbursts like 'Shut your mouth when you're talking to me' were fleeting triumphs won by 'the lads' in an arena in which teachers still had 'the mastery of formal words and expressions'.

The lads' response

When teachers were demeaning or insulting this was always resented, and experienced by 'the lads' as attacks upon their class identities. In an increasingly vicious circle, 'the lads' hit back against the attacks on their culture in any way they could. This meant:

- disruptive and deliberately provocative behaviour designed to wreck lessons, irritate teachers and amuse each other;
- registering, with careful precision, the amount of writing, reading and school work **not** undertaken;
- vandalizing property and doing everything they could to 'go against' those who rapidly came to represent the enemy.

Class conflict in the classroom

According to Willis, the antagonisms were worked out in class terms, and had a good deal to do with different cultural definitions and allegiances. To judge the one in terms of the other, however, is always to find the other wanting. It is just that in education – as in class society generally – the cultural yardstick is usually the 'affronted sensibilities' of middle-class culture when faced with forms of resistance which it cannot understand.

Willis comments:

> It would be wrong to attribute to the teachers any kind of sinister motive such as miseducating or oppressing working-class kids.

It is simply that their behaviour takes the form of class control and is interpreted – if not articulated – by 'the lads' as a class relationship based on notions of 'them' and 'us'.

So far as 'the lads' were concerned, the 'progressive' teachers concerned with 'relevance', 'individual learning', 'self-discovery', etc. were merely variations on a common theme. They provided opportunities for 'the lads' to celebrate their own values and independence, and to perfect their resistance to the official school culture in a way which was largely unmoved by the relative 'kindness' of 'progressive' teachers in comparison with their more 'traditional' colleagues.

Willis dismisses progressive strategies as merely a different way of attempting to exert control by trying to engage the consent (of the governed) rather than renouncing notions of control. One of the effects of this was to legitimize counter-school culture 'and therefore also the processes which it sponsors'. The tactical withdrawal from confrontation actually ensured 'a much more massive and less illicit presence for the articulation and sustenance of counter-school culture' than would otherwise be the case.

The indulgence or impotence of the education system to control the counter-school culture meant that schools not only reproduce success, power, influence and favour, but also resistance – a resistance which contributes to the already 'inherited' characteristics of an oppositional class culture.

'The lads' in Willis's study seemed to have developed 'to a fine degree in their school counter-culture, specific working-class themes: resistance, subversion of authority, informal penetration of the weaknesses and fallibilities of the formal; and an independent ability to create diversion and enjoyment'. This, if it was true, led Willis to an important observation and, of course, to a single and critical question.

The 'strengths' of counter-school culture

The observation was that, although commonplace, explanations concerning educational failure usually relied upon the identification of **individual** problems or personality defects of one kind or another. This did not explain the adoption and development of an anti-school culture which may have regional and generational variations but which showed remarkable consistency when viewed in male, white, social-class terms.

While schools continued to suggest that the attitudes and abilities needed for individual success were necessary 'in general', the contradiction was rarely admitted that, in a class society, not all can succeed. There was consequently no point for the 'unsuccessful' in following prescriptions for success based on hard work, diligence and conformism when, for the majority of working-class men and women, the ideals of equality and opportunity were illusory.

The counter-school culture, in its disdain for the cultural and moral values of the school, provided an illustration, according to Willis, of an important and profound critique of middle-class notions of individualism, meritocracy and equality in our society. It acted as a rehearsal for shopfloor culture and contained within it the important elements of an oppositional class culture; therefore presented the potential for not merely a partial and cultural challenge but for a 'total transformation' of capitalism.

The important question, therefore, is what has prevented this transformation from happening?

The 'weaknesses' of counter-school culture

The main reason, according to Willis, was that, although counter-school culture and shopfloor culture were full of 'political significance' they were, in practice, essentially unpolitical. No political organization associated with the working class, be it the Labour Party or the trade union movement, has attempted to interpret and mobilize cultural opposition.

In addition, there are internal divisions which have prevented the culture from making connections between common interests and from achieving its full potential as a coherent political challenge to the status quo. The most significant of these divisions are between mental and manual labour and those of ethnicity and gender.

Mental and manual labour

The rejection of school by 'the lads' can be seen as a rejection of individualism, but it was also a rejection of mental activity in general.

Since an important cornerstone of the power of ruling groups in our society is based on the distinction made between 'those who are good with their heads' and 'those who are good with their hands', the failure to challenge the authenticity on which these categories are based helps to perpetuate them.

'The lads' consciously disassociated themselves from mental labour, both in schools and as a future job. For them it was 'cissy' and 'effeminate'. The manual labour which they respected was associated with masculinity and strength.

Gender

'The lads' culture was also highly sexist. So long as wives, girlfriends and mothers were regarded as restricted, inferior and incapable of certain important masculine strengths and perceptions, what they provided, and what they did, was undervalued. The suggestion that they did anything, in fact, was rarely conceded.

If women were revalued in the culture by 'the lads' and by women themselves, not only would the sexual oppression and subordination of women in the culture be reduced, but the denigratory association of feminine characteristics with mental labour would be in question.

Racism

Racism provides a third division in the cohesion of working-class culture in general and 'the lads' culture in particular. Racial divisions create a group which Willis referred to as an 'underclass which is more heavily exploited than the whole working class, and is indirectly and partially exploited by the working class itself'. It provided another example (like women) of an 'inferior group' against which the 'superior self' could be measured.

Despite the fact that the subordinate economic position of black Britons closely resembles the economic conditions of working-class whites, a strong sense of difference and antagonism persists between them.

Others have simplified the complexity of inter-racial hostility as the tendency of exploited groups to seek other groups which they can in turn disdain. And clearly, so long as they are prevented from recognizing common conditions of exploitation – despite and sometimes because of cultural differences – and are kept in competition with each other for scarce economic resources, then the challenge to the dominance of ruling economic groups and the ubiquity of mainstream culture is prevented.

Voluntary control

Thus, despite the fact that many of the values of mainstream culture were effectively minced up and defeated by the behaviour of 'the lads', in the end they did not use their 'oppositional potential' as any kind of political challenge to transform the prevailing distribution of power in society, largely because of limitations like sexism, racism and the strong celebration of masculinity, which led to the willing acceptance of manual labour as a legitimate work role.

Willis concludes:

> In contradictory and unintended ways the counter-school culture of 'the lads' actually achieved for education one of its main, though misrecognized, objectives – the direction of a proportion of working class kids 'voluntarily' into semi-skilled and unskilled manual work.
> (Today this might read 'into dubious government training schemes and unemployment'.)

The irony is that, in the end, the culture of 'the lads' seemed to provide the most effective social control of all. While the unruliness of 'the lads' culture could, in one way, be defined as part of the crisis in education which represented them as 'unteachable' and 'unbearable', it could equally be argued that the process which it sponsored helped, in practice, to prevent a different kind of crisis – the challenge to capitalism – from taking place.

The girls

Like most of the studies of school pupils carried out in the 1960s and 1970s, Willis's account was exclusively about white boys. His consideration of girls was simply in relation to 'the lads' and in the role of girlfriends.

The Mill Lane girls   In 1975 Angela McRobbie carried out a survey among 56 working-class, teenage girls who went to the same youth club, the same school and lived on the same estate. As Willis had done, she attempted to identify the ways in which they experienced and made sense of the world they lived in, and to consider in some detail their relationships with each other.

School provided the girls with a number of possibilities:

- It continued the process of socialization concerned with the preparation of girls for careers in domestic labour.
- It was an alienating experience for those who were seen as 'academic failures'.
- They evolved strategies to denigrate as 'snobs' and 'swots' those who were more successful than them in the school's terms.
- They developed a counter-school culture in which they could, on their own terms, develop their social life, fancy boys, learn the latest dance, have a smoke together in the lavatories and 'play up' the teachers.
- They chose sexuality as the main way in which to oppose the mainstream culture of the school – 'to introduce into the classroom their sexuality and their maturity in such a way as to force teachers to take notice'.
- The rejection of authoritarian sexism in schools (neatness, diligence, femininity, passivity, for example) was challenged by the even more sexist stance of sexuality.

McRobbie comments

> Marriage, family life, fashion and beauty all contribute massively to the girls' anti-school culture and in doing so nicely illustrate the contradictions inherent in so-called 'oppositional' activities. Are the girls in the end not simply doing precisely what is required of them? And if this is the case, is it not **their own culture** which is itself the most effective agent of social control for girls, pushing them in exactly the direction that capitalism and the whole range of institutions which support it wish them to go?

To expect working-class girls, conditioned by their class position into gender roles appropriate to their future lives as working-class housewives, to offer resistance to forces in society which have oppressed women, and working-class women in particular, for centuries, is perhaps unrealistic. It is not difficult to see how the process happens, but why they continually allow it to happen, even appear to choose it, is a more complex question.

Most of them realize that for them marriage is an economic necessity, and delusions about romance help them to avoid for a while facing up to the fact that the realities of marriage and child-bearing are not always quite as the magazines and pop songs suggest.

While middle-class girls may enjoy the 'elbow room' of a few years spent at college or university, where thoughts of marriage can be at least temporarily suspended, where the prospect of economic independence via reasonable jobs is offered and where experiences of sexual and other relationships can be enjoyed in relative freedom for a while, the prospects for single, working-class women are not so many. It is not simply a question of economics – though it would mean a life lived on low wages or benefits. It also implies being forced to live as 'a marginal person in working-class society'. According to McRobbie, working-class girls are doubly bound – both by the material restrictions of their class position and by the sexual oppression of women in general.

In 1985 Christine Griffin (*Typical Girls? Young Women From School to the Labour Market*) studied a group of young, white, working-class girls from Birmingham as they entered the labour market. Like Willis, she concentrated on the issues raised by notions of cultural reproduction. She found considerable differences to 'the lads' studied by Willis:

- The 'gang' did not exist – small friendship groups of two or three girls were more common.
- Deviance was defined in terms of 'loose sexuality' rather than 'troublemaking'.
- There was no strong identification with the shopfloor culture or the attraction of factory work.
- A few regarded office work as 'snooty', but office and shop work were preferred to factory work.

Griffin explained the behaviour of the young women using both class and gender analysis. She suggested they were moving in three related markets:

- the labour market
- the marriage market
- the sexual market.

Those who found jobs did so in either manual work or routine office work. They did not associate paid work with their future identities – these were much more bound up in the tension between the marriage and sexual markets.

To behave in a sexually 'loose' manner might damage their marriage prospects. Most sought their identity through romance, marriage and the inevitability of a man. Sue Lees has shown how the use of the term 'slag' has been used 'to control the social and autonomous behaviour of girls and steer them into marriage'. Angela McRobbie has shown how girls' magazines encourage 'an ideology of romance' as an alternative to the 'slag stereotype' for the same reason.

Griffin notes that, while such mythologies are immensely influential, a minority of young women, particularly young black women, are sceptical of them and seek more independent identities.

Carol Buswell's study of girls on Youth Training Schemes (*Training For Low Pay*, 1987) found that:

- option choices in secondary schools during the last two years of compulsory schooling still serve largely to divide pupils by gender. This is partly the result of stereotyped assumptions about 'appropriate' subjects for boys and girls, partly the 'gender-typing' of subjects themselves, and partly because of pupils' own self-identification and assumptions about their eventual place in the world;
- girls gravitate towards gender-specific training schemes, partly because careers officers, teachers, employers and training officers make sexist assumptions and channel girls along particular routes, and partly because, in choosing traditional paths, girls have a grasp of the reality of the labour market and their future positions within it;
- stereotyped definitions of femininity are particularly pervasive in retailing and clerical training schemes. Definitions containing prescriptions about dress and manner appeal to some girls, but they are generated and

maintained by men, for example, decisions made about staff uniforms in chain stores in which white, middle-aged, middle-class men have the authority as managers to decide upon 'their girls'' dress;

● the growth of female jobs in the service sector in recent years, and in part-time and casual employment, is built on assumptions about women's domestic and child-rearing responsibilities. Working-class girls live in families where patterns of part-time working are a fact of life;

● shops and offices tend to recruit young women full-time and adult women part-time. Badly paid jobs are presented with a glamorous image to young, full-time workers, largely through ideals of femininity. These are the same jobs – still badly paid – which are sold to adult women, after childbirth, on a part-time basis, as being 'convenient' enough to fit in with domestic responsibilities.

Buswell comments:

Current ideologies of femininity and domesticity, therefore, far from being historical hangovers, are actually **central** to the restructuring of the economy, labour force and work processes.

● Young women on Youth Training Schemes receive an 'allowance' in lieu of benefits and wages. The terminology is important because it implies that 'training' is the prime goal. In fact, trainees spend only thirteen weeks out of the year 'off the job'. In practice, they work full time for a meagre allowance which soon accustoms them to the experience of having too little money to participate fully in the adult working life in which they are a part.

● They are still dependent on their families during this time. In Buswell's sample three-quarters of the young women were dependent on adults who had only one wage or less to support the entire family.

Buswell comments:

One consequence of training, therefore, is to enmesh young people in a web of dependency and obligations to individuals and families which, for some girls, has the added dimension of an early dependency on a wage earning male.

● The demoralization of low pay is exacerbated by the 'expense' of being 'feminine'. Girls on schemes have to provide their own uniforms, tights and suitable clothes. Many supplement their allowances by part-time babysitting and waitressing jobs – pushing their working hours up to around 50 or 60 a week.

● Low pay at age 16 or 17 has the effect of depressing future expectations. Compared with allowances, even low wages seem preferable.

● The service sector of the labour market, for which most girls are being trained, is increasing but changing.

● In clerical work and financial services, new technologies have contributed to deskilling the work which is done, and casual and part-time contracts are on the increase. Retailing is at best merely a stop-gap between girlhood and matrimony and a part-time job after childbirth. As a means of livelihood it is hopeless.

Buswell says:

> Labour markets which recruit cheap full time youth labour and cheap part time female labour are actually structured around the assumed dependency of these groups within a family context. It is assumed that both of these groups belong to households where the main expenses are borne by a higher earner. The occupations for which girls are currently being trained offer low pay whilst they are young and part time work when they are older. Their training gives them first hand experience of dependency, low pay and 'realistic' – in the light of the actual labour market – expectations.

Young, Female and Black

In *Young, Female and Black*, Heidi Safia Mirza records the experience of young black women as they leave school and begin work. She refutes the widely held myth that young black women underachieve at school and in the labour market.

Whereas in the 1970s Willis talked about the working-class 'reproducing themselves as working class', and in the 1980s Mary Fuller wrote about black girls exhibiting 'sub-cultures of resistance', Mirza, writing in the 1990s, is concerned about kids who actually identify with school, do relatively well, but still fail to attain the jobs to which they aspire. Her study of young black women involved 62 young women aged between 15 and 19 who attended two comprehensives in South London. She compared their experiences with black and white male and female peers. She comments:

> Young black women are not involved in reproducing their inequalities (as Willis suggests) through their cultural values, but, on the contrary, engage in a process which will, according to their specific rationale, ultimately assist them in securing upward mobility ... but they choose a limited range of occupations because they are not given the opportunity to explore other avenues ... the recruitment to YTS is clearly discriminatory ... the existence of a racially and sexually segregated labour market ensures their limited occupational opportunities. ... In spite of their determination to succeed, the career destinations of the young black women and young black men who took part in the follow-up survey, four years on, are characterised by a distinct lack of variety and scope.

Feminist thinking on education

Feminist thinking about the significance of education in the preservation of gender inequalities in society has made a major contribution to the sociology of education in the last twenty years or so.

Key debates

Feminist sociologists have been concerned with:

- differences in the educational achievements of boys and girls;
- questions of bias within the subject matter of the school curriculum;
- the relationship between class, gender and race in the distribution of inequalities in education;
- the school as a location in which boys and girls rehearse the oppressive relationships of a patriarchal society.

Key perspectives

As we have seen, there is not one but a variety of perspectives within contemporary Western feminism. In studies of schooling and education, the perspectives of liberal feminism, socialist feminism and radical feminism have been the most influential.

| Liberal feminism | The basis of liberal feminism is the commitment to equal opportunities in education for all pupils irrespective of gender. It is assumed that wherever inequalities are detected in the treatment of school pupils – for example, in the subject matter of the curriculum and in the subjects offered – these differences should be eliminated. Children should have access to the same schools, the same teachers, the same subjects, the same examinations, irrespective of race and gender. There are no good reasons, according to liberal feminists, why boys should not learn to cook and girls should not play football. |

| Socialist feminism | The basis of socialist feminism is that gender inequality is closely linked to class inequality. Schools exist to serve the needs of capitalism and to reproduce workers for a segregated labour force in the workplace, closely related to an unequal division of labour in the home. As a consequence, boys and girls are socialized and educated differently to fulfil different roles in a sexist and capitalist society. |

| Radical feminism | The basis of radical feminism is the notion that male power over women permeates the whole of society and is deeply embedded in the practices and characteristics of schooling as well as the whole of the education system. In schools, the lessons that are taught and the relationships that exist are saturated in both overt and covert bias which operates to the enormous disadvantage of girls. Boys are not only given preferential treatment by teachers but are also enabled to rehearse attitudes and behaviours which will enable them to exercise power and control over women in later life. In turn, girls learn deference and docility in ways which do not prepare them for the expectation of equality with men in later life. |

| Sexism and sex stereotyping | Since the nineteenth century girls have entered the education system in large numbers, but for the majority their experience at school has confirmed their position within the social relations of capitalism, and particularly with regard to the sexual division of labour. Two concepts are used to analyse the ways in which girls are socialized: |

1 *Sexism*, defined by Frazier and Sadker as 'a belief that the human sexes have a different makeup that determines their respective lives, usually involving:
> the idea that one sex is superior and has the right to rule the other
> a policy of enforcing such asserted right;
> a system of government and policy based upon it.'
2 *Sex stereotyping* This describes the process whereby individuals are socialized into thinking that they have to act and think in a way appropriate to their sex.

Both sexism and sex stereotyping can be seen in the school curriculum, in the way that pupils interact with each other and with teachers, in reading schemes and textbooks, in the allocation and distribution of resources, in curriculum content, in games and play facilities and in uniform and behavioural expectations.

Gender and
educational
achievement

It is usually assumed that there is a vast discrepancy in the educational achievement of boys and girls. It is assumed that girls 'under-achieve' in relation to boys. Increasingly, however, the evidence seems to disprove these assumptions.

Those girls who leave school at 16 do so with marginally better qualifications than boys. According to DES figures for 1987–8, for example, 42 per cent of girls left school with one or more GCSE Grade 1 passes, compared with 34 per cent of boys. While 55 per cent of boys left school with lower-grade GCSE passes, or no qualifications at all, the figure for girls in the same category was 37 per cent.

When ethnicity is also a factor the picture is slightly more complex. According to government statistics reproduced in *Social Trends*, Vol. 20, 1990, in the British population as a whole 16 per cent of white men held a higher qualification of some description, compared with 20 per cent of Indian men and 31 per cent of 'other' men. (In these statistics 'other' refers to African, Arab, Chinese and mixed race.) So far as women are concerned, 14 per cent of white women in comparison with 13 per cent of Indian and 19 per cent of West Indian and Guyanese women held a higher qualification.

In 1991 the proportion of 16-year-olds staying on at school rose by 10 per cent on the previous year. Girls were more likely (68 per cent) than boys (55 per cent) to stay on; and black (77 per cent), Asian (76.5 per cent) and Chinese (73.4 per cent) youngsters were more likely than their white counterparts (63.3 per cent) to continue in school beyond the official school-leaving age.

Analysis of GCSE and A Level results for 1995 indicates that this improvement on the part of girls is continuing. Girls achieved a higher proportion of top grades in GCSEs and showed signs of challenging boys' monopoly of higher achievement in maths and sciences. However, this does not mean that sexism is no longer an issue in the education system.

Subject choice

The disparity between boys and girls is more a matter of differences in subject choice than girls' under-achievement. At school, three times as many boys as girls study physics, and 90 per cent of exam entries in technical subjects are from boys. Girls do not do any of the sciences in large numbers and choose commercial and artistic subjects rather than technology. Sociologists refer to the choice of school subjects being 'gendered' and being based on gender assumptions made by, and held about, the 'natural' and 'most appropriate' aptitudes of boys and girls.

Liberal feminists argue that the introduction of the National Curriculum with its core of compulsory subjects will go a long way to ensuring that girls and boys get equal access to subjects like science, maths and English. Others, however, argue that 'equal access' arguments mask more deep-seated gender inequalities. Maths, science and technology are the subjects most usually regarded as male subjects, and the under-representation of girls in these subject areas occurs in other European countries with education systems which are otherwise quite unlike our own. Employment in scientific and technological areas of life are similarly monopolized by men.

Alison Kelly (*The Missing Half: Girls and Science Education*, 1981) claims that science is 'masculine' because of the way it is presented, the content of its curriculum, the types of employment to which it is related, and because of the sex of those who study, teach and use it. So long as science and technology have a masculine image, it is more likely that boys rather than girls will choose to study these subjects.

In fact, the content of science is not arbitrary or fixed, it is the product of selection, and could be made more gender-neutral.

Similarly, the jobs in which an expertise in science and technology are important are in part prestigious because of the status and exclusivity of those – i.e. men – who perform them. Hussain (*The Economic and Educational Systems in Capitalist Societies*, 1981) argues that the status of jobs, and the determination of what counts as skill, happens in the economic system and not the education system. If girls were suddenly to become well-qualified in science and technology, it is possible that the basis for selection to these occupations might change or the occupations might decline or change in status.

Computers are probably the best example of contemporary technologies that are being monopolized by men. A mystique built upon the dubious assumption that men are 'naturally' better at maths and using technical equipment than women, and because computer studies was originally taught in schools by teachers of technology and maths, has helped to introduce the subject into schools in a gendered way. Just as in science and practical subjects generally, where boys are renowned for grabbing and monopolizing equipment while girls wait patiently by until they lose interest or confidence, computers have become the latest technology to be monopolized by boys in schools.

Boys are also more likely than girls to have access to computers and computer games at home. The growth in the multi-billion-dollar computer games industry is excessively gendered in favour of what are assumed to be male traits and interests.

It is not surprising, therefore, that in the workplace, although women who were once typists may now be keyboard operators, they are much less likely to be data processing managers or program developers.

Education and capitalism

Rosemary Deem, in her pioneering book *Women and Schooling* (1978), combined the Marxist perspectives of Althusser with socialist feminism to argue that schools are part of the system of ideological state apparatuses which exist to transmit ideology. Whereas boys in schools learn their appropriate place in the class and work hierarchy of society, girls are more likely to learn that their primary responsibilities lie in the home and the family and not in the labour market.

The hidden curriculum and sexism

Feminist sociologists have also drawn attention to the ways in which the 'hidden curriculum' of schooling contributes to the socialization of boys and girls into different gender roles. The hidden curriculum refers to values, attitudes and ideas which are not always made explicit in the content of subjects, but which contribute hidden messages about appropriate behaviour for boys and girls.

Glenys Lobban

Considerable research by feminist sociologists such as **Glenys Lobban** (*Sex Roles in Reading Schemes*, 1987) has pointed to the excessive use made of both gender and race stereotypes in textbooks throughout the education system. As early as primary school, images in reading schemes portray a gender-stereotyped world, in which women as mothers rarely escape the confines of domesticity and the home, and men as fathers go out to work. Although feminist criticism has gone some way toward modifying the worst excesses of the white, middle-class, gender-stereotyped world presented in children's reading schemes, the criticisms themselves have become the focus of a right-wing backlash in educational and political thinking about 'politically motivated extremists' supposedly taking 'political correctness' in matters of gender and ethnic representations 'too far'.

At secondary school level, feminists have pointed to the continued stereotyping of gender relations in textbooks – especially in books which are still in frequent use although considerably out-of-date. Indeed, some have argued that the absence of women in maths and science textbooks, for example, goes some way towards explaining the male gendering of these subjects and the under-representation of girls choosing to study them at examination level.

The role of the teacher

The role of the teacher is also seen as influential in transmitting the ideas and values of the hidden curriculum in schools.

Dale Spender (*Invisible Women: The Schooling Scandal*, 1982) found that, in mixed-sex classrooms, boys received on average two-thirds of the teacher's time and attention.

Taking a radical feminist position, she described the education system as one controlled by men for men, in which the kinds of experience defined as important, and the kind of knowledge passed on, are precisely those which reflect male history, male ideas, male values and male culture. Women who have made important contributions to human history, literature and ideas are ignored or deleted from the record as if they were of no importance. The subject matter of most subjects in the school curriculum reflects male achievements and male preoccupations. Subjects which are directed specifically at girls, like commerce and home economics, operate according to limited and stereotyped assumptions about girls' domestic and servicing roles.

Probably the major problem caused by male bias in education, according to Spender, is the tendency for teachers to give boys 'preferential treatment'. Boys take up more space in the classroom, receive more attention, are asked more questions and have more subject matter chosen to engage their interest than girls. Because they are generally more noisy and troublesome than girls, part of their monopolization of teachers' time and energy is in the attempt to manage and control them. In the process girls are ignored, praised only for being quiet, passive and undemanding. Frequently ridiculed by the boys when they do speak or answer questions, girls learn in mixed-sex classrooms to play subsidiary roles and to tolerate assumptions about their inferiority.

Michelle Stanworth (*Gender and Schooling: A Study of Sexual Divisions in the Classroom*, 1983) examined, among other things, teachers' attitudes to girls. She found that teachers' attitudes actually helped to impede girls' progress. In her study of seven different A-level classes, teachers found it more difficult to remember the names of girls than boys in their class. They tended to think that education was less important for girls than boys, since girl pupils were still regarded principally as future wives and mothers rather than potential breadwinners. In her study boys were given more attention than girls even in classes in which girls outnumbered boys by 2 to 1. Girls consistently underestimated their abilities, while boys consistently overestimated theirs.

Classroom behaviour and social interaction

Pat Mahony (*Schools For the Boys*, 1985) described mixed-sex schools as arenas in which boys are trained in 'social maleness'. She based her study on six London-based comprehensives, and found that boys:

- took up more space than girls in the playground and the classroom;
- demanded constant servicing from girls by borrowing rulers, rubbers, etc.;
- used physical and verbal aggression, hostility and ridicule to dominate, diminish and harass girls as a matter of course;
- regularly received more attention and preferential treatment from teachers.

Mahony described the verbal abuse and sexual harassment of girls by boys in schools as 'woman-hating' behaviour, which is part of the training in 'social maleness' by which boys are allowed to rehearse the relationships of oppression they will later exercise with greater effect in adult life. Like Spender, she adopts a radical feminist analysis to relate the interaction in schools to male power in the wider society. In this sense, mixed-sex schooling is a preparation for life – a life in which men dominate and control women. Mixed-sex schooling does not provide for equality of opportunity but for indoctrination and practice in the experience of domination and subordination.

Carol Jones (*Sexual Tyranny: Male Violence in a Mixed Secondary School*, 1985) also reported on the heightened levels of violence initiated by boys in mixed schools against women students and teachers. She argued that schools, by overlooking and condoning the sexist and oppressive nature of boys' bullying and sexual harassment of girls, helped to legitimize male violence against women and make it seem part of the cut and thrust of every day life.

Equal opportunities initiatives in schools

Persuaded by the arguments of feminist sociologists, and increasingly aware of the issues raised by researchers on gender and education, attempts have been made to develop practical responses to counteract some of the most obvious examples of inequality in the treatment of boys and girls in schools.

Recent success by girls in GCSE and A Level examinations has led some to doubt the validity of earlier feminist analysis. If boys 'get preferential treatment' or 'cause trouble to get girls' and teachers' attention' it doesn't seem to be resulting in boys doing better in school. Should we now be concerned about boys' low achievement and why girls are increasingly doing better? In fact, the evidence continues to support the validity of feminist analysis about male and female socialization. While boys are being 'laddish' girls are getting on with their work more conscientiously. In learning situations that reward the ability to 'work quietly and conscientiously on your own' girls – because of their socialization – are likely to do better than boys.

The National Curriculum

1988 Education Reform Act

The passing of the **Education Reform Act** in **1988** has been responsible for introducing some of the most dramatic changes in state schooling since the end of the Second World War (see below). One of these has been the introduction in September 1990 of the National Curriculum. It is now intended that girls and boys at both primary and secondary level will be taught the same core curriculum, ensuring that all pupils have 'equal access' to the same subjects.

Feminists argue that 'access' is not the same as 'outcome', however, and that equal access on its own does not take account of the persistence and deep-rooted effects of the hidden curriculum in schools. The gender bias and sex stereotyping presented in educational materials, content and resources are not tackled by the National Curriculum, nor is any priority given to training teachers to confront and change the kinds of attitudes and practices which, as we have seen, impede the progress of girls. Without some understanding of the effects of the hidden curriculum, and some commitment to changing the sexist culture of schools, it is likely that the National Curriculum will continue and exacerbate the role of the education system in making gender inequalities appear to be legitimate.

Without some recognition of difficult and serious problems like sexual harassment and social maleness in schools, and the readiness to make links between male power in the wider society and the ways in which patriarchy operates in the education system, superficial adjustments at the level of 'curriculum access' will be largely irrelevant.

Ethnicity and education

In studying the connection between ethnicity and education, sociologists have been concerned with two main issues:

- the educational achievement levels of black children;
- the extent to which the school curriculum and the hidden curriculum take account of the cultures of black children.

Educational achievement

In the 1960s and 1970s concern was expressed about the generally low attainment levels of children of Afro-Caribbean origin. They were found to be less likely to pass examinations, more likely to be concentrated in low streams and more likely to be referred to special schools and withdrawal units of various kinds than white children. Explanations for this varied.

Innate ability

Hans Eysenck & Arthur Jensen

Hans Eynsenck in Britain and **Arthur Jensen** in the USA argued that the problem was to do with lower levels of inherited intelligence, a form of genetic inferiority. These views were subsequently criticized as racist and inaccurate.

- They were derived from the effects of 200 years of systematic prejudice and discrimination against black people in societies like Britain and the USA which has led to black people in general living, working and learning in inferior environments to whites.
- The explanations were also based on tests purporting to measure intelligence, which were themselves seriously flawed. The tests were biased against the language and culture of ethnic minority groups. In **1985** the **Swann Report** found that there was no significant difference between the IQs of black and white children.

1985 Swann Report

Language

When English is not the child's first language, or when a culturally different form of English is spoken, this may account for educational under-achievement. But recent research suggests that language differences are not particularly significant. Geoffrey Driver and Roger Ballard's study of Asian children, for example, found them to be just as competent as their English classmates.

Family life

This explanation is similar to the one which relates educational failure to class and cultural deficiencies (see above) and which is manifested in lack of parental competence and interest in educational matters. Black children, it is argued, are likely to experience a variety of detrimental social conditions, such as poor-quality housing, overcrowding, single-parent families, working mothers with inadequate child care facilities, etc. Ken Pryce describes black family life as 'turbulent'.

But lack of economic and other material resources are not the consequence of cultural deficiency. They are the consequence of poverty – poverty exacerbated by the effects of racism in society. To depict black families as 'turbulent' and problematic is to ignore the extremely close-knit and supportive nature of Asian family life, for example, and the ways in which West Indian families frequently act as a strong and supportive bulwark against the racism of the wider society. (See *Heart of the Race* Beverley Bryan *et al.*, 1985.)

Roger Ballard found that parental attitudes in the Asian community positively contributed to the educational success of Asian children. In a report published by the Inner London Education Authority in 1990, after an analysis of the 1987 examination results of 18 314 London schoolchildren, it was found that children of Pakistani and South East Asian origin, including children from Vietnam, China and Hong Kong, scored well above children of English, Scots, Welsh and Irish origin in GCSE examinations. The study found that children of Afro-Caribbean origin did less well – which may reflect low expectations among teachers rather than lack of parental support.

Young Children at School in the Inner City, 1988

A survey carried out by Barbara Tizzard *et al.* (*Young Children at School in the Inner City*, 1988) was based on evidence gathered over a period of three years between 1982 and 1985. The children were mainly working class. The survey found that the parents of both black and white children were interested in their children's schooling, and that this was especially true of black parents. The report concluded:

> there is a widely held belief amongst teachers that black parents are particularly likely to fail to provide adequate support for their children. This proved to be a myth. We found that black parents gave their children even more help with school work than white parents and had a more positive attitude to giving this help.

Tizzard also found that gender was of some significance in the attainment of black pupils:

> At the pre-school stage we found no significant differences in early reading, writing and maths skills. The only sex difference at this stage was that both black and white girls were superior to boys in writing. This superiority continued throughout the infant school. At the end of infant school there was still no overall ethnic difference in attainment but the black girls had emerged as ahead of all other groups in both reading and writing, whilst black boys were doing worst. Both black and white boys made more progress than girls at maths.

Geoffrey Driver's survey of school-leavers in five multi-racial, inner-city schools found that Afro-Caribbean pupils, especially girls, achieved results that were better on average than those of their white counterparts. He suggests that the relatively independent and central role of women in the Afro-Caribbean community, both as heads of single-parent families and in paid work, may act as an inspiration and a motivation rather than be detrimental to their children's achievement.

Social class

A further explanation accounts for differences in the achievements of different ethnic groups in terms of social class. Children of Asian origin are more likely to come from small-business and middle-class families than children of Afro-Caribbean origin. However, the alleged characteristics of white British social class groups are not necessarily transferable to other cultures. The Swann Report attributed about 50 per cent of the causes of educational under-achievement of some black children to the effects of social class, but said that the rest was due to prejudice and discrimination in British society.

Racism in the classroom

The Swann Report attributed some under-achievement to racism in the classroom. While most teachers are not consciously racist, there is a good deal of unintended racism. Teachers' attitudes and expectations and school textbooks and teaching materials frequently endorse negative images of ethnic minorities.

The hidden curriculum

Bernard Coard argues that black children become 'educationally subnormal' by making them feel inferior, dirty, ugly and fit only for menial jobs. The language and spoken English of black children is defined as second-rate. In English culture, white is associated with goodness and black with badness or evil. The content of textbooks frequently ignores the history and culture of black people or portrays them only in stereotyped and subservient roles. Images of Britain's Imperial past, and current explanations of third world poverty and malnutrition, often serve to confirm racist prejudices about inept and inferior cultures.

Prejudice and racism are a daily occurrence in British classrooms and playgrounds. The racist name-calling and harassment of black children by white pupils contributes to feelings of inferiority, low self-esteem, low expectations and hostility.

The low expectations of teachers can act as a 'self-fulfilling prophecy', in which children expected to do badly respond in ways which confirm negative predictions.

Diversity

A recent PSI study written by Trevor Jones (*Britain's Ethnic Minorities*, 1993) and based on the changing experience of various ethnic groups in the 1980s, concluded that it is inaccurate to talk about ethnic minorities as if they are a single group. According to Jones, 'the disparity can no longer be adequately summarized by a simple contrast between relatively well off "whites" and poorly off "blacks" '.

His study found that during the 1980s, despite continuing discrimination, some ethnic groups have made real progress. For example, the gap between white men and men of Indian, African, Asian or Chinese origin, so far as unemployment is concerned, is now virtually closed, and men from these groups are at least as likely as white men to hold professional jobs. However, little improvement has taken place in the West Indian community, while Pakistanis and Bangladeshis remain a highly disadvantaged underclass.

Higher proportions of young people of Indian, African, Chinese and Asian origin stay in full-time education after age 16 than their white counterparts. This in turn leads to higher qualifications and better prospects in the job market. Jones attributes the change to:

● the shift away from manufacturing and the expansion of the professional service sector;
● the development of business networks within the south Indian and Chinese communities;
● the skill shortages in the south-east in the late 1980s.

Young people from the West Indian, Pakistani and Bangladeshi communities are also more likely to stay on at school than their white counterparts, but this has not been translated into improved levels of educational attainment or any improvement in their job chances on leaving school.

● Only 5 per cent of Bangladeshis and 18 per cent of Pakistanis were educated to A level or above, compared with 30 per cent for Afro-Caribbeans and 33 per cent for whites in 1990.
● Afro-Caribbeans were twice as likely and Pakistanis and Bangladeshis were three times as likely as whites to be unemployed.
● In the Afro-Caribbean community there is a sharp contrast between men and women. Women have similar job levels to those of white women, better educational qualifications than women of other ethnic minorities and are generally more likely to be involved in paid employment. Women of other groups do less well. High proportions of Pakistani and Bangladeshi women do not work outside the home.
● They all face considerable discrimination, but their relative positions in education and the job market are also affected by cultural background, gender, skill levels, class structure and time spent in Britain. Currently, the Bangladeshi community is both the fastest growing and most dis-advantaged group in Britain. 'It remains to be seen whether they will catch up in the next ten years', the report concludes.

Racism in education –
The black response

An increasing response to white racism among second- and third-generation black Britons is anger. Although the consequences of anger may be difficult to deal with in the classroom, and may intensify the problems of disorder associated with life in the inner city, anger is probably a more healthy response to prejudice and discrimination than internalized feelings of inferiority and low self-esteem. Whereas in the 1960s researchers in the United States and Britain repeatedly came across images in which black children represented themselves as dowdy and damaged in comparison to white children, the influence of black power movements, Rastafarian culture and Muslim fundamentalism have altered the images available to the young people of ethnic minority groups.

Stuart Hall argues that there is a 'culture of resistance' to dominant power structures among Afro-Caribbean youth groups who choose to develop alternative ways of achieving opportunities and self-expression. Indian middle-class youth groups also display resentment and anger to incipient racism and an increasing willingness to defend themselves against intimida-tion, but they are differently placed within the economic system. They may be able to make use of the business and professional resources in their own communities to advance their progress despite the prejudice and discrimina-tion of white society.

Racism and the school curriculum

The other main focus of sociological research into ethnicity and education has concentrated on the character of the school curriculum and the ways in which it might be used to alter racist attitudes and behaviour in society. There are four main approaches to this issue: assimilation, multi-culturalism, anti-racism and educational needs. Some black and Asian groups have added a fifth possibility, which we can call **separatism**.

Assimilation

This approach was typical in the 1950s and 1960s and was based on the expectation that black immigrants to Britain would come to adopt the language, culture and values of British society. It confirms the racist belief that 'all things British are best', and does not account for the persistence of discrimination despite attempts by black Britons to 'fit in' with the odd cultural practices of an often hostile society. Nor does it account for the persistence of racism against black British residents whose country of origin and nationality are British.

In the 1980s the New Right returned to this philosophy by re-emphasizing the need for children from ethnic minority groups to be schooled in British history, English literature and the Christian religion.

Multi-culturalism

This approach derives from liberal thinking in education, and is based on the belief that the school curriculum should reflect the diversity and richness of different cultures in a multi-cultural society like Britain. While this approach has helped to broaden and rethink the content of the school curriculum in some respects, critics argue that the emphasis has been on the superficial recognition of different customs at the level of dress, food and music. It can contribute to the creation of stereotypes ('All blacks play in steel bands or like reggae music', 'All Asians eat samosas and wear saris'). As an approach it has not taken seriously the central problem of racism in British society.

Anti-racism

This approach is based on the belief that British society, including the education system, is 'structured' in a racist way. The power to make laws and decisions is in the hands of predominantly white personnel, while the school curriculum reflects white British history, values, ideas and priorities over generations. Not only is the curriculum biased against the culture of working-class people generally and the interests of girls in particular – it is also uninformed about, and partial in its account of, other cultures. Attempts to confront racism in schools needs both the wholesale employment of more black law makers, teachers and administrators at every level and a curriculum which includes a critical approach to Britain's racist past and the problems of racism and discrimination in contemporary society.

Special needs

This approach is based on the assumption that 'what is good education for white children is also good education for black children'. Liberal attempts to 'popularize' the school curriculum with multi-cultural music and festivals, and socialist attempts to use the curriculum as a vehicle for attacking racism, detracts from the business of 'real education' – that is, making sure that children are competent in the three Rs. While this approach has been used to criticize some of the rather superficial achievements attributed to multi-culturalism, it has also been used to endorse New Right demands for higher standards and more competition in schools at the expense of critical thinking.

Separatism

This approach has been advocated and adopted in some communities in which it is felt that either insufficient or inaccurate consideration is given to black culture and values in the education system or as a way of preserving particular religions and cultural identities 'in exile'. This has led to the setting up of 'weekend schools' in various communities to learn about Afro-Caribbean history, for example, or to promote religious education in Muslim communities. Government policies, influenced by New Right thinking in education and attempts to provide 'greater parental choice' and 'opting out' of local authority control, provide opportunities for separate communities, at least theoretically, to set up separate schools. The extent to which the Government will, or should, allow these developments to happen remains to be seen.

Education and the New Right

The decline in manufacturing and rising unemployment throughout the late 1970s and 1980s led some to blame the education system for failing to produce skilled, motivated young workers. Increasingly, industrial unrest, the demise of the Labour Party and the rise to prominence of the New Right all contributed to a decline in social democratic concern for the politics of progressivism in education and for attempts to create greater equality of opportunity.

Since 1979 the concern of successive Conservative Governments has been to link education, almost exclusively, to arguments about promoting economic growth and concentrating on the skills needed in the workforce. They blamed former liberal and progressive approaches for reducing standards and promoting 'sloppy' and 'dangerously lunatic' ideas about egalitarianism in society and claimed that increasing numbers of young people were unemployed because they were unemployable.

The two major contributions of New Right thinking to government education policy in the 1980s and early 1990s have been:

● the ideas associated with New Vocationalism;
● the changes brought about by the Education Reform Act of 1988.

New Vocationalism

New Vocationalism, closely associated with New Right thinking in education, refers to a concern about the ways in which the education system can best be used to serve the needs and interests of the economic system. The ideas are closely associated with Conservative Government education policies in the 1980s and 1990s although initial concern that education was not adequately meeting the contemporary needs of the economy is usually attributed to James Calaghan, the Labour Prime Minister, in a speech at Ruskin College, Oxford in 1976.

Under the Tories it has been the influence of the business world in the affairs of education that has been encouraged.

Employers, through organizations like the Confederation of British Industry (CBI) have been widely consulted about what they require in terms of skills and attitudes in young workers.

Schools have been encouraged to include representatives from local employers on their governing bodies.

Industry has been encouraged to sponsor appropriate projects and developments in schools.

Schools have been encouraged to adopt the strategies of business management, competition and marketing to improve the quality of their 'product' and 'sell it' more effectively and efficiently to 'customers' in the 'education marketplace'.

Training and Enterprise Councils and YTS

Government employment training schemes, formerly organized by the Manpower Services Commission (MSC), then by the Training Commission and currently by **Training and Enterprise Councils**, have taken over responsibility for the vocational education of young workers. These are organizations which are controlled by employers and responsible to the Department of Employment rather than the Department of Education. Young people leaving school without jobs are now required to attend Youth Training Schemes (**YTS**) of one kind or another. The reputation of these schemes, however, is not good with either young unemployed workers or government critics.

- Critics have accused them of sexism and racism in their assumptions about training needs and priorities.
- Training components concerned with inculcating positive attitudes to work, discipline, good time-keeping, getting on with others at work, etc. are all said to favour the interests and control of employers, at the expense of education about workers' rights, health and safety at work issues, trade union organization, etc.
- Many of the schemes are held to be spurious. There is no evidence that they lead to full-time employment.
- Often they provide local small employers with temporary cheap labour.
- The obligation to attend training schemes keeps large numbers of young people out of the unemployment statistics – thereby disguising the real level of unemployment – and therefore not entitled to state benefits other than their nominal training allowance, thereby effecting a seemingly legitimate reduction in social security spending.
- Youngsters dependent upon, and obliged to attend, YTS, especially in areas of high youth unemployment, are uniformly cynical about their experiences. Disenchantment with the capacity of YTS to manufacture non-existent jobs, however well-motivated, punctual and disciplined the potential workers might be, and the lack of entitlement to state benefits, are two reasons why increasing numbers of youngsters stay on at school after 16. The implication that more schooling and better qualifications will, in the long run, lead to less unemployment has not yet been proven, however.

Research findings

Dan Finn carried out research in Coventry and Rugby among fifth-form pupils (*Leaving School and Growing Up*, 1984). He found that unemployment is not the consequence of youngsters being unemployable. In his survey 75 per cent of them already had experience of part-time jobs of various kinds and were not ignorant of the world of work. He concluded that YTS was a way of artificially reducing the unemployment statistics and keeping young people in competition with each other for scarce resources, in turn making them vulnerable to employer exploitation and low wages.

John Clarke and Paul Willis (*Schooling For the Dole*, 1984) argue that YTS is a way of contacting people who want to work but who are kept in 'suspended animation' until real jobs become available. The schemes are a result of a 'crisis in profitability' in British industry. Trainees are used as 'cheap labour' to increase profitability at the expense of properly paid full-time workers. Unlike full-time workers, trainees can be laid off or sacked at the end of their training, with no obligation to pay them redundancy pay or add them to the statistics of unemployed workers.

Phil Cohen (*Against the New Vocationalism*, 1984) has analysed the educational component of YTS courses. Rather than providing 'social' and 'life' skills as they claim, Cohen argues that they contribute to the deskilling of young people. The emphasis is on good behaviour and etiquette and creating a favourable impression. The implication that 'not getting a job' is the result of incompetent behaviour in some way, rather than structural unemployment, is a myth perpetuated by such approaches.

Carol Buswell (*Training For Low Pay*, 1987) found that YTS aimed at young women was still underpinned by the ideology of domesticity and femininity. Girls were being offered training primarily in retailing, clerical work and the service sector. In general, girls' experience on training schemes prepared them to accept low wages as future workers, to have limited expectations about the kinds of jobs that are available to them and to give them first-hand experience of dependency in ways which anticipate their future roles as wives and mothers and low-paid, part-time workers.

Although all these criticisms are probably valid, they fail to explain what young people should do in a time of high unemployment and fail to suggest any alternatives. While most sociologists would be critical of the philosophy which underpins such schemes, there needs to be a different set of directions at government level and different economic policies to tackle unemployment and industrial recession rather than to expect employers' organizations to make token adjustments in the curriculum of employment training schemes.

1988 Education Reform Act

As we have suggested, New Right thinking in education tends to ignore the effects of social class, gender and ethnicity because it is not particularly interested in questions of equality of opportunity or cultural relevance in the curriculum. Competition is seen as the driving force that links individual and national achievement. Education, it is felt, cannot compensate either for society or individual incompetence. Rather, the system should treat everyone the same – assuming, of course, that this would be possible – in the belief that those who work hardest and make most progress will automatically rise to the top. It is a reinvention of old ideas derived from Darwin about the 'survival of the fittest', together with New Right commitment to 'enterprise' and the creation of a 'meritocracy'.

The Education Reform Act is probably the most significant piece of education legislation since the end of the Second World War. Its main provisions have been:

National Core Curriculum and SATs

- the establishment of the **National Core Curriculum**, ensuring that all pupils study the same essential subjects with more or less the same subject contents until the age of 16;
- the introduction of **National Standardized Attainment Tests** (SATs) in key subjects, to be given to pupils at ages 7, 11, 14 and 16. The government has also made it clear that it would like the results of these tests published so that parents can assess which schools are achieving the best test results;
- the introduction of the **Local Management of Schools** (LMS). This gives greater control of school budgets to headteachers and governing bodies

rather than the local education authority. Money for teachers, books, school building repairs, etc. is awarded according to the number of pupils on the school roll. How individual schools decide to spend the money and arrive at their priorities is left to the discretion of the head and the governors;

Open Enrolment

● the introduction of **Open Enrolment**, meaning that schools can expand their pupil numbers and thereby increase their entitlement to additional funding. It is likely that schools will choose to expand only in ways which enhance their reputation. In practice, they will become increasingly in competition with each other for the most desirable pupils. Schools which do not attract sufficient pupils will be unable to balance their budgets and have to close;

Opting Out

● the introduction of **Opting Out**, a system whereby schools can choose to receive their money directly from the government, thereby placing themselves totally outside the control of the local education authority. In these circumstances schools will become responsible for hiring and firing staff and deciding their terms and conditions of employment, making their own arrangements and striking their own deals with regard to school supplies, catering and domestic services;

● the introduction of **City Technology Colleges** in some selected cities, financed jointly by government and world business, and operating totally outside the control of the local education authority;

ILEA

● the abolition of the **Inner London Education Authority** (ILEA) officially on grounds of its size and consequent unresponsiveness to the needs of individual schools in different London boroughs. Government critics regard the abolition of ILEA, like the Greater London Council (GLC) before it, as a politically-motivated move on the part of a right-wing government to get rid of possible sources of opposition that were well known for their egalitarian and progressive policies;

● the Act also arranged for the removal of polytechnics (now called universities), further education colleges and tertiary colleges from the control of local education authorities. These are now funded nationally on the basis of their student rolls and separately managed by their heads and governing bodies.

The two main issues arising from these changes are to do with:

● the nature and delivery of the school curriculum;
● the reclassification of education as a form of 'business' which must operate in an increasingly competitive 'marketplace'.

The National Curriculum and testing

The idea of the National Curriculum is not particularly contentious because most educationalists recognize the usefulness of a core curriculum up to age 16. But the content has been vigorously criticized for being too nationalistic, too ethnocentric, too sexist and too racist. The concentration on 'English-ness' in, for example, the teaching of literature and history discounts not only the culture and heritage of other regions of the UK, but also the increasingly multi-cultural nature of British society. Insufficient recognition is made in the content of the curriculum to Britain's place in Europe, the new world order and in relation to the third world.

The fact that all children have access to the same curriculum does not take account of feminist criticisms about the ways in which standard curriculum contents ignore and/or stereotype women, or help to tackle the ways in which conventional classroom interaction helps to ensure that boys receive on average two-thirds of the teachers' energy and time in mixed-sex classrooms.

Testing remains a contentious issue, and led in 1993 to a confrontation between teachers required to administer the tests and government ministers seeking to enforce and publicize them. Teachers argue that tests have not been properly piloted, do not take account of the diversity among pupils and schools, are open to manipulation and require excessive amounts of work on the part of teachers who are already fully stretched. Government ministers, on the other hand, justify the tests in terms of raising educational standards and providing information for parents about how well different schools are doing their job.

Educationalists argue that crude comparisons between the success rates of schools filled with relatively privileged middle-class children in leafy suburbs, compared with those of dilapidated schools in inner cities in which children come from poor and difficult home circumstances, made simply on the basis of SATs results, gives a very biased and incomplete picture of the nature and quality of the schools in question.

Education and the marketplace

Increasing the management responsibility of headteachers and governing bodies and reducing the control of local authority 'bureaucrats' is claimed by the New Right as a victory for variety and choice in the educational marketplace.

● Schools will be in competition with each other for pupils and will need to convince parents that they are doing a good job.
● The responsibility for managing tight budgets, which like everything else in the public sector has been the subject of government cuts under the Tories, will force individual schools to make their own decisions about cost cutting and fund raising.
● Those schools which are well managed and are effective competitors in the education marketplace will attract the best pupils and secure additional funding from sponsorship deals with industry. As a consequence, their SATs and examination results will compare extremely favourably with those of other, 'less effective' schools, which will in turn allow them to be even more discriminating in their selection of pupils.

Criticisms

The main problem with all of this, however, is that, in order to compete for 'customers', schools are being required to think more about financial matters, balancing budgets and effective marketing techniques than educating children.

Just at the point at which comprehensive schools were becoming established, were beginning to make real gains in the battle for greater equality of opportunity and were coming to recognize and tackle some of the problems associated with gender relations in schools and combating racism, the Tories have set about dismantling the entire system and weakening the power of local authorities to develop some kind of parity of esteem between the schools in their localities.

Individual schools touting for customers and balancing budgets will have little time to think about educational philosophy and practice.

Children being systematically prepared for the discipline of work or the cynicism of unemployment will be deprived of an education which encourages social awareness and critical thinking.

A two-tier system will again develop, in which those parents with economic resources and appropriate cultural capital will ensure that their children get the best possible start in life. Parents who are less well informed, lacking in social power or merely poor will have little choice other than to send their children to the nearest school – always supposing that the school is prepared to accept them. In schools in which children come from poor homes, in areas of multiple deprivation and poverty, it is highly unlikely that the test and examination results will compare favourably with those of more privileged schools. The morale of pupils and teachers in such schools will deteriorate, making them increasingly difficult to manage.

We shall have returned to the situation which social democrats and progressives in education set about changing in the late 1950s and mid-1960s, when divisions of social class, ethnicity and gender were paramount and children were clearly recognizable as either winners or losers.

7　Work

The issues
Sociological studies of work carried out at a time before the re-emergence of feminism in the late 1960s described work as a mostly male concern. Work was defined as something which was done in return for wages, in places other than at home. Work, it was said, affected where workers lived, how they voted, their membership of trade unions, their attitudes to education, what they did in their spare time. Leisure was defined as free time spent away from the workplace. If work was monotonous, leisure time was often defined by the researchers as unproductive – concerned with immediate pleasures and short-term goals. If work seemed more challenging, skilful or rewarding, leisure time, it appeared, was also spent in useful hobbies, creative pursuits and long-term interests.

Today these definitions of work and leisure seem totally inappropriate. Even at the time of their sociological popularity, they were seriously flawed. Students of sociology studying work in a previous generation could be forgiven for thinking that work was exclusively the pursuit of men – and white, working-class men at that, working mainly in factories and dangerous occupations such as coal mining and deep-sea fishing.

Studies of work were closely related to studies of industry, to the effects of changes in industrial strategies and to the industrial relations forged between management and workers. In some ways these preoccupations were not surprising. Social behaviour, as Marx knew very well, is considerably influenced by the methods and economic relationships of production. Whether people work or not, the kind of work they do and what happens at work does have enormous significance for the rest of their lives.

Workers in an industrial society can expect such a society to be very different from one in which most of the production and labour is associated with agriculture. But the sociological emphasis on a male workforce, principally engaged in manual labour, did little to consider the working practices of those in other workplaces – in powerful jobs in politics, business, finance, the law, medicine, academia, for example. It also failed to recognize the position of black workers in the labour force, especially as their numbers increased after recruitment drives in the 1950s and 1960s in the Caribbean and the continent of Asia, and it ignored almost entirely the participation of women in paid work, or their relationship to capitalism as a kind of 'reserve army of labour' to be moved in and out of the labour force as the economy required.

It was an approach which concentrated quite properly on the characteristics of capitalism, and on the changes taking place because of the development and spread of capitalism. But the definitions which were used assumed that capitalism was merely about relationships of production. The great contribution of feminism to the study of work and leisure was to point to the dual nature of womens work – badly paid, part-time and essentially unrecognized in the workplace; unpaid, unregarded and largely invisible at home. It was left to feminism to remind us that childcare and domestic labour, although carried out at home and unpaid, should still be regarded as work; work which is just as important and significant in its relationship to capitalism as waged labour because it ensures the reproduction of the labour force – the creation, maintenance and regeneration of new armies of workers, both male and female.

Pre-feminist assumptions about useful and less than useful leisure pursuits undoubtedly reflected the cultural bias of those recording the descriptions, and, of course, leisure defined as 'free time away from the workplace' was barely adequate when applied to women. Feminists introduced the notion of the 'double shift '– one shift at work, a second at home. When the home is also the workplace, but without the regulation of clocking on and clocking off, it is much more difficult to measure the moment when work ends and lesiure begins.

New technologies and the restructuring of the labour market

Since at least the 1970s, changes in technology, especially the introduction of new technologies, have significantly influenced patterns of employment and leisure pursuits. Although part of the problem associated with British industry over the last twenty years or so has been its failure to respond as quickly and creatively to the opportunities presented by new technologies as some leading competitors, these developments have contributed to changing the character and composition of the workforce in this country.

The old industries like coal, steel and shipbuilding, on which the early prosperity of Britain was based, are now pale shadows of their former selves. The solid manufacturing base, which after the Second World War was supposed to guarantee full employment and produce the wealth to fund capital expenditure and social reforms, as part of a post-war settlement, based on Keynesian economic policies and democratic aspirations, is now considerably reduced in size and significance. The last twenty years or so has seen a shift towards new technologies in manufacturing, white-collar employment and office-based activities, and towards service industries and retailing.

'colour bar'

Now women account for half of the total workforce. Black workers have also made some gains, given the widespread **'colour bar'** operating in most British workplaces in the 1960s. But black workers are still most likely to be concentrated in a narrow range of jobs in which the pay and conditions are among the worst in the labour market. They are more likely than white workers to be unemployed, and they continue to experience racism, both in terms of discrimination and hostile attitudes, in all institutions and at all levels of achievement. Unemployment running at between 3 and 5 million – depending on how the statistics are collected – has become a permanent feature of the economy.

equal opportunities

It is much rarer in the 1990s for women to subscribe to the old adage, 'I don't work, I'm only a housewife' – and not only because there are now increasing numbers of women in the paid workforce. Attitudes and identities have changed as a consequence of feminism, and the significance of women's work is now much more widely acknowledged. Policies of **equal opportunities**, and the recognition that women ought not to restrict their employment horizons to jobs traditionally assumed to be 'women's work', has shifted public attitudes to women's role in the workforce. But, as with black and black women workers, the gains are far less than they might be. The majority of women workers still work in less influential, less well paid and less secure jobs than men, and, while the expectations of women regarding paid work, and the assumptions in society generally about women's right to paid work, may have become more enlightened, there is the tendency to regard token inroads into traditionally male occupations such as train driving, engineering, the judiciary and plumbing as evidence that equality between the sexes at work has now been achieved.

Key perspectives and debates

Sociological studies of work have their roots in industrial sociology and in the analysis of industrialization put forward by Marx, Weber and Durkheim. The relationship between capitalism and industrialization has been developed to show how changes in both have affected working processes, working relationships and the kinds of work that are available.

This emphasis led, in the post-war period, to studies of workers' attitudes and motivations and to the consideration of scientific versus human relations management theories. Studies concerned with workers' affluence, alienation and power relations within industry also derive from this period.

With the emergence of the service sector as a major source of employment, and the increase in white-collar work, emphasis shifted to theories about professionalization and proletarianization and to theories about the labour process in post-industrial society.

More serious criticisms of the sociological preoccupation with industrial and manual labour as the only kind of work came with feminism. Feminist theory has been concerned to extend the debate about work to include the interrelationship between paid and unpaid work, productive and domestic labour, capitalism and patriarchy and work and society.

As a consequence of these criticisms, the focus of industrial sociology has shifted from industry to work. Contemporary studies of work now include more discussion of the relationship between work and society, gender and race issues and unemployment.

Industrialization and capitalism

- An industrial society is one in which industrialization and modernization has occurred. Manufacturing becomes increasingly important, and most people become employees.
- Capitalism is an economic system in which the means of production (capital) is privately owned. Workers provide their labour in return for wages paid by the owners of capital (capitalists). The aim of production is to make profit for the capitalists by selling goods (commodities) in a competitive free market.

Industrialization, the growth of capitalism and social change: beginnings

Britain was the first industrial nation and British capitalism was the first to develop. A number of conditions contributed to its early growth and development.

Britain had built up a considerable empire overseas by the middle of the nineteenth century which provided both cheap raw materials and a range of markets in which to sell manufactured goods. Britain had created this empire by invasion, colonization and genocide.

At home, the 'enclosure 'of agricultural land had made many land-holding peasants homeless, and they became the first labourers attracted to the new industries and the towns which sprang up around them.

In the first half of the nineteenth century most manufacturing was still organized on a small scale in workshops, making full use of hand craft and individual skill.

As railways and shipbuilding developed, trade increased. Larger factories were built and machinery was increasingly introduced to speed up and multiply the production of goods.

The spread of machinery, railways and shipbuilding in turn provided a new demand for iron, steel and engineering. Without significant developments in the quality of iron production, mechanization in other industries would have been greatly reduced. But as a result of technical improvements in mining, smelting and purifying steel, Britain soon outstripped all her rivals in iron and steel production.

The other important innovation was the introduction of steam-driven machinery, which made it possible for manufacturers to have greater choice in where they set up their factories and made them less dependent on water and human energy. The development of steam engines and the increased demand for iron in turn affected the production of coal. Almost without exception, new industries and the manufacturing towns which serviced them grew up near to plentiful supplies of coal.

By 1850, therefore, Britain was without equal in terms of industrial production and trade. Her exports multiplied three and a half times between 1850 and 1870, when she was generally considered to be the 'workshop of the world'. In 1870 the total amount of British trade in manufactured goods was greater than Germany, Italy and France combined, though industrial developments in the USA and Germany were soon to challenge her supremacy.

The organization of labour

Prosperity for the owners of factories and those who profited from trade was not without cost to those who provided the raw materials and the labour, however. British rule in the colonies relied on exploitation. Working conditions in the factories and heavy industries at home were notoriously bad. Women and children were exploited by the same insensitive greed as exploited men.

In the end, appalling conditions and repressive measures designed by employers and government to restrict workers' rights encouraged the development of trade union ideas. Small unions and working men's associations were established, and in 1868 the TUC was formed.

Skilled workers were the first to get organized, although many of the early craft unions were little more than *'friendly societies'*. Unskilled workers in the docks, fishing and gas industries, for example, took longer to form trade unions. They lived on low wages with little protection from the law so far as their rights at work were concerned and they had no state benefit to rely on if they lost their jobs. Chronic unemployment, ill-health and poor living conditions were permanent features of their lives in the late nineteenth century, and not the most effective base from which to demand better working conditions and higher wages.

From its early beginnings the trade union movement was a very male affair. Throughout the nineteenth century the majority of skilled unions excluded women in an attempt to protect the jobs, status and wage levels of male workers. Employers were keen to take advantage of developments in mechanization which might enable them to replace skilled workers with cheaper (female) machine operatives and to use women as strike breakers. The solution was not to banish women from the unions, however, but to organize all workers effectively against the divisive strategies of employers.

Working-class men did not accept that women had a right to work – although many did in dirty, hazardous and sweated trades, usually considered 'women's work'. Women had to make their own trade union arrangements. Between 1874 and 1886 the **Women's Protective and Provident Society** (later to become the Women's Trade Union League) helped to establish between thirty and forty women's branches. The League was active in campaigns for the vote, and carried out considerable lobbying of the TUC for women's participation. However, it was not until after the First World War that unions generally opened their doors to women, although the Amalgamated Engineering Union (AEU) – despite women's employment in munitions and the like – excluded them from membership until 1943.

Women's Protective and Provident Society

Industrial change

Meanwhile, in the older industrial areas, those in which the Industrial Revolution had begun, the decline in the traditional economic base had already started. The repercussions of industrial change proceeded at different rates in differents parts of Britain, but the pattern of decline, redevelopment and diversification became a familiar one over the next three-quarters of a century. A significant watershed was the First World War.

> In 1914 Britain still controlled about one third of the world's trade, and there seemed to be no shortage of ways in which money could be made, especially by investing abroad. Eighteen months after the war ended, however, the short-lived, post-war boom in industry collapsed.
>
> Between 1920 and 1940 there was never less than a million unemployed, and those who suffered most were workers in the long-established industries of coal mining, steel production, heavy engineering, textiles and shipbuilding.
>
> Some areas, like Saltley in Birmingham, were able to avoid the worst effects of industrial decline for a while by the development of new industries like car production and the introduction of new manufacturing techniques. In other areas, electrical goods, chemicals and artificial fibres were some of the new developments which helped to change the face of industrial Britain.
>
> The problems of the older areas were dismissed as 'regional problems', and were rarely analysed as the consequences of significant shifts in the growth and expansion of capitalism which might, in time, spread their effects into other areas. A major characteristic of the development of capitalism until the late 1970s was the decline of small independent capital and the growth, centralization and concentration of capital in large national, and then multinational, organizations. During the 1980s and 1990s this process has become still more complex, with international capitalism operating on a transnational basis.

Fordism

In 1931 Henry Ford, an American car maker, opened his first British car plant at Dagenham in Essex, using techniques of mass production perfected in the United States, which soon spread to all kinds of other industries producing everything from canned foods to furniture, clothes, cookers and even ships, after the Second World War. This kind of industrial organization became known as Fordism, and had several specific characteristics.

Small, individual and family-run businesses merged and were acquired to form industrial giants like ICI and GEC.

Purpose-built machinery was formed into assembly lines, on which standardized goods could be mass-produced in enormous quantities.

Mass production required mass consumption. Consumers had to be willing to buy standardized products. Mass advertising was necessary to encourage a mass market.

Mass markets were protected at home from foreign competition. Credit facilities and hire purchase were introduced to assist sales in times of recession.

Taylorism

Mechanization and automation took the skill out of work. It broke up working tasks into a series of repetitive movements which were tied to assembly lines and could be measured by time and motion studies – a process known as **Taylorism**. The system established a rigid division of labour between mental and manual labour and tended to treat human beings like the bits of machinery to which they were attached. Since their function was specific, they could easily be replaced. Workers were paid according to the job they did rather than who they were. Work was boring, and resistance to its monotony took many forms, including time wasting, absenteeism and strikes. There was a high turnover of workers.

Those employed were easily replaceable because little skill was required. There was also a ready supply of cheap labour available in the form of women, rural workers and those specially recruited and encouraged to settle in the 1950s and 1960s from former British colonies in the Caribbean and the continent of Asia.

The rigid demarcation of work tasks encouraged the separate development of different unions, with perhaps as many as eight organizations representing different workers in a single industry. This gave rise to complex negotiations, resulting in different pay scales, contracts and terms and conditions of employment being applied to different categories of workers in the same industry.

Although the lines of competition and conflict between management and workers were well entrenched, they operated within shared assumptions about the essentially male, white culture of the workplace. The inferior wages and restricted opportunities reserved for women workers, and the colour bar operating against black workers in many industries, were based on a tacit agreement about white male dominance in the workplace – be it in the boardroom or on the shop floor.

The type of industrial organization associated with **Fordism** was not only typical of capitalist economies of the period. Soviet-style socialist economies were also greatly influenced by large economies of scale, the rigid demarcation of tasks and the measurement of time and motion by the stopwatch. So embedded in Soviet economics was the notion of giant plants and mass production that there is a hairdresser's in Moscow, even to this day, with 120 barbers' chairs.

Organized capitalism

Urry & Lash

The industrial organization associated with Fordism is also associated with a form of centralized or organized capitalism typical of British society in the middle part of this century. Organized capitalism has several characteristics, according to **John Urry and Scott Lash** in their book *The End of Organised Capitalism* (1987). These characteristics are as follows:

- The power of large national, economic, social and political institutions over people's lives.
- An increase in the average size of workplaces.
- Rising rates of capital concentration.
- Banks, industry and the state working together.
- Residence and plant locations becoming more and more urbanized.
- Collective bargaining taking place on an increasingly national scale.
- The industrial male working class reaching its largest size as a proportion of the population.
- People living in neighbourhoods with others of the same social class.
- Politics and culture reflecting the conflicts and struggles of nationally organized social classes.
- Political behaviour and party membership greatly influenced by social class.
- Relationships within the workplace greatly influencing social conflict and political life.

Post-Fordism

Post-Fordism is a term increasingly applied to industrial changes which have taken place in the 1980s and is seen as characteristic of industrial organization in the 1990s. Post-Fordism has a number of characteristics:

There is a shift away from electronic and chemical-based technologies towards new information technologies based on computers.

The break-up of huge industries mass-producing standardized commodities in favour of computerized work processes flexible enough to create diverse and varied products.

Flexible machines, programmed by new technology, which can switch from product to product with very little waste of energy or time. Benetton's automatic dying plant, for example, allows it to change its colours in relation to demand. Toyota can now change the dye in its presses in two minutes – a task which took General Motors nine hours to complete in the early 1980s.

The hiving-off and contracting-out of parts of the production process to smaller subsidiaries located in other parts of the country or other parts of the world. For example Benetton clothes are made by 11 500 workers in Northern Italy, but only 1500 of them work directly for Benetton. The rest are employed by small firms of between thirty and fifty workers. Benetton provides the designs and colours and computers send back daily sales returns from shops all over Europe to the Italian headquarters so that decisions can be made about which styles need to be replaced. Benetton headquarters instructs the various subcontractors what to make and in what quantity, and orchestrates the supply of stock to 2000 retail outlets, all of them franchised. Components for Toyota cars are made all over the world in the same way. Most are assembled on the same day that they are produced, in an efficient system which supplies components to the assembly point 'just in time' for them to be fitted.

In post-Fordist workplaces the workforce is used differently. Post-Fordist capitalism has understood that deskilled and alienated manual workers are unlikely to be committed to produce quality goods. At Toyota they talk of how routine automation wastes 'the gold in workers' heads'. In Japan the government has stuck to a policy of full employment, and trade unions do not exist as powerful organizations. Core workers are trained to perform many skills, including manufacturing and maintenance as well as monitoring quality and statistical analysis. They gather knowledge and experience over a considerable number of years and are no longer viewed as expendable or interchangeable. Education, training, welfare provision and payment by seniority are all features of the employment contract of these workers. In Britain the EETPU's agreements with Japanese car firms to accept private pension schemes, private health schemes, security of employment and union-organized training, in return for flexible working and single-company unions, represents a significant shift away from British trade unions' traditional conflictual relationships with management. Apollo is an American computer company with a European base in Scotland. Here the company has attempted to unite the workforce by calling everyone 'staff', offering them the same holidays, providing free cancer screening, a smart gym on site and private health insurance. In such circumstances, it is argued, trade unions are unnecessary.

The other side of better wages and working conditions for core workers is the reduction in size of the core workforce, and the hiving-off, or contracting-out, of less significant work to a peripheral workforce. The other side of the Japanese 'jobs for life' arrangements is the parallel development of low-paid, peripheral workers with no in-company welfare and education benefits, relying on an underfunded and inadequate welfare state. This division in the labour market is very closely related to the guiding principles of Thatcherism. The restructuring of industry and the related rewards which accrue to core workers are balanced by the further deskilling and casual nature of peripheral work, tempered by a barely adequate support system of welfare benefits.

In post-Fordist industries, the key word is **flexibility**. Computerized machines are costly to install, but are complex in their capabilities. Programmed to stop automatically when a fault occurs, they can eliminate waste. They can also be programmed to produce a variety of products in a shift from scale to scope. In response to increasingly varied and lucrative markets, the emphasis shifts from quantity to quality. Toyota turns out its cars ten times more quickly than the average Western car producer, saving unnecessary waste and energy in the process.

Market research targets groups of consumers whose lifestyle, taste and culture can be related to the style and significance of different products. The market is now broken down by age, household type, income, occupation, housing and locality. This allows manufacturers to produce special lines for special groups – to cater for the Laura Ashley type, the

Habitat type, the Marks & Spencer type. Even supermarkets like Sainsbury and Tesco know which 'niche in the market' they aim to satisfy. The diversity of Sainsbury's products is deliberately planned to satisfy several different niche markets within the same enterprise.

Emphasis has shifted from standardized goods to innovation and scope. Product life is shorter and obsolescence is endemic, creating continuous demand for new styles. Designers create shops which are described as 'stages for the act of shopping'. It is the synthesis of the 'shopaholic', 'shop till you drop', 'retail therapy' notion of consumer consumption. Instead of 'keeping up with the Jones', consumers are encouraged to be different from the Jones and to develop group identities based not on class but on age, region or ethnicity.

Although specific companies produce specific goods for a particular market, they do it on a world scale. The Body Shop, for example, taps into the same concern for cruelty-free cosmetics, environmentally friendly packaging and production and the conscience of green and third world politics in Europe and the United States as well as in Britain. The image of vitality and upward mobility associated with Benetton fashions also finds its niche in related pockets of affluence and aspiration across Europe. But a Benetton sweater is a Benetton sweater whether you buy it in Siena or St Malo. Coca-Cola is now franchised throughout the world, to a 'niche market' within a mass market. Coca-Cola and McDonalds use the franchising practices of post-Fordism to complement the standardization associated with Fordism. Coca-Cola tastes the same in Mississippi and Marrakesh. The size, shape and composition of a Big Mac is identical whether it is eaten in Moscow, Tokyo or Minnesota.

Disorganized capitalism

The industrial organization associated with post-Fordism is also associated with decentralized or disorganized capitalism, according to Urry and Lash in *The End of Organised Capital*. Disorganized capitalism has several characteristics:

There has been an increase in multinational corporations whose annual turnover is often greater than the entire national income of individual nation states. They cannot be controlled by individual nation states. They plan for profit on a global scale and their loyalty is to increasing profit rather than to the specific interests of their country of origin. Financial organizations such as banks and stock markets also operate across national boundaries. They are able to respond to developments in London, Tokyo and New York at the touch of a button.

There has been a globalization of economic, social and political relationships. The growth of electronically transmitted information can link production units anywhere in the world to the same computer terminal at company headquarters. Advances in technology can now facilitate mass communication on a world scale – 30 per cent of the world's population can share the same pop concert or Olympic final at the precise time at which it is taking place.

The possibility of technological disasters such as nuclear meltdown or destruction of the ozone layer by unregulated pollution by CFCs now creates havoc across national boundaries.

Production is now organized on a global scale. The components that make up an Apple microcomputer are produced in a bewildering array of factories in the United States, Europe and South East Asia. The forty-two chips that are finally put together in the same computer will have travelled at least a million miles to reach their destination.

The mass production of standardized products in huge manufacturing plants, employing thousands of predominantly male workers, is becoming a thing of the past. Manufacturing is increasingly being carried out using more sophisticated equipment and fewer key workers. Large firms are giving way to smaller, decentralized units with franchising and subcontracting arrangements. Large companies appear like federations of small enterprises, not because 'small is beautiful' but because 'large is expensive, wasteful and inflexible'.

Peripheral workers are increasingly likely to be women and black people, often working part-time and for low wages.

There is a shift away from manufacturing employment towards white-collar work and services.

Goran Therborn

Unemployment is on the increase. There are new patterns of social divisions within societies – between those people who have jobs and rising expectations and those who are poor, unemployed and left behind in every significant way. Mass unemployment is likely to become a feature of most advanced capitalist societies, producing what **Goran Therborn,** in his book *Why Some People are More Unemployed than Others*, calls a 'two thirds–one third society' – meaning that the bottom third of the population will be more or less permanently unemployed and dependent on meagre welfare benefits which will be reduced over time. Social controls will be increased. Feelings of despair will also increase – breeding riots, repression and contempt.

The divisions between core workers and peripheral workers also operate on a global scale. As new systems of flexible production and organization are growing in the West, they are connected to peripheral labour markets in newly industrializing economies such as South Korea, Taiwan and Singapore. In this way, much of the routine, monotonous and dangerous work is allocated to countries without protection procedures for workers or a strong trade union presence.

As employers are becoming more mobile and innovative, workers appear to be increasingly reactionary, afraid about changes which will lead to unemployment. Workers who can see a future for themselves in flexible working and multi-skilled occupations are more likely to identify with the priorities of their firms, while those who fear deskilling and unemployment are likely to work to preserve or return to outmoded patterns of industry, technology and values.

Social life, culture and politics are no longer simply related to social class. Inequalities of income, neighbourhood identities and voting patterns are now more complicated. The shared experience of class membership is now overlaid by perceived differences associated with gender, race and age, for example. Social and political movements have emerged in struggles associated with women's liberation, racial discrimination, the environment, nuclear weapons, urban inequalities, the poll tax, etc. These groups are not necessarily united by common class interests. They are organized in a relatively decentralized way and with no automatic allegiance to any of the major political parties.

Culture has also changed. Popular music, fashion, TV and cinema have all responded to demands begun in the 1960s and 1970s for individual identity and self-expression. Uniformity and sameness, associated in its extreme with white, middle-class, middle-aged suburbia in the West or socialist conformity in the East, is now seen as a form of coercion in which the cultural diversity of minorities is subsumed in the unthinking and uncritical sameness of 'the masses'. Such developments lead to radical individualism and to suspicion of centralized organization. These are developments which make primary allegiance to large homogeneous groups increasingly unlikely and help to multiply the situations in which struggle and opposition might take place.

Studies of work

Studies of work carried out before the impact of the 1980s and everything we have come to associate with post-Fordism and Thatcherism tended to concentrate on the relationship between work and its significance in people's lives. In retrospect, the studies tended to assume an essentially male workforce and the existence of large, fairly homogeneous groups described as middle- or working-class. These studies still have sociological importance, however. They provide ways of analysing the meaning of work and they have historical significance at a time when the nature of work and study of it are both changing.

The 1960s and 1970s

The studies of work undertaken in the 1960s and 1970s were varied. Some concentrated on the personal experiences of different kinds of jobs (*Work; Twenty Personal Accounts*, ed. Ronald Fraser). Others examined the impact of extremely dangerous occupations like coal mining (*Coal is our Life*, Norman Dennis, Ferdinand Henriques and C. Slaughter) and trawler fishing (*The Fishermen*, Jeremy Tunstall) as a way of understanding the wider family, social and community life of those involved. In their studies of affluent workers in the Luton car industry in the early 1960s, John Goldthorpe and David Lockwood (*The Affluent Worker in the Class Structure*) set out to investigate the embourgeoisement thesis of Mark Abrams and Richard Rose (*Must Labour Lose*, 1960), Ferdinand Zweig (*The British Worker in an Affluent Society*, 1961), and Josephine Klein (*Samples from English Culture*, 1965) – in other words, to find a typically affluent working-class population and to discover how middle-class it had become in terms of its political and social allegiances and general lifestyle.

Huw Benyon's study (*Working For Ford*) is also about what it was like to work in a car plant, but reveals in a vivid and direct way the processes by which conflict was managed in large companies, and how shopfloor workers and their shop stewards expressed their political and economic aspirations through their unions.

Others tried to identify the characteristics of work which provide job satisfaction – sometimes in an attempt to advise about improvements in working conditions or to make comments on the quality of industrial relations between different employers and their workers (*Job Satisfaction*, ed. Mary Weir, 1976).

Job satisfaction and alienation

People attach different meanings to their work and derive different amounts of satisfaction from doing it. In trying to identify the factors which make for job satisfaction, sociologists carried out a number of surveys. In general, it was thought that people with professional jobs and skilled workers get more job satisfaction than others, especially if they enjoy a fair degree of independence and responsibility. Those jobs which involve a caring responsibility for other people, such as nursing, social work and teaching, are often referred to as 'vocations', and it is assumed that such workers are more committed to the people they care for than arguing about wages and working conditions. However, the connection was not always made at the time that these were also jobs most typically undertaken by women. It took a later generation of sociologists, influenced by feminism, to point to the gender segregation of the workforce, to the concentration of women in jobs related to their supposed 'natural' inclination to 'care' and to assumptions about 'women and pin money' that led to policies of low pay. The idea that certain people have a 'sense of vocation' is often used to persuade workers in these jobs to be less trade-union-minded than other employees. In recent years, however, the low pay of nurses and social workers in particular, and the enormous demands made on teachers in a rapidly changing and underfunded school system, has made many of them feel that their sense of responsibility to their patients, clients and pupils has been exploited by employers and government, and they are now more likely to consider using trade union tactics to improve their wages and working conditions.

Other kinds of jobs which seem to provide a fair amount of satisfaction are those done by skilled workers and craftspeople. Sociologists found that if workers were involved in making something themselves, like a piece of furniture or a clay pot which involved judgement and skill, they were much more likely to find the work satisfying, than if they were continually pulling levers or fixing screws on an assembly line without ever seeing the finished product they had helped to assemble.

alienation

The term **'alienation'** was borrowed from Marx to describe the kind of dissatisfaction which comes from boring, repetitive work. At its simplest, alienation refers to feelings of unhappiness and lack of involvement at work. Marx believed that within capitalism workers do not work to express themselves or develop their interests or find intrinsic satisfaction. They work because they need to earn wages, and they are controlled and disciplined by those who employ them. The commodities they produce do not belong to them and their labour produces wealth and power for a class which oppresses them. The more uninvolved, dispossessed and exploited the workers feel themselves to be, the more likely they are to experience alienation.

Lateness, absenteeism and skiving of various kinds are typical responses to unrewarding jobs. For many, there is the sense of never really achieving anything, and a dreary sameness which makes work something to be endured rather than enjoyed.

Contact with other people has also been seen as crucial in studies of worker satisfaction. If relations at work are friendly, and if employers are considerate and fair, workers are likely to be much more contented with their jobs than if they are treated unjustly or are working with people they do not like.

Jobs which involve hard, physical labour or dangerous and unpleasant conditions, such as coal mining and deep-sea fishing, are hardly likely to produce much job satisfaction either. But sociologists found a special unity and sense of mutual support among workers in such jobs which spread over into their family life and leisure time and was seen as a response to the awfulness of the conditions and the frequent dangers experienced at work.

One of the consequences of automation, as we have already seen, has been the reduction in the need for skilled labour and the increasing use of machines and computers to do the jobs once done by people. In terms of job satisfaction, such developments have produced mixed blessings. Working conditions have become easier, and the working week has become shorter, but many feel reduced to the role of machine minders. Jobs have disappeared at an alarming rate.

Those fortunate enough to be retrained and to be reskilled in new technologies may have retained satisfying employment. However, the working conditions of peripheral workers display all the characteristics of alienating employment. Others have moved into white-collar and service industries while increasing numbers have become unemployed.

Although work can be tedious, unemployment in a society in which everyone needs to work to ensure a decent standard of living and in which persistent unemployment is caricatured as a deficiency or indication of laziness can be a debilitating and depressing experience. Because the jobs people do affect so many other aspects of their lives, and influence the ways in which they are regarded by others, to be without work can reduce a person's status, self-image and identity as a useful member of society. The unemployed are so often pitied or denounced as scroungers, and neither stereotype provides a very attractive image to live with.

The influence of work on leisure activities

Ask most people about themselves and they will tell you what job they do. Whether they enjoy their work or not, it is certainly one of the main ways in which people establish their identities. Work also has an influence on people's non-working lives, in a variety of obvious and less obvious ways.

Since people's jobs determine their income, they also determine where they can afford to live and how much money is available to spend on leisure pursuits. Hobbies like skiing, yachting and parachuting, for example, are obviously reserved for the relatively affluent (and energetic!), whereas fishing, watching sport, dancing and drinking can be enjoyed by more or less anyone.

For some workers, leisure time seems to be almost an extension of their work. It would be difficult for professional writers and cricketers to know where work stops and leisure begins, for example. This will also be the case for women engaged in any of the catering, caring or domestic industries or, indeed, any woman worker for whom unpaid work at home is still regarded as her responsibility.

For low-paid workers generally, leisure time can be something of a precious commodity. Much of it gets eaten up by the overtime and shift work necessary to ensure a living wage. Male workers in routine and boring jobs are most likely to make the sharpest distinction between their work and leisure. Many may feel they only really come alive as people when they leave work.

Studies of workers in dangerous and demanding jobs such as coalmining and trawling have shown how the comradeship of working relationships, in which people often have to depend on each other for their own safety, spills over into leisure-time friendships. Although Hull trawlermen in the heyday of the fishing industry had, on three-week trips to Iceland, only a day or two at home with their wives and children between trips, they spent a good deal of it in the local pubs and clubs with their shipmates. And in traditional coalmining communities, the men's world of the pubs and working men's clubs was still one that was only grudgingly shared with wives and girlfriends on certain days of the week. In both of these traditional communities the lives of men and women could be described as deeply segregated. Just as the men had their workmates, women formed strong friendships and allegiances around their work and their domestic lives. However, the strength and solidarity of women's networks in mining communities have always been underestimated in favour of socialist and romantic notions about the place of miners in labour history. It took the long battle with the Thatcher Government in 1984, and again with the Major Government in 1993, to remind many in the miners' union, their supporters on the left and sociologists commenting on the relationship between dangerous jobs and closely-knit communities that the women of those communities also develop strong bonds of mutual commitment, and that some of those bonds are also developed in opposition to the particular solidarity of the male culture from which they are excluded.

For some, leisure time is an escape from the tedium of routine jobs. But for many, the monotony of work spills over into the monotony of leisure, with television viewing and tinkering with the car becoming the main demonstrations of activity. In recent years, in-house entertainment in the form of television, cable television and video has become an increasing focus of leisure activity. In 1988, average television viewing for all age groups was 25 hours 21 minutes per week, with 77 per cent of the population watching every day and 94 per cent watching at least once a week. People aged 65 and over watched half as much again as the average viewer (*Social Trends* 20, page 153).

Leisure activities in the home are now much more popular than any other form of leisure activity. Cinemas belong almost entirely to the young, as do other forms of non-work activity outside the home. Concern about safety on the streets at night, and in some public places like bars and clubs, is a deterrent to women in particular.

Workers engaged in professional jobs, and those who experience a good deal of job satisfaction, are more likely to have an active and varied social life than manual workers. This is partly a matter of income and the ability to afford foreign holidays, theatre tickets, expensive equipment, etc. However, workers in professional occupations are also more likely to have had satisfactory educational experiences in the past. Interests kindled in school or college in the arts, theatre, music or painting may well continue into adult life. Certainly the adults who continue with part-time study, evening classes of various kinds and 'educational' hobbies are more likely to be those who have already experienced a good deal of educational success.

For women workers, leisure time is less likely to be something they call their own. Interests may vary between occupational, age and ethnic groups, and those who are more affluent may have more resources to spend on domestic and childcare support than others, but for those who live in relationships in which they have responsibility for others – be it children, partners or elderly relatives – the experience of leisure time may be heavily circumscribed by other kinds of unpaid work.

In addition, it has been common to regard voluntary work as something which is mostly undertaken in their spare time by women who don't have 'real jobs' to occupy them. And yet in a political climate in which the services and provisions for people in need in society are being cut back, and in which much is made of the 'user-friendliness' of community care, it is inaccurate to diminish voluntary work as something of a 'spare-time hobby'. The contribution of voluntary work to the general welfare and well-being of disadvantaged groups in society is vital, and yet goes unrecognized in the everyday definition of work and unacknowledged by the usual reward called wages.

The culture of work

Paul Willis, in his article 'Shop Floor Culture' (in *Working Class Culture*, ed. John Clarke, C. Critcher and Richard Johnson, 1979), stresses the importance of understanding the culture of work, precisely because it is so central to the cultural identity of individuals. By culture, he is not referring to 'artifice and manners, the preserve of Sunday best, rainy afternoons and concert halls' but to 'the very material of our daily lives, the bread and butter of our most commonplace understandings, feelings and responses' – in other words, to the whole of our way of life.

In one sense, there are as many cultures as there are jobs and workers involved in them, but at the risk of over-simplification it is possible, according to Willis, to distinguish between two main cultural responses to work: that of the working class and that of the middle class. The two are different from each other in most respects, and in many ways are opposed to each other. They are certainly not of equal force when measured in terms of social power. So far as society is concerned, the middle-class culture of work is part of the dominant or mainstream culture of society and the working-class culture of work is subordinate to it. Both terms are used in a neutral fashion by Willis, but neither assumes that there might be additional significant differences if we have in mind a women's culture of work or a black person's culture of work.

Middle-class culture of work

The middle-class culture of work is described by Willis in 'ideal type' terms. It is not based on actual experiences of work but on the values, assumptions and framework within which various middle-class experiences of work are usually understood. It has three main characteristics:

1 It is 'dead straight' – that is, the 'private world' of the workers' values, attitudes and aspirations is just the same as that of the 'public world' of the enterprise in which they are engaged. The concepts of career, job satisfaction, staff, etc. all belong to the middle-class world in which work and non-work selves are in harmony. The possession of 'professional identity', 'intrinsic satisfactions' and even 'vocation' are central to the experience of work.
2 The second characteristic is based on a sense of rationality, the knowledge that future career prospects and promotion can be accurately plotted by 'careful assessment and the rational analysis of ability and opportunity' – set your target, aim at it, monitor your progress, correct course, achieve it. This explanation of choice and control is, of course, quite different from the resignation with which most shopfloor workers accept that the same thing will happen to them whatever they decide to do.
3 The third characteristic reflects the monopoly over definitions which the members of dominant groups in our society have established in everything from the educational system to the mass media. Applied to work, this monopoly is able to present itself as 'the way things are', the 'only sensible way' of looking at things, against which all other views are misguided, unreasonably subversive or just plain silly. You cannot beat the system, nor should you try, since it represents the best of all possible worlds. The conscious view of society, in which all are engaged in a common enterprise concerned to 'increase the national cake', rarely asks itself the questions which might interest others such as, 'How and on what terms is the cake

made? Who chose the ingredients? Why is the cake cut horizontally to give icing to some and sponge to others? Why do those who weren't even in the cookhouse get the biggest portions?' (Willis). If you ask any of these questions, you are a troublemaker.

Working-class culture of work

The extent to which people accept or subscribe to the middle-class culture of work is largely academic so far as Willis is concerned. Having recognized that, for good or ill, it is the one which reflects the values of ruling groups in society, his concern is rather with the culture of the subordinate class. He concentrates his attention on the working-class culture of work for three reasons – because it relates in number terms to the vast majority of people; because, he claims, it is systematically misrepresented by middle-class culture and the media; and because it is important to know the life experiences which go into the production of commodities in a consumer-oriented society.

Although the surface features of working-class culture may have changed since Marx first discussed the relationships of production in the nineteenth century, the essential characteristics of people working in conditions set by others – to make goods for the profit of others in return for wages – still holds true. The major reason for this kind of employment is not to provide fulfilment and the satisfaction of a job well done – though this may result incidentally, depending on the work – but to create profit. If this means boring, repetitive or physically hazardous employment, there is nothing in the moral code of capitalism to prevent it.

One of the main themes consistently repeated in the personal accounts of manual work collected by editors like Fraser is the alienation described by the workers in mindless, routine jobs in which time hangs heavy on their hands, in which no intelligence or control over the work process is required and in which nothing, except wages, is expected from the drudgery of work – a job which is done not out of interest but merely as a way of earning money. An assembly line worker interviewed by Huw Benyon (*Working for Ford*, 1975) sums up the view exactly:

> You don't believe anything here. A robot could do it. The line here is made for morons. It doesn't need any thought. They tell you that. 'We don't pay you for thinking', they say. Everyone comes to realize that they're not doing a worthwhile job. They're just on the line. For the money. Nobody likes to think that they're a failure. It's bad when you know that you're just a little cog. You just look at your pay packet – you look at what it does for your wife and kids. That's the only answer.

They all tell the story about the man who left Ford to work in a sweet factory where he had to divide up the reds from the blues, but left because he could not take the decision making. Another said, 'When I'm here, my mind's a blank. I make it go blank'.

It is not surprising, therefore, that many such workers have little sense of loyalty to the work; a fear of redundancy, maybe, but no sense of 'hard work and commitment' which permeate the definitions of vocation and responsibility in middle-class jobs.

Shopfloor culture

A common fallacy of sociological accounts of alienated labour (though not Benyon's), which concentrate on the 'meaninglessness' of boring work is the failure to recognize that, despite bad conditions, lack of control and frequent exploitation, people do look for meaning, they do impose frameworks, they do seek enjoyment in activity, they do exercise their abilities. In practice, this response occurs in spite of, rather than merely as a result of, the prevailing conditions of work. In many respects, it is in opposition to the prevailing ideas of work which characterize middle-class culture. Willis identifies two of its main strengths:

1 The strength of the sheer mental and physical power to survive in hostile conditions. Not much, you may say, if you have never had to face the prospect of hard physical labour, but it provides the basis of other forms of response, and also the focus of a good deal of pride, self-esteem and the mystique of masculinity in working-class culture. It may be that new technologies are increasingly replacing the need for physical strength in many jobs, although such jobs do still exist in abundance. But, even where mechanization predominates, in the so-called light industries, considerable endurance is still required and images of physical strength persist to make factories very masculine institutions. This association between self-esteem and masculinity based on strength is very much a part of traditional working-class culture. But it is a characteristic which helps perpetuate sexist attitudes to women in the home and divisive competition between male and female manual workers in the labour force.

2 The strength of profound confidence expressed in the culture of the shopfloor, based partly on common sense, partly on ability and partly on cheek. In one way, it is a means of regaining control over a process which others really control, by joining with fellow workers in an informal resistance against a good deal of the formal organization of the workplace. A bit like the counter-school culture of 'the lads' (see page 144), shopfloor culture has a solidarity and a sense of camaraderie which enables those involved to manage a good deal of their time at work 'on their own terms' and 'in opposition' to what is considered ideal by the formal management structure. This includes the distinctive language and humour of the shopfloor. Willis estimates that up to half of the verbal exchanges on the shopfloor are not serious or concerned with work activities; they are practical jokes, 'pisstakes' or 'kiddings' – some are sharp, others cruel, sexist or racist, and many are about disruption of production and the subversion of the bosses' authority and status.

Cultural weaknesses

The culture Willis describes is vigorous and strong and, like the counter-school culture of 'the lads' is full of political significance. But like their culture also, it is equally limited. Because it exists as a subculture in a context dominated by the decisions of others (about investment policy, the organization of production, marketing and the extraction of profit, etc.), it is ultimately unable 'to challenge the middle-class culture of work which sits on top of it and obscures it'.

The shopfloor, like the school and the neighbourhood, is an arena for economic and cultural conflict, but it is very parochial in its vision: 'its riveting concern for the workplace – and specific workplaces at that – prevents the connecting up of work experiences, issues and social structure'. It is not political; even in its relationship to, and representation by, the trade union movement, shopfloor culture is largely unpolitical.

Just as the Labour Party 'in theory' represents the interests of the working class, but draws some of its support and most of its personnel from other groups, so, too, does the trade union movement act as a form of working-class political representation which is 'one remove' from the majority of those it represents. It presents the institutionalized form of the opposition culture of the shopfloor but, although it is close to that culture, and has been born out of it, it is also distant from it.

In becoming organized, in defining ends and means and in entering into negotiations with management 'in a responsible way', the trade union movement has frequently become another kind of authority over the worker. It often intervenes to cut out time-wasting practices – the seedbed of shopfloor resistance – and can even 'put over' the management's case to workers in order to abide by agreements it has already made with the management negotiators. Frequently, therefore, trade unions acting as a kind of cultural go-between, and in the process of 'responsible negotiation with management', concede a good deal of strength held by the shopfloor.

Clearly, this tendency is greater in the higher echelons of the union structure, and local organizers and shop stewards are likely to be closer to shopfloor culture. Willis sees this as the unions having lost touch with, and even as a betrayal of, the real radicalism of the shopfloor – a process which has intensified with the determination of Thatcherism to destabilize the trade unions as a potential source of opposition to an increasingly reactionary government agenda.

Just as the mystique of masculinity also sustains the most reactionary of attitudes to women, so, too, can other aspects of shopfloor culture be seen as something short of radical. A significant number of shopfloor workers are dominated by, or deferential to, those who employ them. It is a well known fact that Conservative Governments which consistently represent social and economic interests not particularly in sympathy with the class interests of manual workers are repeatedly returned to power with the considerable support of working-class voters. A major reason for the electoral victory that swept Thatcher into power in 1979, for example, was that a vast number of shopfloor workers, among others, blamed the Labour Government for the behaviour of the unions and resented the increasing power which they seemed to be appropriating 'on behalf of the workers' but which the workers did not agree with. It was this same tendency that the Thatcher years exploited to legislate against the strength of trade unions, end closed shop agreements, curtail picketing and the legality of strikes and set the scene for single and non-union agreements in a growing number of workplaces.

An undue tolerance of the media provides another challenge to Willis's romantic notion of shopfloor radicalism. Again, it is well known that the media in general are owned and controlled by middle-class people with economic interests different from those of the working-class. And yet the working class provide a huge and largely uncritical audience for reactionary and often disparaging media messages on television and in the popular press.

Because those who create the television programmes and write the news copy are, with few exceptions, middle-class, their distance from the realities of working-class life means that they rely on stereotypes and prejudice for most of their assumptions. The irony is that the real cultural meanings are taken by the media, transformed and caricatured, and returned to the working class – the mass audience – in unrecognizable forms. Indeed, the misrecognition is so great that, despite what working-class people know of their own lives, they are often prepared to accept contrary media images as an authentic picture of how other working-class people live.

It is not difficult in these circumstances to persuade working-class people, as Thatcher did, that, on the one hand, affluence is within their grasp, and on the other, that the destructive behaviour of trade unions has to be prevented and opposed. Or, as in the general election of April 1992 – in the midst of an extremely bad recession, high unemployment, mortgage debts and repossession of homes on an unprecedented scale – that most of those living on benefits were 'scroungers', economic recovery was just around the corner and a Labour Government would put up taxes and in any case should never be trusted because of its socialist (i.e. extremist) disposition. This after a decade of some of the most extreme government legislation ever.

These are perhaps arguments for conceding that national unions and the Labour Party had lost touch with the shopfloor, but not for assuming that shopfloor culture is automatically a radical one.

Strategies of scientific and enlightened management

F. W. Taylor

The scientific management movement originated in the United States in the 1890s, and was associated with the views of **F. W. Taylor**. His basic assumption was that human beings are essentially lazy and can only be motivated by the promise of economic reward. He advocated procedures in which individuals should be motivated by money and paid in relation to their individual efforts. Ideally, this would remove any need for trade unions. With proper scientific management in the workplace, cooperation could be ensured by the organization of the work process in such a way that individuals were rewarded for pursuing their own self-interest. This led to the introduction of **piecework** – i.e. payment related to the volume of work completed in a set time, for example the number of cartons manufactured or labels attached to tins or seams sewn on trousers.

piecework

time and motion

It also led to **time and motion** studies, i.e. the arrangement whereby work is broken down into a number of tasks or physical motions which can each be accurately timed as a way of arriving at the precise amount of time each job should take. It is then possible to programme the assembly line to run at the necessary speed to achieve this end, thereby ensuring that the output of the workers is dictated by the speed of the machine, rather than by the variability of different workers working at different speeds, or individual workers varying their speed in relation to their mood, inclination or degree of tiredness.

Scientific management advocated:

- the fragmentation of work into simple routine tasks;
- the timing and standardization of each task to cut out any wasted time;
- the separation of mental from manual labour so that the design and control of the operation became a management task and the execution of it became an employee task.

Taylorism

Sociological studies of **Taylorism** or scientific management have tended to concentrate on two issues:

- its significance as a form of management ideology justifying tight management control;
- the extent to which it has been applied in capitalist societies at various stages of their development and over a considerable period of time.

As an ideology, scientific management has had a considerable influence up to the present day, despite opposition from trade unions and employers. It contrasts strongly with the rather more paternalistic attitudes of earlier management theories associated with employers like Jesse Boot, Cadbury and Rowntree in the late nineteenth century.

However, it was later criticized by the Human Relations approach to management as being too individualistic and too economistic in its assumptions about human motivation.

Human relations theory

Hawthorne Studies

Tony Topham (*Approaches to Workplace Organisation in Industrial Studies*, 1975) describes how pyschologists in America in the 1920s and 1930s (the famous Hawthorne Studies undertaken at the Western Electric Company) first discovered that the social bonds between small groups greatly influence their attitudes and help determine production levels, and that relationships in informal work groups are much more influential on worker behaviour than the physical conditions of work. Workers in small groups tend to have loyalties and allegiances and to make up their own rules in a way which is not always in the best interests of their employers.

From this 'discovery' arose a 'human relations' breed of social investigators – academics and others – employed by management to find solutions to their problems of low productivity and lack of cooperation on the shopfloor. Their advice to management – considerably elaborated and extended over the succeeding decades – has been to find ways of manipulating the social relationships of informal groups to achieve cooperation, improve morale and encourage greater productivity. The best known and most influential group of theorists of the human relations school of management are the Harvard and Chicago business schools represented by **Elton Mayo.**

Elton Mayo

Whereas Taylor's solution to worker resistance was to provide financial rewards in return for routine tasks completed in a timed and efficient manner, the various human relations theorists have suggested strategies which include making the work more interesting; appealing to desires for friendship, challenge and variety; matching workers with the tasks needing to be done; encouraging loyalty to the company by promoting competitive attitudes to rivals, especially foreign competitors; 'counselling' uncooperative workers; and providing loyalty-inducing perks such as special recreational facilities and clubs.

Willis describes this process as 'the colonization of shopfloor culture' which, like other colonizations, is based on an attempt to destroy the culture already existing. Thus innovations concerned with 'employee-centred supervision', 'worker participation' and 'job enrichment' programmes have been employed to harness the strength and neutralize the opposition of shopfloor culture. The illusion of self-control given to the workers by these innovations has distracted many from the fact that the basic structures of power remain exactly the same as before, and that much of the potential power of the shop floor culture has been destroyed in the process.

Recent applications of these principles in relation to improving the working conditions and related loyalty of core workers in post-Fordist workplaces have included private pension schemes and private health insurance. Not only do these kinds of inducements undermine the need for protection from trade unions but, once trade union organization has been forfeited in specific plants, it is much more difficult to re-establish their presence. This then leaves the workers directly at the mercy of the management and the market. When workforces are unprotected and without strong union representation, these are precisely the circumstances in which working conditions and pay agreements can deteriorate and perks can be withdrawn. In the interim, it makes the recipients of private pensions and private health insurance less vociferous in defence of state pensions and state health provision as they become increasingly under attack from Conservative forces keen to cut public spending.

Labour process theory

deskilling

An influential source of criticism of management theories was sparked off in 1974 with the publication of Harry Braverman's book *Labour and Monopoly Capital*. Writing from a Marxist perspective, Braverman argued that Taylorism, along with widespread mechanization, automation and computerization, led to **deskilling** and degradation of work for both manual and non-manual workers. It has led to the simplification of complex labour and the reduction of workers' control over what they do, resulting in increasing levels of alienation at work.

He identified the process of deskilling in a number of occupations. In engineering, for example, rationalization and the simplification of tasks assisted by mechanization has made traditional skills as unnecessary as in any other mass occupation. This is also true, Braverman argues, of the newer, white-collar occupations – technical and scientific work, lower-ranking management and supervisory grades in marketing, finance and administration, as well as schools and hospitals.

Considerable attention has been paid to his comments as they relate to clerical work, service and retail trade operations. For example, clerical work has been reorganized so that tasks are broken down into small specialist jobs which follow set routines and are increasingly done by women. The introduction of computers has completed this process.

Braverman argues that the class structure has been transformed in the process:

- There has been a reduction in the proportion of manual workers employed in industry, and a relative growth in the proportion of workers in the service occupations.
- This has implications for the sexual division of labour, since industrial workers were predominantly male, and service and clerical workers are overwhelmingly female.
- The typical division of paid labour in the working class family, according to Braverman, is now that of a male operative and a female clerical worker.
- Fewer and fewer workers own capital and must therefore sell their labour to an employer. As one-time middle-class occupations have experienced the separation of conception from execution (mental from manual labour), they in turn have become deskilled.

Criticisms of Braverman's book sparked off renewed interest in Marx's original ideas about labour process theory. While some have been sympathetic to what he has had to say, others have been less so.

One criticism has been the extent to which deskilling is a necessary and extensive part of the capitalist labour process.

Veronica Beechy

According to **Veronica Beechy** (*Unequal Work*, 1987):

His definition of skill comes from the idea of the male artisan/mechanic as the original kind of skilled worker whose skills have been wrenched away by the subordination of labour to capital and the separation between the mental (conception) and the manual (execution) nature of a task.

The notion of the skilled artisan/mechanic implies a number of skills, and it is unclear to which of these Braverman is referring. For example, does skill mean the combination of responsibility for conception and execution and the possession of particular techniques? Or does it mean having control over what is produced? Or is it related to conventional definitions of occupational status? These different conceptions of skill do not necessarily co-exist in the same occupation. For example, some kinds of work, such as cooking, require complex techniques and control over the labour process but, unless the work is performed by a master chef, cooking is not usually defined as skilled. On the other hand, aspects of engineering do not involve conception and execution and lack complex techniques, yet because of trade union control and practice they have become, or have remained, defined as skilled. In the print industry, machine operatives mind machines and yet they are called machine managers, while welding, defined as skilled in Britain, is considered semi-skilled in many other capitalist countries. Thus it can be argued that in failing to differentiate the different aspects of skill, and failing to clarify the aspects with which he is dealing, he over-simplifies the problem of defining skill. He is not, therefore, in a strong position to make judgements about deskilling.

It is also an over-simplification to suggest that capitalism has led to the deskilling and degradation of labour without recognizing that it has also contributed to the creation of new skills. The development of large-scale industries in the nineteenth century also gave rise to new skilled occupations. The development of monopoly capitalism in the twentieth century required newly created skills in terms of planning, finance, marketing, personnel management, for example. Currently, the techniques popularized in post-Fordist industries, involving a revolution in the use of new technologies and computers, have created new skilled occupations such as computer programming and systems analysis. The history of capitalist production is better seen as the destruction and recomposition of skills to suit its changing purposes rather than the wholesale degradation of labour.

The concentration of workers in workplaces doing repetitive and boring jobs does not, as he assumes, automatically lead to a loss of control and power. Attempts made by scientific management strategies to individual-ize work and eliminate collective working relationships has not been particularly successful. It was in these circumstances that workers 'organized resistance via trade unions and informal resistance via shopfloor culture to management interests was most effective.

The assumption made by Braverman that deskilling is also related to the feminization of the workforce is also problematic, i.e. the notion that jobs are made more simple, given to women and then degraded in terms of the market position of those jobs. There are entrenched assumptions about the relative merits of men's and women's jobs. Looked at objectively, nursing could be regarded as an extremely skilled occupation, especially if interpersonal relations and the responsibilities relating to the protection of life are given due recognition. But historically nursing has been diminished by the notion of 'vocation', and seen rather as an extension of women's 'natural' instinct to 'care' – assumptions which have led to nursing not being equated with skilled labour. And if the occupation of clerk has lost its status over the years, it is not simply because it has changed from an essentially male job in the nineteenth century to an essentially female job in the twentieth century. We are not really describing the same occupation. The labour process within which clerical work exists has been extensively transformed over the years.

The industrial reserve army of labour

Braverman also returns to Marx's notion of an industrial reserve army of labour which can be brought into the labour market when it is needed and pushed out again when it is no longer required. Such an army has little power, and is set to work for low wages and in conditions which provide little protection and few guarantees of permanence. Classically women, black and guest workers and third world labour markets have been used in this way.

Braverman links his analysis of the reserve army idea to expanding and declining sectors of the economy. Thus, while manufacturing industries have been declining, service industries and occupations such as retailing and clerical work have been increasing. As male workers have been expelled from manufacturing work, women have been drawn into the service industries and occupations. This trend has been accentuated, according to Braverman, by the increasing inability of families to survive economically on one wage, which has led more women to seek employment outside the home. Braverman sees this tendency as leading to the breakdown of family and community life.

Again, criticisms of Braverman's conclusions relate to his tendency to simplify and to act on assumptions which privilege male interests at the expense of female interests:

● He does not explain why women rather than men have been drawn into the expanding service industries.
● He does not explain why women enter low-paid occupations. Women's low wages need to be explained.

Veronica Beechy (*Unequal Work*) suggests that the specific position of women as part of the reserve army can be explained as follows:

● their labour power is paid for at a price below its value;
● their labour power has a lower value;
● the existence of the family and women's dependency within the family, and the ideological assumptions which surround this, serve to determine the value of women's labour power.

Women's position within a reserve army does not in itself explain a long-term shift in the class structure, as Braverman suggests. It is more to do with capital making use of cheap sources of labour. In addition, when women are expelled from the paid workforce they retreat into unpaid domestic labour at home and are not redundant in the same way as male workers are seen to be. Women can be dispensed with at little cost to the state, frequently without rights to redundancy benefits and often without inclusion in unemployment statistics. As part of the domestic, unpaid economy, they are still, nevertheless, part of the labour process which services the interests of capital.

Braverman on social class (see page 27)

Braverman's work has been used to discuss changes in the class structure. He defines the working class quite broadly – as being all those who lack ownership of the means of production. He argues that changes in monopoly capitalist production have had far-reaching effects on the composition of the working class. As more and more sectors of the population have become property-less and have had to resort to wage labour, they have become increasingly proletarianized as a result of the separation between conception (mental labour) and execution (manual labour) and the process of deskilling.

His conclusions have been criticized as follows:

- He relates the determination of class entirely to occupational status.
- He relies exclusively on an economic definition of social class.
- He fails to analyse class consciousness.
- He fails to explain why women occupy a specific and subordinate position within the class structure.

Veronica Beechy (*Unequal Work*) suggests that:

- It is important to remember that social class is also constituted historically over time. Changes do not happen instantly (as a consequence of someone changing jobs, for example). We need to understand rather how labour (both wage labour and domestic labour) relates to capital in different historical circumstances.
- Social class is not simply the consequence of occupational status. Class is also created in the wider context of the economy, the distribution of wealth and poverty, access to power, the control of ideas, family relations and the like.
- Any definition of social class needs to be able to explain where the sexual division of labour in society fits into our understanding of social class.

Dual labour market theory

This theory is based on the assertion that the labour market is divided systematically into two sections – the **primary** and the **secondary**. The primary sector is made up of relatively well-paid jobs with promotion and career prospects, training opportunities and job security. By comparison, the secondary sector is made up of jobs which lack these characteristics. The reason for the division is based on employers seeking to offset the high costs of employing stable, skilled workers by employing low-paid, non-skilled workers on worse pay and conditions.

John Rex and Sally Tomlinson (*Colonial Immigrants in a British City*) use this theory to describe the economic position of black workers. Asian and West Indian workers are usually recruited to jobs in the secondary labour market. Because such jobs offer few opportunities for training or promotion, and are most vulnerable to unemployment, ethnic minorities occupy a disadvantaged position in the labour market. Rex and Tomlinson go on to argue that, because ethnic minorities are 'systematically at a disadvantage compared with working class whites and that, instead of identifying with working class culture, community and politics, they form their own organizations and become in effect a separate underprivileged class', they

British underclass

form an underclass in British society perpetuated by disadvantage.

R. D. Barron and G. M. Norris (*Sexual Divisions and the Dual Labour Market*) were among the first British sociologists to apply the dual labour market theory to gender inequalities. Women are over-represented in the secondary labour market, where they can be easily replaced and there is little need for employers to offer them decent wages or career prospects.

Feminists have criticized the application of this theory to women because it does not explain why, for example, women in skilled jobs which are similar to primary sector men's jobs still receive less pay than men, or why women doing the same jobs as men are less likely to be promoted.

More recent descriptions of the restructuring of the labour force in post-Fordist organizations to distinguish between core workers and peripheral workers can be seen as a current application of dual labour market theory.

The professions (see also pages 25–7)

To talk of people 'having a profession' is to talk of those that the Registrar-General, sociologists and most members of the general public would agree are middle-class. The definition of a profession is generally held to be an occupation which involves knowledge and a good deal of training, with some kind of advanced education, but it is not a concept which is very precise. The professions have always presented sociologists with problems. What is their real character? How do they differ from each other and in relation to other occupations? And what is their significance in the class system and social structure?

A major weakness of most sociological definitions is to take the professions' own definition of itself too seriously, without looking critically enough at what is being said. The result is that a number of traits or characteristics have been identified as those which the professions are believed to possess and which are often used as a yardstick when assessing the claims of other occupational groups to professional status.

Until the 1970s there was a tendency to discuss the professions on their own terms, reflecting a functionalist analysis. Bernard Barber (*Some Problems in the Sociology of Professions*, 1965), for example, argues that professions are characterized by a systematic body of knowledge; they are motivated by the desire to serve the public rather than themselves; they are regulated by a self-imposed code of ethics; they regulate and recruit their own members; and their high pay and prestige reflects the high regard in which they are held by the general public.

Talcott Parsons (*Evolutionary Universals in Society*,1964) endorsed the familiar arguments about professions having specialist knowledge and being altruistic in their commitment to society, but took the argument one step further by suggesting that this expertise entitled the professions to authority over the lay person.

Others have been critical of functionalist explanations. Ivan Illich, in his attack on the medical profession (*Medical Nemesis*, 1975), argues that, rather than acting in the interests of society, the medical establishment has become a major threat to health. This occurs because it has convinced the general public that it can diagnose and treat illness, whereas ill-heath is actually caused by social factors such as diet, working conditions, housing and hygiene, and can only be improved as social conditions are improved. Doctors, he claims, actually obscure the real causes of ill-health and therefore contribute to its perpetuation. Many of their treatments do more harm than good and distract attention away from the real causes of illness in society.

Noel and Jose Parry adopt a Weberian perspective (*The Rise of the Medical Profession*, 1977), suggesting that the medical profession, for example, manipulates the labour market to enhance its own position and get maximum rewards for itself. By restricting entry it ensures scarcity value; by claiming to regulate its own members it protects the profession from public scrutiny; by creating a monopoly over a particular service it increases its power and improves its market situation. Older, more established professions, such as lawyers, can do this more effectively than professions employed by the state, such as social workers and teachers; they can therefore guarantee higher financial and other rewards. This argument sees professionalization as being concerned with self-interest.

C. Wright Mills, in discussing lawyers in the United States, argues that such professions have become the servants of the rich and powerful, so that, for example, company lawyers advise big corporations on contracts, business deals, tax avoidance, etc. in ways which serve the interests of capital. Their high rewards are related to the demand for their services by the rich *power élite*

and powerful. Some become so powerful that they become part of what Mills calls the **power élite** in society.

Harry Braverman, the American Marxist, disagrees with Mills (*Labour and Monopoly Capitalism*, 1974). He argues that, once professions become employed by large corporations, they are less able to pursue the interests and influence of their profession. In addition, the mass employment of technicians, accountants, teachers and the like has resulted in deskilling and many of these occupations becoming routine.

Martin Oppenheimer (*The Proletarianization of the Professional*, 1973) says that when professions are employed by the state in the public sector, for example social workers and teachers, they become part of the state's repressive mechanisms and contribute to keeping clients quiet and policing potential troublemakers.

Also from a Marxist perspective, Barbara and John Ehrenreich (*The Professional Managerial Class*, 1979) argue that there is a distinctive professional/managerial class in society which has developed into a third class, somewhere between the bourgeoisie and the proletariat. Its main function is to reproduce capitalist culture and capitalist class relations. It does this by organizing the process of production and applying principles of scientific management to the workforce in its capacities as scientists and engineers; by exercising control over the working class as teachers and social workers; by promoting ruling class ideology as entertainers, media people and teachers; and by developing the kinds of consumer goods which ensure that the working class consume the commodities of capitalism. The Ehrenreichs believe that the professional–managerial class has quite different interests from those of the working class. It sees itself as independent of both the working class and the ruling class, but it is paid out of the surplus profits earned for the ruling class by the working class and develops techniques to help control the working class. Thus clients, workers and students do not always regard social workers, managers and teachers as people who necessarily help them.

It is not in the interests of the professional middle class to be directly dependent on the ruling class, however. It helps to maintain the capitalist system, but it attempts to maintain its own independence and freedom of manoeuvre. In the 1960s, the political allegiance of some members of the managerial professional class shifted. The influence of students and the appearance as a political movement of the **New Left** argued against professions saying they had become the tools or functionaries of the ruling class. This led in the 1970s to further political action and splits between those who retained an allegiance to the interests of their profession and those who declared a commitment to their clients. These ideas in social work and teaching, for example, advocated methods influenced by Paulo Friere and Ivan Illich to do with **conscientization** (political consciousness raising) and empowerment of clients, attempting to open up social work processes to participation between workers and clients and to forming broad political alliances among those who had a commitment to advancing the interests of the working class (community groups, client groups, trade unions, political parties).

More recently, a radical, right-wing alliance has emerged in social work, focusing on individual, family and, to some extent, community responsibility for social problems. Greatly influenced by Thatcherism, this trend has been associated with policies leading to the closing of large institutions for the mentally ill and handicapped, the growth of private welfare schemes and low-cost community care initiatives.

New Left

conscientization

Women's work

In their contribution to studying work, feminist sociologists have asked three main questions:

> Why do women usually earn less than men?
> Why do women do different jobs from men?
> Why do women do less paid work than men?

Currently, women earn around three-quarters of the average hourly rate earned by men. Part-time women workers earn around three-quarters of the average wages earned by full-time women workers. In 1988 women constituted around 46 per cent of the paid workforce, of whom 44 per cent were working part-time. Today the labour market is more consciously structured to make way for women than it was twenty years ago when the Women's Movement campaigned for equal pay and an end to sex discrimination in employment.

the feminization of labour

In Britain women now comprise almost 50 per cent of the paid workforce, and sociologists are beginning to talk about 'the **feminization of labour**'. But this is a misleading term, given that women have always worked, and it wrongly implies progress. The renewed interest taken in women by employers in the 1990s has very little to do with equal opportunities and very much to do with exploiting cheap labour and part-time workers.

As in other advanced capitalist societies, women's entry into the labour force in Britain seems to be one of the few growth areas in the economy. As a consequence of post-Fordist industrial organization, the distinction between core workers and peripheral workers in manufacturing has intensified. Rather fewer of the former are required; rather more of the latter.

Peripheral labour is regarded as cheap, casual and easily disposable – just the kind of work identified with women. So it is women – black and white in Britain, and black in the newly industrializing economies of Taiwan, Singapore, Hong Kong and South Korea – who increasingly constitute the peripheral international labour force associated with post-Fordist economics and transnational capital expansion.

More than half of the total employed population in Britain today works in the service sector of the economy. Clerical and administrative workers make up 45 per cent of the total British workforce. Three-quarters of all employed women work in the service sector and 45 per cent of all women are employed on a part-time basis. Almost a quarter of the total employed workforce is now part-time. Roughly 2 million are employed in retailing, of whom 64 per cent are women. Women now constitute the highest proportion of the paid workforce since industrialization.

This does not mean that women have benefited greatly from these developments, however. In 1990 the Council of Europe specified a decency threshold in relation to wages, set at £178 per week or £4.76 per hour. In that year in Britain, 88 per cent of manual and 70 per cent of non-manual women workers in the hotel and catering industries earned less than the threshold. Eighty-three per cent of manual and 34 per cent of non-manual women workers in other services (e.g. shops, hairdressing, etc.) and 40 per cent of women in the banking and finance sector also fell below the approved threshold. Thus over half of the women working full-time and 81 per cent of those working part-time in Britain in 1990 were officially low-paid. What is more, the percentage of women workers coming into this category has steadily increased in every year since the mid-1980s.

The increase in the number of women in the labour force has not been matched by an increase in opportunities, improvement in working conditions, removal of inequalities, reduction in sexual harassment, improvement in childcare facilities or increase in wage levels. The labour market is not merely being 'feminized'; it is being restructured. It is being shifted from Fordism to post-Fordism, from manufacturing to services and from full-time to part-time working. In these circumstances women increasingly get the jobs, but with neither pay nor conditions which are anything like satisfactory. Women now find themselves in paid work largely because their wage levels have been deliberately depressed for years and because they have been consigned to those sections of the job market which men have traditionally preferred not to occupy.

There are four main ways of explaining gender divisions in employment. These are:

- economic and sociological functionalism
- liberalism
- liberal, Marxist and radical feminism
- dual systems theory.

Economic and sociological functionalism

This theory suggests that women get paid less than men because they have less skill, less work experience and fewer qualifications. This is seen as the result of women choosing to give priority to their role within the family. Talcott Parsons, a famous functionalist sociologist writing in the inter-war years, described women's role in the family as 'expressive', while men's was seen as 'instrumental'. The division between men's and women's roles in the family was seen by functionalist theorists like Parsons as complementary, and in the best interests of both the family and society as a whole. He did not acknowledge that power or ideology or inequality might be factors in the social construction and allocation of different roles to men and women.

Liberalism

Liberal approaches have tended to describe the ways in which women are at a disadvantage compared with men in employment. Alva Myrdal and Josephine Klein (*Women's Two Roles: Home and Work*) described the conflicting demands of home and work as role conflict and a dilemma for women. Kanter (*Men and Women of the Corporation*) described how the cultural pressures and organizational features of workplaces make it more difficult for women to 'reach the top'. She showed how male friendships and the **'old boys' network'** operates in management, for example, and how women without suitable 'role models' of the same sex need considerable and extraordinary persistence to continue in non-traditional roles.

old boys' network

Neither of these studies looks very closely at what might be the causes of inequality between the sexes. They fail to explain how such inequalities have come to be considered 'normal' and have become embedded in systems and assumptions specifically designed to protect male jobs from the advancement of women.

When the problem of inequalities in the workplace is expressed in liberal terms as issues of role conflict and absence of role models, etc., solutions are recommended at the level of 'attempting to change attitudes' or 'intervening in the schooling of boys and girls before they become adult workers'. The problem is explained as one of 'wrong attitudes' rather than 'gendered power relations'.

Feminism

The re-emergence of feminism in the late 1960s led to considerable discussion and writing about women's employment. Labour theories popular in the 1970s – for example, the Marxist labour process theory and the Weberian dual labour market theory – were both criticized for adopting a manufacturing model of employment, which was inadequate for analysing women's work, especially in the state welfare and service sectors of the economy. Both theories also ignored the role of trade unions and of white male workers who helped to create and sustain divisions within the working class between skilled and unskilled workers, between black and white workers and between men and women in the workforce.

The impact of feminism has helped to broaden the definition of work, which was synonymous with waged labour, to include unwaged housework, unwaged care work, emotional management work in the family and unpaid voluntary work in the community.

It was housework rather than paid work which preoccupied early feminists, who considered that relations within the family were central to the understanding of women's oppression.

Liberal feminist approaches

Ann Oakley made studies of housework and motherhood (*Housewife, The Sociology of Housework, from Here to Maternity*) in which she interviewed women about their experiences. From the evidence of women's experiences, and with perspectives common in industrial sociology to do with monotony, isolation and alienation, she was able to identify the extent of the serious labour and common oppressions associated with domestic labour. She helped to make 'housework' and 'caring' visible as 'work' in ways which previous, mostly male, studies had completely overlooked.

Marxist feminist approaches

Others borrowed Marxist concepts of labour power, production and surplus value to argue that women, as domestic labourers, engaged in the reproduction of labour power and undertook domestic duties which helped to sustain the capitalist mode of production.

domestic labour debate

The **'domestic labour debate'**, whether it was conducted in Marxist or sociological language, considerably extended the notion of 'work' and helped to show that social relations within the family have a serious economic basis. Other Marxist feminists, for example, Adamson, Harrison and Price (*Womens Opportunities Under Capitalism*), applied Marx's notion of a 'reserve army of labour' to explain the ways in which women's capacity to work was brought in and out of service when required and returned to the home front when it was no longer needed. Jean Gardiner, on the other hand, helped to endorse Braverman's view that women entered the labour process as a substitute for men in the context of jobs being deskilled (*Women and Unemployment*). Ruth Milkman (*Women's Work and Economic Crisis*) described the ways in which the labour force was segregated into men's and women's jobs and how this was deeply embedded in the historical development of capitalism.

The advantages of Marxist feminist approaches to our understanding of women's employment has been to link women's oppression with other kinds of exploitation and oppression, especially social class, and to explain women's position in the labour market in relation to the emergence, growth and development of capitalism. But such an approach has tended to underestimate the significance of family ideology in determining women's position in the labour force, and has also paid undue attention to the influence of capitalism as distinct from patriarchy in explaining the causes of gender inequality.

Radical feminist approaches

Radical feminism has been clear that male power, described in terms of patriarchy, has colluded with capitalism to preserve definitions of skill and associated wage levels which advantage white men, and that, while societies based on socialist, as distinct from capitalist, economies may have distributed some paid work in more egalitarian ways, they have not redressed the problems of male dominance and violence against women in ways likely to bring about revolutionary changes in relationships between the sexes.

Radical feminists have not written extensively on paid work. They have been more concerned with matters of sexuality and violence. The contribution of radical feminism has tended to spring from a concern about violence against women, and has surfaced in studies of, for example, sexual harassment.

Legal definitions of sexual harassment concentrate on the damaging effects of such behaviour on women's lives at work and working conditions. Caroline MacKinnon (*The Sexual Harassment of Working Women*) argues that such behaviour constitutes sex discrimination because men do not experience similar treatment in the workplace. She shows how women are defined by their sexuality for the use of men. However, her work does not attempt to explain why women are to be found in some jobs more than others or why they get paid less than men.

Elizabeth Stanko (*Keeping Women in and out of Line: Sexual Harassment and Occupational Segregation*) argues that women doing jobs traditionally done by men are more likely to experience sexual harassment than women in traditionally female areas of work. Sylvia Walby (*Theorising Patriarchy*) suggests that this is because sexual harassment is used to keep women out of certain jobs (e.g. firefighting) as well as being a more pervasive form of control.

Diana Leonard and Christine Delphy (*Familiar Exploitation*) use Marxist methodology and concepts to argue the radical feminist position that women's oppression originates in interpersonal relationships with men in marriage and family life. Women's labour is appropriated by men and used to keep them in dependent and less powerful roles. It is these forms of already existing domination which have allowed male capitalism to continue the same process in the paid labour market.

Dual systems theory

This approach attempts to combine the class analysis associated with Marxist feminism with the concentration on patriarchy associated with radical feminism. It claims that both systems of oppression – patriarchy and capitalism – are necessary to understand the position of women in society generally and in employment in particular.

Heidi Hartmann

Heidi Hartmann (*Capitalism, Patriarchy and Job Segregation by Sex*, and *The Unhappy Marriage of Marxism and Feminism*) was among those feminists in the late 1970s who introduced the idea of patriarchy into arguments about the relationship between domesticity and capitalism. Much of the early feminist writing, which owed some allegiance to Marx and Engels, tended to reproduce taken-for-granted assumptions about 'human nature' 'strength' and 'skill' in that they failed to observe and analyse the extent to which male dominance and female subordination are socially constructed, and the extent to which these structures contribute to contemporary inequalities in the workforce.

Hartmann's work drew attention to the sexual division of labour in the home and within the family. She helped to account for why women enter the labour market on unequal terms to men, and how women are used by capitalism in different ways from men.

According to Hartmann, segregation on the basis of sex is central to men's control over women in all spheres of society. By being excluded from well-paid jobs, women remain at an economic disadvantage. Men's access to better paid jobs is because historically they have organized themselves in trade unions to secure a **'family wage'** – money which they argued was necessary to support a dependent wife and children. While it is doubtful that average male wages have ever been sufficient in themselves to support family dependants, the idea of the family wage has been used by employers and male workers alike to dismiss women's work as less than serious and as a way of earning 'pin money'.

family wage

Although many women are breadwinners in single-parent families, and not all women are in relationships with men, prejudice about 'pin money' has been used to depress women's wages historically. Because men have been able to earn more than women, they have been able to ensure that women continue to do housework and childcare in return for male financial support in two-parent families.

Hartmann describes this as a vicious circle, in which women's forced exclusion from well-paid jobs leads to them doing a disproportionate amount of domestic labour, which in turn contributes to their lack of access to better paid jobs. However, she does not explain how this circle persists despite high rates of divorce and the increase in single-parent families headed by women who also need, but rarely succeed in earning, a 'family wage'.

It has taken more recent developments of Hartmann's insight to explain how the state also operates to impose patriarchal forms of authority on women, and to make assumptions about women's dependence on men the excuse for low rates of pay and low levels of state benefits, even when men are not immediately evident or present in women's family life.

Unemployment

Unemployment is officially defined by the Department of Employment as 'People claiming benefit – that is, unemployment benefit, income support or National Insurance credits – at unemployment benefit offices on the day of the monthly count, who say on that day they are unemployed, and that they satisfy the conditions for claiming benefit'.

Unemployment has become an important political issue. By 1993 official government statistics identified 3 million workers who were unemployed. The extent and consequences of unemployment are likely to be more widespread, however.

The official definition of unemployment is very precise, and does not take account of people dependent upon income support but not eligible for unemployment benefit, but who would like to work if jobs were available or if the wage levels offered in unskilled and service industries were significantly higher than state benefits.

During the period of Conservative Government in the 1980s and early 1990s there were more than thirty adjustments to the ways in which unemployment statistics were collected, leading to the accusation that the government had attempted to 'doctor the evidence'. Men over 60, young people on government training schemes, workers who were self-employed, people who leave unsatisfactory jobs through choice, and married women who are ineligible for benefits when they lose their jobs, are all examples of unemployed workers who do not appear in the statistics collected by the Department of Employment. It has been estimated by the Unemployed Unit that official statistics underestimate the true level of unemployment by about a million.

Theories of unemployment

According to the British economist Maynard Keynes, unemployment can be managed and controlled by government intervention. According to Milton Friedman, unemployment will disappear as the market forces deliver 'realistic' wage levels by reducing the cost of wage levels to potential employers. According to Karl Marx, unemployment is endemic in the capitalist system. It will become worse and worse until those who are suffering most develop class consciousness and overthrow the system.

Liberal theories

Governments in the post-war period – both Labour and Conservative – were influenced by the ideas of Maynard Keynes, and believed that unemployment was a temporary and minority concern. Between 1948 and 1966 the official unemployment rate never rose above 2 per cent of the workforce, and it was assumed that a mixture of government control over key industries and the consumer demand for goods produced by privately owned industries would more or less ensure full employment. Governments should manage the **mixed economy**. When demand for goods declined and jobs were lost, the government should increase spending, create jobs and cut unemployment. It was assumed that high levels of unemployment – as in the Depression of the 1930s – was a temporary problem, caused by lack of demand in the economy and by governments losing control of their internal economies in periods of worldwide recession. No Labour or Conservative Government in the twenty years after the Second World War expected to face the electorate or win an election with levels of unemployment higher than 2 per cent of the workforce.

mixed economy

Monetarist theories

In the 1970s confidence in the Keynesian ideas about managing a mixed economy were undermined by rising inflation and rising unemployment. Between 1975 and 1978 unemployment rose to 6 per cent of the workforce. In 1982 it was 9.5 per cent and by 1985–86 it peaked at 11.8 per cent of the workforce. In some regions of Britain the figures were higher and, of course, by this time adjustments were being made in the ways in which statistics were recorded. Increasingly, the Thatcher Government adopted monetarist economic theories popular in the United States and based on the ideas of **Milton Friedman.**

Milton Friedman

Inflation was explained as 'too much money chasing too few goods'. The problem should be solved by allowing less money to circulate in the economy. This meant cutting back on government spending and cutting back on jobs. Monetarist views were based on a reverence for the market – and for removing as many regulations and controls as were necessary to allow the market to flourish or flounder in its own way. The spirit of competition and enterprise would enable the best to flourish and the worst to flounder. Governments should cease to subsidize unsuccessful industries. Nationalized industries should be privatized and taxation of successful industries should be reduced.

By freeing the market from government controls and regulations, companies could adopt the measures which would increase efficiency, lower costs and increase profits. The unemployed should be prepared to work for lower wages in order to get a job, and if wages were reduced, it would provide the incentive to employers to take on more workers. In the end, unemployment would disappear.

Two factors stand in the way, however: strong unions which use their power to keep wages high; and a 'generous' welfare state which provides benefits that discourage people from accepting low wages. A related feature of monetarist economic policies, and one pursued by the Conservative Government, has therefore been concerned to:

- introduce legislation designed to curb the power of trade unions;
- reduce the value of state benefits and increase the punitive procedures applied to those dependent on them.

Marxist theories

Boom and decline

Marx regarded unemployment as automatic in a capitalist system, which inevitably goes through cycles of **boom** and **decline.** At a given time there are periods of expansion in which there is full employment. These are followed by periods of crisis in which unemployment increases. He believed that the recovery from periods of crisis was transitory and based on the adoption of short-term solutions. Each succeeding crisis would get worse until capitalism was finally destroyed.

Marx saw the competition between industries as the inevitable cause of their own ultimate destruction. In periods of boom they would invest in new machinery, take on extra workers and pay high wages to attract good workers. As their costs increased, their profits would fall. They would lose confidence in new investment and new technologies. Old machinery would become defunct and inefficient. Profits would fall. Workers would be laid off. Eventually unemployment would force down wages until a pool of cheap labour became available. In these circumstances employers would begin to invest again and expand their businesses and their profits. Workers would be exploited more consistently than before, but not indefinitely.

According to Marx, capitalism requires workers who can be taken on in times of expansion and laid off in times of crisis and recession. He referred to such groups as a 'reserve army of labour'. When they are not in work, they are unemployed. As their circumstances become more precarious and more untenable, they will, according to Marx, organize to defeat the capitalist system.

The unemployed

Although more people are likely to be unemployed today than at any time since the 1930s, including some professional and white-collar workers not previously regarded as vulnerable to unemployment, loss of work is likely to affect some groups in society more seriously than others.

Class

Unskilled manual workers are three times more likely to be unemployed than other male workers. The decline in manufacturing, mining, shipbuilding and the fishing industry have all contributed to high levels of regional working-class unemployment in recent years.

New Right and Enterprise Culture

Encouraged by **New Right** thinking and monetarist economic policies associated with the **Enterprise Culture** of Thatcherism, many workers in the 1980s were encouraged to become self-employed and use their redundancy money to set up small business ventures of their own. The vast majority of these ventures failed within the first two years of operation. By the early 1990s small businesses were going bankrupt at an alarming rate, and the British economy was again in a state of crisis. Those considered to have been self-employed did not, of course, qualify for unemployment benefits and were not counted in the increasing numbers of registered unemployed.

Gender

Official statistics record that more men are unemployed than women. However, the figures are likely to be inaccurate because married women are usually not eligible for the benefits that might encourage them to become registered, and single parents with childcare responsibilities may not be regarded as seriously 'available for work' if they cannot accept job offers made within twenty-four hours. It has been estimated that one in four women who lose their jobs do not appear in the monthly claimant count.

In addition, women who are dependent upon income support, and with responsibilities for housing and childcare costs, would need to find jobs that pay significantly higher wages than are generally available to unskilled women workers if they are to enter the labour force. Sociologists use the term **poverty trap** to describe those circumstances in which, although benefits are low, so are unskilled wages, making it impossible to move from one into the other.

poverty trap

Age

Youth unemployment has been one of the most serious unemployment problems of the 1980s and 1990s – affecting both school-leavers and those under the age of 24. Government education and training policies, influenced by the ideas of the New Right, have tended to blame lack of competition and low standards in education – encouraged, they claim, by egalitarian and social democratic policies in the 1960s and 1970s – for making young people 'unemployable'. This has led to a spirit of **'new vocationalism'** in education (see pages 163–4) and to the development of post-school government training schemes targeted at the unemployed.

new vocationalism

The withdrawal of benefits from 16- and 17-year-olds and the require-ment to be on government training schemes if they have no job has been one way of distracting attention from high levels of youth unemployment and excluding young people from the official statistics of unemployment.

Ethnicity

Surveys concerned with the relationship between ethnicity and unemploy-ment constantly reveal the same information. Black workers experience higher rates of unemployment than white workers. During the period 1985–87 when 11.8 per cent of the labour force were out of work, the figure rose to 16 per cent for workers of Indian origin, 21 per cent for workers of Afro-Caribbean origin and 29 per cent for workers of Pakistani and Bangladeshi origin.

Unemployment is particularly common among younger members of ethnic minorities and women. A survey carried out by the Policy Studies Institute of unemployment and ethnicity in the 1980s, and by the Equal Opportunities Commission in the 1990s, revealed that black women were twice as likely as white women to be long-term unemployed.

The effects of unemployment

According to Swedish sociologist Goran Therborn, the monetarist 'cut down the public sector, strengthen the market economy' approach has been the 'shortest and fastest route to mass unemployment'. He argues that the

New Right who were associated with such policies in Thatcher's Britain and Reagan's United States may not have wanted mass unemployment, but did not care about it as a serious social problem. Norman Lamont, former Chancellor of the Exchequer in the 1992–93 Conservative Government, claimed infamously that mass unemployment was 'a price worth paying' in the battle against inflation.

Because of the growth of transnational capitalism and government policies based on free market economics, Therborn argues that mass unemployment is likely to become a permanent feature of most advanced capitalist countries producing a 'two-thirds, one-third society'. The bottom third will be permanently unemployed and marginally unemployed, dependent on welfare benefits which are certain to be reduced over time and replaced by increasing state and police activity to control potential unrest. Increased social controls and increased desperation will breed a mixture of lawlessness and apathy. Already in the United States the political commentator and social critic **Noam Chomsky** describes large sections of the poor and unemployed as disaffected and disenfranchised – reluctant to get involved in the democratic processes of voting and representation because they have lost all belief in a system which does not attend to their needs or concerns.

Noam Chomsky

In the middle of Therborn's 'two-thirds, one-third' society will be the 'stably employed', making a fairly decent if unspectacular living and priding themselves on the widening distance between themselves and the unemployed.

The third and smallest layer of mass unemployment societies will be those top business managers and capitalists who benefit from the deregulation of the market and whose wealth has increased under New Right economic policies. As a ruling class they will appeal to the middle layer of employees and secure their allegiance so long as the threat of losing their jobs and joining the permanently unemployed can be held over them as a disaster to be avoided at all costs.

The threat of unemployment:

● makes workers feel less secure.;
● makes workers less likely to leave unsatisfactory or unsatisfying jobs in case they can't find others;
● makes workers blame each other for the loss of jobs rather than look for explanations in the wider economy and government policies. For example, men blame women for taking their jobs, while white workers blame immigrants and ethnic minorities – even in circumstances in which blacks are much more likely to be unemployed than whites;
● makes the likelihood of equal opportunities and positive action in favour of disadvantaged groups much less likely. The unemployed act as a source of cheap labour, in competition with each other for scarce resources and jobs. Employers have no reason to take the trouble to recruit women, young people, older people, ethnic minorities or disabled people, or to improve wage levels and working conditions, in such circumstances.

The personal effects of unemployment

The personal effects of unemployment increase in direct relation to the length of time a person is unemployed. The major consequences are:

● financial – leading to a reduced standard of living, a poorer quality of life and the likelihood of debt. During the last ten years there have been more than fifty changes in benefits paid to the unemployed, with cuts generally larger for those on the lowest incomes;

- social – leading to a loss of status in the eyes of others;
- psychological – leading to a loss of purpose and self-esteem. Psychological responses may lead to feelings of anxiety and distress in workers who previously had long records of employment. Young people facing the future without much prospect of employment may develop attitudes of hopelessness and resignation;
- health – leading to increased levels of physical and mental ill-health;
- crime – leading to increases in petty theft and attempted fraud which are in direct relation to increasing personal poverty and the inability to meet financial commitments.

Gender and
unemployment

Unemployment is most usually regarded as a male experience – a bad experience undoubtedly, with terrible repercussions on the lives of all those who are dependent on the earnings of the one who is now unemployed, and much associated with the loss of status, purpose, meaning and self-respect that employment can provide, as well as the slide into poverty. But at least the experience has a name, and becomes the focus around which action and resistance can be organized.

Women, on the other hand, are rarely counted as unemployed or considered to be so. They return to their other workplace – the home – and continue with the business of domestic labour, caring for others and the emotional and financial management of their families in hard and stressful times.

It is ironic that women's unemployment is not regarded as a problem, since women and their families also lose money when women become unemployed – doubly so, for women are often not entitled to state benefits as a consequence and are more likely than men to be in the kind of casual and peripheral jobs which end with no redundancy payments. Unlike men, they may feel they have no right to find paid work in times of high unemployment, and yet there is no reason to suppose that women can cope any better than men with the loss of self-esteem and economic independence which employment helps to provide.

There are few women who do not suffer financial hardship when they become unemployed. Unemployment benefit, if they get it, is spent on food for others. When women are not entitled to unemployment benefit in their own right, they become even more economically dependent on partners or on a state benefit system which assumes that other men are waiting somewhere in the wings to take on financial responsibility for them.

Furthermore, the loss of 'personal money' however insignificant, is a blow to women's sense of independence and freedom – which in turn affects their emotional and social well-being. For women, unemployment means an end to personal consumption, however modest, and the return to putting everyone else first. It cuts out social life and fun and adds to the already isolated aspect of many women's lives. The social interaction and companionship of 'going out to work', together with the confidence and sense of independence associated with job satisfaction and earning power, disappears with unemployment. Although there is always unpaid work at home to fill the 'empty' hours, it carries none of the same status or significance of 'having a job' and is usually much less interesting.

Poverty and welfare

Until the early 1960s poverty was a neglected subject within sociology, partly because post-war affluence created the impression that poverty was now restricted to the third world and rural communities of Europe and had been virtually eliminated from advanced industrial societies. The British Prime Minister Harold Macmillan caught the conservative 'spirit of the times' when he told the electorate: 'You've never had it so good'. It was assumed that, while there might be 'pockets of poverty' such as vagrants and large families, the welfare state had eased the problem of poverty to such an extent that it was no longer an important social issue.

However, since the 1960s there has been considerable sociological attention paid to the study of poverty. Debate has centred around the following key debates and issues.

Key debates

- How to define poverty – the type of definition adopted affects the numbers of people defined as living in poverty and the kinds of solutions suggested in industrial societies.
- Which individuals and groups are considered to be poor.
- Explanations for the persistence of poverty in advanced industrial societies in which they are influenced by the differing perspectives adopted.
- Policies to tackle poverty which are also affected by different explanations and perspectives.

Definitions and numbers

In 1994 the Duke of Edinburgh launched himself into a debate in which politicians and sociologists had been engaged for some time. In a speech to the Charity Commissioners he claimed that poverty, as we have been used to thinking of the problem, no longer existed.

Earlier that same year newspaper headlines announced:

> 'Poverty highlighted by school meals survey'
> 'Bottom 20 per cent are worse off'
> 'Students hounded out by poverty'
> 'Basic benefit will not buy children a workhouse diet'.

The previous year the Anglican Bishop of Liverpool Dr David Shepherd described poverty as 'the country's worst social evil and a national scandal'.

Newspapers carried accounts of research which showed not only that the poor were very much 'still with us' but that the number of people living in poverty had increased and that the trend of the previous fifty years towards a somewhat more equal distribution of income and wealth had now been reversed.

In September 1994 a study published by the Rowntree Foundation revealed that there were more people living in poverty in Oxford than in

Oldham. The study appeared only days after Oxfam, the Oxford-based charity associated with the relief of third world hunger, confirmed that it was considering extending its operations to include Britain. The study recorded an increase of 30 per cent in income support claimants living in Oxford between 1991 and 1993. One in four of Oxford's children was living in a household dependent on income support. In Oldham the worst poverty and deprivation was being experienced by pensioners and ethnic minorities. The report concluded that the gap between poor and better-off families had widened.

A second study, undertaken by Anne Green of Warwick University and published simultaneously, showed how the sharp growth of inequality in the 1980s had left some of the country's richest and poorest living within a few streets of each other, especially in London. She commented:

> economic and social changes in the 1980s appear to be leading to a growth in 'no earner households, neighbourhoods and labour markets' in conjunction with a growth in 'dual-earner households, neighbourhoods and labour markets' in other locations. The gap between rich and poor has increased as a consequence.

Jonathan Aitken

Jonathan Aitken, Chief Secretary to the Treasury, revealed on the same day as these reports were published that benefits were to be the target of a massive Treasury squeeze when MPs returned from their summer holidays in the autumn. He warned against 'the creation of a benefit dependent culture and society' in which people became 'too comfortable on benefits'.

So which view is correct? Has poverty been eliminated as the Duke suggested, along with rickets, TB and smog – all symptoms of an earlier, and less equitable, era? Or do we have a growing underclass of deprived citizens – the homeless and beggars clearly visible on our streets, and families surviving on inadequate benefits in sub-standard housing in our inner cities?

The key to understanding these opposing views lies in the Duke's statement that poverty is 'no longer absolute, it has become relative'. Whether you believe that poverty has been eliminated or not largely depends on how you define what is meant by poverty.

Absolute poverty

The term **absolute poverty** is used to describe a situation in which the resources needed to sustain life – food, shelter, clothing, etc. – are lacking. This is a very narrow definition of poverty which includes only those physical needs which must be in existence for a human being to survive. It takes no account of other needs that people might have, for example social, intellectual or emotional needs.

In this way poverty is defined as **a minimum standard of living** and can be applied to all human beings, wherever or whenever they live, because it is assumed that there are certain basic requirements needed by all human beings.

It takes no account, however, of the differing needs, for example, of a baby in Sudan and a senior citizen in Britain, or of a manual worker in northern Scotland and an office worker in Essex. Nor does it take account of the fact that physical needs may vary according to age, location, sex, work or climate. Neither does it consider that the costs of providing the necessary items may also differ from one region to another – the cost of food, petrol and housing can all vary, even within a small country like Britain.

More significantly, it assumes that our idea of what constitutes poverty never changes from one historical period to another. But yet, imagine for a moment the typical living conditions of working people in Britain 100 years ago – outside toilets were common, hot running water very rare, carpets, electric-powered lights and a choice of clothes still unusual. None of these items would have been considered to be essential to people's survival in those days. But, of course, people living without these erstwhile 'luxuries' today would have to be regarded as 'poor'.

When the Duke of Edinburgh referred to the elimination of poverty it was absolute poverty to which he was referring.

The poverty line

Charles Booth

In 1889 the social researcher and reformer **Charles Booth** established a subsistence level **poverty line** based on his research among London's poor. Using this line, he declared that about one third of London's population was living in poverty. He collected his information by observation and by interviewing school attendance officers, rather than interviewing the poor themselves. He claimed that poverty was caused largely by circumstances beyond the control of poor people, in particular, low and irregular wages.

Seebohm Rowntree

Rowntree carried out poverty surveys in York in 1899, 1936 and 1950 which came to similar conclusions and proved that poverty was not just a problem experienced by those living in the capital. He argued there were three essential items of expenditure necessary to support the minimum provision people needed to maintain their health and themselves as efficient workers:

1 Food
2 Clothing
3 Housing.

Rowntree used guidelines produced by expert nutritionists to detail precisely what food was needed to ensure physical efficiency; the minimum clothing necessary to keep a person warm and dry; and the average rent paid by people living in York. He then added up the amount of money which would be needed and called this the poverty line. It was a very basic list of needs – no allowance was made for travel, stamps, newspapers, etc. He thought that, if he defined the poverty line as being low, no-one would dispute its existence and the findings from his research would be more likely to encourage social reforms. Rowntree obtained his data from contact with almost every working-class family in York, and reckoned that, on the basis of his calculations, 20 302 people, or almost half the working-class population, were living in poverty, which was caused by low wages, sickness and unemployment. He commented:

The wages paid for unskilled labour in York are insufficient to provide food, shelter and clothing adequate to maintain a family of moderate size in a state of bare physical efficiency ... the diet is even less generous than allowed to able-bodied paupers in the York workhouse and no allowance is made for any expenditure other than that absolutely required for the maintenance of merely physical efficiency.

Criticisms

Rowntree was criticized on the following grounds:

- His diet sheet assumed that people bought their food in the cheapest way, there was no wastage and they had extensive knowledge about marketing and cooking methods. In practice, people may well have been poorer than he suggested by using this method.
- He overlooked the fact that most working-class families in York spent less on food than his budget allowed for – possibly to spend on other items.
- Diets are based on custom, convention, class, region, etc. not on expert diet sheets – these could well have been unrealistic and inaccurate.
- His selection of necessities 'for a healthy life' were based on his own views and those of other 'experts', but were very basic, even by 1899 standards. In latter studies he modified them somewhat, and made a small allowance for such things as transport and stamps.

Findings

According to Rowntree's definition, the percentage of people living in 'absolute poverty' in 1936 was 18 per cent and in 1950, 1.5 per cent. This raises perhaps the main criticism of the 'absolute poverty' approach to definitions. As living standards rise generally in society, fewer people lack the 'bare necessities' to sustain life. But this does not mean that poverty has been eradicated. There are still people whose standard of living falls way below the average standard of living in society, which ought to be taken into account.

The relevance of Rowntree today

The Conservative Governments of the 1980s and 1990s have made use of 'absolute' definitions of poverty, arguing that the aim of social security should not be to improve the living conditions of the poor but to make sure that they can afford the bare necessities of life.

Relative poverty

The main problem with the 'absolute' definition of poverty is that it is based solely on 'the minimum resources necessary to sustain life', and takes no account of other kinds of needs. In Britain today the richest in the population earn many times more than the poorest, those on income support, for example. Some families living on low wages would actually be better off on state benefits. Given this kind of discrepancy, critics feel that an 'absolute' definition of poverty disguises the many facets and the real extent of poverty in Britain and fails to recognize the kind of impoverished lifestyle which many people are forced to endure compared with more advantaged groups. For in reality, poverty in Britain is also the absence of a choice of clothes bought new rather than second-hand and more than one pair of shoes; filling a supermarket trolley with a choice of different kinds of foods, not just staples; having a holiday away from home each year; having money for social activities, whatever they may be; being able to afford public transport or owning a small car; having the use of a telephone at home and being able to buy, repair and replace electrical goods like washing machines, fridges and vacuum cleaners when necessary. In other words, the lack of the kinds of material possessions which most people take for granted and which advertisers and the consumer industry promote as indicative of a 'normal', happy and successful 'way of life'.

Relative poverty also means the lack of good schools in the neighbourhood; not having a decent house to live in; a polluted and depressing environment; inadequate play space for children; bad working conditions or no paid work at all. Compared with people who do not experience any of these things, those who do could well be described as poor. And so long as some individuals and groups have high or average incomes, access to material possessions and those opportunities in life which are dependent upon having money to make them possible, all those who do not share in this kind of potential lifestyle are **relatively poor** by comparison.

Considered on a world scale, the differences in affluence and poverty across the globe are clearly enormous. On the whole, countries from the northern hemisphere with Western-style economies are significantly richer than those from the southern hemisphere with 'underdeveloped' economies. Within countries and within continents there are enormous variations, however, which can best be explained in terms of economics, power and imperialism – but which have the effect of magnifying the enormity and scale of relative poverty.

Sociologists studying relative poverty study those people and groups which lack the kind of items which others consider to be essential. They have developed theories to explain the persistence of poverty in apparently affluent societies like Britain with a welfare state which was supposed to have helped to eliminate poverty. Some sociologists relate poverty to inequality and to the unequal distribution of resources in such societies.

The advantages of the 'relative' definition of poverty are:

● It relates the existence of poverty to the expectations of society.
● It gives a realistic picture of deprivation in society.
● It broadens the understanding of what poverty is from the lack of 'basic necessities' to include other kinds of needs which make life bearable.
● It introduces the idea of equity and fairness in society into the argument.

The disadvantages of the 'relative' definition of poverty are:

● Taken to extremes, it means that so long as there is inequality, there is poverty.
● It can lead to people ignoring the vast differences between societies, i.e. should we use the same terminology to define someone who is 'starving' compared with someone who is deemed to be 'poor' in the West? It can also lead to patronising views of third world countries in which, so long as people are not starving, it is assumed that they are not poor (because expectations are said to be 'lower' in those countries), leading to the view that there are 'different standards' of what counts as poverty in first and third world countries.

Rediscovering
poverty

During the early 1960s the government set up a number of commissions to investigate various aspects of life in Britain; for example, London housing (Milner Holland), children and young people (Ingleby), primary education (Plowden) and the personal social services (Seebohm). One after the other the reports emphasized 'areas of bad housing', 'deprived neighbourhoods' and 'families in special need'. The picture that emerged was a challenge to the complacency of Britain's affluent image of itself as a country which had 'never had it so good'. Poverty still existed, and life for many families in Britain was a persistent struggle to make ends meet and a hopeless battle against appalling housing and terrible environments. Furthermore, the figures suggested that the problems were much more widespread than politicians had chosen to recognize.

In 1964 the Labour Party took over government and began a series of initiatives designed to reduce poverty. It changed the Rate Support Grant to give those local authorities with fewer resources more money. In 1968 the Urban Aid Programme was introduced to provide extra grants to voluntary and statutory organizations working to improve the education, housing, health and welfare of groups living in areas of special need.

Educational Priority Areas and Community Development Projects were established. But, like all the initiatives of the period, they were littered with the language of 'experiment' and 'project', emphasizing the essentially temporary and token nature of their provision. Despite a good deal of public relations propaganda about 'positive discrimination', they operated on an incredibly small budget. The whole Urban Aid Programme, of which the Community Development Programme formed only a small part, represented only one twentieth of 1 per cent of total social services spending, and came from money 'redistributed' from other parts of the service.

Researching relative poverty

Abel-Smith & Townsend

relative deprivation

Brian Abel-Smith and **Peter Townsend**, writing in 1965, claimed that people living on what was then called national assistance (now income support), including those with incomes as much as 40 per cent above that level, should be considered poor. This meant that 14 per cent of the population of Britain could be defined as poor – caused mainly by low wages and old age.

Townsend, in a further study, *Poverty in the UK* in 1979, argued for a more sophisticated definition of **'relative deprivation'** to take account of the circumstances in which people lack the resources to take part in the general lifestyle of the community to which they belong. He compiled a list of sixty 'standard of living' indicators, such as household conditions, health, education, diet, clothing, working conditions, etc. He then selected twelve items from the list which he said were 'particularly important' and calculated how much income a family would need to provide all these items for its members. He interviewed 10 000 individuals in 3260 households and claimed to have established a 'deprivation threshold' below which deprivation increased rapidly. The threshold was set at 150 per cent of the basic income support level. All those living at or below this level were counted as poor. The actual research was carried out in 1968–9. According to Townsend, it showed that 22.9 per cent of the population (12.46 million people) were living in poverty, compared with official government figures of 6.1 per cent. He found that those most 'at risk' from poverty were the low-paid, the unemployed, the elderly, the sick, large families and one-parent families.

Townsend, like other researchers before him, claimed that his research method was 'objective', but this claim has been challenged.

Criticisms of Townsend's research studies

David Piachaud argues that Townsend's definition of poverty involved a 'value judgement' and should be recognized as such. He comments:

● The index is inadequate – there is no clear reason why some items, e.g. a Sunday roast, were selected. Townsend did not carry out research to discover whether such items were 'generally thought' to be important. They were based on his own middle-class lifestyle and views. More recent critics would also point to the culturally specific assumptions underlying Townsend's index, relating to a white British lifestyle.
● Setting the threshold at 150 per cent of the income support level was arbitrary, with no clear justification given.

- Using Townsend's index to define poverty meant that any behaviour departing from the norm (e.g. being vegetarian) could be counted as a point on the deprivation index when it may simply be a matter of choice. It was a mistake not to establish whether people lacked items (e.g. televisons) through choice or lack of money.

Nevertheless it was an important piece of research which stimulated other research.

Mack & Lansley

Joanna Mack and Stewart Lansley (*Poor Britain*), writing in 1983 and 1990, in what is sometimes also known as the Breadline Britain research, used Townsend's ideas about an index, but attempted to correct some of the flaws in his earlier approach. They carried out preliminary research to discover:

- what the general public regarded as necessities;
- whether choice or lack of money accounted for the lack of certain items.

They interviewed 1174 people aged 16 and over who were all given a list of 35 items and were asked to indicate which of the items were necessary and which all adults/families **should** be able to afford. Well over half the people asked included a 'decent, well-heated house with all amenities', 'adequate public transport', 'three meals a day for children', 'celebrations for special occasions like Christmas', 'presents for family and close friends once a year'. When more than 50 per cent of those questioned agreed that the item was important, it was defined as a necessity. This part of the study demonstrated that most people rejected the idea of an 'absolute' definition of poverty.

The researchers then questioned people as to which of the 'necessities' they lacked themselves and asked for details of their income. People who lacked three or more of the items on the final list of 22 necessities were defined as poor. Those who lacked seven or more of the items were defined as living in severe poverty.

On the basis of their research they calculated that in 1983 7.5 million people in Britain were living in poverty (5 million adults, 2.5. million children), which represented 13.8 per cent of the population. The income level at which the calculation took place was 133 per cent and below income support level. They also found that the share of national earnings from employment received by the poorest 40 per cent of the population had fallen from 15.6 per cent in 1965 to 10.2 per cent in 1976.

Both this study and the earlier studies by Townsend revealed levels of poverty which were higher than those claimed by official government statistics.

Official definitions of poverty

The British government, unlike in the USA, does not use an 'official poverty line'. in its calculations. It never uses the term 'the poor', instead, it has traditionally used the term 'low-income families'. Previously these were defined as 'those living on or below income support levels'. Because others then used this level to define people as poor, the government regarded it as an implicit criticism of the amount of money provided on income support and has now switched its definition to 'groups living on half the national average income' as its current euphemism for 'the poor'.

In 1989 **John Moore**, the then Minister for Social Security, using the official calculation, claimed that no-one in Britain was poor any longer and that all groups were now considerably better-off than they had been in the past.

The European Commission uses a similar definition of poverty, i.e. 'those living on less than 50 per cent average income'. Using this official definition, the numbers living in poverty in Britain are said to be approximately 10.5 million. Most sociologists now studying poverty consider this figure to be an underestimation, and **John Pilger**, writing in the *New Statesman* in 1993, claimed that one in four of Europe's poor were now living in Britain.

Explanations for the persistence of poverty

The deserving and the undeserving poor

There are many theories to explain why poverty continues to exist in relatively affluent societies like Britain. In everyday discussions, a distinction is often made between the so-called **deserving poor**, who owe their misfortune to circumstances beyond their control such as illness or the death of a spouse, and the **undeserving poor**, whose situation is deemed to be the result of some personal failing or inadequacy.

This distinction has a long history, going back as far as records about poverty have been kept and discussions about poverty began. In the nineteenth century **Benjamin Disraeli**, in his novel *Sybil*, described the rich and the poor as 'two nations between whom there is no intercourse and no sympathy: who are ignorant of each other's habits, thoughts and feelings, as if they were dwellers in different zones, or inhabitants of different planets'.

Popular middle-class mythology explained the widespread evidence of extreme poverty as being confined to the weak, lazy and debased sections of the population, but the inquiries of social investigators and philanthropists like Charles and William Booth and Seebohm Rowntree presented evidence which showed that in York, for example, in 1899 almost half the working-class population was living without enough food, fuel and clothing to keep them in good health.

Maud Pember Reeves and the Fabian Women's Group

In 1913 **Maud Pember Reeves** and the **Fabian Women's Group** published their detailed account of what it was like for a working man's wife to bring up a family on 20 shillings a week (*Round About a Pound a Week*). The families in Lambeth whose daily budgets were scrutinized between 1909 and 1913 were by no means the poorest of the poor. The men were said to be 'respectable, in full work or at a more or less top wage, young, with families still increasing'. Their wives were described as 'quiet, decent, keeping themselves to themselves' kind of women, who were independent, resourceful, hard-working, respectable – but very poor. The conclusions of the Fabian Women about the women of Lambeth was that:

> the cause of infant mortality (which was high and related to malnutrition) was not that mothers were ignorant or degenerate, but that they had too little money to provide for their own and their families' essential needs: that they lacked housing, domestic equipment, adequate food and clothing, and any facilities or opportunities for recreation.

Although the intervention of social reformers and philanthropists helped to raise public concern about Victorian and Edwardian poverty, the justification was often expressed and usually based on the 'otherwise respectability' of the poor which made them 'undeserving' of their plight. All of which helped to prolong the prejudice that others, who were 'lazy and degenerate'

and clearly 'not respectable', somehow deserved all the misfortune which befell them.

This tendency to 'blame the victim' when it comes to poverty, and to seek to distinguish between those who should be helped and those who are simply 'scroungers', persists to the present day. The popular tabloid press is full of articles about so-called benefit scroungers discovered on foreign holidays at the taxpayer's expense, while Conservative Government cabinet spokespersons make speeches about 'young girls' who 'deliberately get themselves pregnant' to 'jump the housing queue'. Even **Tony Blair,** the Leader of the Labour Party in 1994, anxious to compete with the Tories to be 'the party of the family', has been swift to join the debate about 'the problem of single parents' fuelled by the Tory Government and the Tory press in the early 1990s. In arguments reminiscent of nineteenth century distinctions between the 'deserving' and the 'undeserving' poor when it comes to state intervention and support, Blair, like the Conservatives before him, has been quick to differentiate between 'those who have been widowed or abandoned' and who through no fault of their own 'end up' as single parents, and those who apparently choose not to live in conventional families.

Fortunately, not all members of the public are gullible enough to believe these stereotypes, particularly as more and more people become aware of poverty themselves, as a direct consequence of rising levels of unemployment in recent years. The **Breadline Britain survey** in **1990** asked respondents for their opinions on why there are people who live in need, and compared their responses with those of earlier studies. They found a decline in the numbers of people who believed that poverty was the result of personal failings, such as laziness or lack of willpower, from 43 per cent in 1976 to 19 per cent in 1990. By comparison, there was an increase in the numbers of people who believed that poverty is the result of injustices in society, from 16 per cent in 1976 to 40 per cent in 1990.

Tony Blair

1990 Breadline Britain survey

Cultural and structural explanations

Most sociological explanations of poverty fall into one of two categories: those who believe that poverty is the result of attitudes, values and behaviour – known as **cultural explanations** – and those who believe it is caused by economic, social or political factors within the structure of society – known as **structural explanations**.

Cultural explanations suggest that the way people act is the result of the way they are brought up by their families and communities, and the values they are taught during the process of socialization. As a result, cultures develop which provide the guidelines about how people should behave and cope with their situations and surroundings. These cultures are then passed on from one generation to another.

Among certain communities, it is argued, a set of values develops which stresses a fatalistic attitude to life and a tendency to go for short-term pleasures rather than investment in the future. A good example of this idea would be a young person who leaves school to get an unskilled job at the earliest opportunity, only to find that the work was low-paid or casual and has no future, compared with one who stays on to get qualifications in the hope of securing a more permanent and rewarding occupation in the long run.

Such cultural explanations, then, suggest that the way to tackle poverty is to resocialize people in an attempt to foster more suitable attitudes, such as ambition, hard work or thrift, or to force people to change, through the withdrawal of state help such as social security.

Structural explanations suggest that the cause of poverty lies not so much in the attitudes and values of the poor themselves, but in factors which lie beyond the control of individuals within the structure of society. For example, some explanations claim that the reason why some people are poor is because others are multi-millionnaires. In other words, poverty is not the result of insufficient resources within society so much as a direct result of the uneven distribution of those resources.

Others argue that it suits the needs of society to have groups of deprived people who can be drafted into work if needed, and whose precarious plight serves to motivate the rest to even greater efforts. Sociologists and politicians who accept structural explanations believe that the only way to tackle poverty is by making changes to the structure of society in some way.

Cultural explanations

The culture of poverty
Oscar Lewis

This explanation is based on the work of **Oscar Lewis,** an American anthropologist who studied urban communities in Mexico and Puerto Rico in the 1950s. He argued that the culture and lifestyle of the poor differed in certain important respects from that of the majority, claiming that they had developed a set of attitudes and 'associated behaviours' which enabled them to adapt to circumstances which would otherwise have caused hopelessness and despair. He also examined individual attitudes, family patterns and community involvement, and argued that certain key features characterized their way of life: a fatalistic attitude, feelings of powerlessness and resignation; family life based on the mother and child unit, because marriages or relationships between men and women were likely to be short-lived; and lack of participation in community organizations such as trade unions, political parties or community groups, and in major institutions such as banks, hospitals, department stores and theatres. He argued that the **culture of poverty** provided a set of attitudes which helped to perpetuate poverty, so that even if personal circumstances changed people were unable to take advantage of any changes to get out of their poverty. For example, if an unexpected windfall was received, the emphasis on immediate gratification would mean that the money was spent – on drink or jewellery – rather than saved to provide some security against further hardship.

This theory was popularized in Britain in the 1970s by Sir Keith Joseph who, as Minister for Health and Social Security, claimed that there was a **cycle of deprivation** among the poor in Britain. His view suggested that 'inadequate' parents of large families were failing to socialize their children in the values and behaviour needed for success. Their children therefore failed at school, were unable to provide for themselves, or their own children, in turn and so the cycle was perpetuated from one generation to the next.

These ideas dominated social policies aimed at tackling poverty in both the USA and Britain in the 1960s and 1970s.

Operation Headstart &
the Urban Aid
Programme

In the USA **'Operation Headstart'** aimed to provide 'alternative socialization' at an early age to pre-school children in deprived urban areas, and a host of other schemes, aimed at 're-educating' young and unemployed people, were initiated. In Britain Community Education and Community Development schemes were funded under the **Urban Aid Programme,** 'therapeutic' playgroups were set up and Educational Priority Areas were created to identify those areas which were 'run-down' and in which more money would be made available in the schools.

The fact that poverty has persisted, and actually increased in the years during which successive Conservative Governments have been in power since 1979 in Britain, seems to suggest that these schemes did not work.

Criticisms of the culture of poverty theory

Critics argue that schemes based on this theory did not work because none of the schemes involved the removal of poverty by raising the income levels of the poor. Rather, they concentrated on trying to 'change attitudes' in line with those which are more acceptable to a small but powerful minority within the population.

Several other criticisms can be made of cultural explanations for poverty:

This theory 'blames the victim' – as though it is the attitudes of the poor themselves which cause their poverty.

It is debatable whether the attitudes and values of the poor are significantly different from those of other people within the same society to warrant being referred to as a culture of poverty. Lack of material resources and financial security make it difficult, if not impossible, to plan for the future in any realistic way. Relationships are inevitably placed under additional stress where there is financial hardship. Poverty needs to be 'managed' by those experiencing it, which takes time and energy. Waiting for buses, queueing to use a public phone, shopping for bargains, claiming benefits, can be demoralizing and time-consuming activities which leave little space or inclination for other activities. All the behaviours and attitudes cited by Lewis could be the **consequence** of poverty rather than the cause.

Rutter & Madge

Beliefs and values are not always 'passed on intact' to the next generation to produce a cycle of deprivation. Parents rarely bring up children in precisely the same way in which they themselves were brought up. Research by **Michael Rutter and Nicola Madge** suggests that disadvantage and deprivation are not necessarily 'passed on' from parents to children through socialization. Rather, they found that many types of disadvantage, including poverty, could strike people who had never experienced them in their own childhood. For instance, a divorced mother may experience acute financial distress even if her standard of living had been excellent before the divorce. Or a redundant worker may face defaulting on the mortgage, and the loss not just of a job but of a home as well. Similarly, some people from very impoverished backgrounds may find secure employment which lifts them out of the poverty experienced during childhood. In other words, the idea of a 'cycle of deprivation' or 'culture of poverty' is too deterministic, and ignores the fact that both social and economic circumstances, and individuals, can and do change.

The impression given of the poor as being apathetic, passive and uninterested in anything beyond their own immediate existence has been challenged. There are many poor communities throughout the world where residents are actively organizing themselves into self-help groups, or resisting political situations which contribute to their poverty. Anyone who saw on television the millions of impoverished people turning out to vote in South Africa's first multi-racial elections in 1994 must doubt the accuracy of this aspect of the culture of poverty.

New Right
explanantions of
poverty

Charles Murray

This view has been influenced by the writings of right-wing American sociologist **Charles Murray** in *Losing Ground: American Social Policy 1950–80*. In this book he argues that there is a growing underclass of poor people, some of whom may be there through misfortune, but many of whom make little effort to improve their situation, reviving the earlier distinction between the 'deserving' and 'undeserving' poor. He attributes this increase in poverty to the very programmes which were initiated to prevent it, arguing that the poor have been able to 'live reasonably well' on 'welfare handouts' and therefore have had little incentive to find work. He also argues that the increase in single parents is another consequence of 'misguided' welfare policies, as women are not deterred from having children because they expect to receive support from the state.

In 1989 Charles Murray turned his attention to Britain, where he claimed a similar process was happening. However, critics took issue with his claim that Britain was merely ten to fifteen years behind the USA in the development of a class of alienated poor, whose lifestyle of crime, drug abuse and unstable family life posed a threat to social order.

Returning to Britain five years later, he claimed that his predictions were now borne out by the facts. In the *Sunday Times* in 1994 he wrote:

> From 1987 to 1992, property crime in England and Wales rose by 42%. The risk of being burgled in England is now more than twice that in the United States. Violent crime rose by 40%. In 1987 23% of English births were outside of marriage; by 1992 this had jumped to 31%. ... Between 1987 and 1992, the proportion of working-age men not even looking for work rose from 10% to 13%.

For Murray the blame for poverty lies with an inappropriate welfare system which fosters irresponsibility, easy divorce legislation and a legacy of permissiveness from the 1960s and 1970s. He argues for a return to the traditional middle-class values of 'fidelity, courage, loyalty, self-restraint, moderation and other admirable human qualities that, until lately, have barely dared speak their names'.

Contained within Murray's argument is an implicit criticism of the poor themselves, who are seen to lack such qualities, and whom he refers to as the 'new rabble'. Undoubtedly, his views have struck a chord in Britain with politicians on the right and even with some on the left.

In Britain these views have been popularized by sociologist **David Marsland** who claims that:

David Marsland

> The expectation that society, the state, the government, 'they', will look after our problems tricks us into abdicating from self-reliance and social responsibility. This is a major cause of escalating crime, the collapse of the family, inadequate schools and health care, and economic decline.

He claims that the **welfare state** creates a **culture of dependency** and provides an incentive to the poor to remain unemployed and dependent. Although he claims not to blame the poor:

> I cannot emphasise too much that this is **not their fault**. Critics of UWP (universal welfare provision) are not blaming the poor. ... On the contrary, these are the foremost victims of erroneous ideas and destructive policies imposed on them by paternalists, socialists, and privileged members of the professional New Class,

nevertheless his writing is littered with phrases reminiscent of the earlier 'culture of poverty' argument – 'fractured, fatherless families', 'street-wise trickiness', 'short-term gratification' and 'beggar-state mentality' as the alleged attributes of the poor. He argues for an end to universal welfare provisions where the 'welfare needs of the prosperous majority for education, health and pensions etc. should be transferred away from state institutions to market, co-operative and voluntary mechanisms'.

The provision for the remaining 10 to 15 per cent of those who cannot provide effectively for themselves by these means should be by loans rather than grants, by work-fare schemes (i.e. voluntary and community work in return for state benefit payments) rather than automatic benefits, topped up by charity and voluntary organizations rather than by the state. In other words, only when the welfare state is dismantled, and the poor 'persuaded' to become self-reliant, will poverty be eliminated.

Critics of Marsland, whose views are extremely popular with current government ministers, argue that 'universal benefits' are a right of citizenship, and are less socially divisive because everyone gets them as of right. Targeted benefits stigmatize the poor, who are 'looked down on' for being 'on welfare', and are more likely to trap people into poverty and passivity.

If universal rights to education, healthcare, child benefit, etc. were to be abolished, then many low-paid, disabled people and women workers would not be able to afford to work because these services would only be paid to people on benefits. Bill Jordan argues that 'means-tested' benefits are much more likely to create a large underclass caught in the poverty trap because they are unable to afford to work.

Critics argue that Marsland's views do not explain how the causes of poverty, such as recession or low-pay, should be tackled, and fear that an emphasis like his means that the state will cease to have responsibility for the poor rather than that poverty itself will be eliminated.

Structural explanations

Michael Harrington

Since the 1960s the trend in sociology has been to see poverty in structural rather than cultural terms – relating it to the economic structure of society, to stratification, power and capitalism. Elliot Currie (*The Fading Dream*) traced the development of the low-paid economy in the USA, for example, showing how the income of the average worker had dropped by 16 per cent in real terms in recent years. **Michael Harrington** (*New American Poverty*), writing in 1984, claimed that there were deep structural sources of poverty, for example the growth of multinational corporations with the power to drive down wages, the effects of which would persist into the next century.

Poverty as a result of a particular situation

This view of poverty argues that:

● there are certain times in life when poverty is more likely to occur, for example old age, sickness, unemployment;
● the capitalist system is characterized by booms, in which there is full employment and a rise in wages, followed by slumps or recession, when there are job losses and wages are depressed.

In both these types of situations people can slip into poverty as a result of a change in circumstances which is beyond the control of individuals and for which they cannot be blamed.

This view is not necessarily critical of capitalism as an economic system, but argues that in order to prevent hardship, which may result from the unfettered operation of market forces, the state should take some responsibility for the well-being of its citizens. One way in which the state can do this is by redistributing money obtained through taxation into services such as hospitals and schools, and into cash benefits for those unable, for some reason, to provide for themselves.

social democracy

In Britain this view is associated with the establishment of a welfare state in the period after the Second World War. The set of political, philosophical and economic principles upon which this view is based is often called the **social democratic perspective**.

Beveridge Report 1942

In June 1941 the government ordered a special committee, under the chairmanship of Sir William Beveridge, to make a thorough investigation of all 'the existing national schemes of social insurance. ... and to make recommendations' about how they might be improved. The committee's report was published in 1942. It is generally thought that this report created the foundations of the modern social security system, but it is more accurate to say, that the reforms of the 1940s simply improved benefits and rationalized previous policies. Beveridge's proposals were for a comprehensive system of **social insurance** to which all citizens over school age and below the age of retirement – excluding students, non-working wives and self-employed people earning less than a specified minimum – would contribute. The purpose was to tackle the five 'giant evils' of want, ignorance, idleness, disease and squalor.

National Insurance

The 'evil' of want was to be tackled by contributing to **National Insurance** benefits payable in times of sickness, unemployment and old age, and by an additional non-contributory system of means-tested benefits to prevent the poverty of those people who were not fully covered by National Insurance.

Policies to ensure full employment, at least for male breadwinners, were also introduced. In other words, the provisions of the welfare state were intended to tackle 'pockets' of poverty by stepping in to maintain the incomes of those groups which were vulnerable to poverty at particular times.

We have already seen that most people who are actually dependent on state benefits are poor and lack the resources to buy the kinds of items which most other people see as necessities. This is because benefit levels are deliberately set below average levels of income. This suggests that the welfare state has failed in its original objective. Some sociologists argue that it is partly this failure of the welfare state which has contributed to the persistence of poverty in Britain in the late twentieth century. The criticisms are as follows:

Successive governments have failed to use the taxation system to redistribute income from the richest to the poorest groups to the extent needed to prevent poverty.

Julian Le Grand

Even services like health and education, aimed at improving the welfare of citizens, have benefited the middle class more than less privileged groups. **Julian Le Grand** has shown that the middle class tend to use services more effectively, keeping older children in education longer, or making full use of preventative health services such as screening or vaccinations. Owner-occupiers have, until the 1990s, received more in income tax relief on their mortgages than poorer people ever received in housing benefit. Even transport policies have advantaged affluent car users and rail commuters by high public expenditure on roads and commuter rail networks, at the expense of a subsidized public transport system.

The universal provision of benefits, contrary to the original intention, has provided a subsidy to the comfortably off rather than improving the relative position of the poor.

The real value of benefits has gone down and has not kept abreast of increases in average income. For instance, unemployment benefit was worth 17.5 per cent of the average wage in 1974, but only 13 per cent in 1994. The real value of the state pension today is worth only 16.5 per cent of average male earnings.

Fewer categories of people are now eligible for state benefits. For instance, 16- to 17-year-olds are no longer entitled to income support, and fewer than 30 per cent of unemployed people were actually eligible for unemployment benefit in 1994.

Government policies concerned with selling off council houses have created an enormous housing shortage, which means that there are now more homeless people.

Recession has caused long-term unemployment, and all the evidence suggests that the longer a family has to live on benefits the poorer it becomes. Studies by the government in 1990 showed that the disposable income of a family on unemployment benefit dropped by 59 per cent after three months.

Many jobs are low-paid, exacerbated by the abolition of the wages councils and the government's failure to sign the Social Chapter of the Maastricht Treaty on behalf of workers in Britain. An individual or a family may well be 'better off' on state benefits, which include things like free school meals and housing benefit. This represents a way of "trapping' people in poverty from which it is very difficult to escape.

Although there is ample evidence to suggest that the welfare state has not prevented poverty, others would argue that its creation was a major achievement which has removed the fear of destitution. Beveridge, and the other reformers at the time of its inception, could not have predicted the changes which have stretched the welfare state to its limits – long-term recession, the increase in life expectancy and the growing number of single parents have all contributed to spiralling costs of welfare, while reducing the number of earners to generate the wealth needed to fund it.

Poverty and the labour market

There are several types of structural theories which attempt to explain the persistence of poverty. All would agree, however, that poverty is the result of deep, structural sources of inequality, related to the nature of capitalism.

Modern sociologists, following a Weberian perspective, have drawn attention to how the labour market is structured in such a way that some groups are marginalized (e.g. the unskilled, ethnic minorities and women) so that they become trapped in an underprivileged group known as the underclass.

Weberians use the term 'underclass' in a different way from that of the New Right, however. They argue that certain groups (e.g. professionals and highly skilled technical personnel) are able to manipulate the labour market to their own advantage because their skills are in short supply. This gives them a particularly good 'market position' compared with unskilled workers. Throughout the twentieth century the demand for unskilled labour has declined as a result of technological changes and recession.

Weberians apply the dual labour market theory (see page 192) to explain why certain groups fall into the underclass. They lack the status or skill to get out of their situation and are therefore trapped in low paid, part-time or casual work interspersed with periods of unemployment.

New Times theorists writing about post-Fordism have shown how smaller firms are becoming more dependent on larger firms for their survival, providing a peripheral labour market of unskilled, part-time, casual employment, often made up of women and ethnic minorities, which also ties in with Weberian definitions of an underclass.

According to this view, the poor are part of the underclass not because of their 'behaviour or attitudes' but because of changes in the labour market. Michael Harrington links the development of an underclass in the USA to the globalization of the economy, where multinational and transnational companies can shift investment from one country to another where labour is less organized and cheaper to employ. This has the effect of depressing wages in various countries as they compete with each other for investment from multinational corporations.

As a result, there has been an increase in the number of low-paid, part-time jobs in advanced industrial societies like Britain and the USA. Harrington sees the emergence of an underclass of people, who cannot participate in the lifestyle of the rest of the population – the unemployed, poorly educated young people, single parents, ethnic minorities, etc. – as the consequence of this economic restructuring of the labour market and the economy on a massive scale.

The difference between Harrington's view of the underclass and that of Charles Murray is that Harrington sees 'the causes of poverty and marginalization' as lying in the way the economic system is structured, rather than in the behaviour of those who are trapped in the underclass. However, he does point out that these 'structural factors' can have cultural effects, where people feel hopeless and can see no way of improving their situation.

Poor people in employment may not belong to a trade union, but, even if they do, the power of the union to fight on their behalf has been restricted in Britain by legislation in the 1980s and 1990s. Those who are not in employment do not, on the whole, have powerful organizations to represent their interests. Charities and the Church do attempt to put pressure on governments to recognize the needs of single parents, the disabled and the elderly, but do not have strong bargaining power in the way that professional or business groups have.

Weberians argue that these changes in the organization of work have affected the unity of the working class. Those in relatively secure work are unlikely to perceive their interests as being the same as those of marginalized groups, and are therefore unlikely to campaign through trade unions and other organizations on their behalf. This then contributes further to their isolation from the rest of society.

Conflict theories

Conflict theorists (see pages 239–40) argue that there is a basic conflict of interests between the requirements of a free market economy and the provision of social justice. Marxists argue that poverty is 'built into' the capitalist system and cannot be effectively tackled unless that system is abolished. They place less emphasis on distinguishing the poor from the rest of the working class because they regard them simply as the most disadvantaged part of the working class.

J. C. Kincaird

J. C. Kincaird argues that a low paid sector and army of un/underemployed people helps to depress other wages and serves to keep other workers motivated and grateful to have a job. They are therefore less likely to demand better wages and working conditions. In this way, the plight of the poor has a direct effect on the rest of the working class. Neither group owns the means of production, and their interests would be best served by working together to change the system. But because the fear of unemployment and poverty acts as a deterrent to those who are 'slightly' better off, the two groups do not combine forces.

Marxists also point to various government policy decisions in the 1990s such as the abolition of wage councils which helped to fix minimum wage levels in certain industries; the removal of legislative protection for young workers; and the refusal of the Conservative Government to sign the Social Chapter of the Maastricht Treaty, which gives a basic wage and conditions of work protection to workers in all the other countries involved in the European Union except Britain – as symptomatic of the way in which workers' rights can be undermined when there are large numbers of unemployed people around.

Because Marxists argue that the state reflects the interests of capitalism, governments only seek to alleviate and 'manage' the worst hardships of poverty. They are unwilling to tackle the real causes of poverty. John Westergaard and Henrietta Resler argue that the welfare state was never intended to redistribute income from the rich to the poor. The working class always provided the bulk of payments (through tax and National Insurance), but have always benefited least from these services. The welfare state was originally set up to maintain the health and welfare of the working class in order to maintain a more efficient workforce for capitalism and to minimize social criticism of that system.

Marxists such as Kincaird also make the point that poverty can only really be understood by looking at the class system as a whole. Marxists explain poverty as the result of inequality in the way in which resources are distributed within society – the way in which, in a society like Britain, some people earn a million pounds a year while others live in cardboard boxes.

Marxist explanations of poverty are useful for understanding why poverty exists in the first place, but less useful for explaining why certain groups and individuals experience poverty. This is because they are unwilling to differentiate the poor from the rest of society. This failure means that they have not adequately considered other issues, for example, why are women more prone to poverty than men?

The feminization of poverty

In 1992 the Equal Opportunities Commission declared that 'women continue to bear the brunt of poverty under a Social Security system biased towards men'.

Women are at greater risk of poverty than men, and this situation is not new. In 1908 61 per cent of Poor Law beneficiaries were women and in 1992 63 per cent of income support recipients were also women. However, it has only been within the last few years that the phenomenon of the 'feminization of poverty' has been noted. We need to ask, then, why are women more likely to be poor than men, and why has their poverty been hidden for so long?

Women constitute the majority in most of the poorest groups, such as the elderly, lone parents and the low-paid, but their sex is not simply coincidental. Neither are elderly women poorer because they live longer than men, they are poorer than elderly men; just as lone mothers are poorer than lone fathers.

Most poverty research and social policy has looked at the income of the household as a unit when assessing poverty, but not at the distribution of that income among its members.

In 1942 Beveridge stated:

> the great majority of married women must be regarded as occupied on work which is vital though unpaid, without which their husbands could not do paid work, and without which the nation could not continue. In accord with the facts the Plan for Social Security treats ... man and wife as a team'.

Women were therefore allotted a very specific role as wives and mothers. The state would look after the breadwinner (the man), he would provide for his wife and children, and she in turn would provide the domestic and caring services they all required.

Women's dependency on men

It was not expected that a married woman would need or choose to work outside the home. She and any children would be provided for by the 'family wage' earned by the man or covered by his National Insurance payments in times of unemployment, sickness, old age or death. A married woman who did work could claim these benefits in her own right, but she was not encouraged to do so by the provision of a reduced National Insurance contribution which was not abolished until 1977. Beveridge assumed that:

> on marriage a woman gains a legal right to maintenance by her husband as a first line of defence against risks which fall directly on the solitary woman; she undertakes at the same time to perform vital unpaid service ... even if while living with her husband, she undertakes gainful occupation ... her earning is liable to interruption by childbirth. In the national interest it is important that the interruption should be as complete as possible; the expectant mother should be under no economic pressure to continue at work as long as she can, and to return to it as soon as she can. ... To most married women earnings by a gainful occupation do not mean what such earnings mean to most solitary women. ... In sickness or unemployment the housewife does not need compensating benefits on the same scale as the solitary woman because, among other things, her home is provided for either by her husband's earnings or benefit if his earning is interrupted.

cohabitation rule

Child Support Agency

In writing this, Beveridge was merely echoing the commonly held views of the time, namely, that most women would marry and remain so, and that they would become the financial dependants of their husbands. Although this passage now sounds outmoded, the principles enshrined within it inform current social security policy, despite the changed circumstances of most women. The operation of the **cohabitation rule**, where a woman's benefit is stopped if her (male) lover stays more than three nights at her home, assumes that, if a couple are involved in a sexual relationship, the man should be providing for the woman financially. The setting up of the **Child Support Agency** to pursue absent fathers for maintenance also assumes that women and children should be dependent on a man at all costs.

In the area of disability payments there are similar examples of the assumed dependency of women on men. Until 1986 married women were not entitled to claim the Invalid Care Allowance which was available to a married man or single woman looking after a sick or disabled relative, because this kind of service was seen as part of the 'duty' beholden on a married woman provided for by her husband's income. Women (but not men) who were themselves disabled could only claim an invalidity pension if they failed a 'housework' test.

Although these last two examples have been changed in line with (and because of) European legislation, women claiming disability benefits are usually less well off because they are less likely to be covered by national insurance contributions, and so can only claim the Severe Disablement Allowance which is paid at a lower rate than the contributory invalidity benefit claimed by most men.

It is this 'assumed financial dependency' which lies at the heart of women's poverty. Only with the development of feminist perspectives in sociology has attention been drawn to this fact, as being part of the way in which patriarchal power and control operate. It is seen to affect the experiences of women within the family and in the area of paid employment. Women are poor because they lack the same access to economic resources as men.

Historically, the insistence on men earning a 'family wage' and women doing unpaid work has meant that women are disadvantaged in paid employment by their domestic responsibilities, and their earnings have been continuously depressed as a consequence by the assumption that they are only working for 'pin money'. Women now constitute almost half the workforce in Britain, but they earn on average only 70 per cent of male earnings, despite equality legislation. The gap between the average earnings of men and women is greater in Britain than in any other country in the European Union. And yet in many households women are now either the sole or the major breadwinner, as the number of lone-parent families has grown and the recession has hit traditional male employment. In many other families, women's earnings make the difference between getting by and being poor.

When Beveridge wrote of the man and the woman as a 'team' there was an implicit assumption that income would be equally and fairly distributed within the family. The clue to why women's poverty has remained obscured for so long lies in the fact that much poverty research has studied the **income of households** rather than that of the **individuals within those households**.

Feminist analysis has provided a detailed examination of how power relations within the family are negotiated. The ability to determine how money and other resources are distributed within the household is seen as a further aspect of male power. As Hilary Graham puts it, 'while sharing a common address, family members do not always share a common standard of living'.

Recent research suggests that within heterosexual relationships women do not always have an equal share of money, food, goods, space or time within families. They are the ones most likely to 'do without' when money is scarce; to be denied access to funds in bank accounts or to the 'family' wage; or to have to walk rather than use the 'family' car. They are also the ones upon whom the burden of managing an inadequate income often falls.

Women's poverty within marriage has been revealed partly as a consequence of increasing numbers of one-parent families and the fact that 19 out of 20 lone parents on income support are women. For some of these women, being on benefits is their first experience of a regular, independent income, in which the state proves to be a more reliable partner than a spouse.

Jan Pahl found that between a fifth and a third of women in her sample were actually better off when they left their marriages – not a comment on the generosity of the benefit system but on the lack of equality within many marriages.

However, resources may be distributed differently in different kinds of households, and the analysis presented, especially by radical feminism of power relations within households, may be more applicable to traditional, white, heterosexual families than others. Afro-Caribbean women are more likely to head households and so have more control over the distribution of resources. Asian women are more likely to live in larger households with more than two adults present, and this may affect the way resources are divided. For these women, poverty is also a result of the racism that places women in marginal, low-paid work, with fewer employment rights, and makes them more vulnerable to unemployment.

The racialization of poverty

In the USA there is a clear association between ethnicity and poverty. Almost a third of black families live below the poverty line, and half of all black children grow up in poverty. In Britain it has also been argued that:

> there has been an increased racialisation of poverty: blackness and poverty are more correlated now than they were some years ago. (K. Leech and K. Amin in 'A new underclass? Race, poverty and the inner city', *Poverty*, No. 70, CPAG.)

According to the Policy Studies Institute report *Ethnic Minorities* in 1993, Afro-Caribbean people in Britain shoulder a greater burden of unemployment, at almost twice the rate of whites. Pakistanis and Bangladeshis were three times as likely to be unemployed, and nearly 25 per cent of Bangladeshis in the employment market were 'without paid work' at the time of the study.

Afro-Caribbeans and Asians also have lower levels of average earnings and are more heavily concentrated in low-paid sectors of the labour market, in decaying inner cities and in poorer housing. Black people, therefore, are more vulnerable to deprivation and poverty, partly as a result of discriminatory practices within employment and housing markets. But that poverty is also exacerbated by government policies and the practices of the welfare state.

European Commission on Human Rights

British immigration policy has been criticized by the **European Commission on Human Rights** for its bias against black families. Policies directed at reducing the numbers of primary migrants and refusing entry to dependants of people already in Britain have caused economic hardships to some families. Although the vast majority of black people in Britain are fully entitled to claim the same benefits as other citizens, immigration policies create a climate of suspicion in which it is becoming common practice to ask to see passports before benefits are given. This, and other racist assumptions, may deter some members of ethnic minorities from applying for benefits to which they are entitled, thereby exacerbating their relative poverty. For example, the popular assumption that Asian families can 'always be relied on' to give financial help has led to cases where benefits to which individuals are entitled have been witheld.

Jocelyn Mignott

Jocelyn Mignott, writing in *Social Work Today* on 24 March 1988, explains:

There is a racist myth that should be written on the tombstone of every black, elderly person who dies, cold, alone and poor, unaware of the services which could have advanced their later years – they look after their own (quoted in Richard Webb and David Tossell, *Social Issues for Carers*).

Because married women are defined as dependants in terms of both immigration and social security laws, they are in a particularly vulnerable position. If their husband's immigration status is questioned, they may have their rights to benefits stopped. They may experience difficulties in applying for old age or widow's pensions and death grants on the basis of their husband's contribution record if their marriage took place outside Britain. Complicated proof of marriages which took place many years ago in another country can take many months to sort out, and women's rights to benefits can be withheld during this time. In addition, when women's entitlement to residence in Britain is dependent on their husbands, women who experience violence or contemplate divorce are further disadvantaged in ways that other women, and their own husbands, are not.

Although concern about equal opportunities is a central issue for the provision of welfare services, it remains true that provision has not yet fully met the needs of the black community, whose access to both benefits and services can be adversely affected by racism, compounding the deprivation and poverty caused by unemployment and low pay.

Poverty and social policy

Policies to tackle poverty depend upon:

● which definition of poverty is used;
● the prevailing government's political philosophy.

If an 'absolute' definition is used, then policies need to provide a minimum income to ensure subsistence so that poverty can be eliminated. This is a view that has influenced policy makers since the time of Beveridge, and underlies the provision of income support today.

Criticisms

● 'Absolute' definitions are too simplistic and inflexible. They take no account of different needs. They do not relate the living standards of the poor to the rest of the population and tend to evoke a patronising and stigmatizing view of the poor.
● In practice there is no relationship between the 'success' of policies based on this definition and the 'elimination' of poverty. Life on income support does not stop people being poor or malnourished, or prevent their health and life expectancy from being worse than those of others in the population who are not poor.

If a 'relative' definition is used, then it is necessary to provide the resources which will enable people to participate in a full range of social roles and relationships. Using this definition, it is harder to claim that poverty has been eradicated because it is based on the premise that wealth and resources in society need to be significantly redistributed in order to eliminate poverty and wealth. It implies the kind of 'revolutionary' change in society which is resisted by all policy makers, whether Conservative or Labour.

Restructuring the welfare state

The British welfare state has in the past provided one of the most comprehensive systems of welfare in the world, originally covering education, social security, social and health services, housing and community development, together with policies aimed at full employment.

It takes a large proportion of state resources to fund – resources which derive from taxation and National Insurance contributions. Increasing demands made on the welfare state mean that either more tax revenue has to be raised or services have to be cut. This dilemma has been the focus of a debate between two opposing political philosophies.

The welfare state was founded on the basis of what is usually referred to as a social democratic perspective, which assumes that the state should accept responsibility for the well-being of its citizens. In order to do this, it must provide a range of services and benefits to provide a basic standard of living, funded out of taxation, which will help to redistribute income in order to produce a more fair and equal society. In the period after the Second World War until the late 1970s this view enjoyed a fair degree of cross-party support, with all the major political parties in favour of the welfare state.

Opposed to this view is the position taken by all the Conservative Governments since 1979, and often referred to as the New Right perspective. This view argues that the state should step back from 'interfering' in the lives of its citizens and, rather than taxing them to provide universal services for all, irrespective of their needs, there should be a low tax economy, leaving people free to provide for their own needs as they see fit. Margaret Thatcher's famous pronouncement, 'There is no such thing as society, only the individual and his family', not only managed to be sexist, but was also indicative of a philosophy determined to shift responsibility away from the state, on behalf of the tax payer, to the ingenuity and enterprise of the individual.

Both philosophies are concerned with how best to create a 'free and democratic society'. The social democratic view argues that this cannot be achieved unless all citizens have a minimum standard of living, which reduces extremes of wealth and poverty. It believes that the state can operate as a 'benign institution', concerned to 'see fair play' and to redistribute resources and support families and individuals as appropriate. It argues that, as a society, we should be interdependent with each other, sharing some resources, such as air, water, roads, etc.; and as human beings within the same society, we should recognize our responsibilities to each other for our survival and well-being.

The New Right, on the other hand, argues that freedom will only be guaranteed if the state takes a back seat. The state produces 'undemocratic bureaucracies' which sap individual initiative and enterprise and penalizes those who are most successful by imposing high levels of taxation. Those who are less industrious 'get by on the backs' of everyone else and, when 'welfare handouts' are made too easily available, 'social security scroungers take advantage' and develop a kind of dependency mentality. The less the state 'interferes' in individual lives and decision making the better. This will enable the enterprising and industrious to profit from their hard work, and will force the lazy to 'get on their bikes' and become more 'self-reliant'. It will also ensure that individuals have 'more choice' about how to spend their money (if they have any), e.g. on private education for their children and private healthcare insurance for themselves.

New Right theorists, in attempting to answer the criticism that those with fewer resources in the first place are not best placed to exercise enterprise and initiative, suggest that those who are 'successful' in creating wealth also *trickle-down effect*

help to create jobs for others. Increased affluence would **'trickle down'** as a consequence, enabling more people to own property and shares, etc. so that 'unnecessary expenditure' on the welfare state could be cut.

Fortunately, or unfortunately, this version of reality has not materialized because of recession; a widening gap between rich and poor; increasing evidence of what some would call an 'underclass'; and no evidence at all of wealth 'trickling down' to those below. There has, however, been significant evidence of the related cuts in so-called 'unnecessary' provisions and services provided by the state.

The predominance of New Right ideas during the 1980s and 1990s, and the overriding power of successive Conservative Governments to introduce policies which implement them, has led to a substantial dismantling or restructuring of much of the British welfare state.

Policy implications

The post-war consensus on the role of the welfare state has now broken down, and there is strong disagreement about how to deliver welfare and to whom.

Beveridge's ideas maintained a form of compromise about how best to tackle poverty and between those who believed in universal benefits and those who believed in selective benefits. As a result of his recommendations:

- Education, healthcare, national insurance and family allowances became part of universal provision.
- Income support, based on a means test, provided a 'safety net' for those with insufficient resources to live on. In practice, the 'means-tested' benefits have always been more important than Beveridge expected, especially so with mass unemployment, an increase in life expectancy and growing numbers of single-parent families.

In 1976, concern about the increasing cost of these benefits to the Exchequer led to 'severe restraint' in public spending and to a review of the social security system as the main means of tackling poverty.

From 1979 onwards, the shift in emphasis in government philosophy of successive Conservative Governments, adopting New Right views, led to fundamental changes in the social security system, for example, the abolition of grants and payments to meet 'special needs' and their replacement by a 'social fund' providing loans to the poor on a first come, first served basis with repayments deducted at source from benefits.

The aim is now to target benefits in the direction of the 'most needy', especially families with children, but, since no extra money has been provided, a redistribution of resources had to take place. Not from the rich to the poor, as Marxists, and even some social democrats, would have liked, but from the 'fairly poor' to the 'very poor'. At the same time, the so-called 'gains' to those who benefited from this were 'wiped out' by simultaneous reductions in housing benefit.

This policy involved making distinctions between the 'deserving poor' and the 'undeserving or less deserving poor' (see above). For example:

16–17-year-olds, who have had their rights to benefits removed
18–24-year-olds, who have had their benefits paid at a reduced rate.

Both cuts intended to make young people less dependent on the state and more dependent on their families.

Other groups affected by the cuts were:

- Large numbers of the unemployed, who have had their entitlement to unemployment benefit removed, affecting, for example, mothers of young children, those aged over 55 and those unemployed for longer than 6 months. In 1994 only 30 per cent of those who were unemployed were entitled to claim unemployment benefit because of the introduction of more stringent 'availability for work' tests, with tougher benefit sanctions on those who refuse to take a particular job or leave work 'voluntarily'. The government is currently investigating the 'work-fare schemes' used in the United States whereby claimants have to work on community projects in return for benefits. Young people on Job Training Schemes already work for their benefits. There is pressure to extend this practice to the Restart programme.
- Single parents – the Child Support Agency has been established to shift dependence from the state onto absent and/or divorced fathers. Any money recovered from fathers is deducted at source from women's benefits. The refusal to name or supply information about the whereabouts of absent and divorced fathers can lead to the removal of benefits completely, except in cases of extreme violence.
- People claiming invalidity benefits – doctors have been given more stringent guidelines on which to base their diagnosis of invalidity.
- All benefits claimants were to pay additional charges of VAT on fuel – a measure which, in the event, was not implemented because of the public outcry.

Criticisms

Critics argue that all these policies constitute an attack on the social democratic principles on which the welfare state was founded and introduce a 'selective' system of poverty relief which is no longer regarded as 'a right' to those in need. This leads to an increase in the process of labelling and stigmatizing the poor and to a much more divided society.

The Breadline Britain study discussed above suggests that such policies do not relieve poverty by keeping those on low incomes out of poverty, or address the underlying causes of poverty. In fact, it has been the escalation of these policies and their effects, together with changes in taxation, which have increased the gulf between the haves and have-nots in society, so that the numbers of people living in poverty have actually increased during the last ten years.

Marxists argue that the welfare state was never intended to redistribute wealth and resources from the rich to the poor but to:

- buy off the working class with the benefits of a 'social wage' which, although not paid in cash, would act as a supplement to their earned income;
- placate the working class with social rewards which would make them less critical of governments and less ready to argue for more fundamental social change;
- guarantee at least minimum standards of education, health, etc. in order to provide a more efficient workforce for capitalism;
- create an illusion of fairness in order to lend legitimacy to capitalism.

The Child Poverty Action Group

Marxists and pressure groups like the **Child Poverty Action Group**, also argue that the provisions of the welfare state have consistently benefited the better-off. For example, the middle class receive more in mortgage tax relief than poorer groups receive in housing benefit. So-called scroungers, and people claiming benefits to which they are not technically entitled, are always pursued much more assiduously than people who defraud the Inland Revenue. Tax avoidance and tax fraud is arguably a more 'middle-class' crime, which is not stigmatized in anything like the same way as 'scrounging', but which is estimated to be considerably more lucrative than signing on for unemployment benefit when you also have a part-time job, or claiming income support as a single woman when you are having a sexual relationship with a man who should therefore be assuming 'financial responsibility' for you. Would that the laws which make prostitution illegal were viewed in the same light!

More recently, criticisms of the workings of the welfare state made by feminists and anti-racists have claimed that the provision of services and the underlying assumptions which inform policies and the behaviour of officials should be more responsive to the needs and dignity of women and ethnic minorities.

However, criticisms of the welfare state made by Marxists, feminists and anti-racists do not imply approval of New Right policies concerned to shift the responsibility for surviving poverty away from the state and onto the poor, or condone the increasingly punitive ways in which tests and conditions are applied.

State care or state control?

State concern about poverty and welfare during the last hundred years or so has clearly been influenced by a number of considerations. We have noted the desire to satisfy the needs of capital and at the same time to retain the support of the working class, despite being governed in ways which are inconsistent with their class interests. We have seen how politicians influenced by the New Right have been less concerned to 'placate the working class' and more concerned to 'discipline' them with cuts and threats of unemployment and increased poverty. We have also seen how policies affecting women have served to enforce their traditional domestic and dependent roles within the family, and how the administration of policies affecting ethnic minorities has been compounded by racism.

The anxiety on the part of the ruling class has always also been about the relationship between poverty and politics – the anxiety felt by the ruling class, and the hope expressed by various groups on the political left, that poverty, inequality and injustice might serve to politicize those who experience their worst effects, and that economic deprivation, expressed in social class terms, could lead to organized political unrest.

In the period after the First World War, police and troops were used to crush hunger marches and demonstrations of unemployed workers in Glasgow, Liverpool and London. In more recent times, in the 1980s and 1990s, armed police have been used to control striking coal miners and to prevent demonstrations against the poll tax. Legislation has been introduced to make strikes more difficult and virtually illegal, and the **Criminal Justice** legislation passed in **1994**, removes the rights of citizens 'to assemble in public places' in groups of more than five people in ways which could be construed as a 'public disturbance or trespass'. This will effectively illegalize the activities of homeless people on the streets, squatters, New Age travellers, young people attending raves, as well as people gathering together to protest about environmental or social issues.

Criminal Justice Bill 1994

The relationship between capitalism and the welfare state is full of contradictions. From a working-class point of view, it could be seen in part as a former victory in the continuing struggle to improve and secure a decent standard of living, but which is now being undermined and taken away. From a capitalist point of view, state welfare helped in the accumulation of profit, both by assisting in the reproduction of the labour force and containing its revolutionary potential, but now 'costs too much' to be worth the bother when cheap and 'obedient' labour can be provided more easily by keeping people in competition with each other for jobs. From a woman's point of view, the welfare state once provided jobs in health and welfare services and financial support around personal economic survival and children, but on the basis of a continuing dependency on men and the state rather than economic independence in her own right.

However, to assume that welfare merely serves the interests of capital and the government is to ignore the fact that social institutions are dynamic arrangements which can be sustained or changed by human action. **Paul Corrigan** (*The Welfare State as an Arena of Class Struggle*) points out that:

Paul Corrigan

> if we accept that welfare is controlled by capital and acts against the interests of working people, then why should we fight the cuts? We should welcome them ... as a direct cut in the power of the ruling class over the working class.

And yet fifteen years of Conservative-led cuts in public spending on the welfare state have accelerated a marked decline in job security, living standards and the social wage of working people, as well as widening the economic gulf between those who are comfortably off and those who are poor in society, while also increasing the numbers of people living in poverty. The extent to which a future Labour Government will continue or overturn the dismantling and restructuring of the welfare state in the years ahead remains to be seen.

Sociology and the social sciences

Sociology is about social behaviour, why people behave as they do, what factors in society affect their behaviour, how groups of people in society organize themselves and come to be as they are. Of course, 'an interest in people' would be claimed by almost every academic discipline in one way or another. Even nuclear scientists cannot fail to take account of the behaviour and expectations of people in the society in which they work. But sociology is more than an 'awareness' or an 'interest' in people. It is an attempt to study, in as scientific and systematic a way as possible, how societies operate. This means trying to stand back from a society a little – watching, recording, measuring, evaluating and interpreting what is going on – and trying to explain how and why so many of the things we all take for granted about society come to be as they are.

Of course, societies are made up of countless individuals, all different from each other in many respects. The idiosyncrasies of individual behaviour, which in part cause different individuals to think and react differently, are of interest to sociologists, but are probably more the concern of **psychologists**. Both disciplines are closely related, but whereas the psychologist tends to start from the individual, the sociologist usually concentrates on the social groupings to which the individual belongs.

Sociologists are concerned with the similarities and patterns which can be detected in the behaviour of all those who share the same environment or social class or nationality. Sociologists try to make accurate generalizations about the characteristics of human behaviour and social organization, to identify what causes them and to suggest what their implications might be.

Originally the generalizations made by sociologists were very wide-ranging (suggesting, for example, that most women are paid less than most men). While this is no doubt true, it is also the case that some women earn more than most men. White women in our society earn more, on average, than black women, but not in every case. Women in some societies earn more than both men and women in other societies. And so on. In other words, generalizations have to be treated with extreme care because within similar categories of people and groups there is also considerable diversity. The access to power and economic resources of white, working-class men is not the same as for working-class women or black men or black women. The discrimination experienced by Afro-Caribbean men is not exactly the same as that experienced by Muslim women or British-born children of mixed parentage.

Increasingly, sociologists have become more sophisticated and complex in their identification of social difference and diversity within similar groups, in ways which are given their most extreme expression in the writings of post-structuralists and post-modernists (see below).

The interests of social historians, economists and political scientists are often confused with those of sociologists, too. Like psychology and sociology, their areas of work are closely related. In fact, together they comprise the main group of subjects usually referred to as the **social sciences**.

Because each discipline sets out to study some aspect of social behaviour, there is a good deal of overlap between them in terms of subject matter, and they are certainly dependent upon each other's expertise. But there are differences of emphasis which are crucial: the **historian** is principally concerned with recording what has happened in the past; the **economist** with the financial, business and trading arrangements made by societies; and the **political scientist** with the ways in which societies govern themselves and distribute political power and responsibility.

Each discipline has developed its own theories, methods of study, frames of reference and terminology. It is not surprising, therefore, that together they reflect a range of interpretations and points of view, as well as encouraging more than a little professional rivalry. But equally, together they make possible a fuller understanding of the complexities of human behaviour.

Sociology and science

Because the attention of sociologists is focused on all of these areas – social change, the distribution of wealth, political power and many others – critics often ask: 'So what is special about sociology? Is it just a mixture of everything else?' As the work of contemporary sociologists has become more familiar to people, however, their distinctive contribution has become more obvious. Increasingly, people are coming to appreciate that, to study social behaviour properly, a knowledge of different theories, specialist skills and carefully collected evidence are all essential. There is a good deal of disagreement about which theories, what skills and whose evidence, however, as we shall see later.

In addition, because sociologists have tended to concentrate their studies on what society usually regards as 'problems', such as poverty, delinquency and racial tensions, for example, their findings have always been closely related to the absence or imposition of social policies and have been widely debated in the media. It is this connection which has contributed to the belief that sociologists 'help' or 'hinder' people, depending on your particular viewpoint. And since most of what sociology has to say about society seems to be critical, sociologists are frequently regarded as politically radical. Both of these are assumptions which are largely inaccurate.

Some sociologists like to see themselves as 'neutral scientists', who investigate and analyse different kinds of behaviour with reference to relevant theories and supported by evidence which has been systematically collected. Their aim is to accurately describe, explain and understand. They would probably say that it is not the job of sociologists to say what should or should not be done about the phenomena they describe. Taking action is the job of governments, policy makers and other professionals of various kinds.

This sense of 'scientific detachment' has done a great deal to establish the reputation of sociology as a responsible academic discipline, founded on ideals of scientific objectivity and value-free analysis. It has also been the characteristic of sociology which has come under the most persistent attack from within the ranks of sociologists themselves.

Many would reject the scientific and neutral approach completely, and argue that human behaviour is much more difficult to measure scientifically than are natural phenomena. There are so many different social forces affecting social behaviour, and their interaction and influence are shifting and changing all the time. The intricacies and complexities of human society, working on so many different levels and with so many different twists and turns of relationship, demand inspiration, insight and even imagination when it comes to trying to make sense of it all. This is not something that can happen in tightly controlled laboratory conditions. In addition, it is very difficult – some would say impossible – to be neutral about what is being studied. Because sociologists are humans, with human values, prejudices and traditions, they cannot help but be affected by these when they make decisions about what to study, how best to study it and what conclusions to draw from their investigations.

Because society is the subject of their study, they must also have a view of how society might be improved or changed by what they discover and recommend. Inevitably, this will mean disagreement, conflicting theories and controversial interpretations. Present-day social scientists are far less confident about claiming to have discovered 'absolute truths' than their forbears would have been, and talk more about the 'probabilities' and 'likelihood' of things, rather than the certainty. Increasingly, the emphasis has also shifted to the perspective of those who are being studied. How does it all seem to them? What is their interpretation?

But while sociology may not be a science in the same way as we think of laboratory-based experimental physics, chemistry or biology, that is not to say that it cannot be 'scientific'. The tradition of collecting evidence with which to test and refine theories, and the use of this evidence, as distinct from opinion or speculation, on which to base interpretation, are key features of both scientific and sociological enquiry. Interpretations may, in the end, vary, and different people may draw different conclusions from their scrutiny of the evidence. They may, indeed, set out to collect the evidence in rather different ways. But in the end they will have aimed to approach the evidence in as systematic and objective a way as they can. Otherwise they will not have been pursuing sociology.

Early sociology

Sociology today is a very different discipline from the one that emerged at the end of the eighteenth century in Europe, faced the challenges of nineteenth-century social and economic changes, grew in popularity in Britain after the Second World War and has been reviewing and refining itself ever since. It is ironic that, at a time when the name of sociology has never been more commonplace in everyday language, its composition has never been more complex. To understand a little of why this is so we must look briefly to its origins and more recent developments.

The emergence of sociology as a new form of knowledge is usually reckoned to have taken place at the end of the eighteenth century, when social philosophers of the time developed wide-ranging theories to explain the development of different kinds of societies throughout human history. But important things happened to the intellectual climate in Europe in the nineteenth century which affected the direction in which sociology developed and made it much more concerned with the contemporary world in which the sociologists were living.

As a direct result of the French and Industrial Revolutions a rather different kind of society emerged in Europe – an industrial capitalist society. The old social and political relationships based on agriculture, feudalism, religion and small workshop employment gradually gave way to a new order based on industry, urbanization, new forms of communication and international trade.

It was not an overnight change by any means, and it has since developed and changed yet further. But in nineteenth-century Europe it had a startling effect on those who reflected on its implications. Political and social power no longer depended so much on inherited landed wealth as the emphasis shifted to industrial production and power shifted to those who controlled it. At a time when such an arrangement was not so taken for granted as it is today, because it was new, it was an ideal opportunity to devise theories to explain what was happening.

Some feared that social upheavals of such magnitude would lead to the 'breakdown of society' and the loss of the 'community' and 'tradition' which they associated with the feudal order. They saw 'individualism' and 'isolation' as the characteristics of the new age which would together destroy what had gone before.

Others welcomed the challenge to feudal power and traditional authority, and saw the emergence of a new society based on industrial labour as a significant step in the direction of socialist revolution.

The Enlightenment

The other main influence on sociological thought at the time was the legacy of **the Enlightenment**. From this intellectual tradition came the fascination with science and the respect for rational, systematic study as distinct from philosophizing and speculation.

Durkheim, Weber & Marx

The important sociologists of the time – the most famous being **Emile Durkheim, Max Weber** and **Karl Marx** – were very much influenced by the world in which they lived. But this does not mean that they have nothing to say to us today. Until at least the early 1980s most contemporary sociologists still referred back to the writings of these 'founding fathers' of the discipline, to seek inspiration from their theories and methods of study. They refined them, modified them, argued with them and redefined them in a variety of ways, and in relation to contemporary social issues and social conditions. Their influence, either directly or indirectly, still informed most of what was being written in sociology until this time.

post-structuralism & post-modernism

More recently, in the last ten years or so, the large-scale 'meta theories' which have dominated sociology for generations have come under fierce attack by the philosophies and criticisms of **post-structuralism** and **post-modernism**. While these are the theories which are now fashionable in contemporary academia, in a variety of disciplines including sociology, their popularity is not without its critics, as we shall see later.

Although the tendency of post-modernism and post-structuralism is to declare the irrelevance and inaccuracy of most of what has gone before, it would be premature to arrive at the same conclusions, especially as the political character and political implications of the criticisms made are themselves highly contentious.

Before considering these in more detail, we shall return to the theoretical contributions made to the development of sociology as a discipline by earlier intellectuals and practitioners.

Emile Durkheim
(1858–1917)

Durkheim's most famous work did a great deal to establish sociology as a science of social life and something separate and distinct from other studies of human behaviour such as psychology and biology. His work was empirical, which means that he relied on observation and the collection of evidence with which to test theories and make predictions about behaviour.

Set against the background of a changing French society, he was preoccupied by the relationship between society and the human beings who depended on it. He questioned how society held together and how common values and beliefs and patterns of behaviour came to be.

For Durkheim, society was something like a living body, all its separate organs were linked together and dependent on each other. All had to function properly for the general health and well-being of the whole. When this analogy was applied to society he never questioned whether or not society should be preserved as a well-functioning, healthy organism; he simply assumed that this was something that could be taken for granted, just as he seemed to think that there was a recognizable thing called 'society' which had some kind of existence separate from the individuals who comprised it. The function of institutions such as religion, law and education was to provide the common rules, laws, customs, obligations, attitudes, values and climates of opinion which would exercise control over individuals and groups and ensure that they lived together cohesively. His view was of forces external to individuals which nevertheless had considerable control over them.

Durkheim & suicide

One of his most famous studies was that of **suicide**. Not whether it was a good or a bad thing, but an attempt to link the personal act of committing suicide with the social forces in operation which might encourage it. He collected all the available statistics and analysed them in terms of categories like age, sex, religion and family relationship. At the end of his study he was able to show that certain people in certain situations are more likely to commit suicide than others. His method of investigation provided an example to others about how they should conduct investigations empirically, and has been debated, refined and disagreed with almost ever since. By revealing, for example, that a married Catholic woman, with several children, was less likely to kill herself than an unmarried, childless, Protestant man, he claimed to have produced scientific generalizations about human behaviour which were not based on individual idiosyncrasies and which were social facts quite different from what the expertise of biology or pyschology could account for.

But although he claimed to be scientific in his approach, Durkheim was obviously very influenced by his own reactions to the society around him, particularly what he took to be the breakdown of social relationships by the forces of industrial capitalism. He described anomie as a state of social isolation and normlessness brought about by the collapse of common values and social order so that people could no longer relate properly to each other or to society.

**Max Weber
(1864–1920)**

Like Durkheim, Weber was also very influenced by the social climate of his times. He believed that other German sociologists, especially those who agreed with Marx's analysis of society, over-exaggerated the influence of economics and did not take enough account of the influence of ideas and the impact of significant individuals on developments such as the growth of capitalism. In reaction to what he considered to be the political bias of some of his colleagues and contemporaries, he championed the ideals of value-free sociology and the need to 'understand' and explain, rather than merely describe, human behaviour.

For Weber one of the main characteristics of industrialization and social change was the growth of bureaucratic organizations, which he saw as a serious threat to individual freedoms. The Marxist view that capitalism would ultimately be replaced by socialism caused Weber to predict even stricter bureaucratic controls under socialist organization.

Weber always made the starting point for his analysis the behaviour of individuals rather than the large-scale and external institutions and forces upon which sociologists like Durkheim concentrated. Whereas Durkheim seemed almost to attribute society with an existence and an identity of its own, as something 'out there', and somehow separate from the individuals who comprised it, Weber was adamant that society was only an abstraction. For him society was really only the sum total of lots of individuals interacting together. And in the process of interaction, he believed, they exercised a good deal of mutual influence upon each other's behaviour.

Weber and the 'actions' of individuals

Weber's emphasis on the **'actions' of individuals** has had a big influence on the approaches of other sociologists since his death, and his own writings are best remembered for his studies of Protestantism in relation to the rise of capitalism, bureaucracy, religion, music and industry.

Karl Marx (1818–1883)

Not only sociologists but also economists, philosophers, political scientists and even historians claim Karl Marx as an important contributor to the theory and argument of their particular disciplines. Perhaps it is safest not to label Marx, but to refer to him as an analyst of economic, social and political life. Although he was provoked by the industrial and political changes he witnessed in nineteenth-century Europe, and did most of his major writing in Britain, he was not confined to the events of one period of history nor to the social characteristics of one society. In fact, he was concerned with 'changing' society rather than merely trying to explain it. His method of analysis was not to divide politics or economics or history from society, but to try to unite them in theory and in practice.

In showing how the capitalist system of industrial production, and the relationship between its owners and workers, had come to be, Marx always took a historical perspective. He was also concerned to reveal the links between industrial capitalism in one country and economic developments and social relationships in other societies, particularly the 'third world' empires of the industrial nations.

A third characteristic which demonstrated his refusal to be bound by the present and underlined his enthusiasm for 'changing society' rather than merely recording it was the 'predictive' emphasis in his writings. The logic of his historical, comparative and contemporary analysis of society, culminating in the development of capitalism as an economic, social and political means of organization and control, enabled him to predict how this in turn would give way to something else. Capitalism as a means of social organization and a concentration of power would, he argued, ultimately be replaced by socialism.

The political implications of Marx's writings are obvious, and, though claiming to be scientific and systematic, he never adhered to the philosophy of neutrality. He considered the capitalist system to be unjust and oppressive to the workers who had to provide the labour power for it to become established, and predicted, and, indeed, advocated, a time in which the control of wealth and social power produced by the achievements of industrialization would be taken over by workers so that a different type of society, based on social equality, could be established.

Whether or not people agree with Marx's economic analysis of society, and particularly his political sentiments, it is undoubtedly the case that his writings have had more influence, both directly and indirectly, on subsequent social scientists than those of almost any other single theorist. Modern sociology comprises many who base their analysis and their work very much on Marxist ideas and frames of reference. There are also others who are not Marxist in outlook or sentiment, but who have nevertheless incorporated much of his methodology and many of his concepts into their approach. For these reasons his writings have to be taken seriously.

Marx's view of human beings was that we are both 'created by' the social forces around us and at the same time are the 'creators' of those social forces. The tension between the two, being 'determined by' but also seeking 'to determine', was for Marx the dynamic which rendered society always in a state of change. By far the most important relationship in this process was that between humanity and labour. Through work, people could become either 'fully human' – in the sense of being fulfilled, creative and autonomous – or stunted – a person's labour can also help to keep him or her, unfree, powerless and exploited.

The key for Marx was in the 'conditions' under which labour was created and within which work was carried out. Under capitalism the worker does not have an equal relationship with the owner of capital. Workers must work for owners in return for the wages they need to survive. Their survival depends on that work and those wages always being available to them. Workers do not own the tools they use, or the machines or factories in which they work. They do not own what they produce and they have little control over what they produce or how they are required to produce it. Neither do they have control over what becomes of the things they produce. In all these respects the owner is at an advantage. The owner owns the capital and the plant. The owner has the power to hire and fire workers. The owner makes all the decisions about what will be produced, where it will be sold and how much it will cost. Once the owner has paid the workers' wages and invested in new machinery and factories to keep production running smoothly, all the remaining profits belong to the owner. Both workers and owners are, therefore, almost inevitably in conflict. It is in the owner's interest to keep production as high as possible and to get the maximum amount of profits in return. It is in the workers' interests to make sure they do not become slaves to the production process at the expense of their health, leisure and family life, and that the wages they earn are as high as possible. It is this **'conflict of interests'** between those who own and those who labour which Marx saw as crucial in the explanation of social organization and social change. It explains why both sides need to organize to outdo each other.

Important Marxist concepts that you will come across time and again in contemporary sociology are to be found in his explanations of the relationship between human beings and their labour. For example, the notion that, because of the unequal relationships of capitalism, workers cannot achieve their full potential and autonomy, is a condition referred to by Marx as **alienation**. The fact that in industry a worker must do more work than is necessary to satisfy his or her own needs produces **surplus value** for the capitalist. The inherent conflict of interests between the different elements in social relationships provides the **dialectic,** the growth of one thing out of another, that brings about social change. All of these ideas and more are to be found first in Marx's writings and now in sociological writings today.

One of the most important legacies has been to explain the significance of social class – not merely the difference between capitalism and workers or to provide definitions of Marx's use of the terms 'bourgeoisie' and 'proletariat' but a systematic explanation of the links between people's economic circumstances and the ideologies, or sets of ideas, which sustain them.

Different approaches

You will already have realized that sociology is not one simple mutually agreed way of studying society. There are a variety of different approaches within sociology which are based on different theories of society and different methods of investigation. Shifts in emphasis and developments are happening all the time. As more aspects of social behaviour come under scrutiny from sociological inquiry, the discipline inevitably splits up, and areas like family life, education, industrial relations, deviance, popular culture, gender, ethnicity, etc., have all become specialist concerns. But these are not the important distinctions in sociology today. What is more important is the way in which different sociologists approach their work.

In simple terms, the main distinction is between:

those who see the patterns and characteristics of social behaviour as mainly imposed by huge structures, institutions and forces in society that influence and determine how people behave

and

those who believe that social behaviour is created and given some kind of meaning by the conscious and unconscious actions of individuals in interaction with each other.

structural versus interpretive view

In the first view, which we call **systems** or **structural**, social behaviour is created by systems, forces and institutions outside the control of individuals, which mould them into shape. In the second, which we call **social action** or **interpretive**, human beings, as individuals and members of social groups relating together, produce and create the social characteristics of their groups and their societies.

The first view, which derives its inspiration from the ideas of Durkheim and Karl Marx, begins by considering sytems and structures in society and develops a **macro** explanation of social behaviour. The second, which derives its inspiration from Max Weber, begins with the individual and small group and develops a **micro** approach to describing and understanding social behaviour (see Figure 9.1).

In the end, it is probably most useful to see both sets of perspectives as different sides of the same coin. But before we go on to explain why this might be so, lets look at the two sides in more detail. We will see how each has developed over the years and how different contemporary approaches connect into them.

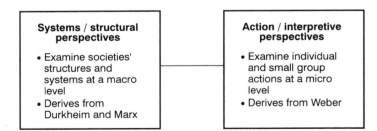

Figure 9.1 Theories of social behaviour

Systems/Structural perspectives

The main characteristic of systems and structural perspectives is that social behaviour is learned via the process of socialization. Human beings learn the kinds of behaviour which are expected of them in the different social settings in which they find themselves. Social behaviour in different societies is different because people have different rules about how to behave and what to think. The behaviour of different groups within societies is different for the same reasons – because they are socialized into the acceptance of different rules. According to this perspective, the systems and structures of society determine the behaviour of its members.

Functionalism

Functionalism was probably the most influential approach in sociology until about the 1950s. Its origins go back a long way in the philosophical tradition of considering social institutions in relation to the contribution they make to the overall functioning of society. We referred earlier to the notion of society as an **organism** – a body whose separate parts had to function properly and in harmony if the whole was to be kept healthy. The English sociologist Herbert Spencer first applied this analogy to society, and much of Durkheim's work assumes this kind of relationship.

More recent functionalists refer to society as a system rather than an organism, but the interest in how various parts of the system relate together is much the same.

Functionalist sociology is concerned, therefore, with analysing the functions of different parts of the system – to question how they relate to each other and to the whole. In practice, this usually means an analysis of social subsystems like politics, economics, law and religion, among others, to identify the links between them and to enumerate the functions they fulfil for society.

There has been quite a reaction against this kind of approach in recent years. The main criticisms stem from the implicit assumptions in functionalist analysis about the persistence and value of social cohesion and the desire for social order – the notion that there are 'common values' in society and 'common interests' which are best served by the preservation of recognized institutions. But these assumptions do not accurately describe the diversity and conflict inherent in most complex societies; nor do they accept the idea that preserving the sanctity of systems and institutions at all costs is extremely conservative. The functionalist perspective, it is argued, disguises the conflicts and contradictions which exist in every society, and underestimates the significance of social change.

There is also the tendency in functionalism to attribute a kind of 'existence in their own right' to social institutions, as if morality or law, for example, are things you can see, keep in a box or hold in your hand. The danger of seeming to make 'things' out of abstractions is called **reification**, and is criticized by those who believe that it ignores the active participation of individuals in creating, redefining and changing society by their behaviour and interaction.

Even when it is accepted that social institutions come to exist, and do serve particular functions for society, functionalism does not explain how these institutions came to be in the first place, or what causes them to change over time. These are considered to be serious weaknesses in the functionalist perspective.

Conflict perspectives

Conflict perspectives derive from similar ideas about the importance and influence of structures in society, but they do not recognize the existence or value of cohesion and cooperation as a way of describing social change or achieving social progress.

Conflict theorists tend to focus on examples of **inequality** in society and the ways in which inequalities operate to the detriment of those who are affected by them. The notion of a conflict of interests between the haves and have-nots in society is also central to this perspective. So far as conflict theorists are concerned, socialization is more likely to be an instrument of oppression, which attempts to produce social order and control by force and indoctrination rather than by consensus.

Marxism and neo-Marxism

The influence of Marx on contemporary sociology is immense, and the distinction made between systems/structural perspectives and action/interpretive perspectives is not altogether helpful because both sides find inspiration in his ideas and methodology.

According to Marxists:

- a state of conflict exists between those who own capital and those who are obliged to work for capitalists;
- the major conflict of interests is in terms of social class;
- the characteristics of the economic system are seen as most important in determining the nature of society and the characteristics of social behaviour.

Living through the development and consolidation of capitalism, and the apparent inability, and even disinclination, of vast numbers of the working class to emancipate themselves, has not been easy for twentieth-century Marxists. Attempts to make sense of why Marx's prediction about the overthrow of capitalism has not happened has led to two main developments in Neo-Marxist thinking:

- Humanist Marxism – associated primarily with the Italian Marxist Antonio Gramsci and the German members of the Frankfurt School. Humanist Marxism is said to have drawn its inspiration from Marx's earlier writings.
- Structuralist Marxism – associated primarily with Louis Althusser, who is said to have drawn his inspiration from Marx's later writings.

Althusser is probably best known for his writing on the state and his separation of the two ways in which the state exercises its power. He refers to organizations like the police, the army and the law as part of the **repressive state apparatus** of power; and to educational, media, religious and cultural institutions as part of the **ideological state apparatus** of power.

According to Althusser, education has taken over from religion in modern society as the main ideological instrument of state oppression. The work of Bowles and Gintis (see pages 141–2), about the correspondence between the needs of capitalism and the workings of the education system, is a practical application of Althusser's Marxism.

Gramsci and hegemony

Humanist Marxists have shifted the emphasis from the economic base of society to the superstructure. Gramsci introduced the notion of **hegemony** to describe the all-consuming way in which ideologies operate to distort a person's view of the world. The effects of ideological bombardment is to create a kind of 'false consciousness' which needs to be replaced by 'class consciousness' before effective political action for social change can be taken. Gramsci advocated education as a form of counter-socialization and as being one of the most likely ways of resisting the strength of hegemonic beliefs.

The Frankfurt School and phenomenological Marxism

The action emphasis is also reflected in the **critical philosophy** of the **Frankfurt School**, most often associated with Theodor Adorno, Jurgen Habermas, Max Horkheimer and Herbert Marcuse. They employ a kind of

phenomenological Marxism to stress the creative and recreative capacities of human beings, and their ability to intervene consciously and deliberately to change the course of social life.

The difficulty of classifying Marxist sociology is further frustrated by the wealth and variety of his writings and the fact that his ideas have been taken on board by many other disciplines. Some regard Marxism as almost a 'world view' – a total explanation of the development and characteristics of human society, whose myriad elements, from political life to industrial relations, and from medicine to literature, can be examined, explained and understood from the perspective of Marxist ideas.

After taking all the modifications and developments into consideration, however, the following characteristics are probably the ones which best describe what is distinctive and most valuable in Marx's contribution.

- The primary significance given to the economic structure and the relationship between labour and production in the analysis of society. Of all the factors which influence what society is like, and the ways in which people behave, economic considerations are regarded by Marxists as the most important.
- The concern to place the society, the phenomenon or the social relationship being studied into a historical and economic context to see where it came from, how it developed and what caused it to change.
- The view that society does not merely 'evolve gradually', but that social progress and change is frequently brought about by revolutionary breaks in continuity as societies change from one form to another.
- The emphasis on conflicting interests and contradictions within structures as the key to the dialectic which serves to produce revolutionary change.
- The link between theory and practice which is usually called **praxis** – the view that action must first be reflected upon intellectually and then carried out consciously.
- Marx's great achievement was to devise a social theory which could be used to analyse society and at the same time provide a guide to action, in that human beings were encouraged to make their own history.

This last characteristic has produced perhaps the most criticism, especially in its commitment to socialism, and it has sometimes been difficult to differentiate between theory, analysis and dogma in the writings of those subsequently influenced by Marx's ideas. Similarly, the prediction that Marx made about the destruction of capitalism, and the characteristics of the socialist and communist societies which would replace it, have not happened quite as he imagined. But as the criticisms and controversies continue to rage – not least those most recently inspired by the fashion for post-modernism and post-structuralism – the effect is to force contemporary sociologists to continually re-examine their assumptions and their approaches, and to produce a stimulating and fruitful climate in which the perceptions and authority of sociology, as a way of understanding society, is continually being extended.

Non-Marxist conflict perspectives

The belief that it is conflict rather than cohesion that typifies the power relationships between different groups in society characterizes the ideas of other – non-Marxist – conflict theories of social behaviour. The best example of such a perspective is Feminism. While some feminists may also be Marxists, and most feminists attribute considerable significance to social class in the unequal distribution of power and resources in society, they also emphasize the conflicting interests bound up with relationships of sex and gender. A similar recognition of group conflict which does not spring simply from social class power relations is that which is located in issues of ethnicity and nationality.

Feminism

For most of the last 200 years or so, in which sociologists have been concerned to explain the nature of society and, in some cases, argue for social progress and social change, they have done so in ways which:

● seem to assume that society is made up entirely of men;
● seem to assume that generalizations made about men can be equally applied to women;
● fail to take account of the variety of disadvantages experienced by women in the world compared with men, and which derive from different experiences and different access to resources.

The re-emergence of the women's movement in the West in the 1960s gave rise to considerable agitation for social and political change on behalf of women. Feminist ideas began to influence the academic debates in a variety of subjects which had previously been dominated by the concerns of men.

Sociology was a fairly male-oriented and male-practised subject before the impact of feminism and before the questions raised by feminism about the lives, relationships and social conditions of women began to be taken seriously. Few studies were undertaken about the social behaviour and experience of women, and descriptions of essentially male experience – for example, 'social class', 'industrial labour' and 'delinquency' – were assumed, by default, to apply equally to women, although they were rarely mentioned.

Now the picture has changed. Not only has the subject content become considerably more concerned with the recognition of gender issues in society, but many more women are studying, writing and teaching sociology in their own right. Feminist perspectives have become an essential element of sociological theory.

Liberal feminism

Liberal feminism (see also pages 44–5) tends to regard gender inequality as the largely unintented consequence of prejudice and ignorance. Unenlightened attitudes and behaviour differences which are detrimental to the ideals of equality of opportunity between the sexes can be changed by education and persuasion. Adjustments and changes to the law should be able to ensure greater equity in matters of pay, for example. Training schemes which encourage women into non-traditional jobs should help to challenge sexist attitudes in the workplace. Ignorance and prejudice can be gradually overcome by re-education and government intervention.

The early work of Ann Oakley helped to provide the kind of information which revealed inequalities and disadvantages in women's lives which could be relieved by re-education and legislation.

Marxist and socialist feminism

Marxist and socialist feminism (see also pages 45–6) takes a more structural view of women's oppression, which is attributed not to individual ignorance and prejudice but to institutionalized ways of distributing power and resources in society.

According to Marxist feminists, women's oppression serves the needs of capitalism. It is in the economic relationships of production that we should look for the root causes of womens' subordination. Marxist feminists have extended the insights about conflicting class interests at the point of production to the study of the relationships of reproduction and the domestic economy. The creation of a sexual division of labour – which gives responsibility to women for unpaid childcare and domestic work at home – provides for the free reproduction and rearing of the future workforce for capital.

Once women are persuaded that their main responsibilities and duties lie in the home, they become discounted as serious workers outside the home, which means they can be paid less than men and treated less favourably in terms of working rights and conditions. Once the myths and inaccuracies have been established that women don't really want or need to work, because they are economically dependent on men and are primarily committed to their domestic roles, their actual presence in the paid workforce can be ignored and discounted. They become like a 'reserve army' of cheap labour, to be moved in and out of the labour market as and when they are needed.

According to this view, two main sources of power operate to keep women in a disadvantaged position – both of them stemming from the relationships of capitalism:

1 Economic power, and women's lack of reasonable access to equal economic resources.
2 Ideological power, and the use made of oppressive ideologies by capital and the state to advance repressive ideas about the virtues of family life, motherhood and femininity.

According to Marxist and socialist feminists, the liberation of women is dependent not simply upon changing attitudes and removing ignorance, but upon the destruction of capitalist economic relations. This will also involve the transformation of ideas about sexuality, gender and family life, so that women and men are no longer coerced into living in oppressive and restrictive ways.

Radical feminism

The main problem with Marxist and socialist explanations of women's oppression under capitalism is that they do not explain the subordination of women in non-capitalist societies; or why, within the relationships of capitalism, non-capitalist men who are themselves oppressed by capitalism choose to collude with capital to preserve the servicing and subservient roles of women.

Radical feminism (see also pages 46–8) sets out to explain the universal nature of women's oppression, which both predates capitalism and operates in very different societies, based on very different economic systems to our own. The explanation favoured by radical feminism is that **patriarchy** – the power of men over women – is the source of women's oppression. It is not the economic system, but men's, that oppress women.

According to radical feminists, men as a group may have internal differences with each other based, for example, on conflicts of class, power, culture and ethnicity. But they share a common understanding and expectation of their own superiority in comparison to women. Over the centuries they have used their control of economic relations, ideas and culture to help institutionalize beliefs, laws, education, religion, state institutions and organizations which protect male interests at the expense of women. Even relatively powerless men benefit from the advantages, arrangements and assumptions made on their behalf by more powerful men.

The exercise of power over women by men is not simply confined to the **public** and political arenas of work, state and society. Just as important is the personal and **private** world of intimate relationships and family life. Politics and the exercise of power also occur in interpersonal relationships, in which individual men exercise power over individual women. This may operate according to a whole series of cultural norms about who does the housework and who makes the decisions; about whose work and whose interests and opinions are considered to be most important and valuable; about who is regarded as the breadwinner and the head of the household, etc.

Frequently, disproportionate amounts of power between men and women are encouraged by sexist socialization and education, as well as by the influence of religion and the media. Men have also organized historically to make sure that they secure more of the money and other resources coming into the household than women.

When all else fails – including indoctrination, persuasion and owning more resources – there are other forms of male power over women to fall back on.

The emphasis on power relations in the privacy of interpersonal relations has encouraged radical feminists to consider sexuality and violence as two of the main ways in which men control women.

It is now a well-known fact that women and girl children are in greater physical danger from the fathers, brothers, husbands and partners to whom they are related than from any other single group. Child abuse, rape, domestic violence and domestic murder are common experiences in families of all cultures, creeds and classes. In the vast majority of cases, women and children are the victims and men the perpetrators.

Male sexuality and violence are frequently experienced as two sides of the same coin in which women and children are viewed as the objects of male sexual attention and gratification, irrespective of the wishes, desires, safety or integrity of their victims. Popular media presentations and pornography present women as sexual commodities for the abuse and pleasure of men. Intercourse and heterosexuality are presented as the 'norm'. For women of different cultures and in different ways, sex is what is done to them by men.

The notion of women defining and determining their own sexual identity, free from the onslaught of anti-woman, male-oriented and pornographic representations about what constitutes sex, and all of which is widely promoted in the interests of patriarchy, would require social changes on a scale that is little short of revolution.

The notion that it is men rather than systems that oppress women, and that oppression operates at both a personal and a public level, has led radical feminists to advocate solutions that are to do with women separating themselves from men.

Separatism can be seen as both a refusal to 'sleep with the enemy' and a political strategy which reduces the power of men to control the lives of women. It may cause some men to alter their behaviour and to rethink their allegiance to patriarchy. But, more importantly, it enables women to develop patterns of survival, self-reliance and independence which confront social attitudes and challenge those arrangements which are designed to keep women in positions of social subordination.

*Dual systems
theories*

Dual systems feminism (see also pages 50–1) make use of the insights of both Marxist feminism and radical feminism to account for the impact of both capitalism and patriarchy on women's oppression. The links are most often made in discussions about marriage and family life, in which men are revealed as colluders in the economic oppression of capitalist economics.

A materialist version of dual systems feminism, associated with writers like Christine Delphy, Zillah Eisenstein and Heidi Hartmann, represents capitalist patriarchy as being in cahoots in ways which maintain the economic and domestic exploitation of women for the benefit of men's profit, personal advantage and home comforts.

A psychoanalytical version of dual systems feminism, associated with writers like Juliet Mitchell, argues that patriarchy is rooted in the unconscious rather than the material world. It is not social systems which exercise coercive male power over women so much as ideas that women develop about themselves at an unconscious level in the process of psychological development – ideas which allow for their domination by men. To make changes in women's self-esteem and patterns of unconscious and submissive behaviour requires psychoanalysis and therapy rather than political action.

Black feminism

A common objection to different versions of feminist theory – be it liberal, Marxist or radical – is that it has come largely from the experience and intellectual traditions of white, Western, middle-class groups, and has tended to assume some kind of 'essential' similarity in the lived experiences of all women, simply because they are women.

This led in the late 1970s and 1980s to considerable discussion about the ways in which social class membership, sexuality, ethnicity and nationality cut across and intersect with gender to create both similarity and diversity in women's experience. Black feminists in particular have felt invisible, misunderstood and misrepresented by the combination of class, race and intellectual oppressions that tended to inhabit white Western feminism.

Amos and Parmar say:

> Few white feminists in Britain and elsewhere have elevated the question of racism to the level of primacy within their practical political activities or in their intellectual work. ... Thus the perception of white-middle class feminists of what they need liberating from has little or no relevance to the day-to-day experience of the majority of black women in Britain.

Ann Phoenix

About black people's invisibility, **Ann Phoenix** says:

> When 'normal' processes are being studied, black people are usually excluded from samples for two sorts of reasons. The first is to do with the strict control over the number of variables in the study ... the other set of reasons ... are the result of what Jennifer Platt (1985) calls 'samples of opportunity'. Researchers frequently study samples that live conveniently near the university. ... Whatever the reason for the exclusion ... the effect is to underline the common-sense view that black people are different from white people.

Hazel Carby

About feminist categories used 'universally', **Hazel Carby** says:

> It bears repetition that black men have not held the same patriarchal positions of power that the white males have established. ... If we take patriarchy and apply it to various colonial situations it is equally unsatisfactory because it is

Combahee River Collective

Post-modern feminism

unable to explain why black males have not enjoyed the benefits of white patriarchy. There are very obvious power structures in both colonial and slave social formations and they are predominantly patriarchal. However, the historically specific forms of racism forces us to modify or alter the application of the term patriarchy to black men. Black women have been dominated patriarchally in different ways by men of different colours.

About feminism itself, the **Combahee River Collective** says:

> Although we are feminists and lesbians, we feel solidarity with progressive black men and do not advocate the fractionalisation that white women who are separatists demand. Our situation as black people necessitates that we have solidarity around the fact of race, which white women do not need to have with white men. ... We struggle together with black men against racism, and we also struggle with black men about sexism.

The notion that the meaning of 'womanhood or 'sisterhood' is not the same for women everywhere encouraged post-modernists to argue for the deconstruction of 'taken-for-granted' terms like 'woman', 'femininity' and 'sexuality' to reveal the variety, diversity and elusiveness of the many forms which these words can take.

Most of the work of feminist post-modernism has focused on what is meant by the term 'woman' and on the exploration of 'femininity' and 'masculinity' as cultural forms. This has led principally to the study of language and of cultural texts such as film, literature, magazines and pictures. It has tended to concentrate on the ways in which individuals are represented. Arguments have also concentrated on the ways in which individuals represent themselves and give meaning to their sense of identity.

So far as feminism as a political movement for social change is concerned, these developments into post-modernism and post-structuralism are to be regarded as highly reactionary. While their origin in 'anti-essentialism', and in criticisms of 'universalistic' statements about the condition of all women, made from the position of very 'particular' kinds of experience, is certainly valid, the focus in post-modernist approaches on cultural and literary forms, philosophy and language is possibly less conducive to interpreting the realities of everyday life than the 'all-embracing approaches' which they set out to criticize.

Equally, feminism as a theoretical perspective is not simply concerned with explaining the world, but is also concerned with trying to change it. This should lead, and has led, to continuing attempts to confront prejudices and ignorance about the diversity of women's experience, and to develop and refine the connections between the theories which explain women's lives and the immense complexity of those lives, in order to pursue effective political change.

Action/interpretive perspectives

The main characteristic of social action and interpretive perspectives in sociological theory is not to be found in the macro systems and structures of society, but in the ways in which small groups of individuals relate together. The spotlight is placed on the interpersonal methods of communication between individuals, how people are treated by others, how individuals come to understand and make sense of each other's behaviour. These perspectives are based on the conviction that part of the quality of being human is the capacity to work out what is going on and then choose to act in a particular way as a consequence.

Social action theorists concentrate on the micro level of social life, and do not consider that societies have any existence or meaning outside the perceptions and behaviour of their members. Societies are the **product** of social interaction, not the origin or cause.

Symbolic interactionism *Cooley & Mead*	The origins of symbolic interactionism are in the writings of **Charles Cooley** and **George Herbert Mead**, two American sociologists who were greatly influenced by Weber's emphasis on social action, but who tended to concentrate on the interaction between individuals and small groups rather than relate the behaviour of individuals to larger, social, economic and political structures, as Weber did.

The starting point for an examination of social behaviour in this approach is the individual, and how the individual is made into the kind of person he or she becomes through interaction with others. It is the view of interactionists, and, indeed, sociologists generally, that while some physical and biological characteristics are inherited by human beings, most of their behaviour is learned and considerably influenced, by the social environment in which they grow up.

Symbolic interactionists are interested in:

- the ways in which humans use symbols in communication with each other;
- the effect that the interpretation of these symbols has on the behaviour of all those involved in the interaction.

George Herbert Mead

Human infants first begin to learn their identity in the family and, according to Mead, this learning is very dependent upon the symbols that mediate between individuals and the others who are important to them in their lives – in Mead's words, their 'significant others'.

The growing child learns, in response to the behaviour and reactions of others, to attach meanings to symbols such as language, facial expressions, dress, gestures and skin colour, for example. Whether it is the difference between a frown or a smile; the knowledge about what kinds of behaviour give pleasure or pain; words which indicate whether he's a boy or she's a girl and what's expected of people in gender roles – the learning is endless. It is 'internalized', or taken into the consciousness of, young children as they gradually come to know who they are and what is expected of them, and as they begin to develop a sense of their own self-image and identity.

Other relationships serve to continue this learning process throughout life, as individual behaviour responds to the reciprocal interaction between an individual's own thoughts, feelings and reactions and those of the significant others with whom he or she comes into contact. Of course, this is not a one-way process. Just as the one is forming, modifying and adapting in response to the reactions and expectations of others, so, too, are the others being affected and making modifications in their turn throughout the interaction.

The 'meanings' people give to situations, and the 'interpretations' they make of social actions and events, are a crucial feature of this approach. An incident like a fight, for example, might be interpreted quite differently by different people. Some might see it as an act of aggression or deviance; others as an act of self-preservation or frustration. For some, it may seem the most logical and normal way to react to emotional disturbance; for others, it may be an indication of weakness or lack of self control. According to this perspective, there is no such thing as only one social reality. There are many realities and each is different, depending on the context in which it occurs and the past experiences and present identities of the different actors and observers involved.

Equally, people attribute different 'meanings' to what might seem to be the same experience. An enquiry into the circumstances of someone's personal life may 'mean' a gesture of friendship or a nosey intrusion. Some people may 'mean' a lot when they offer friendship; others may 'mean' very little.

The same words, looks and gestures exchanged between two people may mean totally different things to each of them. Consider the dynamics of a tortuous love affair, for example. In each case the actors' behaviour is affected by what they differently believe the words, looks and gestures to mean. In such circumstances, 'the truth of the matter', whatever it might be, is hardly relevant. The truth about whether love or a God exists, for example, is of little concern to sociologists. But the ways in which people's behaviour is affected by love or by the belief that a God exists is of considerable interest.

This insight has been developed by symbolic interactionists to discuss the significance of 'labelling' people. As soon as a teacher applies the label 'troublemaker' to a pupil, for example, after perhaps one or two pranks, it often encourages the pupil to 'live up to' the label and all that it implies. Equally, the teacher may come to expect 'nothing but trouble' from the pupil in the future. Whether or not the label was true or justified in the first place becomes forgotten as both the teacher and the pupil behave as if it were. The label becomes a symbol, which considerably influences each one's expectations of the other, and of the consequent behaviour that results from these expectations.

Erving Goffman

In his classic study of mental patients in *Asylums* (1968) Erving Goffman describes the ways in which people labelled as mentally ill become victims of the label in ways which define actions – like hoarding pieces of string and toilet paper and cigarettes – as symptomatic of disturbed behaviour, whereas in situations like mental hospitals, in which these commodities are in short supply and usually kept away from patients and under lock and key, the urge to acquire and hoard them becomes perfectly reasonable and understandable behaviour.

Labels can also be 'generalized' from the behaviour of one or two individuals to the behaviour of entire groups. For example, part of the process of stereotyping groups such as teenagers or feminists or vegetarians is to assume that they all display the same – usually negative – behaviour patterns.

Phenomenology and ethnomethodology

Phenomenology and ethnomethodology became popular in sociology in the 1970s but their origins go back to earlier times and other disciplines. The perspectives of phenomenology derive from the emphasis placed on 'interpretation' and 'understanding' by Weber and the phenomenological philosophy of Edmund Husserl. The two branches came together in the writing of Alfred Schutz, and the outcome, phenomenological sociology, has since been developed by both symbolic interactionists like Peter Berger and T. Luckmann and the more usual (in terms of conventional sociology) ethnomethodology of Harold Garfinkel.

The emphasis in phenomenology is on the intellectual and mental processes by which the individual comes to understand the world and what constitutes reality. According to phenomenology, things and events have no meaning 'in themselves'. They only 'mean' what human beings take them to mean. In society – in which individuals live together – there are developed 'shared meanings'.

The emphasis in ethnomethodology – which means 'people's methods' – is on the ways in which people actually develop these shared meanings – the methods which are used by all those who participate in social encounters to make sense of what is going on and to communicate this understanding to others.

The emphasis in both these approaches is on small-scale investigations, or micro sociology, and the subject matter is 'everyday life'.

One of the main criticisms of functionalism and social interactionism, as we have seen, is based on the unacknowledged assumptions which influence the sociologist's work. Whole areas, categories and attitudes are left unexamined, 'taken for granted' or distorted by reification.

The approach of phenomenology and ethnomethodology has been to try and supply these 'missing elements'. The starting point is to take nothing for granted, to question the commonplace and the ordinary, to treat even the most simple things as 'problematic'. For example, functionalist sociology has been able to relate educational success and failure to social origins and characteristics. Phenomenologists would be unhappy about taking for granted notions like 'success', 'failure' and 'social class' without recognizing that many people mean different things by these terms. 'Whose definitions of success and failure are being applied?' they would ask. 'Where did these definitions come from?' 'Does everyone accept them?' 'What do they mean?'

But phenomenology is not merely a close examination of meanings and commonplace assumptions; it is also concerned to discover how people arrive at these meanings and assumptions in the first place. How do people, as they go about their everyday life, come to construct the meanings, attitudes and responses to society which they then take so much for granted? And what is the significance of other people's perceptions in this process?

Phenomenological sociology has obviously presented a challenge to other forms of sociology because its inspiration has been based so much on the criticism of other approaches and it has forced a re-examination of many old ideas. In some cases it has led to exciting developments – in the sociology of knowledge, for example – and encouraged important breakthroughs in the investigation of individual and small group behaviour.

Taken to extremes, the denunciation of conventional sociology by ethnomethodologists like Garfinkel has been devastating. One of the main reactions of ethnomethodology has been against the mystification of expertise and the apparent insights of 'professional' sociologists. The emphasis in ethnomethodology is on the ways in which 'ordinary people' make sense of their everyday lives and are able to apply meanings and make interpretations which, it is claimed, are equivalent in significance to those made by sociologists.

They are often not in agreement with the definitions made by sociologists either – a factor which is significant enough to make Garfinkel question the credibility of 'so-called' experts. Ethnomethodologists claim that sociologists are merely using complicated language and an exaggerated view of their own professional knowledge to do much the same kind of thing as ordinary people do all the time – that is, make sense of the world around them. If this is true, sociology as such is pointless, and all can be explained by common sense.

Needless to say, not many sociologists would subscribe to this extreme view. The main criticism of ethnomethodology is that, in claiming that the understanding of society is a matter of common sense, and by assuming that all definitions are equally valid, no account is taken of the existence of power and inequality in society.

It is not simply that experts 'know better' than ordinary people, it is that some groups are given the status of experts, and the power and authority that go with it, while others are not. Why this is the case and how it has come to be are the important questions, and ethnomethodological approaches provide no way of answering them.

Neither do they provide a way of moving from an understanding of the particular and the specific towards an explanation of social organization and patterns of behaviour at a societal level. The fact that there are economic, political and social differences in society between different groups, which keep some powerful and some powerless, are not accounted for in the preoccupation with the particular.

Post-modernism

To understand anything of post-modernism it is also necessary to understand what was formerly meant by modernism.

Modernism

The ideas associated with the 'modern' period in history grew out of the decline of medieval society in Europe and the beginnings of the 'Enlightenment'. Modernity is said to have had three main characteristics:

- The development of capitalism as an economic system, together with its related forms of production, profit accumulation and waged labour.
- The consolidation of the centralized nation state as a political system, together with its related forms of centralized bureaucracy and administration and the development of democratic representation and participation.
- The intellectual challenge to traditional beliefs based on, for example, divine intervention, superstition, fate and nature, in favour of progress brought about by a growing emphasis on reason, enlightenment, rationality, scientific and technical knowledge.

The purpose of acquiring knowledge, according to modernist thinking, was to influence and improve the human condition in the pursuit of progress – the view that the world can be changed for the better by overturning tradition and by the application of reason and rationality to solve problems and ameliorate the human condition.

Sociology as a discipline was greatly involved with the development of modernism and of the belief that theories could be created which would help to apply reason and logic to the understanding of society in ways which could also be used to achieve progress – a project which, despite sociology's preoccupation with scientific neutrality, was about constructing theories which were not simply about how people live, but also about how people 'should' live. Marx's view, for example, was that the purpose of knowledge was not only to understand the world but also to help change it.

Language and social action

Language plays a vital role in both modernism and action theory, in that it provides one of the most sophisticated ways of expressing and defining social meanings and communicating them to others in the process of social interaction.

Language, and the ability to use it reflectively to make sense of social life, is, for action theorists, a distinguishing characteristic of human beings. It implies consciousness, the ability to interpret and attach meaning. It is the facility which ensures that human beings are not simply determined and conditioned by the social forces around them. Placed in the context of modernism, language implies the possibility of applying reason and logic to the creation and interpretation of social life, and can be a significant tool in the human struggle for progress and social change.

It is particularly challenging, then, to find the development of post-modernist theories – which have derived partly from the concerns of social action, from interpretation and understanding, from the significance of social meanings and the use of symbols, and from the variety and variability of what constitutes social reality – to find ideas which seem to use the tools of the social action approach to dismantle the very assumptions about human beings and social life to which the approach is committed.

Post-modernism and post-structuralism

Jean Francois Lyotard

In his book the *Post Modern Condition* (1984) **Jean Francois Lyotard** defined post-modernism as 'incredulity towards meta-narratives'. He argued that it was no longer possible to believe in the grand theories of society and the inevitability of progress brought about by the application of science, reason and logic. There were too many flaws in functionalism and Marxism, he claims, to accept their explanations of social processes and social change.

Post-modernism not only questions structural theories like Marxism, but also social action theories which attribute considerable credit to individual consciousness in the creation of social behaviour. Post-modernism asks why we should assume that the individual actor or subject is the source from which meaning is derived, or is the architect of a consciously created social reality.

Wittgenstein

According to the theories of language promoted by the philosopher **Ludwig Wittgenstein** language pre-dates those who use it. In other words, humans learn the words which then allow them to express what they mean to say. If there was no word to express a particular emotion or feeling, there would be no way of saying it. Even the words used by individuals to explain and describe themselves to others have first to be learned from elsewhere. Language is a system which pre-dates and exists separately from any of the individuals who learn it and then use it. When they do come to use it, they are obliged to adopt the meanings, symbols and significance already attached to the words they choose – in which case the role of individual thought and individual consciousness in the creation of meaning is minimal.

For theorists like Wittgenstein, language has the same kind of status as institutional structures have for systems and structural theorists like Marx. Just as institutional structures shape and determine and exercise control over social behaviour according to Marx, so, too, does the language which we habitually use to express our thinking and talking also exercise similar constraints. In other words, the ways in which we 'know' about the world and talk about it are decided for us by the languages which we learn from others who have come and gone before us.

Such views lead to two obvious questions:

Where does the language we use come from in the first place?
Do people who use different languages inhabit different worlds and realities?

Claude Levi-Strauss

According to Levi-Strauss:

Language is a pre-existing structure in society which determines and constrains social behaviour.

The underlying structure of all languages is the same.

Language originates in the unconscious human mind and, since all human minds work in the same way, the languages which emerge are organized according to the same principles.

Culture is also the creation of unconscious thought processes. While cultures may, like language, become manifest in different ways, the processes by which they are created are the same.

There is nothing in social life which is the deliberate and innovative creation of human beings in interaction with each other. Their life histories are written for them in the language and culture which they learn and then use.

This view is clearly very different from the views held by Weber, Goffman, Schutz and Garfinkel.

Michel Foucalt

Foucalt agrees with Levi-Strauss that individuals do not create their own life stories – but he disagrees with the notion that there are universal features underlying the formation of language and culture.

His main interest is in the power relationship involved in the creation and use of language.

By language he does not mean what we commonly refer to as English or French or Chinese, but how different kinds of knowledge are expressed in different ways of thinking and talking – something he calls **discourses**.

Discourses provide us with the ways of knowing about things. Because we have no alternative but to know about reality by means of various discourses, they exercise power over us.

Who we are, what we think and what we know are created by the discourses which are available to us to use. For this reason, the rational, thoughtful, creative actor or subject who is at the heart of social action theories does not exist. As individuals, we are the creation of the discourses which are available to us. They provide us with our thoughts and our knowledge, and which in turn inform any actions we might take.

The origins of different discourses are a matter for historians to uncover, according to Foucalt, and are also concerned with questions of power.

Power is exercised in two ways: firstly, it is exercised so that a discourse is enabled to come into being in the first place; and secondly, it is exercised by a discourse itself in its control over the ways of thinking, knowing and acting of those individuals who use it.

Foucalt's own studies of the origins of specific discourses have led him into accounts of the history of medicine, madness, sexuality, punishment and the body. Once discourses become established – for example, the medical discourse – their concepts and authority become pervasive, commonplace and taken for granted. Once established, the medical discourse which defines health and ill-health has become applied not just to bodies but to societies, desires, sexual orientations, appetites, pastimes, relationships, economies, marriages, families, etc.

For modernists, the purpose of knowledge is linked to social change and progress, freedom and liberation. For Foucalt, knowledge is used to oppress, control and coerce. Social change is not progress – merely the creation of different discourses which in turn oppress, control and coerce in different ways. They are neither better nor worse than what has gone before – they are merely different. Because we live in a world in which, for example, scientific discourse prevails, this does not mean that as a discourse it is any better or worse than previous definitions of truth.

This view is completely opposite to those views underlying modernism, in which it is assumed that the more we know the more chance we have of improving the world and furthering human progress and emancipation.

The views of post-modernists and post-structuralists like Foucalt are highly **relativist** – that is, they believe that there is no such thing as 'objective' truth, merely various and competing ways of looking at things, none of which is more important or more significant than another – merely different.

The commitment to relativism is reflected in the post-modernist belief that we should abandon attempts to produce objective truth and accept that all humanly constructed accounts of reality have equal validity. For this reason, no single theory should be given consideration at the expense of others, and there is limited value in considering that 'meta-narratives', or huge, historical, universal and comprehensive theories like, for example, functionalism and Marxism, have any useful role to play. We live in a post-modern world in which such grand theoretical ideas are obsolete.

Post-modern thinking has been applied to other areas of human production, creativity and activity, such as architecture, art, popular culture and literature, for example, in which the emphasis is also on relativism and pluralism (that is multiple and competing realities). The picture painted is one of a society in which the hallmarks are impermanence, instability and transience rather than the modernist search through reason and enlightenment for truth, progression and emancipation.

The post-modern world is one in which, it is argued, fashion, trend and image have come to matter more than substance and meaning. The media dominates all cultural forms and helps to define multiple realities and various identities using, for example, the discourses of advertising, popular music, and soap opera. Each is ephemeral, and of significance only until it is replaced by another.

Global change

Immanuel Wallerstein

Already the ideas of post-modernism and post-structuralism are themselves under attack from other sociologists, however. The concentration on style, relativism and fragmentation makes post-modernism seem defeatist and decadent.

Descriptions of the growth and development of capitalism into a world system which transcends individual nation states and continents in its exercise of influence and power is being used to counter post-modernist theories of fragmentation and diversity. **Immanuel Wallerstein** in his book *Unthinking Social Science: The Limits of Nineteenth Century Paradigms* (1991), argues that transnational capitalism now provides the forms in which sociology should attempt to make sense of what is happening in society. There are now very few, if any, significant areas of work, organization or culture that are outside the influence of the capitalist world system. Even the day-to-day activity that goes on in the privacy of individual workplaces, households and school classrooms, for example, is affected by global forces. It is increasingly difficult not to place studies of employment, for example, or gender oppression, or education and training, or the influence of mass communications, outside the context of global considerations.

In this respect sociology, on its own, may not be the best way of understanding the many ramifications of globalization. What is more appropriate, perhaps, is a multi-disciplinary approach to analysis and interpretation, which makes use of the interrelated insights of other disciplines within the social sciences.

All kinds of sociologists, whatever their different perspectives might be, agree on the need to base their interpretations of social behaviour on the systematic collection of evidence, though different perspectives have developed different preferred methods of collecting evidence, as you might expect.

The information necessary to be able to explain and understand social behaviour is perhaps more difficult to obtain than the data collected by physical scientists, in that human beings are the 'raw material' and not inanimate objects. They have dignity and rights and expectations about privacy which need to be respected. Public opinion would be loath to condone the kind of experiments on people which natural scientists are allowed to carry out on chemicals and even animal life. And, of course, the involvement of the human researcher in the investigation of human behaviour can cause problems of bias or distortion.

The best that can be expected is that researchers should be as 'scientific' and ethical as possible. They must consider as many aspects of the phenomenon they are studying as possible and, unless there are issues of confidentiality involved, make all the evidence collected, and methods used, available for scrutiny by others. They must be sensitive to their own assumptions and the effects they are likely to have on the questions which are asked and the kinds of conclusions which are arrived at.

The very activity of 'doing research' in the first place is likely to affect what is being studied. Social research, like all social relationships, is a two-way affair. It is a process of interaction between different people who may not share the same gender or ethnic background or possess the same amount of social power. The behaviour of each of them will be likely to affect the behaviour of the other. One of our students, a black woman doing research into Afro-Caribbean women's experiences of racism in Britain, found that being black herself did not automatically 'guarantee access'.

There were many factors to consider, such as class, what sort of background we all came from, which Caribbean island we had originally come from. When I started doing the research I felt that it would be pretty straightforward and that all the women I had arranged to interview would be willing, enthusiastic and almost desperate to tell their story. I was wrong, unfortunately. My first interviewee was very keen to be interviewed when I first approached her, but a few days later, the morning of the interview in fact, she suddenly changed her mind with no warning whatsoever. Her reasons, she says, were that her mind had suddenly 'gone blank'. Then she started saying she wasn't intelligent enough and that she could put me in touch with someone who was more intelligent than her. I explained that I wasn't testing her intelligence and that I only wanted to know about how white people treated her when she first came to Britain. But sadly she still declined. Some of the other women were a bit tense at first because they thought their voices would sound awful on tape. After a few minutes they relaxed and began speaking to me in their natural accents and using patois [a form of dialect used by people in the Caribbean]. One woman said, 'We will always support any student, but especially a black sister, who is trying to put black women in the picture'.

Put simply, a sociologist cannot expect to question a group of people without recognizing that their responses will be affected by how they perceive him or her. And if, as a group, the people happen to be women who have been physically or sexually abused or homosexuals or army officers or tax collectors, it would be unusual for the researcher not to have some pre-formed opinions about them as particular 'types' of people. So the business of collecting human evidence is fraught with difficulties. But these are all problems which the methods of investigation used by different sociologists try to take into account.

When sociologists set out to investigate some aspect of social behaviour, they obviously have available the kind of background information that is generally accessible to any commentator on social life – including official records, government statistics, previous reports, newspaper articles, etc. They may treat them with a fair degree of scepticism, but they provide a starting point. They will probably set the subject being studied into some kind of context, which might be historical or cultural or economic and they may make comparisons with other groups in other societies if this seems relevant. They will certainly be conscious of whether they are investigating something in an urban or rural setting and in an industrial or pre-industrial society and they will probably make some kind of assessment of the political, economic and social characteristics of the group which they are studying and take into account factors to do with social class, gender and ethnicity.

positivist, interpretive, ethonographic & feminist

After establishing the general background, the sociologist has to build up a more detailed picture using a variety of methods and approaches. In an effort to simplify these a little, we can divide the main approaches used into four main types: **positivist, interpretive, ethnographic** and **feminist**. To fix them in your mind right away, it might be helpful to note that positivist research is linked to systems or structural perspectives; interpretative research is usually associated with social action perspectives; ethnography, inspired by symbolic interactionism, has an eye to incorporating the best of all the rest into a fairly integrated approach to research methods; while feminism uses a variety of methods as appropriate, but has a clear commitment to certain feminist and ethical principles in carrying out and making sense of research findings and to identifying what are suitable subjects for feminist research in the first place.

Primary and secondary data

When sociologists begin their research they make a choice about the most appropriate research methods to collect the kinds of data they need. They may carry out their research using **secondary data** or information which is already in existence and which has been produced for other purposes, such as autobiographies and diaries, newspaper reports, studies carried out by other sociologists and government statistics. On the other hand, they may prefer to collect their own new information or **primary data** by using a variety of different methods.

Quantitative and qualitative methods

Quantitative research methods are used to produce numerical and statistical data. Great emphasis is placed on assembling information about how different social phenomena affect large numbers of people and on being objective. The most usual way of gathering quantitative information is by questionnaires and tightly structured interviews. Quantitative methods place less emphasis on individual or subjective experiences, and are favoured by those sociologists who are using systems or structural perspectives.

Quantitative data are most often associated with positivist research methods, and are seen to be more 'reliable'. Reliability in this context means a piece of research which can be repeated and which then produces the same result, i.e. to show that there is consistency in order to arrive at conclusions. In the natural sciences, for example, two gases mixed together may always produce the same result. It is debatable whether this consistency would apply in terms of human behaviour, however, because, unlike in laboratory experiments, sociologists are not able to control all the variables which affect human behaviour. However, quantitative methods are generally held to produce more reliable, and repeatable, results.

Qualitative research methods are used to produce data about personal experience and about the meanings behind social action. Emphasis is placed on individual experience and feelings rather than on how large-scale social structures affect people. What does it feel like, for example, to be a member of a juvenile gang, or a school drop-out, or an inmate of a prison or a mental hospital? The most usual way of gathering qualitative information is by observation and by unstructured interviews which use the interviewee's own words. These methods are most likely to be used by those sociologists using action, interactionist or feminist perspectives. Qualitative data are most often associated with interpretive research methods, and are generally considered to be more 'valid'. Validity in this context means research which gives a more truthful, in-depth picture of the phenomenon being studied. Qualitative data are often seen to be more valid than quantitative data but less reliable, i.e. less easily applied to anyone other than those individuals or specific phenomena being studied.

In practice, there is a continuum stretching between the most commonly used quantitative and qualitative methods, rather like that shown in Figure 10.1.

Figure 10.1 The continuum between the most commonly used quantitative and qualitative methods

Some methods are more useful in some situations than others, depending on what is being studied and what use is going to be made of the evidence collected. However, all the methods have advantages and disadvantages.

Positivist research

It is often the case that systems or structural theories like functionalism use a positivist methodology. The main characteristics of positivism, as we have seen, are that sociology is regarded as being equivalent to the natural sciences, and that social facts are capable of being measured objectively, in the same way as natural facts. The methods most frequently used, therefore, are surveys, questionnaires, structured interviews, attitude scales, controlled clinical experiments and statistical analysis.

Empiricism

The application of scientific methods to sociology, which is associated with positivism and which involves the development of scientific method, is known as empiricism. It is based on the scientific principles of observation, experimentation and reasoning, which in turn involves hypothesizing and theorizing. A **hypothesis** is quite simply a hunch or a supposition made by

hypothesis & theories

a researcher which is then put forward for testing, using a variety of different methods of investigation, in an attempt to prove or disprove the original supposition. **Theories** are sets of ideas which both inform our understanding and seek to explain the reasons for, and connections between, different social phenomena. Each new contribution to research plays its part in substantiating, modifying or revising established theories. Sociological theories derive initially from the attempt to understand and explain social phenomena. Structuralists tend to start with theories and then apply them to whatever it is that is being studied. Ethnographers and feminist sociologists tend to assume that the generation of theory comes from the close observation, interpretation and correlation of human experience. In the process, theories are built up which, in the case of feminist theories, for example, then become applied, tested, modified and developed in the process of doing ongoing and different pieces of research.

The nature of science and scientific method

Science means knowledge, but it tends to be associated with the natural sciences such as physics, chemistry and microbiology.

Scientific method represents the attempt to create knowledge in a **systematic** way, which is true in all circumstances, so that what scientists say can be trusted and because they can predict what, in any given circumstances, is likely to happen. In the intellectual period since the Enlightenment, and particularly during the nineteenth century, science became increasingly powerful in Western thought. It laid claims to being a superior form of knowledge, more so than common sense, religion or experience because it could produce evidence and was based on reason and rational thought. Science became associated with man's capacity to create culture and control nature while nature was considered essentially female and indicative of different, generally inferior, qualities. Science increasingly challenged religion, developing theories of evolution, and also applied science to changing systems of power and technology associated with the Industrial Revolution. As a consequence, radical changes took place in the economy, in family life and in communities.

As the backdrop against which sociology developed, it is not surprising that early sociologists turned to science and used it as a yardstick for their methodology. Comte, for example, attempted to produce scientific 'laws' to explain society, and Durkheim tended to treat social facts as if they were things.

Early sociologists like Comte and Durkheim were both functionalists and positivists. They believed that, although beliefs, customs and institutions could enter into human consciousness, they originated externally in society. Society was not simply the sum of many individual parts, but served to create human behaviour through externally derived laws of nature, norms and values. In setting out to study suicide, Durkheim began to correlate different variables in an attempt to show how suicide was caused. He claimed, for example, that suicide was related to the incidence of economic booms and slumps and to the experience of anomie or general normlessness said to occur during periods of rapid social change, in which the rules and norms governing social behaviour were disrupted, and during which time members of society were no longer so sure what the rules were.

Today there has been a shift away from the simple empirical ideas associated with the natural sciences towards methods which recognize that studying human beings is much more complicated than studying inanimate objects.

Interpretive research

Action-based perspectives in sociology, as we have seen, are sceptical about claiming any allegiance to the natural sciences and of seeing people as 'things' which can be studied like 'objects'. Individuals, it is argued, are conscious beings who are capable of thinking, interpreting and attaching meanings to everyday existence in a complex and varied way.

Some of these ideas can be seen in the influence of Weber and his concern about **verstehen** or the need to understand human consciousness rather than merely describe human behaviour.

Alvin Gouldner was greatly opposed to positivist assumptions applied to sociology. He argued that total objectivity was neither possible nor desirable.

Thomas Kuhn argued that all scientists worked within a particular framework or **paradigm** which channelled their thinking to such an extent that they could not see outside it. They were unlikely to notice other kinds of evidence because they were not looking for it.

The concern to understand human consciousness and the subjective meanings which individuals attach to behaviour affects the choice of methods which social action theorists choose to use most frequently. They are concerned to 'get into a relationship' with those they are studying – a relationship which is not 'cluttered' or 'distorted' by the paraphernalia of formal questionnaires and tightly structured interviews. The sociologist's aim is to be more informal, to meet people on their own territory rather than in a university or a special interview room, for example, to 'observe' things as they happen, and to allow enough time to enable confidence and trust to be built up between the researcher and those being researched. **Interviews** are most likely to be unstructured, open-ended discussions, in which the interviewees are encouraged to expand at length, and in their own words, about their experiences. A tape recorder is often used so that the sociologist has an accurate record of what is said without having to remember or note down specific responses.

Meanwhile, the sociologist's interpretation of what is happening has to pass through three stages. The first stage is to try to identify the subjective meanings which influence the behaviour of those who are being studied, and, with empathy, try to 'see things from their point of view'. The second stage is to observe, analyse and interpret what is said and done, in an attempt to find the reasons for, and the causes of, their behaviour. The third stage is to recognize that the sociologist's participation in the discussion, and observation of the action, in some senses changes it, as he or she is in turn changed by it. So there can be no question of 'objectivity' in the positivist sense. To be 'valid', therefore, and credible, it is necessary to ensure that the research stages are rigorous, logical and consistent. If the procedures are seen to be sound and the deductions convincing, the results will speak for themselves.

Ethnographic research

Ethnography means 'a picture' of the way of life of a social group interacting together, and comes originally from anthropology. A group's 'total way of life' or culture is considered to be 'ongoing' and 'ever changing', and the methods of ethnography aim to capture this as full as possible, in all its various shades and nuances, in as much detail as possible and with full recognition of the 'many levels' at which relationships take place. The ethnographer tries to begin with no preconceived ideas about people's roles or positions or what he or she expects to be happening, but waits for these to be revealed over time.

The main method of ethnography is **participant observation,** which clearly puts the researcher right into the middle of the action. The starting point for the study of a particular family group, for example, would not be to assume that two happily married adults were looking after and bringing up a number of dependent children in a more or less successful kind of way. The researcher would begin by asking rather different questions, like: 'What's going on here? or 'What are these people doing to each other' and would try to build up a picture of the family group by building in what each of them says about it. Obviously there are problems here: the individuals' accounts may differ; they may not know why they do things; they may not be able to put into words what they feel without being misleading. Furthermore, one or other of them may be influenced by what they think they 'should' say, or by what they think, rightly or wrongly, the researcher 'wants to hear'.

How is the sociologist to make sense of all this? Ethnographers take the view that the sociologist gains insight, which an outsider or a positivist would not, from participation – not merely 'sitting in on' an unstructured group discussion, but actually 'taking on a role' within the group or the institution and making some contribution to its day-to-day functioning. Some sociologists have actually joined street corner gangs, spent time in prison, become factory workers or taught in classrooms. As a member of the group, with a role to play, they can actually begin to analyse their own behaviour and feelings and their interaction with others.

Here again, the problems are obvious. If you join a gang, for example, do you reveal to the members that you are a sociologist? And what if you develop loyalties to the gang which prevent you from being detached enough to see clearly what is happening? You may find yourself defending their behaviour rather than studying it. Being a teacher may present fewer problems, except that to gain the confidence of colleagues in order to get their views may prevent the researcher from getting close enough to the pupils to be trusted by them and vice versa.

In the last resort, a great deal will depend on whether or not members of the group believe in the researcher. If the researcher's behaviour is in any way suspect, he or she will have difficulty in continuing with the research and access to information will be blocked. Often the most revealing information is not disclosed because the researcher feels it would be a betrayal of the trust that has been built up.

Ethnographers claim that a 'deep involvement in the action' over a considerable period of time is the best way of building up a picture of the social behaviour of a given group. But it is obviously not the only way. Social relationships exist on a variety of levels and are influenced by a number of interconnected factors. It makes sense, therefore, to 'cross-check', to get as many different accounts of the same experience as possible, and to recognize that in any situation there will not only be one, but many, realities.

Part of the 'picture' will include more structured interviews; a review of 'official' sources of information; a detailed analysis of the legal, economic, cultural or historic factors involved; or a reference to what has been learned from similar studies elsewhere. To understand fully the behaviour of the family group mentioned earlier, it may also mean an analysis of their economic circumstances, an account of the jobs they do, their educational experience, the social characteristics of the environment they live in and the links between all of these and the wider society. Issues to do with social class membership, gender and ethnic origin will be crucial, as will assumptions held by both the family members and the sociologist about the nature of family life. In all these respects the ethnographer has much to learn from other sociological methods, but whereas systems people or tructuralists may take a macro view of society as their starting point and formulate hypotheses about the family's behaviour from an analysis of wider structural arrangements, the ethnographer is much more likely to let these links be revealed in the process of working closely with the group involved over a period of time.

Some sociologists feel that ethnographic case studies are merely 'high-class reporting', and are at best only a very detailed 'description of behaviour without providing a scientific analysis of the 'causes' of behaviour. This is largely because the ethnographer often does not begin in the usual empirical way of starting with accepted theories, formulating hypotheses and working out categories in advance. Ethnographers argue that the danger of this is to predetermine the outcome before you start and risk the possibility of missing potentially crucial factors and subjective meanings, which are not available to the outside observer, until they become revealed in the process of interaction. Being too hidebound by established theories and well-tried methods may actually prevent the generation of new insight, new methods and new theories. In other words, sociologists should 'make sense of what's going on as they go along' and utilize methods to 'discover' theoretical perspectives from the situation itself.

Of course, a lot depends on what is being studied. It may be that the sociologist who is preoccupied with the 'elusive nuances of small-scale interaction between individuals in groups' is blind to the structural constraints of the wider society. Social action does not take place in a vacuum. Alternatively, the sociologist concerned to 'relate economic forces to the distribution of power and control in society' may ignore the effects on small groups, as people experience, and reproduce, the constraints and consequences at a personal level.

Feminist research

Feminist research is principally concerned with researching those experiences, relationships and social institutions which are of direct relevance to women – partly because mainstream sociology over the years has been male-dominated and has concerned itself principally with studying society from a male point of view, or relying on sexist assumptions about women; and partly because of a political commitment to the emancipation of women. What makes feminist research 'feminist' is not simply that it is about women, but that it is about producing evidence and developing theories which reveal the basis of women's inequality and assist in the process of women's emancipation.

There are a number of basic assumptions and principles underpinning feminist research. These are:

- the importance of women's personal and first-hand experience
- a recognition that women's experience is varied and diverse and is in turn affected by class membership, ethnicity, sexuality, age, culture, etc.
- gender is central in understanding how women experience society
- research is a consciousness-raising activity – it is not simply about describing the world; it is about wanting to change it
- there is a rejection of hierarchies between the researcher and the researched, and a conscious attempt to create equality – this influences the research methods chosen and what use is made of the research afterwards

- feminists favour forms of collaborative scholarship rather than the individual and competitive accumulation of knowledge designed to enhance personal reputation and career. There is likely to be greater equality between researchers and research assistants, for example, and the recognition that those who are 'being researched' also have great knowledge and insight to impart, rather than being viewed as the mere 'objects' or 'subjects' of research
- feminist research is not regarded as simply an 'academic exercise' – it is an active engagement with forms of women's oppression. Its aim is to assist in social change which reduces and overcomes women's oppression.

Margaret Eichler

According to **Margaret Eichler** (*Non-Sexist Research Methods*, 1988), there are seven main ways in which mainstream research is sexist and which feminist researchers need to overcome.

Androcentricity

Androcentricity means 'viewing the world from a male perspective'. This occurs when the group studied is assumed to be, or defined as though it consists, only of males – usually white males (e.g. much of the sociology of work, crime and deviance and social class). Women are either invisible (e.g. all the classic definitions of social class), or assumed to be passive objects (the women behind the men who make the decisions and who affect what happens in the world), or have their contribution to social action and the social meanings of their behaviour misunderstood (e.g. housewives aren't workers, motherhood is instinctive).

Over-generalization/ over-specificity

This happens when studies are dealing with only one sex but present themselves as if they apply equally to both. Over-generalization can occur when studies refer to 'parents' when in fact they mean women. Over-specificity occurs when single-sex terms (e.g. 'he', 'mankind', 'man in society', etc.) or single-sex concepts (e.g. doctor, shop steward, industrial worker, the unemployed, etc.) are used although members of both sexes are involved. Many of the problems involving sexist language belong in this category.

Gender insensitivity

This happens when sex and gender are ignored as important social variables – for example, when it is impossible to tell whether male or female subjects are included in a study because the information is missing. The same problem occurs in relation to ethnicity – for example, traditional studies about the relationship between social class and educational achievement spoke simply of working-class and middle-class children. Clearly, the gender and ethnic background of the children involved would have been crucial variables. In addition, in some studies of poverty, for example, families are treated as if they are a single unit. It has taken feminist sociologists to point out that men and women experience poverty differently within the same family or household, and that members of ethnic minorities also experience poverty in different ways from white Britons.

Double standards

A double standard occurs when different measures are used to identify identical behaviour – for example, women who commit crimes, including domestic crimes, are viewed differently from men who commit crimes; women who leave their children are viewed differently from men who leave their children. In terms of sexuality the notions of virility and promiscuity are highly gender-specific.

Sex appropriateness

This involves the uncritical discussion of such concepts as 'appropriate gender roles' or 'appropriate gender identity', and is especially common in studies of childhood socialization, work and the sexual division of labour.

Familism

This involves using the family as the smallest unit of analysis without differentiating between the experiences of different members, e.g. in many areas of social policy. In fact, family membership is a very different experience for men and women, and is also dependent on factors to do with culture, ethnicity, social class, age, etc.

Sexual dichotomy

This involves treating different genders as discrete social categories without acknowledging overlapping characteristics (e.g. school 'failures', people suffering from mental illness, etc.). Sometimes single-sex studies are presented as an answer to gender insensitivity, but they can perpetuate many of the same problems.

Research methods in practice

Sampling

Sampling is used in many social surveys because:

- it is not practicable to study the whole population;
- it is possible to draw reliable conclusions from the study of a smaller group if it is selected with care.

The principles of sampling

The aim is to select a sample that accurately represents the characteristics of the population being studied. For example, if the voting behaviour of the UK electorate is being studied, a sample of 1200 to 1500 can accurately represent the entire electorate if every care is taken to ensure that it is representative.

Representativeness is affected by:

- *size* – if the sample is too small it cannot represent all the necessary characteristics of the population in the correct amounts (e.g. social classes, regions, sex, ethnic groups, age groups, etc.). However, a large sample does not necessarily ensure complete representativeness;
- *selection* – this is the most important factor in ensuring representativeness.

The first step in any survey is to identify the sample to be surveyed. This may be the whole population or it may be a subsection (e.g. young people aged 15–19, married women with children under 5, etc.). For the purposes of the research this is known as the **population**.

The next step is to obtain an accurate **sampling frame**. This is the list from which the sample is to be drawn. It may be a register of electors or a telephone directory or patients on a doctor's list, etc.

There are six main methods of selecting an accurate sample from the sampling frame.

Random sampling

This is where every name has an equal chance of being selected, (e.g. every twelfth name on the electoral register). Problems arise, however, if significant numbers of respondents are unavailable for questioning and the sample becomes biased. It may also provide samples that are too large for most research projects.

Stratified random sampling

This is where the sample is divided into strata or groups (e.g. age, sex, ethnic group, area, etc.), and individuals are selected randomly within these groups. This method ensures that all groups which may have clear and distinct views on an issue are sampled and that their views are recorded.

Cluster sampling

This means concentrating the interviewing in certain areas because it is typical of a certain category rather than the entire population. This can provide a detailed picture of a particular segment of the population, for example, those living in a particular town or suburb. The disadvantage is that it may not be possible to generalize from the findings to the population as a whole.

Quota sampling

This is the main method used by commercial surveys, for example, market research. To make maximum use of limited time and resources, the interviewers are employed with instructions to select respondents according to pre determined criteria, such as age, sex, income group, etc. This can mean that there is bias because interviewers may select people who seem more pleasant or approachable or available at the specified time (e.g. in a shopping centre in the afternoon).

Panel studies

Here the same carefully selected sample is surveyed repeatedly over a period of time to determine changes in their views (e.g. the British Election Survey tracks changes in voting preferences as an election approaches). Sometimes **longitudinal** studies, which are long-term studies of the same sample over several years, are used to track, for example, the effects of educational achievement on employment prospects or divorce on children's social and educational development.

Snowball sampling

This is a means of contacting members of a particular group, for example, drug users. It is not a random method and is not necessarily representative. One respondent puts the researcher in contact with others in the same group. This method is most often used when the sample size is small, and for more 'in-depth' kinds of research.

The way respondents are selected will depend on the type of research being carried out. Those who follow more 'scientific' procedures will be more concerned to be able to generalize on the basis of their results and are more likely to emphasize the representativeness of their respondents. Sociologists who believe that it is more important to get in-depth information about how people react and respond will be less concerned about representativeness – for example, some may study a single case or small group such as a school class or a football team.

Pilot study

Having chosen a research method and selected a sample, some sociologists begin by 'trying out' their research questions and their chosen methods on a small preliminary group. This helps to test the research design and enables the researcher to make any adjustments or alterations before embarking on the full-scale project. A pilot study is simply a small preliminary study, carried out to refine the research design and approach before the real study is begun. It is not particularly appropriate if the main research method to be used is a case study, but it can be very helpful in the use of lengthy questionnaires or structured interviews in order to make sure that the questions asked are not ambiguous and will elicit the kinds of information required.

Case studies

Case studies as a research method make no claim to be representative. A case study involves the production of a detailed examination of a particular individual or a single example of something. It could be the study of an institution, such as a specific school like Hightown Grammar. It could be a particular social group or community. It could be a specific event. They are useful as detailed and specific examples of more general social institutions, phenomena or groups. A case study of one teenage gang, for example, may throw light upon the behaviour of teenagers in gangs generally, but it is impossible to determine how far the findings derived from one case study can be applied to other examples. At best they can provide useful hypotheses which can then be tested out in other situations. They are also useful ways of providing 'in-depth' information favoured by those sociologists who are interested in the specific and the particular rather than the broad ranging and the general.

Surveys, questionnaires and structured interviews

Surveys and questionnaires are the methods most often associated with sociology. They provide the possibility for large numbers of people to be questioned, either in person, according to a previously determined schedule of questions, or by leaving a questionnaire to be filled in by a respondent, returned by post, or collected later by the researcher. The responses are then analysed and turned into statistics with the help of a computer. Sometimes this approach is used with relatively small samples of people, to compare their experiences of education, for example, or their views on abortion, and may be followed up by personal interviews. However, it is a technique which best lends itself to large-scale investigations in which the researcher wants to contact as many people as possible.

Obviously the ways in which the questionnaires are compiled and the surveys conducted are central to the credibility and the success of this method. Postal questionnaires are relatively cheap, but there is a risk of respondents neglecting or forgetting to return them. A personal collection of the forms, and even the presence of the researcher while the questionnaire is being filled in, is often more efficient, but it is also more time-consuming, costly and perhaps more intimidating for the respondent, since he or she may well choose to put down what he or she thinks the researcher wants to know, or will approve of, rather than what he or she really believes.

Interviewing respondents personally is thought to be a more reliable way of getting questionnaires completed and making sure that the respondent knows what he or she is expected to do. Interviewers are trained by sociologists to be as neutral and objective as possible, but, as symbolic interactionists are swift to point out, this is a virtually impossible ideal. Factors to do with social class, gender, ethnicity and age may all play a part in influencing the exchange between the interviewer and the interviewee in ways which are always complicated and not always well understood by the respective participants.

The questions themselves have to be simple enough to be understood by the respondents; they have to be phrased in as unambiguous a way as possible; and they have to be capable of being analysed and turned into statistical presentations. A question which is badly worded, like: 'Do you read books very often?' may produce the response 'Yes' or 'No', but gives no indication of what the respondent means by 'often'. It may also disguise the fact that individuals may mean different things by 'books'. Some may mean hardback or paperback novels; others magazines.

Questions which are so simple and unambiguous that there can be no mistake about them are usually only capable of providing the most simple and obvious information. If sociologists want to find out about feelings, opinions or patterns of behaviour, they must frame their questions in a more open-ended way and encourage their respondents to reply at length. But again, if the sociologist wants to put people at their ease and get them talking naturally about what they really believe, it is unlikely that an interviewer with a clip-board and a set of inflexible questions or a bureaucratic-looking form will remove the barriers between them.

Clearly, these methods do have a number of advantages, especially if sociologists want to contact a lot of people, but they also present many problems. And, of course, the main criticisms made by interactionists and feminists is that they can distort information through unconscious racist and sexist bias, and do not represent the best ways of understanding the idiosyncrasies and complexities of human behaviour.

Attitude scales and clinical tests

If surveys, questionnaires and structured interviews are regarded sceptically by many people, attitude scales, clinical experiments and statistical analysis present even more problems. Again, the aim is to be as scientific as possible and to apply the best tried methods of natural science to social science. All are ways of 'measuring' human behaviour in an effort to relate 'individual' reactions to 'general' categories.

A sociologist investigating racial prejudice, for example, might present a subject with a list of statements about ethnic minority groups with which to agree or disagree. He or she might then give the replies a rating on a scale which ranged from 'extremely prejudiced' to 'totally unprejudiced'. Another sociologist may set up an experiment, under controlled laboratory conditions, to test levels of sexual aggression displayed by men towards women – an experiment which might involve the portrayal of pornography and the monitoring of men's responses to the images viewed. Both of these methods owe much to the influence of clinical psychology, and would only be used by sociologists who have a commitment to socio-psychological explanations of human behaviour.

The problems involved in the two methods are probably clear to you. Definitions of what constitutes prejudice and sexual aggression vary. Members of different ethnic groups experience different degrees of prejudice and racism, as do men and women from minority groups. Explanations of male violence are complicated by controversies concerning the nature of male and female sexuality, both of which are further complicated by pervasive assumptions about the normalcy of heterosexuality and the primacy of intercourse as the dominant form of sexual expression. Controversy also rages about what constitutes pornography, let alone the nature and extent of its damaging effects. All of these concepts and terms may mean different things to different people – they are not terms which can be 'taken for granted' as 'commonly agreed upon' categories. So whose definitions are being used in experiments like these is a fairly critical question.

Also, who is being questioned? The selection of the sample to be tested would need to take into account questions of social class, gender, age and politics, at least, in studies of racism and personal prejudice. Levels of male sexual aggression towards women and men's use of pornography may also vary between different social and cultural groups or it may not. Certainly sociologists would be likely to regard the social composition of the sample as significant. What if all the respondents were convicted rapists, for example, or homosexuals? In neither case could we assume that they would be any more or any less aggressive towards women than men generally, but their social characteristics as a group would need to be taken into account.

There are also questions to be asked about who is carrying out the tests and experiments. Are we to assume that the men are any less prejudiced or woman-hating than the subjects of their experiments? How might the results of the tests be affected if members of ethnic minority groups acted as the testers? Or if women were the ones who measured the levels of male sexual aggression said to be revealed by their response to viewing pornography? In both cases, the interaction between the researchers and the researched would be a variable which would be hard to control in laboratory conditions. The non-presence of the researcher in the room would also create a somewhat artificial situation in which different kinds of human interaction were being measured in conditions in which no human interaction was taking place.

There are so many different social, emotional, personal, historical, economic, gendered and cultural factors influencing people's prejudices and sexual behaviour that they cannot easily be measured in clinical or laboratory conditions which are shut off from the rest of social interaction. The success of scientifically controlled and laboratory experiments usually relies upon the exclusion of confusing external variables, but in social science it is likely that these confusing extraneous influences are the very ones which provide important insights into the phenomena being studied.

Statistics

Statistical analysis always gets a bad press. The notion that you can 'make statistics prove anything you like' dies hard. But ironically, a great deal of emphasis is placed on official statistics when recommendations are being made and new policies introduced. You are more likely to be allowed to introduce changes in legislation if you can show that large numbers of people are affected by the issue than if you provide a handful of detailed but personal in-depth accounts.

Official statistics drawn up by government departments, trade unions, the Census Office and other organizations are obviously a useful source of information for sociologists, but they need to be used carefully. One problem is that official categories are not always the ones sociologists would use. Sociologists are interested in the **social** causes of crime or suicide, for example, but these are not the sort of things which are recorded in police records or on death certificates.

Equally, some kinds of statistical information which would be useful are simply not recorded. It is generally accepted that 'official figures' concerning domestic violence and child sexual abuse represent simply the 'tip of the iceberg' so far as the real extent of these problems is concerned. But the majority of domestic crimes committed within the privacy of families and households are never reported to the police for reasons of fear, shame, powerlessness and low expectations about the ability or the commitment of the police to respond. If the crimes are not reported, they cannot be counted.

A third difficulty is that statistics are not always available in a way that is useful to sociologists. Figures may be presented separately from each other. For example, the statistics regarding people owning the largest amounts of wealth in Britain are notoriously unreliable, neither are they correlated, for example, to people in different kinds of occupations. It might be that the relationship between these two circumstances would be of interest to sociologists, but the link is not made in the original collection of statistics.

Frequently statistics are 'doctored' or 'massaged' in ways which are decidedly 'economical' with the truth. In a recent *Times Educational Supplement* article entitled 'Lecturers Go for Contracts' (TES, June 1994) about the imposition of new contracts on staff in further education, Ian Nash claimed: 'The majority of lecturers have now signed new contracts in at least one-quarter of all colleges'. The issue was quite a contentious one at the time, involving a serious deterioration in the terms and conditions of employment of college lecturers and provoking industrial action by their union on a national scale. A completely different emphasis would have been given about the current state of play if the article had been titled 'Lecturers Reject Contracts' and Ian Nash had reported that 'the majority of college lecturers have **not** signed contracts in three-quarters of all colleges'.

Another example of the 'creative' use of statistics occurs in terms of unemployment figures. The methods used to count the numbers of people unemployed in Britain have been changed so often during the years of successive Conservative Governments beginning in 1979 that members of the public have become quite cynical about the Government's honesty or concern to address the issues posed by unemployment. What is certain is that official figures seriously underestimate the real extent of the problem. By taking so many categories of people off the unemployment register (for spurious reasons of compulsory education and training courses or ineligibility) and therefore out of the statistics, it helps to present the problem of unemployment as being far less serious in numerical terms than it really is.

In providing their own statistics from the findings of surveys and questionnaires, sociologists are often on surer ground because they can cross-reference and interrelate different categories to fit in with what they are trying to find out or prove. But sociologically-derived statistics can still obscure sexist and racist biases and, so long as popular cynicism about the authenticity of statistics continues, sociologists will have to ensure that their sources and procedures are as sound as possible.

Informal or unstructured interviews

Informal interviews provide a way of doing small-scale research on sensitive or contentious issues, using a method which enables people to speak for themselves at length, in their own words.

To use such a method it is necessary to prepare a framework of key questions.

The questions need to be open-ended and enabling, not vague but simple. The method depends upon the interviewer putting the respondent at ease and establishing a good rapport.

Respondents may need prompting with supplementary questions, but in a good interview the interviewer says very little, giving maximum air space to the respondent.

The interview needs to be recorded.

The recordings need to be listened to several times, with useful quotes and extracts transcribed.

Advantages

● Often a good rapport develops between the interviewer and the interviewee, enabling detailed, honest information to be obtained. This is particularly important when the subject matter of the research might be regarded as personal or sensitive.
● It provides an opportunity for people to speak for themselves and gets closer to individual and subjective experience.
● The data are not pre-defined by the questions set. The interviewer can follow up leads and gain detailed information.
● The meanings behind actions can be explored, rather than just discovering the facts.
● When a tape recorder is used, the information is complete and not reliant on memory, which is inaccurate, or rapid note-taking, which is offputting to the respondent. It can then be referred back to during analysis.

Disadvantages

● The 'success' of the interview often rests on the skill of the interviewer.
● There are three potential problems caused by interviewer bias:
  – the interviewer may be consciously biased, giving non-verbal cues (e.g. frowning) which could in turn influence an interviewee's response;
  – the interviewer may only follow up leads which he or she considers to be important – which may not coincide with what the interviewee thinks is important;
  – the interviewer may not be able to resist 'getting into a discussion' in which he or she insists on putting a point of view at length and takes up all the air space!
● It is time-consuming.
● Samples tend to be small, making generalizations or the production of statistics difficult.
● The fact that an interviewer is asking questions about something sometimes changes the situation for the people concerned. They may:
  – have issues raised about their behaviour which they hadn't thought about before. For example, Liz Kelly, in her extensive research into domestic violence and child sexual abuse, established parallel support groups for survivors participating in her research;
  – change their behaviour – which raises ethical questions about the relationship between the researcher and the researched (e.g. questions to women about inequalities in domestic labour);
  – if a relationship of trust and equality is established, the interviewee may 'ask questions back'. If the interviewer answers these questions, this may also change people's behaviour. Maybe this doesn't matter. But maybe it does. In either case it raises questions about the relationship between research and political change.

Participant observation

Participant observation enables the researcher to observe social behaviour in its natural setting (for example, observing the social dynamics at play during a trade union meeting, or the teaching–learning interaction that goes on in a classroom). Sometimes the researchers not only observe but participate in the social interaction (for example, Sallie Westwood spent a year working in a hosiery factory in Leicester researching the culture of the shopfloor (*All Day Every Day*). Others using this method have spent time in schools with teenage pupils (Paul Willis (*Learning to Labour*)) or joined street corner gangs.

To do this, observers need to have a clear idea before they begin the observation as to what kind of things they are looking for – but not so clear that they then ignore or miss other important bits of social interaction which they hadn't bargained for.

They need to devise an efficient way of recording their observations which is not obtrusive and not likely to alter the group dynamic being studied. For example, Sallie Westwood spent each night after work in the factory writing up a lengthy diary containing information and observations noted during the day. She also followed this up with a series of unstructured interviews of her fellow workers and management. Dale Spender, in her extensive research into the part played by gender and sexism in classroom dynamics, used a tape recorder to tape lessons from which she could deduce how much time was spent on responding to boys' needs and questions, etc. compared with girls. Pat Mahony (*Schools for the Boys*) used photographs to show the ways in which boys monopolized space in corridors and playgrounds. An observation concerning a study of sexual harassment at work would not only need to record what people say and do in some way but it would also be relevant to notice and record what kind of pictures and calendars were on display.

Advantages

- Social behaviour is viewed in its natural setting.
- It offers the opportunity for small-scale detailed research.
- It gives validity to the meanings which people attach to their actions.
- It constructs the world according to the actors' values and norms.
- It may be used before carrying out a survey or interview in order to discover what questions it would be relevant to ask.

Disadvantages

- The researcher may become too involved and therefore be a poor observer (e.g. on a hospital ward in which people are chronically sick).
- Recording information accurately without bias is always difficult. Tape recorders and camcorders can be obtrusive. Often too much relies on memory.
- As a method, is it morally/ethically acceptable? Do people know they're being observed for a particular purpose? Does it matter? If they do know, might it affect their behaviour?
- It might be physically dangerous for the observer (e.g. a National Front meeting or a street gang).
- It might take a long time to get in, stay in and get out of the action.
- The researcher's own values will affect what is seen and how it is interpreted. Does this matter?
- The observer's presence may change or influence the behaviour of the group.

Researching the mass media	There are three main types of media research: 1 Content analysis 2 Semiotic analysis 3 Audience research.
Content analysis	The analysis of media contents can be expressed in statistical or numerical form. It is really a counting exercise – asking questions such as: 'How often do murders take place on TV programmes?' or 'How often do news stories feature women in positions of authority compared to men?' The number of appearances in a pre-selected sample of TV programmes or newspapers can then be counted. Content analysis works best when dealing with broad generalizations, and is probably the most popular way of studying the media. The most famous example is the work carried out by the Glasgow University Media Group (*Bad News, More Bad News, Really Bad News and Peace News*) examining British TV news programmes. A sample of news programmes was studied for each piece of research. Particular kinds of items were carefully timed and counted (e.g. industrial and economic news items). The method of presentation was noted and whether film was used, also the point at which the item was placed in the programme and who presented it, etc. This type of research method studies the media message, not its effect, but tends to assume that if the media item is biased in some way it will ultimately affect the viewer or reader. If you wanted to assess the effect of the mass media, an alternative method of research would have to be used. The main difficulty involved in content analysis is how to categorize and record items. For example, if you wished to study how ethnic minorities are portrayed on TV you would need:

- to have a list of possible kinds of portrayal, e.g. shopkeepers, petty criminals, musicians etc.;
- to know whether they are portrayed as major or minor characters;
- to know whether they are portrayed in a positive or negative manner (you would have to decide what constitutes negative or positive portrayal).

Useful categories may be developed by carrying out a pilot study. You would also need:

- a clear data collection sheet to log information;
- a way of recording an item's length, placement, running order, category and presentation.

Difficulties can arise when items fit into more than one category or do not fit directly into any category.

Other examples of studies using content analysis	D. M. Meehan (*Ladies of the Evening*) analysed 33 American dramas from 1950–1980 using videotaped archives. He analysed them in depth, finding that women were portrayed in ten principal ways (e.g. the good wife, the bitch, the victim, etc.). He concluded that the portrayal of women was generally sexist! Marjorie Ferguson (*Forever Feminine: Women's Magazines and the Cult of Femininity*) studied a sample of *Woman's Own* and *Woman's Weekly* magazines 1949–74 and 1979–80. She isolated various dominant themes (e.g.

getting your man, happy families, etc.). She concluded that women's magazines present a cult of femininity.

Evaluation of content analysis

- It tends to be artificial – as viewers we don't normally scan large tracts of the media for particular categories of items. There is therefore a danger of considering items out of context.
- Its strength lies in its ability to take an overall view in which things may be revealed which might otherwise escape notice (e.g. bigoted attitudes expressed about gays).
- Some aspects of the mass media lend themselves to counting more than others.
- Items which appear most frequently are not necessarily the most important.
- It can provide a useful starting point for more detailed and delicate analysis of media messages.

Semiotic analysis

Semiotic analysis is a way of analysing in depth the **meanings** that lie within a particular 'text', i.e. programme or article. It is an approach which has developed from **semiology**, which means 'a science that studies signs within society'.

Semiotic analysis starts from the assumption that direct behaviour between human beings is impossible because we communicate our feelings and attitudes in codes which we give away in gestures, body language, facial expressions, etc. In normal communication we use these codes without thinking so that they become automatic and we are unaware that we are using them. When semiologists study these codes, they begin to question what is 'natural' or 'common sense'.

For example:

In English the use of the pronouns 'him' or 'he' can also be taken to mean 'her' or 'she'. 'Mankind' is meant to include women. Dale Spender (*Man Made Language*) undertook a detailed analysis of language, revealing that it is not neutral or natural but deeply sexist.

Dress can be studied as a code. Bikers, gays or members of different youth cults, for example, use dress to make statements about themselves. There are different dress codes for men and women, and mixing them can mean different things in different contexts, cultures and historical periods. Perhaps you can think of some examples?

Semiotic analysis has been used to study soap operas and magazine advertisements, where the placing, colour, camera shots and music are all analysed as codes conveying and signifying certain messages. Studies have been made of magazines aimed at teenage girls and analysed for the messages contained within them. Can you think what these might be?

Research of this kind can be very complicated, and requires considerable understanding of the topic under investigation. It can generate information about what messages are signified by particular signs, such as images and language, but audience research is needed to cross-check whether such images are really interpreted in the way suggested.

Audience research

The British Audience Research Board uses three types of measures:

- meters attached to TV sets which monitor which programmes are watched and for how long;
- diaries kept by a sample of viewers to record the programmes which have been viewed;
- interviews with a representative sample of viewers.

Questionnaires or interviews can be used to discover the ways in which mass media are used and how messages are interpreted, and to get people's responses to particular programmes, adverts, magazines or newspapers.

Discussion groups can also be used as a research method – for example, in cases where certain media items are shown and a response is elicited through discussion. Taylor and Mullan used discussion groups of nine or ten people using a variety of open-ended questions like: 'Is there any resemblance between your family and the Ewing family in Dallas?'

A second type of audience research uses **controlled experiments**. In controlled experiments researchers try to control as many variables as possible and then alter one variable to assess cause and effect. A key question about the mass media often approached in this way is whether violence on TV causes people, especially children, to become violent. But this is a very difficult question to study. Some researchers have tried using two groups, subjecting one to a piece of violence on television and the other to something more neutral. They have then attempted to measure the responses of each group. What kinds of responses do you think could be measured in this way? What are the problems involved with this kind of research?

What kinds of problems face sociologists in attempting to produce a science of society?

Positivists claim that it is possible and desirable to apply the methods of natural science to the study of society, e.g. Durkheim, Marx).

This view is criticized because it is argued that sociology cannot make use of the main scientific technique, (i.e. experiments) because the 'objects' of research are human beings and because there are practical and moral objections.

Positivists respond by arguing that the comparative method and the social survey offer 'scientific' alternatives from which reliable generalizations can be made and which can be repeated and reproduced in similar conditions.

Anti-positivists argue that these methods do not reveal the real meanings, reasons, and motivation which lie behind people's behaviour. Even official statistics are not accurate because they are socially constructed.

Sociology is criticized because, unlike science, it cannot produce 'laws'. But Karl Popper claims that there are no universal scientific laws anyway because it is never possible to prove that something is completely true. Scientists should be attempting to disprove or refute their hypotheses rather than produce laws.

Thomas Kuhn claims that every science operates within a g~ framework or paradigm. So long as scientists collect data wit⊦· paradigm, they may not see other 'evidence' which fall⸠ Sociology does not have a generally agreed paradigm but rath⸜

of perspectives which provide alternative interpretations of society based partly on subjective values and opinions as well as theories and research (e.g. Marxist, feminist, functionalist, etc.).

According to the realist view of science, much of sociology is scientific because it develops models of the underlying structure and processes of society which are then evaluated and modified in the light of research. Sociologists would argue that there is little difference between social and natural science. Some sciences are more closed and precise; others, like sociology or meteorology, are more open and less able to study their subject matter in experimental conditions.

Claims about objectivity in the natural sciences are also being challenged – opinions, funding, careers, etc. all influence so-called scientific research.

In what ways might sociologists' values and beliefs influence their research?

Values may enter into any kind of research in a number of ways at different stages. First, there is the selection of areas of research – some topics are selected, others are ignored. This process is often guided by the values and interests of the researcher. Peter Townsend spent most of his career studying poverty, presumably because he believed it to be a serious social problem.

Once an area of research is chosen, it is possible that a researcher may become committed to a particular line of inquiry and may consciously or unconsciously seek evidence to support his or her hypothesis. Cyril Burt firmly believed and wanted to prove that intelligence was something which was genetic and could be measured.

In sociology the question of values is even more significant, as the sociologist is usually a member of the society being studied and may be a participant in the processes which are being researched (e.g. domestic labour, trade union membership).

Early sociologists like Comte and Durkheim believed that sociologists could, and should be, value-free because they believed that scientific knowledge was value-free and reflected 'the truth'. Marx also believed that it was possible to study society objectively. Weber was concerned about the question of values, and did not think that complete objectivity was possible; however, once research was underway, he did believe that sociologists could be objective.

It could be argued that the work of all these sociologists was influenced by the values that they held (functionalist, modernist, etc.). Functionalism supported a conservative view of society. Marx believed that revolutionary change was both possible and desirable. Weber clearly disapproved of some aspects of the bureaucracies which he studied.

Some more recent sociologists have argued that complete value freedom is neither possible nor desirable in sociology. Alvin Gouldner argues that all sociology is influenced by some basic assumptions about the nature of society. Functionalism, for example, assumes that societies are fundamentally stable, whereas Marxists believe they are unstable. Gouldner calls these **domain assumptions**, and argues that these kinds of beliefs influence the direction and the conclusions of research.

They determine the methods which are used, i.e. quantitative or qualitative – structuralists favouring the former, interactionists and feminists the latter.

They determine how data are interpreted.

Interactionists such as Howard Becker and Jack Douglas argue that it is pointless to attempt to achieve value freedom because it is unavoidable. Writing in the 1960s, Becker argued that too many sociologists studied the views of officials such as doctors, teachers, police and employers as if they held objective views. Rather, like official statistics, they are partial and subjective. In the pursuit of deeper understanding, alternative points of view need to be studied, for example, those of patients, pupils, prisoners, workers. He argued that much of the research into youth cults, for example, was from the point of view of youngsters 'causing trouble' rather than from questions concerned with the ways in which adult society creates trouble for young people. He argued, like Gouldner, that sociologists should recognize their own values and state them clearly. This is a view which has been substantially taken up and developed by feminist sociology.

There is much evidence to suggest that sociology does involve value judgements. For example, feminists have pointed out the sexist assumptions upon which most of mainstream sociology is based (in studies of stratification, family, work, education, deviance, etc.).

Although it is unlikely that sociologists could ever be completely value-free, neither are natural scientists. All scientists make 'domain assumptions' or work within a particular frame of reference and, like sociologists, are concerned with their careers, reputations and research grants. In addition, there is a growing awareness about the way in which scientific research reflects both cultural dominance and selection and reveals only partial truths rather than objective reality.

Summary

In practice methods of investigation are decided by what is being studied, as well as the theories of different schools of thought. Although some methods are more associated with some perspectives than others, researchers often mix and match the methods they use. For example, Sallie Westwood (*All Day Every Day*) applied Marxist, feminist and structuralist theoretical understandings to an ethnographic study of the shopfloor culture of mainly Asian women hosiery workers. Eileen Barker (*The Professional Stranger: Some Methodological Problems Encountered in a Study of the Reverend Sun Myung Moon's Unification Church*) in her study of Moonies used questionnaires to provide quantitative data about numbers, ages, backgrounds, etc., unstructured interviews to find out why people joined, and participant observation to see what the way of life was like inside the cult. John Goldthorpe, in his study of affluent car workers (*The Affluent Worker in the Class Structure*), used a questionnaire to assess social mobility, but also collected personal biographies from a smaller sub-sample of the workers interviewed. It would be wrong to assume that one method is always right, or that another is always wrong. In some circumstances, surveys and questionnaires will be more appropriate than participant observation; in others, unstructured interviews and the personal involvement of the researcher will be more revealing. They are all, to some extent, versions of the same practice – the attempt by sociologists to make their studies as accurate and illuminating as possible and to provide the evidence which will allow them to make interpretations of the complex social causes and characteristics of human behaviour.

Index